IGNORANCE OF LANGUAGE

Ignorance of Language

MICHAEL DEVITT

CLARENDON PRESS · OXFORD

OXFORD
UNIVERSITY PRESS

Great Clarendon Street, Oxford OX2 6DP

Oxford University Press is a department of the University of Oxford.
It furthers the University's objective of excellence in research, scholarship,
and education by publishing worldwide in

Oxford New York

Auckland Cape Town Dar es Salaam Hong Kong Karachi
Kuala Lumpur Madrid Melbourne Mexico City Nairobi
New Delhi Shanghai Taipei Toronto

With offices in

Argentina Austria Brazil Chile Czech Republic France Greece
Guatemala Hungary Italy Japan Poland Portugal Singapore
South Korea Switzerland Thailand Turkey Ukraine Vietnam

Oxford is a registered trade mark of Oxford University Press
in the UK and in certain other countries

Published in the United States
by Oxford University Press Inc., New York

British Library Cataloguing in Publication Data
Data available

Library of Congress Cataloguing in Publication Data
Data available

Typeset by SPI Publisher Services, Pondicherry, India
Printed in Great Britain
on acid-free paper by
Biddles Ltd., King's Lynn, Norfolk

ISBN 0-19-925096-0   978-0-19-925096-7

1 3 5 7 9 10 8 6 4 2

Preface

This is a book in the philosophy of linguistics. In a way it began a long time ago in 1968–69 when I was a graduate student and had my first experience of generative grammar. I audited a syntax class at Harvard given by George Lakoff and then a philosophy and linguistics class at MIT given by Noam Chomsky and Sylvain Bromberger.

Those were heady revolutionary times in linguistics. Papers were poured out, passed excitedly from hand to hand, and declared "way out of date" months before they were published. This samizdat frenzy was easy to understand. Generative grammar was revealing, at a furious pace, a wealth of fascinating facts about the syntax of natural languages. I was very impressed (and still am). But I was also very puzzled. For, along with the claims about deep structure, surface structure, and transformations, went the claim that this was all, somehow, an account of the mind. Surely, I thought, all the talk of generations and transformations could not be descriptions of *mental* processes. Yet it often seemed as if this was indeed what linguists intended. And if this wasn't what they intended, what exactly *did* grammatical descriptions have to do with the mind? Surely, I thought, the grammar is describing the syntactic properties of (idealized) linguistic expressions, certain sounds in the air, inscriptions on paper, and the like. These items are produced by minds, of course, and presumably get many of their properties somehow from minds, but they are not themselves mental. It rather looked to me as if linguists were conflating a theory of language with a theory of linguistic competence. That was the idea from which this book sprang.

Still, it was a very long time springing. My first book, *Designation* (1981), makes passing mention of the idea and criticizes a related philosophical conflation of the theory of meaning with the theory of understanding. The first real step in developing the idea was in the mid 1980s when Kim Sterelny and I wrote *Language and Reality: An Introduction to the Philosophy of Language* (1987). Naturally this included a discussion of generative grammar. And, in chapter 8, we addressed the issue of what linguistics is about and the issue of the place of language in the mind. We took a very unChomskian position on these issues. We developed this position into a paper, "What's Wrong with 'the Right View'" (1989) ('the Right View' being Jerry Fodor's witty name for the received Chomskian view of what linguistics is about). The paper did not go down well in certain circles.

The next step came in June 1996 when I was invited to a conference in Maribor on naturalized semantics, focused on my book, *Coming to Our Senses* (1996). I wrote a long paper for the conference, "Chomskian Linguistics and

Referential Semantics", which had most of the main ideas for this present book. Within a year or so, I had a draft of most of the book. This was the basis for a much revised chapter 8 in the second edition of *Language and Reality* (1999). Progress since then has been very slow. Partly this was because I got distracted by other projects, philosophical and administrative. But I think it was largely because I needed to have some familiarity with a great range of literature, literature not only in linguistics but in psycholinguistics and in the psychology of skills. I frequently found this task a bit overwhelming.

The book is concerned with the psychological reality underlying language. I arrive at some "major conclusions" and some "tentative proposals". The conclusions I am fairly confident about, the proposals, very much less so. A central theme of the book is that we have nowhere near enough evidence to be confident about many psychological matters relevant to language; we are simply too ignorant. Still I do think that the tentative proposals are promising guides to the future, and more so than their alternatives. These conclusions and proposals are very much at odds with standard Chomskian views. For example, I urge that linguistics is not part of psychology; that the thesis that linguistic rules are represented in the mind is implausible and unsupported; that speakers are largely ignorant of their language; that speakers' linguistic intuitions do not reflect information supplied by the language faculty and are not the main evidence for grammars; that the primary concern of linguistics should not be with idiolects; that there is little or nothing to the language faculty; that language processing is a fairly brute-causal associationist matter; that the rules specified by "Universal Grammar" are largely, if not entirely, innate structure rules of thought; that if the language-of-thought hypothesis is false the rules of a language are not psychologically real, and the rules specified by Universal Grammar are not innate, in a speaker. Though many of my conclusions and proposals are radical, the assumptions that lead to them are often familiar, sometimes even relatively uncontroversial; for example, that a competence should be distinguished from its products; that a rule can govern a process without being represented; that language expresses thought; that linguistic competence is a skill or ability. I sometimes felt that I was arguing for something that should be fairly obvious.

Over the years of writing the book, I have delivered some parts of it in talks. I gave a talk based on Chapter 2 in very many places, starting at Kings College London in March 1997. The talk was initially entitled "Ignorance of Language" but in 2000 I changed the title to the more apt "Linguistics is not Psychology". This turned into the publication, Devitt 2003. In 2001, I delivered a talk in Dubrovnik, "Language Processing", which was the beginnings of Chapter 11. I have delivered "Intuitions in Linguistics" (2006), based on Chapter 7, in several places since 2002. Finally, I wrote "Deference: A Truth in Linguistic Relativity" (2002), the basis for sections 8.6 and 8.7, for the Society for Philosophy and Psychology conference at Edmonton in 2002.

As one would expect, I received a great variety of responses to this material. Among this variety, three sorts deserve comment. The first sort is to my many attributions to linguists, sometimes to Chomsky, sometimes to other linguists. With surprising frequency I received responses along the lines of: "Nobody believes *that*." An extreme example was the response of an anonymous reviewer, clearly a linguist, to an attribution in my 2006 of what I call, "The Representational Thesis": the thesis that the rules/principles of a language are represented in the minds of its speakers. The response was: "it is beyond doubt that [the Representational Thesis] is not any view in linguistics". What to say? One does one's best to get people right, citing evidence in support. In this case, I cite a great deal of evidence. If the evidence really is misleading and the attributions false, one wonders why people write in such misleading ways. In any case, the main point in making the attributions is not to score points but rather to set the stage for a positive discussion of the psychological reality underlying language. If we can clearly identify, and reject, a view of this reality that is *at least suggested* in the literature—for example, the Representational Thesis—then we can move on to consider better ideas. We have made progress. The truth of the matter about psychological reality is much more important than the truth of the matter about what people have claimed about that reality.

The second sort of response simply restates a view, vigorously and with references to Chomsky's work, that is precisely the one criticized. But, of course, the issues here, as elsewhere in science, cannot be settled by vigorous restatements and appeals to authority; they should be settled by answering criticisms and by offering evidence and argument.

The third sort of response draws attention to this or that grammatical discovery that I have not mentioned. Usually the discovery is truly fascinating and so it is not hard to empathize with enthusiasm for it. But what needs to be asked is whether the discovery is relevant to the issue in question. That issue is the psychological reality underlying language. So we are concerned with what, in general, syntactic theories, grammars, might tell us about that psychological reality. We are concerned, one might say, with "the interpretation" of linguistics. But we are not much concerned with what is going on "in the engine room" of linguistics, with the syntactic details. Our concern raises questions like: Suppose that this or that part of a generative grammar *were* true, what would it show us about the place of language in the mind? A fascinating grammatical discovery might indeed throw some light on such a question, but it might not.

Although I am not "doing linguistics" but talking about it, I am a philosopher treading on linguistic turf and this can cause resentment. Occasionally, indeed, it has led to anger and abuse. Part of the problem is, of course, that the views I am criticizing are held passionately by many. Another part is that my style is brusque. I have a tendency to, as we say in Australia, "call a spade a bloody shovel". It is too late for me to try to change that. I don't mean to offend and I am sorry if I do. But I do mean to state views clearly and provocatively. I think that Chomskian views of the place of language in the mind are seriously mistaken and that we should be exploring other options.

The inspiration for some of the ideas in this book, particularly the positive ones in Part IV, came from the Gricean view that thought is explanatorily prior to language and from the language-of-thought hypothesis. The *locus classicus* for the latter is, of course, Jerry Fodor's, *The Language of Thought* (1975). I reread this masterpiece after developing these ideas and was reminded that Fodor also embraces a Gricean view and urges a view of the relation of thought to language that is rather similar to mine. Yet we are not led down the same path by these similar views; indeed, we are in sharp disagreement over the Representational Thesis, the matter of what a grammar is about, the language faculty, and various other matters. Despite my tendency in this book to harp on the differences rather than the similarities, I should like now to acknowledge a large debt to Fodor.

I have many others to thank: Kim Sterelny, my co-author in some of the works that led to this one; already acknowledged helpers with Devitt and Sterelny 1989; the audiences at the above-mentioned talks; Stephen Crain and Juan Uriagereka, with whom I taught a course on the philosophy of linguistics in Fall 1997 at the University of Maryland; students in classes at Maryland and the CUNY Graduate Center; Sara Bernal, Jeff Bub, John Collins, Fiona Cowie, Jerry Fodor, Cynthia Haggard, Paul Horwich, Dunja Jutronic, Guy Longworth, Bob Matthews, Paul Pietroski, Geoff Pullum, Bill Ramsey, Gurpreet Rattan, Philip Robbins, Barbara Scholz, Robert Stainton, and Steve Stich, all of whom have given me advice on parts of the book, and, especially, Alex Barber and Eric Margolis who commented on drafts of the whole book; my research assistants Fritz McDonald and James Dow for valuable help. Most of all I am indebted to Georges Rey for comments on drafts and very many discussions of the topic over the last few years. Very likely I have forgotten some others who have helped in the long time it has taken to write this book. If so, I apologize.

It is conventional in a preface to admit to errors in the book to follow (thus generating the paradox of the preface). I think there is an unusually high chance of errors in this one because of the risk of errors of commission and omission concerning linguistic, psycholinguistic, and psychological literature. I just hope that the errors are not crucial to the arguments.

Contents

I. LINGUISTICS IS NOT PSYCHOLOGY

1. Introduction   3
2. A Grammar as a Theory of Linguistic Reality   17

II. POSITIONS ON PSYCHOLOGICAL REALITY

3. Some Possible Positions on Psychological Reality   45
4. Some Actual Positions on Psychological Reality   62

III. "PHILOSOPHICAL" ARGUMENTS FOR THE REPRESENTATIONAL THESIS

5. The Rejection of Behaviorism   87
6. Folk Psychology   89
7. Intuitions   95

IV. THE RELATION OF LANGUAGE TO THOUGHT

8. Thought Before Language   125
9. A Case for the Psychological Reality of Language   142
10. Thought and the Language Faculty   163

V. LANGUAGE USE AND ACQUISITION

11. Language Use   195
12. Language Acquisition   244

Glossary of Named or Numbered Items   273
References   277
Index   295

Full Contents

I. LINGUISTICS IS NOT PSYCHOLOGY

1. Introduction   3

  1.1 Chomsky's View of the Linguistic Tasks   3
  1.2 The Plan   8
  1.3 Clarifications   14

2. A Grammar as a Theory of Linguistic Reality   17

  2.1 Competence vs. Outputs   17
  2.2 Structure Rules vs. Processing Rules   18
  2.3 Respecting Structure Rules   21
  2.4 Application to Linguistics   23
  2.5 The Contemplated Task and the Linguistic Enterprise   30
  2.6 Four Methodological Points   35
  2.7 Interesting Psychological Matters   38
  2.8 Conclusion   40

II. POSITIONS ON PSYCHOLOGICAL REALITY

3. Some Possible Positions on Psychological Reality   45

  3.1 Represented vs. "Simply Embodied" Rules   45
  3.2 Structure Rules Used as Data in Processing   53
  3.3 Rational–Causal vs. Brute–Causal Processes   53
  3.4 Some Possible Positions on Psychological Reality   56
  3.5 Conclusion   60

4. Some Actual Positions on Psychological Reality   62

  4.1 Chomsky and Positions (i) and (iii)   62
  4.2 Chomsky and Position (ii)   68
  4.3 Fodor, Bever, and Garrett   72
  4.4 Bresnan and Kaplan   76
  4.5 Berwick and Weinberg   79
  4.6 Matthews   81
  4.7 Conclusion   83

III. "PHILOSOPHICAL" ARGUMENTS FOR THE REPRESENTATIONAL THESIS

5. The Rejection of Behaviorism   87

6. Folk Psychology   89
  6.1 Philosophers vs. Chomsky   89
  6.2 The Philosophers   91
  6.3 Chomsky   92
  6.4 Conclusion   93

7. Intuitions   95
  7.1 Introduction   95
  7.2 Evidence for Linguistic Theories   98
  7.3 Tension in the Linguists' View of Intuitions   100
  7.4 Intuitions in General   103
  7.5 Linguistic Intuitions   108
  7.6 Comparison of the Modest Explanation with the Standard
      Cartesian Explanation   112
  7.7 A Nonstandard Cartesian Explanation of the Role of Intuitions?   117
  7.8 Must Linguistics Explain Intuitions?   119
  7.9 Conclusion   120

IV. THE RELATION OF LANGUAGE TO THOUGHT

8. Thought Before Language   125
  8.1 Intentional Realism   125
  8.2 Language Expresses Thought   127
  8.3 Ontological Priority of Conceptual Competence   128
  8.4 Explanatory Priority of Thought   132
  8.5 Priority of Theoretical Interest in Thought   134
  8.6 Linguistic Relativity   135
  8.7 Reference Borrowing   138
  8.8 Conclusion   141

9. A Case for the Psychological Reality of Language   142
  9.1 Representational Theory of the Mind (RTM)   142
  9.2 Language-of-Thought Hypothesis (LOTH)   145
  9.3 Linguistic Competence   147
  9.4 The Public-LOTH   149

9.5 The Syntax of Mentalese   152
9.6 "Communicative" vs. "Cognitive" Conceptions   160
9.7 Conclusion   161

10. Thought and the Language Faculty   **163**

10.1 Brain Impairment and the Independence of Language   163
10.2 Brain Impairment and the Language Faculty   165
10.3 Thoughts and the Language Faculty   172
10.4 Chomsky on Thoughts   174
10.5 Chomsky on Conventions and Idiolects   178
10.6 Rey on "the Intentional Inexistence of Language"   184
10.7 Conclusion   189

V. LANGUAGE USE AND ACQUISITION

11. Language Use   **195**

11.1 Introduction   195
11.2 "The Only Theory in Town"   198
11.3 Background on Linguistic Competence   201
11.4 Implausibility of Represented Rules in Linguistic Competence 203
11.5 Psychology of Skills   210
11.6 Brute–Causal Processing   220
11.7 Psychology of Language Production   230
11.8 Psychology of Language Comprehension   234
11.9 Conclusion   241

12. Language Acquisition   **244**

12.1 Innateness Theses   244
12.2 Evidence for Nativism   248
12.3 "The Only Theory in Town" and I-Representationalism
      (Thesis 3ʀ)   252
12.4 Embodiment of UG-Rules (Thesis 3)   256
12.5 Language Faculty (Thesis 1)   260
12.6 Implausibility of I-Representationalism (Thesis 3ʀ)   266
12.7 Bearing on the Representational Thesis (RT)   270
12.8 Conclusion   271

Glossary of Named or Numbered Items   273
References   277
Index   295

PART I

LINGUISTICS IS NOT PSYCHOLOGY

1

Introduction

The major concern of this book is to investigate the respect, if any, in which the rules or principles of a language are "psychologically real" in its competent speaker/hearer.[1] Naturally enough, the views of Noam Chomsky will loom large in this enterprise.

1.1 CHOMSKY'S VIEW OF THE LINGUISTIC TASKS

The wonderfully successful research program in linguistics initiated and sustained by Chomsky starts from the assumption that a person competent in a language *knows* that language. The program then defines the linguistic tasks in terms of this knowledge. Thus, at the beginning of a book called, appropriately enough, "*Knowledge of Language*" (1986), Chomsky claims that 'the three basic questions that arise' in the study of language are:

> (i)   What constitutes knowledge of language?
> (ii) How is knowledge of language acquired?
> (iii) How is knowledge of language put to use? (p. 3)

In general, talk of "knowledge" is very loose. This has led to some initial difficulty in interpreting (i) to (iii). However, there is a natural interpretation which takes Chomsky pretty much at his word. On this interpretation, his answer to question (i) claims that competent speakers of a language have propositional knowledge of its rules.[2] This knowledge underlies the speakers'

---

[1] Earlier versions of generative grammar talked of "rules", later ones emphasize the far more general "principles". Such differences as there may be between rules and principles are unimportant to my discussion. I shall mostly just talk briefly of rules. I shall abbreviate "speaker/hearer" to "speaker".

[2] Thus Chomsky describes the knowledge as a "system of beliefs" (1969a: 60–1; see also 1980a: 225) and says that a child's acquisition of a language is the discovery of "a deep and abstract theory—a generative grammar of his language" (1965: 58). See also his more recent 1986, pp. 263–73, which includes the following: "Knowledge of language involves (perhaps entails) standard examples of propositional knowledge" (p. 265); "it is proper to say that a person knows that R, where R is a rule of his or her grammar" (p. 268). Jerry Fodor describes Chomsky's view as propositional (1983: 4–10); it is the view that "your linguistic capacities . . . are . . . explained by reference to the *content of your beliefs*" (p. 7).

intuitive judgments about the syntax of expressions; it underlies their "linguistic intuitions".

The key point concerning the rules of the language is that a speaker stands in *an unconscious or tacit propositional attitude to these rules which are represented in her "language faculty"*, a special "organ" or "module" of the mind. I shall call this "the Representational Thesis" ("RT"). Chomsky puts the claim about representation with characteristic firmness: "there can be little doubt that knowing a language involves internal representation of a generative procedure" (1991a: 9; see also 1965: 25; 1975a: 304; 1980a: 201; 1980b: 9; 2000a: 50). The term 'know' is mostly used for the propositional attitude in question but, when the chips are down, Chomsky is prepared to settle for the technical term 'cognize' (1975b: 164–5; 1980a: 69–70).

The key point concerning the intuitions about particular syntactic matters is that speakers *derive their intuitive judgments from their representations of rules* by a causal and rational process like a deduction:

> it seems reasonably clear, both in principle and in many specific cases, how unconscious knowledge issues in conscious knowledge... it follows by computations similar to straight deduction.   (Chomsky 1986: 270)

The intuitions are, we might say, "the voice of competence". So, *simply* in virtue of being competent, speakers have propositional knowledge of syntactic facts; their competence gives them "privileged access" to this reality. Because of this, these intuitions provide the main evidence about the nature of the rules.[3] This is not to say that the intuitions are infallible: performance error can lead to mistakes (Chomsky 1986: 36). Still, apart from this "noise", intuitions reflect the underlying representations of the rules of the language.

To be competent in a language is to be able to produce and understand the expressions of that language. According to Chomsky, on our natural interpretation, this competence involves representations of the rules of the language. So those representations determine what expressions the speaker produces and understands. According to the point about intuitions, those representations also determine what the speaker says *about* those expressions in her intuitive judgments.

On our interpretation, task (i) for a language comes down to the study of the system of rules that is the object of the speaker's knowledge. Chomsky calls this object, an "I-language". Since the speaker's knowledge about this I-language constitutes her competence, task (i) is, in effect, the study of that competence. In attempting this task, the linguist produces a "grammar", which is a theory of the I-language. That theory, hard-won by the linguist, is precisely what the speaker tacitly knows. Task (ii) is concerned with how the speaker acquires her competence. How much of her knowledge of the language is innate and how

---

[3] This view of intuitions is widespread in linguistics; see section 7.1 for evidence.

much learned from experience? Task (iii) is concerned with the role played by this competence in performance. What role does her knowledge of the language play in understanding and producing expressions of the language?

It is surely indubitable that speakers of a language do "know the language", in the ordinary sense that they are competent in the language. Furthermore, the intuitive judgments that they make about the language are generally reliable. Still, I think that the just-described view of this knowledge and of its relation to the judgments is highly dubious. In particular, we should doubt RT, doubt that speakers must have *propositional* knowledge of the language or that they must have representations of linguistic rules in the language faculty or anywhere else in the mind. Rather, I shall argue, a person could be competent in a language without representing it or knowing anything about it: she could be totally *ignorant* of it.[4]

Because of this, and the aforementioned looseness of talk of "knowledge", I think that linguistics would do better to avoid the talk: any purpose served by talk of knowledge seems better served, by talk of "competence".[5]

The talk of representing rules raises a question: What sense of 'represent' do I have in mind in RT? The sense is a very familiar one illustrated in the following claims: a portrait of Winston Churchill represents him; a sound /the President of the United States/ represents George W. Bush; an inscription 'rabbit' represents rabbits; a certain road sign represents that the speed limit is 30 mph; the map on my desk represents the New York subway system; the number 11 is represented by '11' in the Arabic system, by '1011' in the binary system, and by 'xɪ' in the Roman system; and, most aptly, a (general-purpose) computer that has been loaded up with a program represents the rules of that program. Something that represents in this sense has a *semantic content*, a *meaning*. When all goes well, there will exist something that a representation refers to. But a representation can fail to refer; thus, nothing exists that 'James Bond' or 'phlogiston' refer to. Finally, representation in this sense is what various theories of reference— description, historical-causal, indicator, and teleological—are attempting to partly explain.[6]

There are, of course, other senses of 'represent' in ordinary English. Thus, if we were to say that Hillary represents New York, Fido represents dogs, Jerry Fodor

---

[4] I think that we should be similarly dubious of the thesis that speakers must have tacit propositional knowledge about the meanings and truth conditions of sentences of their language (1981: 95–110; 1997a: 270–5). This thesis is ubiquitous in philosophy and common in psychology (see, e.g., Anderson 1983: 268) and elsewhere.

[5] Chomsky resists talk of "competence" because it suggests that linguistics is concerned with an *ability*. I discuss this resistance later (Ch. 6). Zenon Pylyshyn makes a plea to confine talk of knowledge to cases where what is known is represented (1991: 248). This is surely a move in the right direction but I think that we should go further. I think that we should drop talk of knowledge from serious science, even from naturalized epistemology. There is always an alternative way of talking that is less vague and that lacks the unfortunate connotations of talk of knowledge.

[6] For a critical discussion of such theories, see Devitt and Sterelny 1999.

represents cognitive science, or Olivier represents Henry V, we would be using 'represent' in one of these other ways. But these are not the ways in which I shall be using 'represent'. I shall always be using it with the sense illustrated in the last paragraph. Thus RT is to be understood in light of this.[7]

Chomsky is naturally interpreted as urging RT, with 'represent' understood in this way, because doing so nicely accommodates his talk of "beliefs", "theories", "propositional knowledge" and of intuitions being "deduced" from representations. RT is the core of what Jerry Fodor (1981b) calls "the Right View" of what a grammar is about. RT is certainly widespread in linguistics.[8] Still the interpretation of Chomsky may not be right.

Chomsky's frequent talk of speakers standing in a propositional attitude to the rules of their language would alone amount to RT if we could be confident that he subscribed to the popular "Representational Theory of the Mind" ("RTM"). For, according to RTM, any propositional attitude (or thought) involves standing in a certain functional relation to a mental representation; thus a certain belief in my head represents that Nixon was malevolent and a certain hope in Milosevic's mind represented that NATO would give up. Fodor confidently attributes RTM to Chomsky, taking him to assume "that the intentional objects of [propositional attitudes] are *ipso facto* 'internally represented' as a matter of nomological (or maybe metaphysical) necessity" (2001: 109). Still one wonders whether this confidence is misplaced.

Even Chomsky's frequent talk of speakers *representing* the rules of their language does not settle the matter because we cannot be confident that he is using 'represent' in the familiar and relatively clear sense that I have endorsed (which is also the sense relevant to RTM). Aside from its other senses in ordinary English, 'represent' (and its cognates) is used fairly indiscriminately in linguistics, psychology, and AI. Thus the cognitive psychologist John Anderson describes the *behaviorist's* S-R theory of a rat's maze-running skill as a theory about how that skill is "represented" in the rat (1980: 235–6). In the sense of 'represent' that I am

---

[7] I am attempting to clarify my sense of 'represent' (and its cognates) by distinguishing that sense from other ordinary ones. I am not, of course, attempting a theory of representation, a theory of what 'represent', in that sense, refers to. The concerns of this book do not require such a theory (which is just as well given how difficult it is proving to come up with one!).

[8] (i) A recent encyclopedia article endorses the view (attributed to Chomsky) that "the human language faculty is a system of knowledge". "This knowledge is formal, specific to the language capacity (as distinct from other cognitive capacities), and cerebrally represented. It constitutes a biological module, putatively distinct from other knowledge bases and mental processes" (Grodzinsky 2003: 741). (ii) In discussing the distinction between knowing how and knowing that, Fodor remarks: "my linguist friends tell me that learning how to talk a first language requires quite a lot of learning that the language has the grammar that it does" (1998a: 125). (iii) All but one of the views discussed in Chapter 4 seem to take RT for granted. (iv) Two philosophers influenced by Chomsky, Susan Dwyer and Paul Pietroski, base a theory of belief on the view that "ordinary speakers believe the propositions expressed by certain sentences of linguistic theory" (1996: 338). (iv) Alex Barber takes Chomsky and others to hold that a linguistic theory is "the explicit statement of certain aspects of the *content* of knowledge states possessed by ordinary speakers". This is "the default conception many linguists have of the project they are engaged in" (2003b: 3).

deploying, the very essence of the behaviorist's theory is, of course, that the rat runs the maze *without* using representations. And the critics of behaviorism who argued that the rat uses an internal map of the maze are insisting that the rat *does* use a representation in this sense. Chomsky himself often seems to have some technical sense of 'represent' in mind that is different from the familiar one.[9]

So, natural as it is to attribute RT to Chomsky and other linguists, it may not be right to do so. And some sympathetic to his research program think that this natural interpretation is not right (as I have discovered when proposing it). Indeed, some even go so far as to hold that the view is not to be found in linguistics, despite the massive evidence to the contrary.[10] If the interpretation is indeed not right, what is? Chomsky must hold that the rules of the language are *embodied somehow* in a speaker without being represented (in my sense, of course) just as, say, arithmetical rules are embodied somehow in a simple mechanical calculator without being represented (see section 3.1 below). Furthermore, these embodied rules must be responsible somehow for the speaker's use of language and intuitive judgments about it. I would, of course, like to interpret Chomsky correctly but I want to emphasize from the beginning that interpreting Chomsky is not my major concern. My major concern is to evaluate a variety of ways in which language might be psychologically real in the speaker, whether or not they are plausibly attributed to Chomsky (or his followers). So I shall take no firm stand on this matter of interpretation.

The natural interpretation attributes RT to Chomsky. If this thesis is right then the language is psychologically real in the speaker in a strikingly robust way: the rules of the language are represented in the speaker's language faculty; the language is psychologically real because the theory of the language—its grammar—is psychologically real. Indeed, a language simply is this system of rules encoded in the mind. Those represented rules are the reality that a grammar is theorizing about. If that interpretation is wrong then Chomsky must hold that a language is a system of rules embodied somehow in the language faculty without being represented. Then those embodied rules are the reality that a grammar is theorizing about.

It can be seen that, according to Chomsky, the reality of a language is in the mind, whether as represented rules or as otherwise embodied rules: the reality is psychological:

Linguistics is simply that part of psychology that is concerned with one specific class of steady states, the cognitive structures that are employed in speaking and understanding. (1975b: 160)

---

[9] On the issue of what Chomsky means by 'represent' and other apparently intentional expressions, see the fascinating exchange: Rey 2003a; Chomsky 2003; Rey 2003b. I do not have the heart to enter into this debate.

[10] "it is beyond doubt that RT is not any view in linguistics" (anonymous reviewer of Devitt 2006).

He has persuaded many others of this. As Robert Matthews says:

It is a measure of the depth of the conceptual revolution wrought by Noam Chomsky in linguistics that few linguists would quarrel with his notion that theoretical linguistics is a subfield of psychology. (1991: 182)[11]

So it is not surprising that Chomsky is irritated by the oft-raised question: "Are the rules described by a grammar 'psychologically real'?" (see e.g., 1980a: 189–201). He points out that a grammar is a scientific theory and so should be treated just like any other scientific theory. And a scientific theory should be treated realistically, for the alternative of treating it instrumentally has surely been discredited. This yields a very fast argument for the psychological reality of the rules described by the grammar. We have good, though not of course conclusive, evidence for a grammar's truth and so we have good evidence for the reality it concerns. And, in Chomsky's view, that reality is psychological.

Yet, on the face of it, this view of linguistics seems implausible. In any case, Kim Sterelny and I (1987, 1989) have argued against it. Jerrold Katz (1981, 1984) and Scott Soames (1984) have argued independently along similar lines.[12] Our point seems simple, even rather obvious.[13] Chomsky (1986: 34–6; 1991b: 31; 1995b: 33–4; 2000a: 139–40) responded to it briefly and dismissingly. Susan Dwyer and Paul Pietroski (1996) made some critical remarks in passing. Louise Antony (2003) responded critically to Soames in a 1991 talk that has been published in a recent volume. Stephen Laurence (2003) has mounted a lengthy attack in the same volume. Some people stopped talking to us. Beyond this, there is no evidence that our arguments have had any effect.

1.2   THE PLAN

My earlier argument now seems to me to have many errors. So my first aim, in the rest of Part I, is to argue the matter somewhat differently and, I hope, better. I claim that there is something other than psychological reality for a grammar to be true of: it can be true of a *linguistic* reality.[14] One might think that this claim

---

[11] John Collins' recent claim is typical: "the job of linguistic theory is to understand the nature of the language faculty" (2004: 516). (With surprising confidence Collins interprets Chomsky as *not* proposing the Fodorian view that the language faculty comprises propositional structures known by the speaker.) Some do quarrel with the psychologistic interpretation of linguistics, however: "We make no claims, naturally enough, that our grammatical theory is *eo ipso* a psychological theory" (Gazdar *et al.* 1985: 5). The Bloomfieldian linguistics that preceded Chomsky's revolution was very antimentalist. Chomsky's psychologistic interpretation was not apparent in his early works. He claims that this was because the approach seemed to him "too audacious" at the time (1975c: 35). There is some controversy about this claim; see Harris 1993: 268–9n.

[12] See also related views in Dretske 1974; Sampson 1976 (crediting Margaret Gilbert); Cummins and Harnish 1980; Stabler 1983; and George 1989b.

[13] Thus, Fiona Cowie thinks that the point "should be...accepted as utterly uncontroversial" (1999: 246).

[14] Earlier (1981: 92–5) I argued an analogous point against philosophers who identify semantics with the explanation of linguistic competence or understanding.

was uncontroversial and yet Chomsky and others seem to resist it. So I shall start by arguing for the claim carefully with the help of three quite general distinctions. Next, given the weight of evidence, it is plausible to think that the grammar is indeed more or less true of that linguistic reality. Furthermore, this reality is worthy of theoretical study in its own right, whatever the case may be with psychological reality. So a grammar is about linguistic reality not the language faculty. Linguistics is not part of psychology. This is my "*first major conclusion*". The grammar might *also* be true of a psychological reality, of course, but to show that it is requires an explicitly *psychological* assumption. And, I shall argue, it is hard to find evidence for an assumption that will do the trick.

If this is right, the very fast argument for the psychological reality of linguistic rules—we have good evidence for the grammar and so we have good evidence for the psychological reality it describes—is revealed as not only fast but dirty. It remains an open question whether the rules hypothesized by the grammar are psychologically real.

In the rest of the book I shall argue that it is hard to establish psychological assumptions that show that linguistic rules are indeed psychologically real. My general concern will be to explore the nature of the psychological reality underlying language, whether that reality embodies the rules or not. Putting this another way, my general concern is with the nature of linguistic competence.

As I have indicated, it is common to believe RT: speakers of a language embody its rules by representing them. I shall argue that there is no significant evidence for this thesis and, given what else we know, it is implausible. This is my "*second major conclusion*". Should a linguistic rule be embodied it is unlikely to be represented (in the sense illustrated in section 1.1). Those who are already convinced of this can skip Chapters 5 and 6, and some of 7, 11 and 12.

Part II starts the investigation of the psychological reality issue by describing some positions on the matter. In Chapter 3, against a background of further distinctions, particularly the distinction between rules that govern by being represented and applied and those that govern by being simply embodied, I describe some alternative *possible* positions on psychological reality. These vary according to whether or not the rules of the language are embodied in the mind; whether or not some processing rules for language are represented in the mind (cf. RT); whether or not some processing rules operate on metalinguistic representations of syntactic and semantic properties of linguistic items. And there is an uncontroversial minimal position that is committed only to there being a psychological reality that "respects" the linguistic structure rules. Given the Part I conclusion that linguistics is *not* psychology, no position stronger than the minimal one can be sustained without some powerful psychological assumption that is independent of anything revealed by the grammar of a language. Such an assumption is needed to conclude that the rules of the language are present one way or another in the mind.

In Chapter 4, I attempt to place some historically interesting *actual* positions among these alternative possible positions on psychological reality. Chomsky's own position is hard to determine. There is strong evidence that he is committed to RT, but even that commitment is open to question. In their classic work, *The Psychology of Language* (1974) Jerry Fodor, Tom Bever, and Merrill Garrett subscribe to RT despite finding no work for RT in explaining language use. Joan Bresnan and Ronald Kaplan (1982) seem to take RT for granted. They seek a grammar that is psychologically motivated and so abandon 'transformational' grammars in favor of 'lexical-function' grammars. In contrast, Robert Berwick and Amy Weinberg (1984), who also seem to take RT for granted, defend the idea that a transformational grammar is psychologically real. Robert Matthews (1991) finds no evidence for RT and rejects it. Still he claims that the rules of the language are psychologically real in another way.

I turn next to the assessment of evidence from various quarters for positions on psychological reality. In Part III I begin my case for my second major conclusion by rejecting what we might call 'philosophical arguments' for RT. (The main arguments for RT are those from language use and from language acquisition and will be rejected in Part V.) Chapter 5 considers, *very* briefly, the argument from the rejection of behaviorism. But this rejection is compatible with many alternatives to RT. Chapter 6 considers the argument from the folk psychological view that a person competent in a language 'knows' the language. But, despite Chomsky's objections, this knowledge could be mere knowledge-how. Chapter 7 considers the most interesting of the three arguments. The intuitive judgments of speakers are treated as the main evidence for a grammar. Why are they good evidence? The Chomskian answer involves RT: the intuitions are derived by a rational process from a representation of linguistic rules in the language faculty. I argue for a different view based on a view of intuitions in general. Linguistic intuitions do not reflect information supplied by represented, or even unrepresented, rules in the language faculty. Rather, they are empirical central-processor responses to linguistic phenomena differing from other such responses only in being fairly immediate and unreflective. And I argue that they are not the main evidence for a grammar. These views about intuitions constitute my *"third major conclusion"*. The conclusion yields an explanation of the evidential role of intuitions without any appeal to embodied rules of the language.

Part IV strikes a more positive note by attending to thought. I start in Chapter 8 with the folk idea that 'language expresses thought'. This idea seems irresistible once one has accepted that people really have thoughts, once one has accepted "intentional realism". The idea leads to my *"fourth major conclusion"*: the psychological reality of language should be investigated from a perspective on thought. The idea also leads to the view that conceptual competence partly constitutes linguistic competence and so is ontologically prior to it. I next argue, following Grice, that thought is explanatorily prior to language. These ontological and explanatory priorities have some interesting temporal consequences. Finally, on the basis of these priorities, I argued that our theoretical interest in thought is prior to that in language. I sum up these priority claims roughly as follows: thought has a certain priority to language ontologically, explanatorily, temporally, and in theoretical interest. That is my *"fifth major conclusion"*. The assumptions of the arguments in this chapter are, it seems to me, relatively uncontroversial and yet their repercussions for the issue of the psychological reality of language are both considerable and strangely unnoticed.

This discussion lays the groundwork for a decidedly speculative proposal in Chapter 9. The argument for this begins with the popular RTM described a few pages back. On this view a thought involves a mental representation. The crucial next step in the argument is the controversial "Language-of-Thought Hypothesis" ("LOTH"): the representation in thought is language-like. On the basis of this hypothesis, I argue that the syntactic structure of this representation is likely to be similar to that of the sentence that expresses it in the thinker's language. So, a language is largely psychologically real in a speaker in that its rules are similar to the structure rules of her thought. Linguistic competence should be seen as an ability to translate back and forth between the speaker's 'Mentalese' and her natural language.

The argument for this proposal depends on an assumption about thought that is far from indubitable. So the proposal is tentative; it is my *"first tentative proposal"*. If we were to adopt a different assumption about thought—for example that mental representations are map-like—then we could not draw this conclusion about the place of language in the mind. Indeed, I doubt that we could draw any positive conclusion about this. So this argument illustrates the point that some powerful assumption about the mind is needed to support a robust view of the psychologically reality of language.

In Chapter 10, I first consider the bearing of these views of thought on a belief in the language faculty. The view that conceptual competence is part of linguistic competence already places a considerable part of linguistic competence in the central processor. I argue that this view is not undermined by the well-known dissociation of cognitive impairment and linguistic impairment. The rest of linguistic competence consists in processing competencies for spoken language, written language, and so on. If there is to be a modality-neutral, relatively central, language faculty, it must be found in some commonalities between these modality-specific processing competencies. I argue that, contrary to the received view, the evidence from brain impairment counts much more against there being the required commonalities than for there being them. Aside from that, if we adopt my first tentative proposal, we should not expect to find these commonalities. I am led to the view that there is little or nothing to the language faculty: this is my *"second tentative proposal"*. I say more in support of this in Chapter 12.

I turn next to Chomsky's views of thought and its relation to language. It is surprisingly difficult to say what these views are. I offer some reasons for thinking that they are very different from the ones I present. I go on to look critically at some puzzling claims that Chomsky makes against linguistic regularities and conventions, against the need for shared and discoverable meanings in communication, and in favor of idiolects rather than common languages as the objects of research. I emphasize that it is because of shared conventional meanings in a group that language can play its important role of making the thoughts of each member of the group accessible to the others. It is the task of linguistics to explain the nature of these conventional meanings. This yields my "*sixth major conclusion*": the primary concern in linguistics should not be with idiolects but with linguistic expressions that share meanings in idiolects. I develop these views by contrasting them with Georges Rey's rather startling antirealism about linguistic entities.

Finally, in Part V, I attend to language use and language acquisition. My main argument in Chapter 11 is that a consideration of language use provides no persuasive evidence for RT and that RT is implausible. Not only is RT not now part of a good explanation of language use, it is unlikely to be so in the future. So, this argument rejects the apparently popular 'only-theory-in-town' abduction for RT. Indeed, I claim that this abduction fails all the main criteria of a good abduction. My argument places a lot of weight on what we can learn from the general psychology of skills and their acquisition. For, linguistic competence is a skill apparently acquired by "implicit learning". This argument against RT is the main step in the case for my second major conclusion. Suppose, then, that we drop RT. It might still be thought that language processing is governed by the *un*represented structure rules of the language. I argue against this thought: the structure rules are the wrong sort of rule to govern the translation process of language use. This is my "*third tentative proposal*". The proposal has to be tentative given the consensus that we know so little about this processing. Still, the proposal seems much more plausible than the alternative view that the structure rules are processing rules, a view for which the study of language use seems to provide no evidence. Finally, the chapter considers whether language processing involves metalinguistic representations of the syntactic and semantic properties of linguistic expressions. The received view, even among those who do not clearly hold RT (that the linguistic *rules* are represented), is that the processing does involve these representations. I present a case that this view is wrong, that the speedy automatic language processes arising wholly, or at least partly, from linguistic competence are fairly brute-causal associationist processes. This is my "*fourth tentative proposal*". The proposal must be particularly tentative but it is, in my view, better supported than the contrary view that these processes do involve metalinguistic representations.

This proposal, together with the second major conclusion rejecting RT, arises from a principle introduced in Chapter 3: "Representations are not to be multiplied beyond necessity." I call this "Pylyshyn's Razor". I am not against representations in general, as Part IV shows. However, I think that we should posit them only if they do explanatory work. I doubt that representations of linguistic rules and properties do any work in explaining linguistic competence.

The received Chomskian view is that the rules of a language are psychologically real in a speaker, whether they are represented or not. In Chapter 9 I made my first tentative proposal, based on the controversial LOTH, that a language is indeed largely psychologically real in a speaker in that its rules are similar to the structure rules of her thought. The arguments in Chapter 11 are against a language being otherwise psychologically real. This yields my "*fifth tentative proposal*": if LOTH is false, then the rules of a language are not, in a robust way, psychologically real in a speaker.

The last chapter, 12, is concerned with language acquisition. I set aside for a moment the bearing of this issue on the nature of "the final state" of linguistic competence, the main concern of this book. The issue raises a related concern, the nature of "the initial state" of competence, that is very interesting in its own right. The innate initial state enables humans to learn natural languages. What is it like? This question dominates the chapter. I take the familiar arguments for nativism to establish the interesting nativist thesis that the initial state is sufficiently rich that humans can naturally learn only languages that conform to the rules specified by "Universal Grammar" ("UG"). Can we establish stronger nativist theses? For example, can we establish the very exciting thesis that the rules specified by UG are represented in the initial state? According to this thesis the initial state includes UG itself. So the thesis is the initial state analogue of the final state Representational Thesis (RT). I call it "the I-Representational Thesis". Fodor has urged an "only-theory-in-town" abduction in favor of this thesis. This abduction is poor, lacking detail and evidential support. I propose an alternative nativist thesis to I-Representationalism based on my first tentative proposal: humans are predisposed to learn languages that conform to the rules specified by UG because those rules are, largely if not entirely, innate structure rules of thought. This is my "*sixth tentative proposal*". The proposal has to be tentative because it rests on the highly speculative first proposal and because we are nowhere near a persuasive explanation of language acquisition. Suppose then that LOTH and hence the first proposal are false and so we have to adopt some other view of thoughts. This yields my "*seventh tentative proposal*", the initial-state analogue of the final-state fifth proposal: if LOTH is false, then the rules specified by UG are not, in a robust way, innate in a speaker. Next, I argue that, without RT, Chomsky's well-known argument for placing the initial state in a distinct language faculty rather than in the central processor collapses. And if my sixth proposal is correct that state very likely *is* largely in the central processor. This completes the argument for my second proposal (Chapter 10) that there is little or nothing to the language faculty. The proposal has to be tentative but, I argue, the contrary view that there is a substantial language faculty seems to lack any significant evidence. Finally, I return to the I-Representationalist Thesis according to which the rules specified by UG are not simply embodied in the initial state, as in my sixth proposal, but represented in it. I have earlier rejected Fodor's only-theory-in-town abduction for the thesis. I now argue against the thesis. On the basis of a comparison of linguistic competence with other skills and attention to the nature of thoughts and thinking I claim that there is no significant evidence for the I-Representational Thesis and, given what else we know, it is implausible. This is my "*seventh major conclusion*". It arises from another application of Pylyshyn's Razor. If the conclusion is right, the arguments for nativism do not support the traditional doctrine of innate ideas.

The chapter ends by considering the bearing of this discussion of the nature of the initial state on the nature of the final state, the main concern of this book. It has less bearing than one might have expected. Even if I-Representationalism were true it would give no direct support to RT. And if it is false, as I argue it is, then RT is left, once again, with no support. That finishes my argument for my second major conclusion.

My fourth major conclusion urges us to investigate the psychological reality underlying language from a perspective on thought (Chapter 8). We can now summarize some significant results of that approach. It yields my first tentative proposal, based on LOTH, that a language is largely psychologically real in a speaker in that its rules are similar to the structure rules of her thought (Chapter 9); and it yields my fifth tentative proposal that if LOTH is false then the rules of a language are not, in a robust way, psychologically real in a speaker (Chapter 11). These proposals concern the final state of linguistic competence. The approach yields two analogous proposals about the initial state: my sixth tentative proposal that humans are predisposed to learn languages that conform to the rules specified by UG because those rules are, largely if not entirely, innate structure rules of thought; and my seventh tentative proposal that if LOTH is false then the rules specified by UG are not, in a robust way, innate in a speaker. Finally, the approach yields the second tentative proposal, which concerns both the initial and final state: there is little or nothing to the language faculty (Chapters 10 and 12).

In sum, I shall be arguing that a number of Chomskian views about the psychological reality of language are ill-supported by evidence and argument and are probably wrong.

For convenience, the seven major conclusions and seven tentative proposals are listed at the end of the Glossary of Named or Numbered items. The Glossary also lists, for example, the Representational Thesis (RT) and some possible positions on psychological reality.

1.3   CLARIFICATIONS

(i) A person's I-language, according to Chomsky, supervenes on intrinsic properties of the person's brain: it is, as philosophers would say, "narrow" and individualistic. It does not involve language-world connections and so does not involve semantics proper. In effect, an I-language has only syntactic properties, in a broad sense of the term. This restriction reflects Chomsky's doubts about the scientific study of reference.[15] I do not share these doubts and so think that the object of study should not be an I-language but rather something "wide", a "wide-I(ed)-language": the study should include the referential properties which, together with syntactic properties, determine the truth-referential meanings of expressions. But this difference of opinion is largely beside the present issue and so, for the sake of argument, I shall *mostly* go along with Chomsky's restriction to an I-language and to syntax (although, as Chapter 2 makes clear, my view of the nature of language, whether I- or wide-I(ed)-, is very different from Chomsky's).

(ii) A grammar posits various "levels" in an I-language. My concern is largely with the level of "Logical Form" ("LF"), a level that describes all the syntactic properties that contribute to the meanings of sentences, hence a level that makes the scope of all quantifiers explicit. So the main issue is about the psychological reality of the rules at that level. I am hardly concerned at all with the (fascinating) level of "Phonological Form" ("PF") partly because, in an important respect, it is concerned with something that is not essential to language: "the cognitive abilities supporting language and its acquisition in humans are not restricted or specialized to speech but rather permit the development of signed as well as spoken languages" (Newport and Supalla 1999: 759).

(iii) Chomsky's revolution in linguistics has really been a series of revolutions moving from the early Standard Theory to Government and Binding and recently to Minimalism. The concern of this book is not with the linguistic issue of which rules of a language are right, it is with the place of the right rules, whichever they may be, in the mind. The concern is not with the linguistic details but with an issue raised by the whole enterprise. So, for the most part, I shall abstract from the differences between the members of this series.

(iv) Consideration of the psychological reality of language raises issues that are undoubtedly difficult. How important are they? What hangs on the outcomes of this consideration? One accomplishment of generative grammar certainly does *not* hang on them: the extraordinary progress in providing explicit statements of the linguistic rules with the aim of deriving complete structural descriptions of all the possible sentences of a language. This accomplishment strikes me as a triumph and none of the outcomes of this book is intended to cast any doubt on it whatsoever. What about psycholinguistics? The outcomes are clearly at odds with the early determination of psycholinguistics to show that the linguistic rules— transformations, for example—themselves govern language processing. But that determination seems to have largely disappeared. I suspect that the vast majority of the present day-to-day psycholinguistic work would not be affected by the outcomes. One thing is clear, however: our overall picture of the place of language

---

[15] These doubts are nicely expressed and motivated in Pietroski 2003.

in the mind does hang on the outcomes. If I am right, the Chomskian research program is revealing a lot about language but, contrary to advertisements, rather little about the place of language in the mind (beyond the idea that, whatever that place, it may be largely innate). Ordinary speakers are ignorant of language but *theorists* are not; they are ignorant of linguistic competence.

Quantum mechanics provides extremely successful physical theories. Yet it is notoriously difficult to "interpret" the theories. What picture of reality are they giving us? Controversy rages over the answer. Similarly, generative grammar is providing extremely successful linguistic theories. There is not a similar controversy over how to "interpret" these theories but I think that there should be. For, according to the standard Chomskian interpretation these theories are directly about the mind and that, I argue, is a mistake. The reality that these grammars are primarily describing is linguistic not psychological. The grammars leave the nature of the psychological reality underlying language largely undetermined.

Finally, a brief word about the naming conventions in this book. Philosophers and linguists follow different conventions for naming a linguistic expression: philosophers surround the expression with single quotation marks; linguists italicize the expression. I mostly follow the philosophical convention but occasionally follow the linguistic one where linguists are under discussion. I name a mental expression by surrounding a linguistic expression with corners. I name meanings, contents, or propositions by capitalizing and italicizing an expression. I name properties and relations by simply italicizing an expression.

2

A Grammar as a Theory of Linguistic Reality

My first aim in this chapter is to argue, with the help of three quite general distinctions, that there is something other than psychological reality for a grammar to be true of: it can be true of a *linguistic* reality. Next, given the evidence, it is plausible to think that the grammar is indeed more or less true of that linguistic reality. Furthermore, this reality is worthy of theoretical study in its own right. So, linguistics is not simply a branch of psychology. The grammar might *also* be true of a psychological reality, of course, but to show that it is requires an explicitly *psychological* assumption.

2.1 COMPETENCE VS. OUTPUTS

A competence is a competence to produce a certain sort of output/product; or it is a competence to process a certain sort of input; or it is both.

1. Distinguish the theory of a competence from the theory of its outputs/products or inputs.

For convenience, in the early parts of my discussion, I shall focus on competencies to produce certain sorts of outputs.

I shall draw the distinction first with a simple example, distant from the concerns of linguistics: the competence of a blacksmith and the horseshoes he produces. Horseshoes are obvious parts of the physical world. A study of them will quickly conclude that they are made of iron, have a certain shape, have holes for nails, and so on. The blacksmith's competence is some state of his mind or body that plays the central role in explaining his behavior in producing horseshoes. Goodness knows what a study of it would conclude. The key point is that the "theory" of the horseshoes is one thing, the theory of the competence, another, because horseshoes are very different from the competence to produce them. Of course, given the causal relation between the competence and the horseshoes it produces, we can expect a theory of the one to bear on a theory of the other. But manifestly this does not make the two theories the same.

With an eye to two important features of grammar construction, we note that there are two respects in which a theory of the outputs of a competence is not simply about the *actual* outputs of that competence. First, there can be perform-ance errors in the exercise of a competence. Thus sometimes what a blacksmith produces is not a good horseshoe. The theory is only concerned with the nature of the outputs of a competence when it performs as it should; the theory idealizes by abstracting from error. Second, the theory is concerned with any *possible* output of the competence (when working well). Thus, the theory of horseshoes is concerned not only with the actual outputs of competent blacksmiths but with any of an indefinitely large number of outputs that they might produce.

The discussion to follow provides several other illustrations of distinction 1.

2.2   STRUCTURE RULES VS. PROCESSING RULES

The theory of a competence explains what it is about an object that makes it competent. Part of the explanation must be that the object embodies rules that govern the process of producing the appropriate output when the competence is exercised. Call these rules "processing rules". Sometimes the *outputs* of a com-petence are also rule-governed, but in a different way: their natures are consti-tuted by their place in a "structure" defined by a system of rules. Call these rules "structure rules".

2. Distinguish the structure rules governing the outputs of a competence from the processing rules governing the exercise of the competence.

In characterizing the output of the blacksmith we will not appeal to rules, but in characterizing other outputs we will. Thus, consider the output of a chess player: chess moves. The characterization of chess moves must appeal to a rather elaborate system of rules: a bishop may only move diagonally; the king may only move one square; no piece except a knight may move through an occupied square; and so on. Chess moves are rule-governed in that something counts as a chess move at all only if it has a place in the structure defined by the rules of chess. Something counts as a particular chess move in virtue of the particular rules that govern it, in virtue of its particular place in the structure. (This was an insight of the structuralists, of course.) A "theory" of the nature of chess describes these structure rules.[1] In doing so it describes constraints on the appropriate output of a chess player. A chess player should only make moves that have a place in the system the structure rules describe. That is, a chess player should make only legal moves. The structure rules *may* also be among the rules governing the psycho-logical process by which she produces chess moves. They *may* be among the processing rules activated in the exercise of her chess competence. However, this is not necessary and may be unlikely. In any case, the key points are that *being a*

---

[1] An *interesting* theory of chess will describe good strategies, of course. But that is a different matter.

structure rule, a rule governing outputs, is a very different property from *being a processing rule*, a rule governing the psychological production of outputs; and governing outputs is a very different matter from governing the production of outputs.

Some examples will help to bring out the distinction. Let us start by considering chess a bit more. It is a structure rule of chess that bishops move diagonally. If this rule were also among a player's processing rules then the player would, when appropriate in figuring out a move, go through a process of inferring '*x* moves diagonally' from '*x* is a bishop'. A player may not do that. In particular, given what we know about grand masters, it seems unlikely that they do: they combine a prodigious memory of chess configurations with strategies that may well not involve any such simple inferences. And we can imagine a machine that has a massive data base with an appropriate response to every possible chess configuration and that plays chess by simply applying this data base. This machine never goes through *any* inference that corresponds to a structure rule.[2] (If this is a bit hard to imagine because there are so many possible chess configurations, imagine a machine that plays a simpler game like draughts/checkers in the same way.)

A nice example of our distinction is provided by the distinction between the *formation* and *transformation* rules of a formal logic (the latter are not to be confused with the very different transformation rules of grammar). The *formation* rules are structure rules characterizing the *wffs* (well-formed formulae) of the system: nothing counts as a *wff* unless it accords with those rules. In this way, *wffs* are rule-governed. Each *wff* has its particular syntactic structure in virtue of the particular formation rules that govern it, in virtue of its particular place in the structure defined by the system of rules. The *transformation* rules are processing rules governing the move from one *wff* to another; they govern a process of valid derivation (if the rules are good). Nothing is both a formation and a transformation rule.

Think of the formal logic as embodied in a "logic machine". The machine takes *wffs* as inputs, processes them according to the transformation rules, yielding *wffs* as outputs (so it embodies a proof procedure). The outputs of this machine are all in accord with the formation rules, but those rules are not the ones that govern the process of producing them. The governing of *wffs* by formation rules is a very different matter from the governing of transformations by processing rules.

Of course, we could build *another* machine, a "*wff* machine", that simply generated *wffs*: it constructs *wffs* out of the basic symbols, the lexicon. *This* process must be governed by the formation rules although in all other ways, including selection from the lexicon, it would be random. Thus, in generating a

---

[2] I owe this nice example to suggestions from my students, Michael Maumus and David Pereplyotchik. It reminds one of ELIZA, the early AI program that (mostly) gives the responses of a "competent therapist" but does so in a mechanical way without applying any theory of the mind.

wff, it might start by picking a certain syntactic form. This selection is constrained by the formation rules but is otherwise random. Next, for each category of term in the selected syntactic form, it randomly selects an item of that category from the lexicon. This process might yield a simple *wff* like '*Fa*' or a more complex one like '*Fb* & (*Gc* v *Hd*)' or '(*x*)(*Gx* --> *Hx*)'. The particular syntactic structure of each *wff* would be determined by the particular formation rules involved in generating it. But notice that the logic machine does not generate *wffs* by this process.

Bees provide another good example of the distinction between structure rules and processing rules. A bee returning from a distant food source produces a "waggle dance" on the vertical face of the honeycomb. The positioning of this dance and its pattern indicate the direction and distance of the food source. These dances form a very effective symbol system governed by a surprising set of structure rules. It is the task of a theory of the dance symbols to describe these structure rules. Karl von Frisch completed this task in the 1960s.[3] In contrast, the processing rules by which the bee performs this rather remarkable feat remain a mystery.[4]

Here is a description of one of the structure rules of the bee's dance:

> To convey the direction of a food source, the bee varies the angle the waggling run makes with an imaginary line running straight up and down ... If you draw a line connecting the beehive and the food source, and another line connecting the hive and the spot on the horizon just beneath the sun, the angle formed by the two lines is the same as the angle of the waggling run to the imaginary vertical line.   (Frank 1997: 82)

How *might* the bee manage this? To start with it must "remember where the food source is" when it gets back to the hive. How? Two popular ideas are that the bee uses variations in Earth's magnetic field or in the polarization of the sun's light. A wilder idea is that the bee is sensitive to quantum fields (p. 84). Whatever the truth of this matter, the real mystery remains: what process does the bee go through to turn this memory into an appropriate dance, a dance governed by the structure rule? We should not rush to the judgment that the structure rule itself must govern this unknown process. It may be the *wrong sort* of rule to play this role. Nature faced the design problem of adapting the pre-existing structures of an insect to produce (and respond to) the message of the bee's dance. We have no reason to suppose a priori that nature solved this problem by making the bee go through the structure rule "calculation". Indeed, it is not at all clear that the bee could plausibly be seen as performing this calculation: can the bee even manage

---

[3] Any kcepticism there may have been about von Frisch's discovery should disappear in light of its confirmation by a recent study that involved putting radar transponders on bees (Riley *et al.* 2005).

[4] "Scientists have known of the bee's dance for more than seventy years, and they have assembled a remarkably complete dictionary of its terms, but one fundamental question has stubbornly remained unanswered: "How do they do it?" (Frank 1997: 80).

the necessary representations of the food source, of the spot on the horizon, and of the angles?[5]

In sum, to be a processing rule that governs the activities of a chess player, logic machine, or dancing bee is one thing, to be a structure rule governing the outputs of such activities is another. And a structure rule of the outputs may have no place among the processing rules that produce those outputs.

With an eye to important features of grammar construction, we have noted, first, that our theory of outputs idealizes by abstracting from performance errors. So we are not concerned with the chess player's moves when he is drunk, with any "noise" produced by the logic machine, or with the bee's dance when it is shaken off course. We have noted, second, that we are concerned not only with any actual output but with any possible output. So we are concerned with any of an indefinitely large number of *wffs* that the logic machine might produce and of dances that the bee might perform.[6] We now note, third, that we also abstract from properties of the outputs that are irrelevant to our concerns. For example, consider a collection of logic machines each embodying the same formal logic. One machine may produce a "written" *wff* in one script, another, in another script; one may produce a fast high-pitched "spoken" *wff*, another, a slow low-pitched one. We might be interested in these differences and so distinguish these *wffs* and the competences that produce them. But we might well not be. We may be simply interested in the rule-governed syntactic structures of the *wffs*, structures shared by the outputs of all these machines. So in our theorizing we abstract from these differences.

Still with an eye to important features of grammar construction, we note, fourth, that although our theory is of the idealized output we can use it to make distinctions among the nonideal. Moves that are not chess moves, formulae that are not well-formed, and maneuvers that are not proper bee dances, can differ in their *degree* of failure. For, they can differ in the sort and number of structure rules of chess, *wffs*, and bee dances that they fail, respectively, to satisfy.

2.3 RESPECTING STRUCTURE RULES

Although processing rules need not include any of the structure rules, they must, I shall say, "respect" them.

---

[5] According to C. R. Gallistel (1990), the bee can: "the bees must represent the angles and distances of food sources not only with reference to the sun but also with reference to prominent features of the terrain surrounding the hive" (p. 132). Gallistel's account of the extraordinary navigational skills of insects makes this plausible.

[6] This talk may appear to commit theories of outputs to the existence of unactualized possibilia, but the talk can be, and in my view should be, a mere manner of speaking. It is a convenient way of capturing that these theories, like all interesting ones, are lawlike. Strictly speaking, the theories quantify only over actual entities but the theories are, in some sense, necessary. So the talk captures the modal fact that if something *were* a horseshoe, a chess move, a *wff*, a bee's dance, or whatever, then it *would have* the properties specified by the appropriate theory of outputs. (How are we to explain modal facts? I don't know but, *pace* David Lewis, surely not in terms of unactualized possibilia.)

3. Distinguish the respecting of structure rules by processing rules from the inclusion of structure rules among processing rules.

I have mentioned that there is a causal relation between a competence and its output. There is also a "constitutive" relation. This arises from the fact that the *very nature* of the competence is to produce its outputs: producing them is what makes it the competence it is. Thus, the blacksmith's competence is (partly) the ability to produce horseshoes; the chess player's, to produce chess moves, things governed by the structure rules of chess; the logic machine's, to produce *wffs*, things governed by the formation rules; the bee's, to produce dances, things governed by the dance rules. So a theory of the outputs of a competence is automatically, to that extent, a contribution to the theory of the competence, for it tells us about the outputs the production of which is definitive of the competence. And we can say that a competence and its processing rules must "respect" the nature of the appropriate output in that, performance errors aside, the processing rules must produce outputs that have that nature. Where we have to appeal to structure rules to characterize that nature, as we do with the outputs of the chess player, the logic machine, and the bee, these structure rules must be respected by the processing rules. Thus, whether or not the chess player actually goes through a process of inferring 'x moves diagonally' from 'x is a bishop', whatever processes she does go through must respect the structure rule that a bishop moves diagonally; any moves she makes must be in accord with that rule. And even if I am right in suggesting that the processing rules governing the bee's dancing cannot plausibly be seen as including the previously-described structure rule for the direction of the food source, the processing rules must respect that structure rule in that they produce dances that are governed by it.

I emphasize that 'respecting', as I am using it, is a *technical* term applying primarily to a relation between a competence and its processing rules on the one hand, and the structure rules governing the outputs of that competence on the other hand. Occasionally I shall extend the use of the term to talk of the competent person herself respecting those structure rules, but this should not be confused with her respecting them in any ordinary sense. She respects them in that her competence produces outputs that are governed by those structure rules. Finally, note that this technical sense of 'respecting' is very different from either of the senses of 'governing' we have mentioned, the governing of a process by processing rules and the governing of an object by structure rules.

On the strength of the fact that these structure rules must be thus respected it may be appropriate to say that the competent object behaves *as if* those rules were embodied in the object, but it is surely not appropriate to say *solely* on those grounds that the rules *are* embodied in it. The respecting might, of course, be the *result* of the rules being embodied; for example, the rules might also be processing rules. But the respecting alone does not require that the rules be actually realized in the speaker; for example, it does not require that they be processing rules. For there may be many other possible ways that a competence might respect the rules, as the chess and logic machines illustrated. So the claim that a competence and its processing rules respect the structure rules is the minimal claim on the internal reality issue. In a sense, this claim tells us little about the competence because it tells us nothing about *the way in which* the competence respects the structure rules. Still, we should not minimize the minimal claim. We know something quite substantial about a bee when we know that there is something-we-know-not-what within the bee that respects the structure rules of its dance. And were the respected rules richer and more complicated than those of the bee's dance we would know something even more substantial.

It follows from the minimal claim that a theory of a competence must posit processing rules that respect the structure rules of the outputs. Similarly, a theory of the outputs must posit structure rules that are respected by the competence and its processing rules. Let us capture this by saying that both theories must meet the "Respect Constraint".

I have remarked that a theory of the outputs of a competence must be a contribution to the theory of the competence. I think that we should go further: the theory of a competence must *begin* with a theory of its outputs. A competence is a competence to produce outputs with certain natures; those natures are partly constitutive of the competence. How then could we make any significant progress studying a competence until we knew a good deal about the natures of the outputs that it is supposed to produce? How could we start trying to solve the mystery of the bee's competence to dance until we knew the previously-described structure rule for the direction of the food source? In brief, the theory of outputs has a certain epistemic and explanatory priority over the theory of competence.

2.4   APPLICATION TO LINGUISTICS

I shall now apply this discussion to linguistics, arguing that we should see grammars as primarily theories of linguistic not psychological reality. In the discussion I have had an eye to certain important features of grammar construction. This was in anticipation of a certain objection to the view of linguistics I am urging. The objection is that this view cannot be right because it cannot account for those features. We shall see that it can and does.

Observing distinction 1, we distinguish the theory of a speaker's competence in a language, a psychological state, from the theory of the outputs of that competence, sentences in the language. The competence in the language is not the language any more than the blacksmith's competence is a horseshoe, the chess player's competence is chess, or the bee's competence is its dance. The linguistic competence is in the mind/brain, the language is not.[7] The construction of the

---

[7] This difference from standard ways of talking in linguistics and psycholinguistics is not, of course, a merely verbal one over the use of the word 'language': it reflects a disagreement over the subject matter of linguistics, whatever that subject matter is called.

theory of the competence is Chomsky's task (i), described in section 1.1. The construction of the theory of the language is a different task, one that I wish to promote. What can we say about it?

Like the theory of the outputs of the blacksmith, chess player, logic machine, and bee, the theory of the outputs of linguistic competence is not concerned simply with the actual outputs. It abstracts from performance error to consider outputs when the competence is working well. Thus we account for the first important feature of grammar construction. And our theory of outputs is concerned with any of an indefinitely large number of these idealized outputs that the competence might produce, with any possible output.[8] Thus we account for a second important feature. Like the theory of the outputs of the logic machine, our theory can abstract also from a range of properties of the outputs—for example, form of script and pitch of sound—focusing simply on the syntactic properties that we are interested in. Thus we account for a third important feature.[9] The outputs of a linguistic competence, physical sentence tokens, are governed by a system of rules, just like the outputs of the chess player, the logic machine, and the bee. Something counts as a sentence only if it has a place in the linguistic structure defined by these structure rules.[10] Something counts as a particular sentence, has its particular syntactic structure, in virtue of the particular structure rules that govern it, in virtue of its particular place in the linguistic structure. Like the theory of the idealized outputs of the chess player, logic machine, and bee, our theory can be used to make distinctions among the nonideal. Strings that are not sentences can differ in their *degree* of failure. For they can differ in the sort and number of linguistic structure rules that they fail to satisfy. Thus we account for a fourth important feature.

Observing distinction 2, we distinguish these structure rules from processing rules involved in the exercise of linguistic competence. These two sorts of rules have very different roles. The processing rules produce sentences of the language in the exercise of linguistic competence. It is because those sentences are governed by the structure rules that they are indeed sentences of the language. It may be possible that a structure rule will also be a processing rule, but it is not necessary that it be.

The linguistic structure rules are like the formation rules for the *wffs* of a formal logic. Since we know the formation rules for the *wffs*, we could build a *wff* machine that generated *wffs* from the lexicon. Similarly, if we knew all the

---

[8] And, as with the earlier theories (note 6), such talk need not be construed as a commitment to unactualized possibilia but rather as a way of capturing that the linguistic theory is lawlike. So if something *were* a sentence, a wh-question, a passive, or whatever, it *would have* the properties specified for such items by the theory.

[9] We might sum up the point of this paragraph so far in the terms of Ferdinand de Saussure (1916): our interest is in *langue* not *parole*.

[10] The analogy of language with chess was a favorite of Saussure's (1916: 20, 107). This reflected his mistaken view of language as an autonomous system and his related rejection of reference (Devitt and Sterelny 1999: 266).

linguistic rules, we could build a "sentence machine" that generated sentences from the lexicon. This process would be governed by the linguistic rules although in all other ways, including selection from the lexicon, it would be random. Thus, in generating a sentence, it might start by picking a certain syntactic form. This selection is constrained by the rules for combining words of the various syntactic categories but is otherwise random. Next, for each category of word in the selected syntactic form, it randomly selects a word of that category from the lexicon. This process might yield a simple sentence like 'Aristotle admired Plato', or a more complex ones like 'Frege believed that Aristotle taught Alexander the Great' or 'Every dog has fleas'. The particular syntactic structure of each sentence would be determined by the particular linguistic rules involved in generating it. We noted that the processes by which the *wff* machine generates *wffs* are very different from the processes by which the logic machine does. Similarly, I shall emphasize that the processes by which the sentence machine generates sentences are very different from the processes by which humans do (4.2).

Finally, observing distinction 3, we note that although the structure rules governing sentences may not be among the processing rules that govern the exercise of linguistic competence, they must be respected by the competence and its processing rules: performance errors aside, the outputs of the process must be sentences of the language and hence must be governed by the rules of the language. For, it is the very nature of the competence to produce such sentences. The claim that the structure rules of the language must be respected by the competence and its processing rules is the minimal claim on the issue of the psychological reality of language. In this sense, at least, we might say that the grammar describes "what the competent speaker knows". And on the strength of this minimal claim we might say that the speaker behaves *as if* those linguistic structure rules were psychologically real in her, *as if* she embodied them. But it is surely not appropriate to say *solely* on the strength of that minimal claim that those rules *are* psychologically real in her, *are* embodied, for the claim does not require that the rules be actually realized in her. In a sense, the claim tells us little about linguistic competence because it tells us nothing about *the way in which* the competence respects the linguistic rules. Still, we do know something substantial about a person when we know that there is something-we-know-not-what within her that respects the rich and complicated structure rules of a certain natural language.

Both a theory of a person's linguistic competence, of her knowledge of her language, and a theory of her linguistic outputs must meet the Respect Constraint. A theory of the competence must posit a psychological state that respects the rules governing the linguistic outputs. And a theory of the linguistic outputs must posit rules that are respected by the competence and its processing rules.

On my view, a language is composed of the outputs of a linguistic competence, symbols that are governed by a system of linguistic structure rules. That is the reality of a language. And the task we have been contemplating, and that I wish to promote, is the study of the nature of this reality. This is not Chomsky's task (i), the study of the nature of the competence itself. Indeed, at first sight, the contemplated study may seem to be alien to Chomsky's enterprise. It may even seem to smack of studying an "E-language", of which Chomsky takes a dim view: "the concept [of an E-language] appears to play no role in the theory of language" (1986: 26); an E-language has "no corresponding real-world object" (p. 27). But it is not obvious that the outputs of linguistic competence fit Chomsky's description of an E-language. According to him an E-language is "externalized ... in the sense that the construct is understood independently of the properties of the mind/brain" (1986: 20). And it sometimes seems as if an E-language for Chomsky is essentially Platonic. In any case, the outputs I have identified, physical sentence tokens governed by a system of linguistic rules, are certainly not divorced from the mind/brain since they are the symbolic outputs of the mind/brain. In studying them our *object* of study is not the mind/brain, of course, but their linguistic properties are surely largely *determined* by the mind/ brain. Finally, the theory of them is as much concerned with real-world objects as the theories of horseshoes, chess moves, bees' dances, and *wffs*. It is often convenient to talk of the objects posited by these theories as if they were *types* not tokens, as if they were abstract Platonic objects, but this need be nothing more than a manner of speaking: when the chips are down the objects are parts of the spatio-temporal physical world.

Here I part company with Jerrold Katz (1981, 1984, 1996). He also favors a linguistic task that is quite different from Chomsky's task (i), but the one he favors is the study of a system of Platonic objects.[11] For him talk of sentence *types* is not a mere manner of speaking but essential to the task. He calls Chomsky's view "conceptualism" and my sort of view "nominalism". He takes nominalism to have been refuted by Chomsky's criticisms of Bloomfieldian structuralism. Yet, so far as I can see, these criticisms are not of the *nominalism* of the structuralists but rather of their *taxonomic methodology*, a methodology in the spirit of positivism. According to Chomsky, this methodology imposed "arbitrary and unwarranted" limitations on linguistics: it insisted on defining "lower levels" before "higher levels"; it was inductive instead of explanatory (abductive); its epistemology was localist instead of Quinean holist. Indeed, despite the explicit nominalism of the structuralists, Chomsky is prepared to

---

[11] Dwyer and Pietroski take linguistic generalizations to be about non-mental abstract objects but "nonetheless ... hold that linguistics is properly construed as a branch of psychology, in that linguists ascribe [linguistic] beliefs to agents" (1996: 349). This is not a good reason for placing linguistics in psychology. (They have another reason, discussed in section 2.7 below.) According to Dwyer and Pietroski, the ascription of beliefs is to explain *the use* of language and to explain *intuitive judgments* about language (p. 340). Yet, the former explanation is the proper concern of psycholinguistics and the latter is the proper concern of epistemology (or so I shall argue; 7.7 below). On their Katzian view of what linguistic generalizations are about, neither explanation should be the concern of linguistics itself.

take the structuralists as implicitly concerned with the psychological reality of language and hence not really nominalist at all (Chomsky 1975c: 30–6).[12] Yet he still thinks his methodological criticisms stand. In any case, Chomsky's methodological criticisms can be and, in my view, should be embraced by the nominalist. In particular, we should not demand that the linguistic properties of tokens be reduced to "brute-physical" intrinsic properties of the tokens. The linguistic properties that concern us are "high-level" relational properties.[13]

There are likely to be lingering doubts about my contemplated task. One doubt is about how the domain of study is to be determined: How do we select the tokens to be studied from all the other behavioral outputs of speakers? And the answer is: in the way science usually determines domains. That is, guided by folk linguistics, we start with an intuitive idea of the domain of grammatical tokens to be studied. We do not include many items that seem "unacceptable" to speakers. As our linguistics goes scientific, we modify our view of the domain, accepting some strings that we had thought ungrammatical because they were, say, too hard to parse or "meaningless". We may even reject some strings previously thought to be grammatical. Linguistics, like other sciences, largely determines its own domain.

A second doubt may arise from the rather curious view that there aren't really any linguistic tokens. This view is a mistaken reaction to two facts. The first is the just-noted fact that the properties in virtue of which something is a linguistic token are all relational. The second is the fact that tokens of the one linguistic expression can appear in a variety of physical forms: a variety of sounds, a variety of inscriptions, and so on. I shall discuss the view in section 10.6. Meanwhile, I note briefly that something can really have a certain linguistic property just as something can really have the property of being Australian even though neither have these properties intrinsically and even though things that have them can differ greatly in their physical forms.

Another doubt arises out of attitudes to Bloomfieldian linguistics. From the generative perspective, the Bloomfieldian approach often appeared to be somewhat superficial and instrumentalist, concerned merely with describing

---

[12] In taking this line, Chomsky follows a common and effective pattern in realist philosophy of science: arguing that scientists who claim to be instrumentalists follow practices that are implicitly realist.

[13] Katz has another objection to nominalism: grammars are about an infinite number of sentences but there cannot be an infinite number of tokens. If there were a problem for my sort of nominalism it would lie in its apparent commitment to nonactual possible sentences, a problem that would arise even if we were dealing with a finite language (e.g. English with a limit of one million words to a sentence). The only significance of any apparent commitment to an infinite number of sentences is that it would *guarantee* that some were nonactual. But talk of there *being* nonactual possible outputs of a competence can be a mere manner of speaking (notes 6 and 8). So too can talk of there *being* an infinite number of such outputs. The truth behind the talk of the nonactual can be simply that the grammar is lawlike. And the truth behind the talk of the infinite can be simply that there is no limit to the number of different sentence tokens that might be governed by the rules the grammar describes.

regularities in the corpus of observed utterances rather than with the language's underlying generalizations. The generative focus on the psychological reality of language is seen as the way to avoid this instrumentalism and be a realist about linguistic theory.[14] So there may be doubts about how my contemplated task can be realist about language. But, as I have emphasized, the study of linguistic tokens is not concerned only with actually observed tokens: like any other scientific theory it is modal, concerned with any possible token. And the approach should indeed be realist, concerned with the underlying generalizations of the language. Linking language to the mind is important, of course—and I shall do plenty of it—but it does not require that we collapse the contemplated task into task (i). And the link to the mind is not needed for realism. We should be realist in linguistics as everywhere else in science,[15] as Chomsky has frequently insisted. But we can be realist in linguistics without taking the grammar to be true of psychological reality, but rather taking it to be true of linguistic reality: all being well, linguistic symbols really do have the properties ascribed to them by the grammar; some really are c-commanded, some really are co-indexed, and so on.

Here is a more disturbing doubt. I have talked of studying the nature of a sentence token, a nature that we reach by abstracting from properties that are irrelevant to our concerns. But what are these concerns? *What is our theoretical interest in the token?* It would not be enough to argue for what Soames (1984) calls the "conceptual distinctness" of this task from the study of competence. We have to show that the task is worthwhile. I suspect that the presupposition, often the conviction, that there is no such worthwhile task is the main reason for thinking that the linguistic task is Chomsky's (i). The view is that we need to take the task to be about competence for it to be worth doing.[16]

Here are four reasons for thinking that my contemplated task is worthwhile. First, it must be worthwhile *if Chomsky's task (i) is.*[17] For, although we have distinguished the two tasks we have also related them in a way that makes

---

[14] For example, consider the following quotes and the texts that surround them:

On other grounds, it is difficult to explain why investigators continually found it necessary to revise and modify their procedures in the light of results that were, in some unexplained sense, "unacceptable" though in no way inconsistent with the corpus of data. (Chomsky 1975c: 36)
we are interested in linguistic analyses primarily insofar as they may be claimed to represent the knowledge speaker–hearers have of the structure of their language. (Fodor, Bever, and Garrett 1974: 40)
The shift of focus from language itself to the native speaker's knowledge of language is the major feature of the Chomskian tradition. (Haegeman 1994: 7)

[15] See my 1997a. I frequently do missionary work for realism. (I sincerely hope that McGilvray 1999 is wrong in going beyond the usual attribution to Chomsky of the nativist view that our biology determines our language to the attribution of the appallingly antirealist view that our biology determines *the world itself*.)

[16] See Laurence 2003, sec. 5, for a vigorous argument to that effect.

[17] I owe this reason to Roblin Meeks.

completing the contemplated task *necessary* for completing task (i). For, the nature of the speaker's competence studied by task (i) *involves* the nature of the symbols studied by the contemplated task: those symbols are what the competence produces. Indeed, our earlier discussion (2.3) shows that the contemplated task has a certain epistemic and explanatory priority over task (i). How could we make any significant progress studying the nature of competence in a language unless we already knew a good deal about that language? Just as explaining the bee's dances is a prerequisite for discovering how the bee manages to produce those dances, so also explaining the syntax of sentences is a prerequisite for explaining how speakers manage to produce those sentences.

A second reason for thinking that my contemplated task is worthwhile is that analogous ones are. This may not seem so obvious with the horsehoe, chess, and the logic machine, but it is surely obvious with the bee's dance. A serious researcher spent years "cracking the code" of this dance, working out how it indicates the direction and distance of the food source. His findings were certainly interesting to scientists.[18] The study of human language must surely be more worthwhile and interesting than the study of the bee's.

A third reason for thinking the task worthwhile would be that substantial and interesting theories are fulfilling the task. In the next section I shall argue that generative grammars are such theories.

The fourth and most important reason starts from the intuition that our concern with sentence tokens, as with bees' dances, is with their *meanings*. This is a widely held view[19] but it is unsatisfactorily vague. I have argued elsewhere that we should be concerned with the properties of sentence tokens that enable them to play certain striking roles in our lives, including the role of informing us about reality; these are the "meanings" of tokens (1996: 2.3–2.8).[20] Analogously, the properties of bees' dances that concern us are the ones that enable them to play their role of indicating food sources. Sentence tokens have their meanings partly

---

[18] "Von Frisch's *Dance Language and Orientation of Bees* was some four decades in the making. By the time his papers on the bee dance were collected and published in 1965, there was scarcely an entomomologist in the world who hadn't been both intrigued and frustrated by his findings. Intrigued because the phenomenon Von Frisch described was so startlingly complex; frustrated because no one had a clue as to how bees managed the trick" (Frank 1997: 82). Von Fisch's work was so interesting that he was awarded the Nobel Prize. We should also note, as Michael Maumus pointed out to me, the great interest in the work of Jean Francois Champollion and other scholars who spent years studying the Rosetta stone to crack the code of a "dead language", the language of Ptolemaic-era hieroglyphics.

[19] Randy Harris calls the definition of linguistics as "the study of the links between sound and meaning" "one that virtually all linguists would agree to" (1993: 5).

[20] Fodor poses the "fundamental question" of the theory of language thus:

under certain conditions the production by speaker S of an acoustic object U which is a token of a linguistic type belonging to the language L suffices to communicate a determinate message between S and any other suitably situated L-speaker. How is that fact to be explained? (1975: 103)

in virtue of their syntactic properties and partly in virtue of the meanings of their words. So, accepting the restriction to syntax for the sake of argument, the nature of the sentence token that we need to explain is made up of the syntactic properties in virtue of which the token can play those striking roles.

Our first reason seemed to make our theoretical interest in the contemplated task dependent on our theoretical interest in Chomsky's task (i). On the basis of our fourth reason, I shall soon argue for the opposite dependency (2.6: "fourth methodological point").

We need to say much more about the theoretical interest of studying linguistic symbols and I shall attempt to do so later (8.5). I think that this interest does indeed arise out of our interest in the mind, in particular from our interest in thoughts and their role in explaining behavior.[21] But, once again, this does not make our study psychological: in particular, it does not turn it into task (i), the study of competence.

Doubts about my contemplated task may still linger. One aim of the Part IV discussion of the relation of language to thought is to set such doubts to rest; see particularly Chapter 8 and sections 10.4 to 10.6.

Is my contemplated task appropriately characterized as nominalistic? It takes all the objects that linguistics is about to be concrete tokens, and so to that extent it is nominalistic. Where it stands ultimately on the nominalism issue depends, of course, on what we make of its ascription of meaning *properties* to those objects. However, it seems unlikely that the nominalist would have any *special* difficulty paraphrasing away this property talk. My contemplated task for linguistics is likely to be as nominalistic as tasks in physics, biology, or economics.

2.5 THE CONTEMPLATED TASK AND THE LINGUISTIC ENTERPRISE

Whether or not this study of the outputs of competence is the study of an E-language in Chomsky's sense, and whatever the case about the psychological reality of languages, I want to argue that there is nothing alien to the linguist's enterprise in the contemplated task.

There are two parts to this question. (a) What property does U have that enables it to convey the message? (b) How are S and the other L-speaker able to exploit that property to communicate? (a) is about L. My contemplated task is to answer (a). (b) is about competence in L which is, as I am arguing, a different but related question.

[21] It is this theoretical interest that is likely to make a grammarian of English as concerned with the outputs of Laurence's Martians (2003: sec. 5) as with our own outputs. And it will prevent her concern from spreading to the outputs of parrots, tape recorders, and the like (Devitt and Sterelny 1999: 145), a spread that Laurence argues is a likely consequence of not taking the Chomskian view (2003: sec. 5).

First, these actual and possible idealized outputs, governed by a system of rules and fitting into a structure, *are* what we would normally call a language. Indeed, wherever there is a linguistic competence there *has* to be such a language, for the language is what the competence produces: the language is what the speaker is competent *in*; it is definitive of the nature of the competence.

Second, we note that Chomsky himself often describes his task in ways that suggest it is the one we have been contemplating. For example, consider the following from the early pages of *Syntactic Structures*:

> The fundamental aim in the linguistic analysis of a language L is to separate the *grammatical* sequences which are sentences of L from the *ungrammatical* sequences which are not sentences of L and to study the structure of the grammatical sequences. (1957: 13; see also 1980a: 222)

Third, *prima facie*, a great deal of the work that linguists do, day by day, in syntax and phonology is studying a language in the nominalistic sense I have described.[22] Work on phrase structure, case theory, anaphora, and so on, talk of "nouns", "verb phrases", "c-command", and so on, all appear to be concerned, quite straightforwardly, with *the properties of symbols* of a language, symbols that are the outputs of a competence. This work and talk seems to be concerned with the properties of items like the very words on this page. The traditional view of phonology is that it is concerned with "external physical phenomena produced by behavior we call 'speech' ... phenomena external to mind/brain (for example, sounds)" (Burton-Roberts *et al.* 2000: 3).[23] And, we have already noted, four important features of grammar construction are also part of the contemplated study: the idealization of outputs; concern with all possible outputs; abstraction from irrelevant properties; the making of distinctions among the nonideal.

Fourth, the linguistic evidence adduced for a grammar bears directly on a theory of the language in my sense; evidence about which strings of words are grammatical; about the ambiguity of certain sentences; about statement forms and question forms; about the synonymy of sentences that are superficially different; about the difference between sentences that are superficially similar; and so on.

---

[22] Or in Katz's Platonic sense, which can be taken as simply a convenient manner of speaking of language in my sense (2.4).

[23] Burton-Roberts *et al.* go on: "It is difficult to square the traditional view of phonology and its rationale" with Chomsky's internalist view of language (p. 4). They describe four responses to this difficulty. (A) Isolate the externalist phonological part of the language faculty from the internalist rest; the phonological part is simply "different". (B) Reject the internalist view of language, taking the theory of language to be "the theory of communicative behaviour and its perceptual products" (pp. 4–5). (C) Reject the externalist view of phonology, thus purging it of "phonetic substance" (p. 5); it is concerned with "mental objects" (p. 9). (D) Accept the internalist view of language but exclude phonology from the language faculty (pp. 5–6). The view of language I am urging clearly goes nicely with the traditional view of phonology and response (B). The other responses indicate the contortions that the Chomskian view of language has brought upon phonology.

Objection: "But this so-called 'linguistic' evidence is largely the intuitions of the native speaker. These arise from her underlying competence. So the evidence bears directly on task (i) not your task." **Response:** It is indeed true that if the speaker's knowledge of her language consists in her representation of its rules and if her intuitions are derived from those representations by a causal and rational process, then those intuitions are direct evidence for task (i) because they are direct evidence of what rules are represented. I shall later argue against this view of these intuitions and against the view that the linguistic evidence largely consists in these intuitions (Ch. 7). But whatever the truth of these matters, the point to be made now is that the intuitions are direct evidence about language in my sense provided that we have good reason to think that they are accurate. It does not matter to this point whether we think that they are accurate because they are derived from representations of the rules or for some other reason. If they are accurate they are evidence about language because language is what they are about: they are about the grammaticality, ambiguity, etc. of linguistic *symbols or expressions*. So if the intuitions are indeed derived from a representation of linguistic rules, then they will be direct evidence for *both* task (i) and my contemplated task. If, on the other hand, they are not so derived but are nonetheless generally accurate, as I shall argue they are, then they will still be direct evidence for my task even if only indirect evidence for task (i).

Fifth, the *psycholinguistic* evidence about language comprehension and acquisition, offered to support the view that a grammar is psychologically real, bears directly on a theory of the language, in my sense.[24] Thus, concerning comprehension, evidence that speakers are sensitive to a proposed syntactic property in parsing an expression is evidence that the expression really has that property, for it is evidence that their competence respects the structure rules that determine that property; see the later discussion of a "click location" experiment for an example (4.3). The right theory of a language must ascribe rules to the language that competent speakers of the language respect: the Respect Constraint. In this way, the psycholinguistic evidence bears directly on our theory of the linguistic reality.[25] And, concerning acquisition, evidence about nature and nurture showing that a

---

[24] Adapting Chomsky's terminology (1965: 24–7), we might say that a grammar that is justified by psycholinguistic evidence as well as linguistic evidence is "explanatorily adequate".

Laurence (2003: sec. 5) names one of my earlier arguments (Devitt and Sterelny 1989: 514) "The Martian Argument" and takes it "to question whether *in principle* [psycholinguistic] data are even *relevant* to the evaluation of linguistic theories" (p. 95). I doubt that I ever questioned this but I certainly do not question it now. One of the two advantages that Laurence claims for the Chomskian view of linguistics over its rivals is that it brings psycholinguistic data to bear on linguistic theory. The Chomskian view does not have this advantage over the view I am urging.

[25] Cf: "A parser which is well-attuned to the competence grammar can be a source of information about the properties of the grammar" (J. D. Fodor 1989: 174). My point is that the parser *has* to be a source of information for the grammar because it has to be sufficiently well-attuned to assign the right syntactic structures, performance errors aside. Of course, on the received assumption that the grammar is psychologically real and applied in parsing, evidence about parsing will obviously be seen as bearing on the grammar; for example, see Chomsky 1980a: 200–1; Berwick and Weinberg 1984: 35. My point is that the evidence bears on the grammar even without the assumption.

language with a certain structure could or could not have been learnt by a person from the "primary linguistic data" is direct evidence for or against any theory that ascribes such a structure to a language that has been learnt by the person.[26]

In light of responses to a related point that Soames made about evidence (1984), I should guard against possible misunderstandings.

(a) I am making the empirical claim that, as a matter of fact, the linguistic and psycholinguistic evidence bears directly on a theory of language in my nominalistic sense (whatever its bearing on anything else). This sort of claim about the bearing of evidence on a theory is a familiar part of science and ordinary life. The claim is *not* an attempt to impose a priori restrictions on the domain of evidence relevant to Chomsky's task (i) or to my contemplated task (cf. J. A. Fodor 1981b: 199–200; Chomsky 1986: 34–6; 1995: 33–4; Antony 2003; Laurence 2003: 101–4). I go along with the Duhem-Quine thesis which allows, roughly, that anything might be evidence for anything. But it is clearly not a consequence of that thesis that a piece of evidence bears with equal directness on all theories. It is not a consequence, for example, that the experience of green grass bears equally on the theory that grass is green and the theory that echidnas have spikes.

(b) I am not claiming that the linguistic evidence mentioned in my fourth point *is* irrelevant to task (i). Indeed, since the processing rules of linguistic competence must respect the structure rules, any direct evidence about the structure rules must to that extent bear on task (i). For the same reason, the psycholinguistic evidence mentioned in my fifth point must also bear on task (i) to that extent. Of course, we hope that this evidence will bear on task (i) to a much greater extent, throwing light on *the way in which* competence respects the structure rules. However, I do plan to argue that the psycholinguistic evidence now available does not in fact throw much light on this matter and gives no support to the view that competence respects the structure rules by representing them; it gives no support to the Representational Thesis (RT).[27]

---

[26] This evidential point seems to me to be the truth underlying the view, attributed to Chomsky, "that language acquisition is the key to understanding the nature of language" (Pinker 1995a: 108).

[27] The second of the two advantages that Laurence (2003) claims for the Chomskian view of linguistics over its rivals is that it confers *explanatory power* on linguistic theory, in particular the power to explain language use and acquisition. (1) On the view I am urging, the power of a linguistic theory is to be found primarily in its explanation of the properties of linguistic tokens. (2) Still, the theory does contribute to the explanation of language use and acquisition because competence must respect the linguistic rules ascribed by the theory. So use and acquisition phenomena that would be predictable if those rules were the ones respected—for example, the phenomena Laurence describes (sec. 2)—are indeed partly explained by a theory that ascribes those rules. (3) Of course, the theory would make a greater contribution to the explanation of use and acquisition were it the case that competence respected the linguistic rules by representing them. I shall be arguing that the psycholinguistic evidence does not support this thesis (nor even the more modest thesis that competence respects the rules by embodying them without representing them). But the point to be made in response to Laurence is: if the psycholinguistic evidence were ultimately to support the thesis, thus expanding the explanatory power of linguistic theory, this expansion would not count against the view of linguistics I am urging. Rather, the expansion would be welcomed as an explanatory bonus: the theory not only explains language, it plays a larger role in the explanation of language use and acquisition than we had any reason to expect.

In brief, my evidential point is simply that evidence that has played a big role in linguistic and psycholinguistic theorizing bears directly on the task that I have distinguished from Chomsky's task (i), whether or not that evidence, or any other evidence, bears on task (i). And my general point is that linguists appear to be studying, partly at least, a language in my nominalistic sense.

Sixth and finally, the appearance that linguists are studying language in this sense is just what we should expect *given Chomsky's assumption (on the natural interpretation) that the competence that is the concern of task (i) is knowledge of the language, involving the representation of its rules; i.e., given RT* (1.1). For, *the language that would be thus known and represented would be the very same language that is the output of the competence.* Chomsky assumes that competence consists in knowledge about the I-language. The point I am emphasizing is that this very I-language is, indeed *must be* at the appropriate level of abstraction, the output of that very competence. So, *given Chomsky's assumption*, task (i) requires just the same study as we have been contemplating. So it is no surprise to find Chomsky moving straight from an account of the task like the one quoted from *Syntactic Structures* to the following version of task (i):

The problem for the linguist ... is to determine ... the underlying system of rules that has been mastered by the speaker-hearer ... Hence, in a technical sense, linguistic theory is mentalistic, since it is concerned with discovering a mental reality underlying actual behavior. (1965: 4)

Given the assumption of RT, task (i) and the contemplated task are much the same.[28] At one and the same time we study the symbolic system that is the output of the competence and the competence itself which is a representation of that very system.

If this is so, the contemplated task is not open to objection from Chomsky. Given his assumption, it is a task that must be performed in performing his task (i). The contemplated task acknowledges the link between competence and language but differs from task (i) in being neutral about the precise psychological nature of that competence.

Not only must Chomsky accept the contemplated task, we should all accept it. A competence is a competence to do something. So whenever there is a competence to investigate there is also a product of that competence to investigate. When the output is a language, it should go without saying that its investigation is theoretically interesting. Still, we can say why it is and I have started to do so in the last section.

Chomskian linguists believe that the grammars they produce are about psychological reality. But believing that it is so does not, of course, make it so. In this

---

[28] A similar assumption yields a similar conflation in some philosophers of language; hence Michael Dummett's slogan, "a theory of meaning is a theory of understanding" (1975: 99).

section I have produced evidence that it is not so: the grammars are about linguistic reality.

2.6 FOUR METHODOLOGICAL POINTS

If this discussion is right, it has a great deal of methodological significance. I have pointed out (1.1) that Chomsky is irritated by the issue of the psychological reality of language. For him the only issue here is the truth of the grammar: if the grammar is true then of course it is true of psychological reality because that is what the grammar is about.

First methodological point. There is something theoretically interesting for a grammar to be true about other than the internal reality of speakers just as there is something theoretically interesting for a theory of chess moves, *wffs*, or bees' dances to be true about other than the internal reality of chess players, logic machines, or bees. The grammar might be true about a symbolic system, a *linguistic* reality. Contrary to received opinion, language is not a "type of mental entity" (cf. Harris 2003: 717). And Chomsky's claim that "the language has no objective existence apart from its mental representation" is false (Chomsky 1972: 169). So we can take the grammar realistically without taking it to be true of *psychological* reality. Furthermore, given the weight of evidence adduced for a grammar, it is plausible that it *is* (more or less) true of linguistic reality.

In light of this methodological point consider the following defense of the psychological reality of structural descriptions:

Hypotheses about structural descriptions are true when they correspond to the relevant facts, and the relevant facts concern the internal representations that speaker/hearers compute when they produce and understand the sentences of their language. But if it isn't internal representations that make structural descriptions true, what is it? (Fodor, Fodor, and Garrett 1975: 244)

On the view I am urging, the answer to the authors' question is: The facts that make structural descriptions true are the properties of the expressions described by the descriptions. Still, my view allows an underlying truth to the authors' claim preceding their question. For, the competence of the speaker/hearer must respect the rules that constitute those structural properties of expressions. So what the speaker produces and the hearer comprehends must have those properties (performance errors aside). That truth underlies the claim that the facts that make the structural descriptions true "concern the internal representations that speaker/hearers compute".

Second methodological point. The view that a grammar has any more to do with psychological reality than the amount allowed by the minimal claim requires a powerful psychological assumption about competence, if not Chomsky's assumption then one of similar strength. Without such an assumption, the grammar simply concerns a language system. This system is the output of something psychological but it remains to be argued that it is itself psychological.

Of course, this does nothing to show that the grammar is *not* true of the psychological reality, that the rules of the language are *not* actually realized in the speaker. The point is that whether the grammar is true of psychological reality is a *further* question to its being true of the linguistic reality. Settling that further question depends on settling the truth of a powerful psychological assumption. *The psychological reality of language is not something "you get for nothing" with the truth of the grammar.*[29] I fuss about this because I think it is hard to find evidence for a psychological assumption that will do the trick.[30]

Third methodological point. According to the Respect Constraint, a theory of competence in a language must posit processing rules for comprehension and production that respect the structure rules of the language. And the grammar must posit structure rules that are respected by the competence and its processing rules. So, the Respect Constraint makes the justification of the grammar partly dependent on the justification of the theory of competence, and vice versa. Beyond that, however, *the grammar and the theory of competence are independent of each other.* So there should be no a priori demand that an acceptable grammar must meet some further constraint concerning psychological reality, for example what Robert Berwick and Amy Weinberg call "transparency" (1984: 38). And a grammar should not be dismissed—as, for example, transformational grammars were by Joan Bresnan and Ronald Kaplan (1982)—for failing to meet such further constraints. And we should not decide which linguistic theory is right, as Janet Fodor suggests we might, "by considering the sorts of parsing procedures that each linguistic theory implies" (1989: 181). A grammar that attributes rules that are respected by users of the language may be a perfectly adequate theory of the language however little it can be incorporated into a model of language use. Nor, in setting out to examine psychological reality, should we look to the grammar for any insights beyond those arising from the Respect Constraint. So far as the grammar is concerned, "the psychological cards can fall where they may", subject only to the Respect Constraint. Similarly, the theory of the bee's dance, including the previously-described theory of how the dance indicates the direction of the food source (2.2), provides no help to the theory of the bee's competence to dance beyond that arising from the fact that the competence must respect the rules of the dance.

---

[29] Cf. "Obviously, every speaker of a language has mastered and internalized a generative grammar that expresses his knowledge of his language" (Chomsky 1965: 8).

[30] In Devitt and Sterelny 1989, our case for the thesis that a grammar is about linguistic reality rested heavily on the view that it was very likely not true of psychological reality. This is what Laurence (2003: sec. 4) criticizes as "The Methodological Argument". I am still doubtful that the grammar is true of psychological reality but my present case for the thesis does not rest on that doubt.

This bears on a popular criticism of the claim that a grammar's rules are psychologically real.[31] The criticism is that we lack evidence as to *which* grammar's rules are psychologically real: "If we can come up with one grammar for a language, we can come up with many which, though they posit different syntactic rules, are equivalent in their explanation of meaning: they are equally able to capture all the syntactically determined facts about meaning. We need psycholinguistic evidence to show which grammar's rules are in fact playing the role in linguistic processing, evidence we do not have." This criticism is not quite right. We need evidence that the syntactic rules of *any* grammar are processing rules. These rules may simply be the *wrong sort of rules* to be processing rules, just as the rules of the bee's dance very likely are, and the rules of the logic machine's language certainly are. Suppose, as seems quite likely, that the human language capacity is an adaptation. Then nature faced the problem of designing this capacity out of pre-existing structures in our ancestors. We should not think, in advance of empirical discovery, that nature solved this problem by making humans go through processes governed by linguistic rules. We should not suppose a priori that a correct account of the linguistic reality will describe the psychological reality. A grammar may have nothing more to do with psychological reality than comes from its meeting the Respect Constraint.

So it was a mistake to assume that psycholinguistic evidence would decide which of many meaning-equivalent grammars was true of psychological reality: perhaps none of them are. We might be tempted to think that something interesting still remains of the criticism in that we need psycholinguistic evidence to decide which of many meaning-equivalent grammars are true of *linguistic* reality.[32] For, we need the psycholinguistic evidence to tell us which grammar meets the Respect Constraint, which one posits rules that are respected by the competence and its processing rules. The syntactic properties determined by rules that are respected are the ones that linguistic tokens really have. But this tempting thought is also mistaken. If two grammars positing different rules really do "capture all the syntactically determined facts about meaning" then they must both meet the Respect Constraint. For, there can be nothing more to a competence respecting rules than its producing and responding to sentences that have the syntactic properties determined by those rules. The two grammars specify rules that determine the same syntactic properties because the grammars are meaning-equivalent. (We shall later find that something interesting does still remain from the criticism; 11.4.)

Fourth methodological point. We have noted (2.4) that a grammar as a theory of a language has a certain epistemic and explanatory priority over a theory of the psychological reality underlying language. We cannot make any significant

---

[31] Devitt and Sterelny 1989 is an example. The criticism is related to what Laurence (2003: sec. 5) calls "The Martian Argument". It has its roots in Quine 1970.

[32] I was tempted (2003: 133).

progress studying competence in a language until we know a good deal about that language. So it is appropriate that, from the start, much of the work in generative grammar has been directly concerned more with the linguistic than with the psychological reality.[33]

I think that we can go further. Our *theoretical interest* in explaining competence in a language surely starts from our theoretical interest in that language. Think of the bee once more. Were it not for our interest in the nature of the bee's dance, we would never have become interested in the state that manages to produce that dance: it is because that state produces something so theoretically interesting that the state itself is so theoretically interesting. I think that the same goes for the state that produces language. If so, our theoretical interest in a language is prior to our interest in its psychological reality.

Earlier (2.4) I suggested that our theoretical interest in language arises from our interest in thoughts. I will attempt to support this later (8.5) but suppose, meanwhile, that it is right. Now put it together with what I have just claimed. We have the following "direction of theoretical interest": from thoughts to language to linguistic competence. The relation between theories of these three relatively distinct realities will be discussed in Part IV.

2.7   INTERESTING PSYCHOLOGICAL MATTERS

I trust then that it is obvious that I am *not* suggesting that the psychological reality underlying language is unworthy of study. Indeed, the theoretical interest in a language leads immediately to an interest in two matters psychological.

(i) It is not enough to know that there is something-we-know-not-what within a speaker that respects the rules of her language, any more than it is enough to know that there is something-we-know-not-what within a bee that respects the rules of the bee's dance. We would like to go beyond these minimal claims to discover the ways in which the competence of the speaker, and the competence of the bee, respect these rules.[34] But in studying these matters, to emphasize my third methodological point, it is a mistake to insist on finding, or even to expect to find, embodied in the organism, processing rules that are also structure rules of its outputs. The processing rules and structure rules have very different jobs to

---

[33] Cf:

many generativists assert that they aim to account for how children master their native languages, but the vast majority of their analyses do not contribute to that aim.   (Hornstein and Lightfoot 1981b: 7)

it is possible, and arguably proper, for a linguist (*qua* linguist) to ignore matters of psychology. But it is hardly possible for a psycholinguist to ignore language.   (Gazdar *et al.* 1985: 5)

[34] Hence the frustration of entomologists mentioned in note 18.

do. We should keep a totally open mind about how the organism manages to respect the structure rules.

The rest of this book will in fact be devoted to considering the way in which a person competent in a language respects the rules of the language.

(ii) The language a person is competent in has one structure and not another. We should like to know *why* the person speaks such a language, why the something-we-know-not-what that she embodies respects the structure rules of that language and not other structure rules:

> we want to know why there are these social regularities and not others, or why we consider these abstract mathematical structures and not others. Surely the facts might be otherwise. (Chomsky 1980c: 57)[35]

The bee's competence to dance is surely innate. To what extent is this also true of a person's linguistic competence and to what extent is that competence the result of the person's environment? We shall address this question in Chapter 12.

Our interest in language will surely also lead us in the end to an interest in a very different psychological matter. (iii) It is impossible to give deep explanations of linguistic reality without appeal to the psychological: for, surely, psychological facts together with social and environmental facts determine linguistic facts. So in the end we will need to study the psychological in order to explain the linguistic. But in the beginning we do not. Syntactic investigations of *being c-commanded*, *being doubly embedded* and the like, the sort of investigations that linguists do every day, are not psychological. Even when, in the end, we have to appeal to psychology to explain in virtue of what tokens have these properties, the object of our study remains linguistic. Analogously, a study of the property of the bee's dance that indicates the direction of the food source is not a study of the bee's "psychology" even though the explanation of in virtue of what the dance has that property appeals to inner states of the bee. A linguistic symbol, like a bee's dance or a horseshoe, really has its properties whatever the explanation of its having them. The symbol objectively exists with its linguistic properties "apart from its mental representation".

There seems to be some confusion on this point. (a) Consider one of the reasons that Dwyer and Pietroski offer in support of their view that "linguistics is concerned with psychology" even though its generalizations are about linguistic types. The reason is that we must appeal to mental states to answer the question: "by virtue of what is a (concrete) utterence *u* an utterance of an (abstract) linguistic type?" (1996: 350). (b) Similarly, Barry Smith, describing "the cognitivist position advanced by Noam Chomsky", takes linguistics to be "a branch of cognitive psychology" because "facts about the meaning and form of expressions are determined by the psychological states of speakers" (2001: 284). (c) And

---

[35] So the view of languages that I urge does not lead, as Jerry Fodor anticipates it might, to any lack of interest in "counterfactuals about what languages there could be" (2001: 118n). (Fodor is criticizing Cowie for her inclination to endorse the view in Devitt and Sterelny 1989.)

Laurence suggests that "someone with broadly Chomskian sympathies" might accept that "linguistics *is* about symbols" and yet still maintain that "it is, in the first instance, about competence". She can do this because

the important properties of these symbols—the properties in virtue of which symbols have their linguistic properties—are properties pertaining to our linguistic competence, and perhaps aspects of how these symbols are processed in language comprehension and production ... The important issue is not over whether linguistics is about symbols but over the nature of the facts which determine the linguistic properties of symbols.   (2003: 87–8)

This sort of reasoning is erroneous. Even if symbols had their properties in virtue of certain mental facts that would not make the theory of those symbols about those facts and so would not make the theory part of psychology. Indeed, consider the consequences of supposing it would, and then generalizing: every theory—economic, psychological, biological, etc.—would be about physical facts and part of physics because physical facts ultimately determine everything. A special science does not lose its own domain because that domain supervenes on another.[36]

I emphasize that in claiming that linguistics is not part of psychology I am not divorcing language from the mind. Linguistic competence, a mental state, is *causally* related to language: that state produces and responds to linguistic symbols. Furthermore, the Respect Constraint rests on the fact that the nature of those symbols is partly *constitutive* of that competence. Finally, as we have just noted, the linguistic partly *supervenes* on the psychological.

2.8 CONCLUSION

Linguistics has something worthwhile to study apart from psychological reality of speakers: it can study a linguistic reality. This reality is in fact being studied by linguists in grammar construction. The study of this linguistic reality has a certain priority over the study of psychological reality. A grammar is about linguistic reality not the language faculty. Linguistics is not part of psychology. This is my *first major conclusion.*

The extraordinary advances in syntax in recent decades leave the question of the psychological reality of language largely open. To close the question we need other arguments and evidence, including psycholinguistic evidence about language production, comprehension, and acquisition. That will be the concern of the rest of this book. I shall argue that this evidence leaves the Representational

---

[36] In my view, Laurence is making another error in assuming that the determining facts for linguistic properties are facts about linguistic competence rather than facts about thoughts and social and physical environment. I shall propose such a Gricean explanation later (8.4, 9.5).

Thesis (RT) unsupported and implausible. And it makes it hard to choose among a range of other positions on the question of psychological reality.

In the next part I describe some positions on the psychological reality of language and attempt to place the positions of Chomsky and others among them. In doing this, I will often draw attention to ways in which writers diverge from my methodological points.

The distinctions and methodological points made in this chapter, along with the Respect Constraint, are listed in the Glossary.

PART II

POSITIONS ON PSYCHOLOGICAL REALITY

3

Some Possible Positions on Psychological Reality

3.1 REPRESENTED VS. "SIMPLY EMBODIED" RULES

Our argument in Part I that linguistics is not part of psychology rested on three distinctions. To make progress now in describing alternative positions on the psychological reality of language, we need some more distinctions. The first of these is not controversial,[1] yet it does not have the prominence it should have in the debate over psychological reality.

4. Distinguish processing rules that govern by being represented and applied from ones that are simply embodied without being represented.

This is a distinction between two ways in which certain processing rules might be psychologically real, two ways in which the rules might be embodied in the speaker. Neither of these ways should be confused with a situation where an object simply behaves *as if* it is governed by those processing rules. For that situation is compatible with those rules *not* being embodied in the object at all.[2] Consider a pocket calculator, for example. Its operations are governed by rules, the rules of algorithms for addition, subtraction, and so on. Now let *R* be a rule for addition. So the calculator should behave *as if* it is governed by *R*: its outputs given inputs should be just what we would expect if it were governed by *R*. But, of course, this does not mean that it *is* governed by *R*. There are many ways to add and the calculator may have been so designed that it is governed by a rule other than *R*; for example, *R* might be in the decimal notation and the governing rule might be in the binary notation. For it to be governed by *R* it has to not only

---

[1] Pylyshyn says that it "is not a distinction that Chomsky has endorsed" (1991: 233) and yet occasionally it does seem to play a role in his discussions; see section 4.1 below on his response (1980c: 56) to Elliott Sober's peer commentary (1980).

[2] On the strength of the fact that the *structure* rules of an object's output must be respected by the object's competence I allowed earlier (2.3) that it *might be* appropriate to say that the object behaves *as if* those rules were embodied in the object. I am here saying something a bit different that certainly *is* appropriate: the object behaves as if certain *processing* rules are embodied.

have the appropriate outputs for inputs but *an appropriate internal organization.*[3] Distinction 4 is between two sorts of appropriate internal organization.

In section 1.1 I pointed out that it is natural, although perhaps not right, to interpret Chomsky as holding RT. According to RT linguistic rules are psychologically real in that they are represented (in the sense illustrated) in the speaker. If these rules were processing rules then the representations of them would be applied in processing; they would be "read". Distinction 4 draws attention to another possibility: the rules might govern processing without being represented.

The first point to be made is that any system *has* to have some processing rules that govern it without being represented and applied.[4] For, if there is a rule that governs by being represented and applied, *there has to be another rule that governs the application.*[5] That rule might also govern by being represented and applied but then *its* application has to be governed by a further rule; and so on. If this regress is to end and any rule is to govern by being represented, there must be some rules that govern without being represented, without being *encoded*; that is a moral of Lewis Carroll's famous dialogue between Achilles and the Tortoise (1895). The upshot of this point is that, given any system that is governed by a rule, it is *an empirical question* whether the system represents and applies the rule or the rule is simply embodied in the system without being represented.

Computers demonstrate the point nicely. Software rules encoded in RAM can govern the operations of a computer only because there are rules built into the hardware that enable them to do so.

The folk seem to recognize these two forms of rule governing in two of their many uses of the loose term 'know'. Sometimes the term is used for *knowing-how*, as in 'Ralph knows how to swim'. Knowing-how is in the same family as skills, abilities, and capacities. Sometimes, it is entirely cognitive; for example, knowing how to play chess. Othertimes, it may be hardly cognitive at all; for example, knowing how to ride a bicycle. Sometimes, it may involve representation of rules; for example, some cases of chess know-how. Othertimes—and this is the important point for us—it is, as the folk would say, "*mere*" know-how and *prima facie* does not involve the representation of rules; for example, knowing how to ride a bicycle. In contrast, 'know' is sometimes used for *knowing-that*, as in 'Ralph knows that R is an algorithm for addition'. Knowing-that is essentially cognitive and propositional. According to the popular, and in my view correct

---

[3] Pylyshyn (1980a, 1991) calls systems or processes yielding the same input/output behavior "extensionally equivalent" or "weakly equivalent". "Strongly equivalent" systems or processes produce that behavior in the same way, by the same algorithm.

[4] Analogously, a logical calculus that has axioms has to have inference rules that govern the application of the axioms. (It might have no axioms, only inference rules.)

[5] "knowledge doesn't eventuate in behavior in virtue of its propositional content alone. It seems obvious that you need mechanisms to put what you know into action." (J. A. Fodor 1983: 9)

(1996), Representational Theory of the Mind (RTM), this knowledge involves representation. For example, it requires that Ralph represent R.[6]

In the light of this, there can be no swift move from ordinary talk of a speaker's "knowing the language" to the view that speakers have any knowledge-that about the language and represent its rules; the knowledge may be mere know-how. I shall consider the case for a slow move later (Ch. 6).

The distinction I am emphasizing is related to the distinction between "declarative" and "procedural" knowledge involved in performing tasks. This distinction, originally in AI, is widely acknowledged and frequently applied in psychology, and is sometimes compared to the folk one between knowing-that and knowing-how.[7] The distinction is described, rather inadequately, as follows: where declarative knowledge is explicit, accessible to consciousness, and conceptual, procedural knowledge is implicit, inaccessible to consciousness, and sub-conceptual. What about the representation of the processing rules for a task? It is clear that psychologists think that a subject has declarative knowledge of these rules only if she represents them. So this knowledge matches one half of my distinction. Does procedural knowledge match the other half? The answer to this question is not so simple. First, the psychological consensus is that we still have a lot to learn about procedural knowledge. Second, although some psychologists clearly think that procedural knowledge does not involve represented processing rules (e.g. Sun *et al.* 2001)—thus matching the other half of my distinction—some others seem to think that it does, albeit representations of a different sort from those involved in declarative knowledge (e.g. Anderson 1983, 1993). I shall discuss this later (11.5).

Finally, the distinction is *not* one between processing rules that can be modified and those that cannot. Both represented and simply embodied rules can be modified, but they are modified in different ways. A represented rule can by modified by changing the representation; in the case of a computer, by reprogramming the software; in the case of a human, by changing, for example, a belief. A simply embodied rule can be modified by rebuilding; in the case of a computer, by an engineer changing the hardware; in the case of a human, by experience changing the wetware.

We shall now consider some systems where the processing rules that govern their operations are not plausibly seen as represented in the systems, let alone propositionally known by the systems.

[6] This needs qualification because, strictly speaking, this knowledge, like belief, is dispositional: a person knows a lot of things she has never entertained. So the view should be that "core knowledge" involves representation; see Dennett 1978 and Field 1978. This qualification is unimportant to the argument and so will be ignored.

[7] "The distinction between *knowing that* and *knowing how* is fundamental to modern cognitive psychology. In the former, what is known is called *declarative knowledge*; in the latter, what is known is called *procedural knowledge*." (Anderson 1980: 223)

(i) Think of a really simple calculator, a mechanical one. When the calculator adds it goes through a mechanical process that is governed by the rules of an algorithm for addition. We have already noted that we cannot assume that the calculator embodies a particular rule simply because the calculator behaves *as if* it does. The present point concerns the rules that do, as a matter of fact, govern the operations of the calculator. Perhaps these rules operate on representations of numbers like 28 and functions like addition, but the rules themselves are not represented in the calculator. The rules are hardwired but not encoded in the calculator. And, of course, the calculator does not *know* that the governing rules are rules for addition, subtraction, etc. We can be quite confident about this because the calculator is not the sort of thing that can know about anything. Finally, in virtue of the calculator being governed by those rules we can say, if we like, that the arithmetical "information" that those rules reflect is embodied in the calculator even though the calculator does not represent the information.[8]

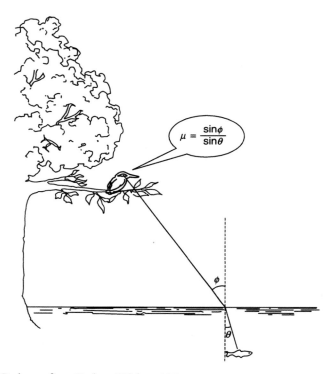

$$\mu = \frac{\sin\phi}{\sin\theta}$$

Figure 1. Redrawn from Boden, 1984, p. 153.

[8] Dwyer and Pietroski wonder, surprisingly, how having a mechanism in a speaker that is "correctly described by a linguistic theory is not tantamount to [the speaker's] having the relevant beliefs" (1996: 341). It is not tantamount because the theory could correctly describe the algorithm that is embodied in the mechanism in the way that an arithmetical algorithm is embodied in the calculator.

(ii) Consider the cartoon Figure 1. The kingfisher catches fish by diving into water. It does not dive vertically, nor does it pursue fish underwater. So, in diving, it must make suitable allowance for the refraction of light: the light deflects as it leaves water for the less dense medium of air. The point of the cartoon is that it would be absurd to suggest that the kingfisher goes through the following process: it represents (tacitly knows) that μ for water-to-air refraction is such and such; it represents that the angle ϕ is so and so; it represents that $\mu = \sin \phi / \sin \theta$; it uses this information to calculate the angle θ. Applying this new representation it dives into the water at the appropriate angle. It is not plausible to suppose that the kingfisher represents any of these facts about refraction and angles. No more does it represent whatever rules do govern its fishing: "mechanisms that perform certain tasks need not embody theories of those tasks" (Schank 1980: 35). Those mechanisms, reflecting information about water-to-air refraction, are simply built into the kingfisher "by nature" just as the rules for the calculator are simply built into it by an engineer.

(iii) Think of the vast amount of simple behavior, including much insect behavior, that can be adequately explained in terms of behaviorist dispositions. This behavior is governed by a simple S-R rule which the organism does not represent. And think of more complicated insect behavior like the bee's dance. Whilst there may be some plausibility to the idea that the bee represents its food source, there is little to the idea that it represents whatever rules may govern its dancing (2.2).

(iv) I take the next example from Zenon Pylyshyn's discussion of "early vision" (drawing on Marr 1982). The visual system accurately recovers a 3-D layout from a 2-D image. How? It "behaves as though it were making certain assumptions about the nature of the physical world"; for example,

that most of an image consists of light reflected from surfaces, that the distance of the surfaces from the perceiver varies gradually in most of the image, that certain kinds of discontinuous visual features in the image usually arise from physical discontinuities on the surface of smooth rigid 3-D objects, that contour discontinuities usually arise from occluding edges, that the light illuminating the object usually comes from above, and so on.

Yet, "nobody actually believes that the visual system uses an explicit representation of these constraints" (1991: 237). In Pylyshyn's terminology, the explanation of what is going on here appeals to "intrinsic functional properties" not to "the content of representations" (p. 241), to a "cognitive capacity" not to "representation-governed regularities" (p. 242).

(v) Consider a vast range of human skills. We know how to swim, ride a bicycle, touch type, and so on. These activities are governed by rules that have been built into us largely by learning. Even if representations of some of these rules can play a role in the acquisition and improvement of the skills, it is not plausible to suppose that those rules must be represented in a person once she has achieved competence, nor to suppose that many of them are, as a matter of fact, usually represented in her. Consider, for example, the skill of catching a fly ball. An essential part of this skill is being at the right place when the ball descends to catch height. An experiment showed that skilled fielders "ran at a speed that kept the acceleration of the tangent of the angle of elevation of gaze to the ball at 0" (McLeod and Dienes 1996: 531). It is not known how they manage this (p. 542) but they surely don't manage it by *representing* the algorithm for being in the right place and applying it to a series of representations of the acceleration of the tangent of the angle. As Pylyshyn says, "clearly, cognitive processes are relevant to motor skill. Equally clearly, however, certain aspects of their execution are purely bio-logical and physical" (1980a: 119). This is even true of some cognitive skills. Ralph *may* know how to add up by R because he knows that R is an algorithm for addition and can apply it. If so then this piece of knowing-how is largely knowing-that. But Ralph is quite likely to be simply governed by R without representing it to himself: R is psychologically real in him without being represented. Finally, consider the most cognitive skill of all, the skill of thinking, of inferring one thought from another. We can, of course, learn "laws of thought"—that is what we do in logic classes—but most of us know hardly anything about these rules. Most thinking in most people surely does not involve applying representations of these rules, representations involved in higher-level thoughts about the rule-governed thoughts; and *all* thinking could not, as Lewis Carroll showed. I shall discuss motor and cognitive skills at some length later (11.5).

(vi) Finally, consider the contrast between a universal Turing Machine using a program for addition and a special-purpose Turing Machine built for addition. Or, getting more real, consider the contrast between a general-purpose computer loaded up with a word-processing program and a dedicated word-processor. The computer is governed by the rules of that program because the rules are represented in its RAM and it operates by reading and applying them. In contrast, the rules that govern the operations of the dedicated word-processor—perhaps the very same rules—are largely hardwired without being encoded. Similarly, the rules for addition are represented on the universal Turing Machine's tape but hardwired into the special-purpose machine. The universal Turing Machine and the com-puter are analogous to a human who knows that certain rules form an algorithm for addition and applies them to add. The special-purpose Turing Machine and the dedicated word processor are analogous to a human who knows how to add by those rules without having any propositional knowledge of them.

This example points to an important generalization. Any processing rule that governs the behavior of one object by being represented and applied could govern that of another by being embodied without being represented as Edward Stabler points out:

Any program that can be computed by a program-using system can be computed "directly" by a system that we would clearly not want to call a program-using system....

networks of electronic circuits can be hardwired to compute even very complex programs directly, without having control states to govern their operation according to an encoding of a program.   (1983: 392)

If rules are rules for processing information, then either way of embodying them in an object enables the object's behavior to be explained in terms of the flow of information.[9] So whenever such an explanation applies there is a further empirical question about the way of embodiment.

In contrasting "connectionist" with "classical" mental architecture it is sometimes assumed that the latter is committed to the explicit representation of rules (see, for example, McClelland 1999). But this is a mistake, as Terence Horgan and John Tienson point out:

although programs are explicitly represented as stored "data structures" in the ubiquitous general-purpose computer, stored programs are not an essential feature of the classical point of view. In some computational devices—including, for example, many hand-held calculators—the rules are all hardwired into the system and are not explicitly represented. According to classicism, cognition must conform to representation-processing rules that constitute a computer program; but a cognitive system could conform to such rules simply by being hardwired to do so.   (1999: 725; see also J. A. Fodor and Pylyshyn 1988: 142–3)

In cognitive science, Pylyshyn has rightly urged, "one must attribute as much as possible to the *capacity* of the system . . . to properties of the *functional architecture* . . . one must find the least powerful functional architecture compatible with the range of variation observed" (1991: 244). I think that we should draw a moral from this that I shall call "Pylyshyn's Razor": "*Representations are not to be multiplied beyond necessity*". Sometimes we already know enough about how a system works to be confident that the rules that govern certain behaviors are represented in the system; thus we know that many rules are represented in the general-purpose computer. But we are mostly not in this position; we are not, for example, with the rules that govern the diving kingfisher, the dancing bee, and various human skills. Pylyshyn's Razor demands that we posit representations of these rules in the systems *only if the representations do explanatory work*. I have, in effect, been applying the Razor in suggesting that these rules are not plausibly seen as represented. In general, the Razor places heavy evidential demands on any view that a processing rule is represented in a system. It will play a large role in the rest of this book.

If we could look into the brain and simply "see" if there were representations of this and that, as we can look in a book and see if there are representations of

---

[9] Fodor seems to overlook this in his defense of information flow psychology: "What distinguishes what organisms do from what the planets do is that a *representation of the rules they follow constitutes one of the causal determinants of their behavior*" (1975: 74n). What distinguishes what organisms do may be that rules operating on representations *of their environment* constitutes one of the causal determinants of their behavior. Whether they represent the rules by which they process that environmental information is surely another matter and not essential to what organisms do.

Peter Ustinov, then that would of course settle the matter. But we cannot: we don't even know enough about what to look for. As Jerry Fodor says, "there isn't one, *not one*, instance where it's known what pattern of neural connectivity realizes a certain cognitive content" (1998b: 145). So we should only posit such representations if we can find some serious causal work that they have to do. Sadly, it is often difficult to tell when we have found causal work for representations: the issue is simply not that clear. Consider, for example, these cautious words from Pylyshyn:

> whenever behavior is sufficiently plastic and stimulus-independent, we can at least assume that it is somehow mediated by internal functional states. Such states may be further viewed as representational, or epistemic, if certain other empirical conditions hold. For example, we would describe the behavior as being governed by representations and rules if the relation between environmental events and subsequent behavior, or the relations among function states themselves could be shown to be, among other things, a) arbitrary with respect to natural laws, b) informationally plastic, or c) functionally transparent.   (1980a: 120)

The rationale for Pylyshyn's Razor is not an a priori assumption that the world is mostly representation-free. The rationale is primarily epistemological. If we fail to posit representations where there are some, we are likely to come across evidence that there are some: our explanations are likely to be inadequate. In contrast, if we posit representations where there are none, it may be difficult to come across evidence that there are none, because with enough representations almost any behavior can be explained.

In sum, the behavior of a machine, an animal or a human can be governed by a hardwired rule that it does not represent (encode), or know about.[10] So, even if structure rules of the language are processing rules, they may not be represented (encoded), or known about in the way required by RT. Pylyshyn's Razor puts an onus on a theory that posits represented rules: *should we have good reasons for supposing that a system is governed by a rule, we need further reasons for supposing that the rule governs by being represented and applied.*[11] The general-purpose computer is a misleading model for the mind because it leads immediately to the idea that the mind operates by applying represented rules. Yet the truth may well be that the mind is more like a set of special-purpose computers.

---

[10] Clearly more needs to be said than I have about what exactly it is for a system to be governed by a rule that the system does not represent. On this see Davies 1995.

[11] Fodor's delightful 1968 paper, "The Appeal to Tacit Knowledge in Psychological Explanations" (1981a: 63–78), fails to accept this onus. Fodor argues for the intellectualist view that we tie our shoes by representing the rules for so doing but he gives no reason for supposing that the rules governing shoe tying are represented rather than simply embodied. He seems to presuppose that only *very simple* rules are hardwired (pp. 66–9). But there is no reason a priori to suppose that complicated rules are not simply embodied in an object. The most plausible thing to say about shoe tying and other human skills—see (v) above—is that underlying them are complicated but unrepresented rules of some sort, often acquired by arduous practice.

3.2   STRUCTURE RULES USED AS DATA IN PROCESSING

This discussion is all about processing rules. We have left open the general possibility that a structure rule might also be a processing rule. If one is then, like any other processing rule, it can either be represented or simply embodied. Either way the structure rule would be embodied, internally real. Edward Stabler (1983) has drawn attention to another way in which rules might be internally real. They might be represented in a system and used by processing rules as *data*.

5. Distinguish the representations of structure rules used as data in processing from the representations of structure rules that are applied in processing.

So RT might hold not because the represented rules *are* processing rules but because they are *data for* processing.

Suppose that we have good reason to think that a system encodes a representation of structure rules. It may, nonetheless, seem rather implausible that these rules *are* processing rules. The problem is that structure rules often seem to be *the wrong sort* of rules to be processing rules: they do not seem to be the sort of rules that would govern a process that the system actually goes through. Consider the chess player. It is plausible to think that the player represents the rules of chess, for example, that the bishop can only move diagonally. Yet it seems somewhat unlikely that the player would actually go through a process of inferring '*x* moves diagonally' from '*x* is a bishop'. This does not seem to be the right sort of rule to be among the strategies and heuristics that the chess player tries out in deciding a move. However, with the help of distinction 5 we can see another role for the represented rule. The strategies and heuristics captured by the processing rules may require "consulting" the chess rules stored in memory. In the process of assessing possible chess moves, these structure rules are included in the data used by the processing rules, with the result that only proper moves are contemplated. In this way the encoded structure rules constrain processes without themselves being processing rules. This story may well be true of some actual chess player. In any case it seems more plausible that an encoded structure rule should thus constrain processes rather than specify them.

3.3   RATIONAL–CAUSAL VS. BRUTE–CAUSAL PROCESSES

We have paid a deal of attention to whether processing rules are represented. But what about whether processing rules *operate on representations*? The distinction we need here is hard to characterize precisely but it also is not controversial. And it also does not have the prominence it should have in the debate over psychological reality.

6. Distinguish processing rules that govern a "rational-causal" operation on syntactically structured representations (or symbols) from ones that govern "brute-causal" operations that may or may not involve representations.[12]

What do we have in mind as a "rational-causal" operation on representations? We have in mind a process that manipulates representations in virtue of their syntactic structures. The rules that govern the process are sensitive to those structures. The causal link between a stimulus input and a behavioral output is mediated by representations of each and of stored "background knowledge". The process starts with some symbols and yields others in "a flow of information". The process is, or is analogous to, one of *thinking about* the input and possible outputs. The role of background knowledge in this process leads to flexibility in the relation between inputs and outputs: the one input can yield different outputs and different inputs can yield the one output. Pylyshyn illustrates the point nicely:

seeing that the building you are in is on fire, smelling smoke coming in through the ventilation duct, or being told by telephone that the building is on fire, can all lead to similar behavior, and this behavior might be radically different if you believed yourself to be performing in a play at the time.   (1980a: 121)

Paradigm examples of rational–causal operations are yielded by the "classical" von Neumann architecture of the standard general-purpose digital computer. And, according to the "classical" view of the mind, the practical decision making that takes place in a situation like the one Pylyshyn describes is also a paradigm.

The standard computer operates on symbols because it represents and applies processing rules that govern such operations. Still, an object's behavior may be governed by a rule that operates on symbols even though that rule is not itself represented. A special-purpose Turing Machine is an example. Our discussion (3.1) suggests some others: simple electronic calculators that operate on representations about numbers; dedicated word-processors that operate on representations about expressions; and, most interesting of all, human thinkers who operate on complex mental representations that might be about anything at all.[13]

A rule for language use might govern a rational–causal process by operating on *metalinguistic* representation of the syntactic and semantic properties of linguistic items; thus it might operate on the likes of 'This input is a VP' and 'That input means *CLINTON*'.

---

[12] I take the terms "rational–causal" and "brute–causal" from Fodor (1981a: 273) but my usage is somewhat different.

[13] Would the operations on cognitive maps that are alleged to explain the navigational behavior of animals (Gallistel 1990) count as rational–causal? I think not but I confess to being far from confident about this. These operations are sensitive to the "syntax" of the cognitive map but do not seem to involve any manipulation of symbols. Rather, given an appropriate stimulus—for example, an ant obtaining food—the map leads "automatically" to a certain behavior—heading straight back to the nest.

What is the contrast? What operations do *not* manipulate structured representations? Here we have in mind operations that are *a*rational and more "brute–causal" and "primitive". In such an operation, the processing rule is directly responsive to the input/output: the input directly triggers a fairly brute–causal processing operation and the output is the direct result of that brute–causal operation. There are a variety of examples of such rules.

(i) Associationism provides paradigm examples. The elements of classical associationism are mental, experiences and ideas. Learning is a matter of pairing these according to certain laws. Mental processes are simply a matter of moving from an experience to an associated idea, or from an idea to an associated idea. Association is a primitive relation in the theory. Behaviorism is nonmentalistic associationism: the mental elements are replaced by physical ones, environmental stimuli and behavioral responses. Mental processes are replaced by processes from stimuli to associated responses, processes that are like reflexes in their brutal simplicity. Daniel Dennett finds what seems to be a nice example in the "simple, rigid and mechanical" behavior of the wasp *Sphex* as it drags a previously paralyzed cricket to its burrow (1978: 65–6). The wasp leaves the cricket on the threshold of the burrow whilst "checking" inside. If the cricket is moved back from the threshold whilst the wasp is inside then, on emerging, the wasp will drag it back to the threshold and repeat the "checking" procedure. If the cricket is moved again, then the wasp will check again. And so on indefinitely.

(ii) More complicated examples are posited by the moderate Hull–Tolman behaviorism: sensory stimuli and behavioral responses can be linked in this direct way not only to each other but also to internal states, perhaps representational ones. These are examples because the rules governing operations are not sensitive to the syntactic properties of representations.

(iii) Moderate behaviorism is the first step toward positing a complex functional organization within the object that intervenes between the stimulus and the response. This organization, however complicated, might be governed by rules of the sort in question because its causal operations might not manipulate structured representations. Perhaps the rules governing addition in an old-fashioned mechanical calculator are of this sort. Perhaps most of the rules governing motor skills like those of the diving heron, the bee dancing, and human bicycle riding, swimming, catching, and touch-typing are too (11.5).

(iv) Wherever a system is governed by rules for processing representations there have to be transducers that take physical inputs and transform them into representations for processing and take representations that are the result of processing and turn them into behaviour. The rules governing transducers are further examples of processing rules that do not manipulate structured representations.

(v) Finally, the rules governing connectionist networks are notoriously of this sort for connectionism is a complex form of associationism: "associative learning is what neural networks implement" (Macintosh 1999: 183); "simple associationism is a particularly impoverished and impotent corner of the connectionist universe" (Smolensky: 1991: 165).

We note that representations may be involved in a brute–causal process. Thus the processes of Hull–Tolman behaviorism and of connectionism may involve representations[14] as surely do those of many skills. But these processes are not governed by rules that manipulate representations according to their syntactic structure in the rational–causal way.

If a rule for language use governs a brute–causal process then it may respond to and produce items that have properties like *being a VP* and *meaning CLINTON* without there being any complex metalinguistic representations of those items as having those properties. This stands in contrast to our earlier example of a rule for a rational–causal process that operates on these metalinguistic representations. Pylyshyn's Razor (3.1) requires us to find an explanatory need for supposing that language use is rational–causal before positing the metalinguistic representations. (Note that, unusually, the inputs/outputs of language use *are* representations of a certain sort. Still they might be processed without being *represented as* representations of that sort.)

I appreciate that this characterization leaves distinction 6 somewhat vague,[15] particularly on the brute–causal side. But this cannot be avoided without an overcommitment to a particular view of fairly brute–causal processes.

3.4   SOME POSSIBLE POSITIONS ON PSYCHOLOGICAL REALITY

We can apply these six distinctions to yield a range of possible positions on the psychological reality of the structure rules of language. These are by no means the only possible positions. Indeed, in the next section, we will discuss actual positions that "back away from" these positions in interesting ways. Still, the positions are clear and straightforward and serve as useful benchmarks.

For convenience, our focus so far has been on language production, mostly ignoring language comprehension. We must now take both types of language use into account.

---

[14] William Ramsey (1997) argues that connectionist models do not really involve representations.

[15] Note that we cannot characterize it as the distinction between computational and noncomputational processes because, although computational processes are frequently taken to be those of a "classical" architecture, there are a variety of views of computation: "It is surprisingly difficult to find an answer within the cognitive science community to the question of whether there is a univocal notion of computation that underlies the various different computational approaches to cognition on offer." (Wilson 1999: xxix; see also Brian Smith 1999)

We have already seen (2.4) that distinction 3 yields a minimal position that should be uncontroversial:

(M) A competence in a language, and the processing rules that govern its exercise, respect the structure rules of the language: the processing rules of language comprehension take sentences of the language as inputs; the processing rules of language production yield sentences of the language as outputs.

The processing rules are of course psychologically real but position (M) does not require that those rules involve the structure rules that the processing rules respect nor that the structure rules are psychologically real in any other way. Perhaps (M) entitles us to say that the speaker behaves *as if* her behavior were governed by those structure rules but not that it is so governed. (M) meets the Respect Constraint, as any theory of competence must (2.4-2.6), but it does nothing more.

Now, of course, there *must* be more to be said about the psychology: there must be some true account of a speaker's competence that explains *how* it respects the structure rules of the language. And, in light of the claims of Chomskian linguists, we are particularly interested in positions that say more by giving *those very rules* a role in the psychological explanation.

I have argued that, in the first instance at least, the grammar describes linguistic reality, the structure rules of the language. That was the first methodological point (2.6). The second methodological point was that any view that the grammar also describes psychological reality, describes linguistic competence and its processing rules, needs a powerful psychological assumption. The third point was that there should be no a priori demand that our theory of psychological reality be tied any more closely to the grammar than the uncontroversial minimal position (M). There is no need to constrain that theory in any other way.

We shall now describe five possible psychological positions on language use, some positions with two versions. The first three positions do take the grammar to throw more light on this psychological reality, in particular to be true of that reality as well as linguistic reality. And so they each involve a powerful psychological assumption. Each position is a robust view of the psychological reality of a speaker's language, placing its rules one way or another in the mind. The final two positions explain language use without placing the linguistic rules in the mind.

Distinction 5 yields two possible positions. In both of these, the language is psychologically real in that the grammar itself is: so they entail RT (the Representational Thesis):

(I) The structure rules of the language are also processing rules that are represented in the speaker and applied in language use.

(II) The structure rules of the language are represented and used as data by the processing rules of language use.

Stabler characterizes position (II) as follows (G being the rules of the language):

> the language-processing system has a representation of G in memory to which certain computational processes are sensitive; parts of G are taken as arguments to functions that are computed.[16]   (1983: 400)

(I) *identifies* the represented processing rules with the rules of the language but we shall count a position as (I) if it takes the processing rules to be isomorphic to or to "mirror" the linguistic rules.

(I) faces an immediate and obvious problem: language use "runs in two directions", producing sentences in speech and parsing them in comprehension. How could the one set of structure rules be processing rules for these two opposite processes? To avoid this problem let us count a structure rule as a processing rule even if it is "run backwards" in processing. ((II) does not face the problem because the representation of the rules can be consulted by processors running in either direction.)

We could distinguish two versions of each of (I) and (II). For a reason already noted (3.1), it cannot be the case that *all* of a system's processing rules are represented. Wherever a processing rule is represented and applied, there must be underlying processing rules that govern applications without being represented: there must be some hardwiring. Still, in the case of (I), it might be the case that some of the processing rules that are *not* structure rules are represented or that none of them are. And in the case of (II), more simply, it might be the case that some of the processing rules are represented or that none of them are. I shall not bother to distinguish the two versions.

In considering the chess player earlier (3.2), we noted the unlikelihood of a represented structure rule being a processing rule and hence found the position analogous to (II) more plausible than the one analogous to (I). When we consider the logic machine and the bee (2.2) the analogues of both positions are surely false because there is no serious question of the machine or the bee representing structure rules.

Attention to distinction 4 yields a position which abandons RT:

(III) The structure rules of the language are also processing rules for language use but the processing rules are not represented.[17]

---

[16] One of Stabler's "peer commentators" points out that we think of a conventional computer as running a LISP program even though the machine uses the program as data to simulate a LISP machine (Davis 1983: 404). In such a case, the distinction between doing this and running the program directly loses some of its interest. Still, the distinction remains. Our discussion of the chess player and the language user suggests that in other cases where the data used may not be representations of processing rules—hence not a program—but representations of structure rules, the distinction is very significant. (Some other commentators make similar points to Davis: Berwick 1983, Gross 1983, Lipton 1983, and Thompson 1983.) Ray Jackendoff describes three possible positions on the relation of grammars to processing. The second is: "the rules of the mental grammar are explicitly stored in memory and ... the language processor 'consults' them or 'invokes' them" (1997: 7). Consulting the rules seems to amount to position (II). Perhaps invoking them is position (I).

[17] (III) is Jackendoff's third possible position: "the rules of mental grammar are 'embodied' by the processor" (1997: 8).

So, the language is psychologically real even though the grammar is not. We shall count a position as (III) if it takes the embodied processing rules to be iso-morphic to or to "mirror" the linguistic rules. Such a position faces the same immediate and obvious problem as (I) and we avoid it in the same way: count a structure rule as a processing rule even if it is "run backwards" in processing.

In considering positions (I) and (II), we did not have to attend to distinction 6 because if the rules of the language are represented and applied or used as data, it goes without saying that processing must operate on metalinguistic representa-tions of the syntactic and semantic properties of linguistic items. However, distinction 6 is very relevant to position (III), yielding two versions. According to version (a), the unrepresented structure rules process metalinguistic *represen-tations of* the syntactic and semantic properties of linguistic items, representations like 'This is a VP' and 'This means *CLINTON*', and there is a rational information flow. According to version (b), the rules are directly responsive to items that *have* properties like *being a VP* and *meaning CLINTON*. There are no metalinguistic representations and the process is of a fairly brute–causal associ-ationist sort.

The analogue of (III) is certainly false for the logic machine because the structure rules of its language are the wrong sort to be its processing rules. I have suggested that the analogue for the bee is very likely false for the same reason (2.2). The analogue for the chess player is somewhat unlikely but certainly not inconceivable. Perhaps for some chess players, the structure rule that the bishop can only move diagonally is a processing rule: the players actually go through a process of inferring 'x moves diagonally' from 'x is a bishop'.

(I) to (III) place the rules of the language in the mind of a speaker, represented in (I) and (II), unrepresented in (III). So they are ways to capture what seems to be the received view of Chomskian linguistics: that these rules are embodied somehow in the mind. The following positions on language depart from that view. If they are correct, the grammar throws no more light on language processing than is captured by (M).

(IV) Some processing rules for language use are represented but they are largely unlike the structure rules of the language and do not use the structure rules as data.

(For the reason given in discussing (I) and (II), not all processing rules could be represented.) Once again we do not need to apply distinction 6: since the processing rules are represented they must operate on metalinguistic representa-tions of the linguistic properties.

Analogues of (IV) for the bee and the logic machine are no more plausible than were the analogues of (I) and (II). However the analogue of (IV) for the chess player may have some plausibility.

We move now to a position on language use that not only gives no place to the structure rules of the language but also no place to represented rules.

(v) The processing rules for language use are unrepresented and largely unlike the structure rules of the language.

Distinction 6 is relevant here, yielding version (a) that is committed to some of the rules operating on metalinguistic representations and version (b) that is not. (For a reason already noted (3.3), it cannot be the case that *all* of a system's processing rules operate on metalinguistic representations. For, if some did, others would have to supply representations of the input and take the results of operations on representations to produce a behavioral output.)

An analogue of (v)(a) is very likely true of the logic machine: its transformation rules are unrepresented, are unlike its formation rules, and operate on *wffs* to yield an information flow. An analogue of (v)(b) may be true of the bee's dance and other insect behavior.

We have described a range of possible positions on language use, starting with the highly intellectualist (i) and (ii) and ending with the fairly nonintellectualist (v)(b).

There is one further position on the psychological reality of the language that I shall emphasize:

(t) The structure rules of a speaker's language are similar to the structure rules of her thought.

This position arises from the controversial "Language-of-Thought Hypothesis" ("LOTH") according to which thoughts involve *language-like* mental representations. (t) is not a position on language use but on the relation of language to thought. It differs strikingly from (i) to (iii) in claiming that the structure rules get their psychological reality not from being rules used in processing but from being similar to the structure rules governing mental representations. Analogously, the formation rules for the *wffs* of a formal language get their "internal reality" in a logic machine not from being processing rules but from being the structure rules governing the *wffs* that are processed by the machine.

Position (t) encourages, although it does not require, the view that the structure rules are not psychologically real in any other respect than being similar to the structure rules of thought. And it has lots of other interesting consequences. I shall explore this position in Part IV.

3.5 CONCLUSION

This chapter began with a series of distinctions. First, there was the distinction between processing rules that govern by being represented and applied and those that are simply embodied without being represented. Discussion of this led to the important "Pylyshyn's Razor": representations are not to be multiplied beyond necessity (3.1). Next, there was the distinction between representations of structure rules being used as data in processing and rules being applied in processing (3.2). Finally, there was the distinction between processing rules that govern "rational–causal" operations on syntactically structured representations from ones that govern "brute–causal" operations (3.3). Against the background of these distinctions, I have described some alternative *possible* positions on psychological reality. These vary according to whether or not the rules of the language are embodied in the mind; whether or not some processing rules for language are represented in the mind (cf. RT); whether or not some processing rules operate on metalinguistic representations of syntactic and semantic properties of linguistic items. And there is an uncontroversial minimal position, (M), that is committed only to there being a psychological reality that respects the linguistic structure rules (3.4). Given the Part I conclusion that linguistics is *not* psychology, no position stronger than the minimal one can be sustained without some powerful psychological assumption that is independent of anything revealed by the grammar of a language. Such an assumption is needed to conclude that the rules of the language are present one way or another in the mind. And, we shall see, it is hard to justify such an assumption.

In the next chapter, we shall consider some historically interesting *actual* positions on the psychological reality issue and relate them to these possible positions. This will demonstrate that later criticisms of positions (i) to (iv) are not criticisms of straw men. In describing an actual position I shall often advert to the earlier methodological points (2.6). We shall see that most of these writers seem to subscribe to RT. *That* is a powerful psychological assumption of the sort that, according to my second methodological point, is needed in taking the grammar to be true of psychological reality. This thesis is so taken for granted that these writers do not seem to contemplate the idea that the grammar might simply be true of linguistic reality, as urged in my first methodological point. Finally, we will see that most writers take the constraints that the grammar and the theory of competence place on each other to be much greater than the Respect Constraint of my third methodological point.

The distinctions and possible positions mentioned in this chapter, along with Pylyshyn's Razor and LOTH, are listed in the Glossary.

4

Some Actual Positions on Psychological Reality

4.1 CHOMSKY AND POSITIONS (I) AND (III)

What is Chomsky's view of the psychological reality of language? This question is surprisingly hard to answer. Chomsky is insistent that language is psychologically real but is very noncommittal about how it is. And what he does say suggests several different positions. In this section and the next I shall present cases for attributing to him some of the positions described in section 3.4; in this section, for attributing position (I) or (III); in the next section, (II). According to both (I) and (III), the structure rules of the language are also rules for language use. So, in language use a speaker actually goes through a process governed by those rules. According to (I) this is because the rules are represented in the speaker and applied in processing; according to (III) the rules are simply embodied. According to (II), the structure rules are represented and used as data by processing rules but are not themselves processing rules. Clearly both (I) and (II) are committed to the Representational Thesis (RT).

The evidence that (I) or (III) is the right interpretation of Chomsky can be put simply. On the one hand, a language is said to be psychologically real in its speakers. On the other hand, this language is described as a *process*. Thus, there is much talk of "generation", "computation", "derivation", and "transformation", and there are diagrams with arrows suggesting processes. Consider the following, for example:

The I-language consists of a computational procedure and a lexicon. The lexicon is a collection of items, each a complex of properties (called "features").... The computational procedure selects items from the lexicon and forms an expression, a more complex array of features. (Chomsky 1995b: 15; 2000a: 120)

And these procedures are persistantly presented as psychological (e.g., 1993a: 36). So, the structure rules of the I-language are the rules of these procedures:

I know of no proposed explanation for the fact that our judgements and behavior accord with certain rule systems other than the assumption that computation involving such rules and the representations they provide takes place in the mind... (Chomsky 1980a: 130)

So those rule systems govern processes that really go on in the mind. Indeed, if language really is a computational process, where else could this process plausibly be but in the mind?

Consider also the following two pieces of evidence. (i) In an early work (Miller and Chomsky 1963), Chomsky proposed a very direct relation between the grammatical rules, in particular the transformational rules, and the rules of the parser. However the rules could not be the same because grammatical derivations "run in the wrong direction". So the proposal was that the parser runs the inverse of those rules; it undoes the transformations; it runs the rules backwards. (We counted this as running the rules in section 3.4.) (ii) In a later work, Chomsky discusses *wh*-movement (1980a: 192–202;1980b: 4), a classic transformation from deep structure (later D-structure) to surface structure (later S-structure) that forms questions and relatives. He argues for the psychological reality of this transformation: there is a mental process of moving expressions like 'who' and 'what' to the left of clauses; "We attribute psychological reality to the postulated representations and mental computations" (1980a: 197).[1]

If we take literally such claims about the mental reality of grammatical computations then we must see Chomsky as demanding a much closer relation between the grammar and the theory of competence than is appropriate according to my third methodological point (2.6). For, according to that point, we should demand only that the grammar and the theory meet the Respect Constraint: the grammar should posit structure rules that are respected by the competence; and the theory of competence should posit processing rules that respect the structure rules. And it seems that we must adopt (I) or (III) as the interpretation of Chomsky. In the next section, I shall consider the possibility of not taking the claims literally. Meanwhile, what about the choice between positions (I) and (III)? According to (I), the speaker performs an I-language's computations as a result of applying representations of the language's rules, applying the grammar. I began this work by claiming that the natural interpretation of Chomsky, the one that takes him pretty much at his word, ascribes RT to him. If he does hold this thesis, then position (I) not (III) seems to be the right interpretation. But many think that Chomsky does not hold RT, despite his words suggesting he does (e.g. Matthews 1991: 192; Collins 2004).[2] If not, (III) should seem to be the right interpretation. According to (III), the speaker performs an I-language's computations because its rules are embodied without being represented.

Chomsky seems to acknowledge the distinction between (I) and (III)[3] but he gives it strangely little attention. An example of his acknowledging the distinction

---

[1] Consider also his comparison of the computations of a language "to the complex calculations of the mind/brain that inform me that I am seeing a group of people sitting in a lecture hall" (1988: 91).

[2] On this matter, I direct the reader once again to the exchange: Rey 2003a; Chomsky 2003; Rey 2003b.

[3] Although according to Pylyshyn (1991: 233) he does not.

is to be found in his response to Elliott Sober's peer commentary (1980) on Chomsky 1980b. Chomsky supposes that R is a rule and that "H(R) attributes R to the mind/brain and asserts that computations eventuating in behavior use R". He then criticizes Sober for equivocating between two distinct psychological realities: "psychological reality of a theory and its hypotheses, such as H(R), and psychological reality of entities such as R attributed by the theory to the mind/ brain" (1980c: 56). The distinction between these two psychological realities is in effect the distinction between (i) and (iii). Yet his earlier response (p. 44) to Dennett's skepticism about the "claim that universal grammar is innately fixed *in the form of explicit rules*" (1980: 19) seems to miss the distinction entirely.

Despite Chomsky's persistant talk suggesting that linguistic derivations are psychologically real, there are problems in taking him to believe this and hence to hold (i) or (iii).

First, scattered through Chomsky's writings are warnings against taking his accounts of language as accounts of a psychological process. For example, talking about the arrows in a diagram depicting the "levels of representation" of a language, he says that "their orientation expresses structural relations and entails nothing about temporal order of speech production or processing" (Chomsky 1986: 67). Earlier he remarks that

it seems absurd to suppose that the speaker first forms a generalized Phrase-marker by base rules and then tests it for well-formedness by applying transformational rules to see if it gives, finally a well-formed sentence. But this absurdity is simply a corollary to the deeper absurdity of regarding the system of generative rules as a point-by-point model for the actual construction of a sentence by a speaker.... To think of a generative grammar in these terms is to take it to be a model of performance rather than a model of competence, thus totally misconceiving its nature.... it can be regarded only as a characterization of the intrinsic tacit knowledge or competence that underlies actual performance. (1965: 140–1; see also p. 9)

Furthermore, what Chomsky finds absurd here surely is so. This may not be *so* obvious when we consider what the grammar of that time claims about trans- formations but it is surely obvious when we consider what it claims about the formation of the initial D-structure phrase-marker. This formation starts with an 'S', rewrites this as 'NP + VP', goes through various other rewrites many of which are optional, and finally terminates with lexical insertion and semantic interpretation. It is hard to see how this *could* be the story of a psychological process because it could not be part of any plausible view of the way a thought is turned into language, the way a "message" is conveyed, in language production.[4] The problem with the story was foreshadowed in our earlier discussion of the *wff* machine and the sentence machine (2.2, 2.4). On this story of language produc- tion, as on that earlier account of *wff* production and sentence production, the

---

[4] For roughly this reason, according to Jackendoff, "back in the 1960s, we were firmly taught not to think of rules of grammar" as embodied processing rules (1997: 8).

selection from the lexicon is random apart from syntactic constraints: these constraints may demand the selection of a noun not a verb at a certain place in a string, but hardly the selection of 'lion' not 'tiger'. (Note that meaning—"the semantic representation"—does not become part of the story until after the formation of the D-structure.) Similarly, the selection of one syntactically appropriate structure over another is random; thus a required 'NP' might be a simple 'N' (say, 'Fred') or it might be a complex 'D + Adj + N' (say, 'the bald man'). In language production, humans do not generate sentences by making selections of structures and words that are random apart from the constraints of syntax. Humans generate a sentence *from a thought*, intending to convey a message that is the content of that thought. What selects syntactic structures and items from the lexicon to form sentences is *primarily* the thoughts the sentences express not the language used to express them. (I shall make much of this point later in Parts IV and V.)

I remarked that treating the grammar as a model of performance in the way Chomsky criticizes may not seem *so* absurd when we focus on transformations. Still, taking transformations to be psychologically real does seem *prima facie* odd. Is it psychologically plausible that on the way to producing a passive sentence a speaker must produce an active-like D-structure which she then transforms into a passive S-structure by NP-movement? Mightn't her thought have been passive from the start? And what about questions, whether *wh-* or *yes-no*, which require transforming an indicative-like D-structure into an interrogative S-structure by moving items? Surely a person who asks a question would be "thinking a question" from the start.[5] Finally, if we were right a moment ago to agree with Chomsky that it is absurd to think that a speaker runs through the rules for forming a D-structure in language use, we should wonder why it is appropriate even to *look for* transformations being run in language use. If it is absurd that some linguistics rules are run by the language processor, why expect others to be? Why expect that any of these rules will govern processes in the mind?

The absurdity we have been discussing comes from taking grammatical derivations as psychological processes of language *production*. But, of course, if it were appropriate to take them as such processes then it would be appropriate to take their inverse as psychological processes of language *comprehension*. So the idea would be that, in parsing, a person "runs backwards" through the grammatical rules. Some think this is a "natural" first guess about parsing (Fodor, Bever, and Garrett 1974: 313; Berwick and Weinberg 1984: 39). Indeed, psycholinguists once devoted considerable energy to investigating the psychological reality of transformations in parsing (as we shall soon see). Certainly, since parsing always starts with a particular sound, the idea of running the process backwards does not have the randomness problem that brought absurdity to the

---

[5] "the input to the process of question-formation is not a declarative sentence, but rather a desire for information" Schank 1980: 36).

idea of running the process forward in production. Still, running transformations backwards in comprehension seems no more psychologically plausible than running them forwards in production. And the idea that, in comprehension, we run backwards through the rules for forming a D-structure until we reach 'NP + VP' and finally 'S' would be as absurd as the idea that, in production, we run forward through those rules. Intuitively, once a hearer has extracted the D-structure plus semantic interpretation of an utterance she has gone as far as she needs to go in language comprehension. Finally, if, in language use, running D-structure rules forward or backward is absurd why should we even expect transformation rules to be so run? This looks like the wrong model of language use.

I shall be arguing, in effect, that the moral we should draw here is broader than Chomsky's. Not only does the process talk not provide a plausible model of performance but, taken literally, it does not provide a plausible model of competence either. First, there is a *prima facie* problem in supposing that it does provide such a model: competence is a *state* and so it is odd to think of it as consisting in processes at all. Second, competence is exercised in performance. And this link to performance is not accidental: the competence is a competence to use language; that is the very nature of this psychological state. So a theory of competence must be at the center of a theory of performance. (Chomsky's task (iii) in section 1.1 was "How is knowledge of language put to use?") It is hard to see how the view that a speaker literally selects from structures and the lexicon in the largely random way described could fit with any plausible theory of performance. In general, not only are the computational procedures identified with an I-language not plausibly seen as a point-by-point model of sentence construction, they are not plausibly seen as such a model at any level of abstraction; for the most part, they are not plausibly seen as psychologically real processes at all, as processes going on in real time in the mind.

Finally, we should take account of Chomsky's allusion to David Marr's famous "levels". Chomsky takes "the study of grammar to be at the level of the theory of the computation" (1980c: 48). This is the first of Marr's three levels for understanding an information-processing device: it specifies *what* is computed and *why*. The second is the algorithmic level: it specifies *how* the computation is done. The third is the level of implementation: it specifies the way the computation is realized physically (1982: 22–5). Marr also thinks that a grammar is at the computational level (p. 28). For this to be so, the grammar must be a theory of a function that the speaker actually computes. That leaves open *how* the speaker computes the function—the algorithmic level—but it does entail that the speaker goes through some psychological process or other of computing the function specified by the grammar.

But if the grammar is a theory of an I-language as described in the quote from Chomsky (1995b: 15; 2000a: 120) at the beginning of this chapter, it is hard to see how it could be a theory at the computational level. On the strength of that description, we might say that the grammar is a theory of a function for generating sentences from a lexicon but, for the reasons already indicated, that is not a plausible view of the function that a speaker computes in language use. What a speaker computes are functions turning sounds into messages in comprehension and messages into sounds in production.[6]

Chomsky has another way of describing a language that may seem a more promising way to accommodate the allusion to Marr: a language is said to be "a generative procedure that associates sound and meaning in a specific way" (Chomsky 1996: 48). Can we then take a grammar to be a theory of a function for associating sounds and meanings? If so then we could indeed think of a speaker as computing this function (for associating sounds with messages amounts to associating them with meanings). We could see a grammar as describing, at an abstract level, psychological processes actually going on in speakers during language use.

The problem is that we surely cannot take the grammar to be a theory of a function for associating sounds and meanings. We might say that the grammar is a theory of a function for generating sentences from a lexicon, where the lexical items all *have* sounds, syntactic characters, and meanings, and where each sentence generated has its sound, syntactic character, and meaning in virtue of the way it is generated from the lexicon. That is very different from a function for associating sounds and meanings.

From my perspective, the underlying truth of the claim that the grammar is a theory of a function for associating sounds and meanings is that it is a theory of the rules that are respected by this function. Perhaps we should see the allusion to Marr as demanding no more.

Let us sum up. First, it is hard to see how the view that a language is literally a computational process can be combined plausibly with the view that the language is psychologically real (whether in virtue of having its rules represented or in virtue of having its rules simply embodied).

Next, my third methodological point (2.6) was that the grammar and the theory of competence are largely independent of each other: the only epistemic constraint that they place on each other arises from the Respect Constraint. It might still be the case, of course, that some structure rules posited by the grammar are processing rules posited independently by the theory of competence. However, I raised the possibility that the structure rules are the *wrong sort* to be

---

[6] Is a grammar a theory of the speaker's competence at Christopher Peacocke's "level 1.5", as he claims (1986, 1989)? Perhaps so. A level 1.5 explanation states information that the competence draws on. This information must be a consequence of the grammar. I have emphasized that a grammar must meet the Respect Constraint: it must posit rules that are respected by the competence (2.4–2.6). This seems rather like claiming that the grammar must provide level 1.5 explanations of competence. Peacocke takes the grammar to be psychologically real simply in virtue of this claim (1989: 114). I do not take it to be psychologically real simply in virtue of its meeting the Respect Constraint. But this difference may be just verbal.

processing rules just as, in our examples, the rules of the bee's dance very likely are, and the formation rules of logic certainly are (2.2). The present discussion suggests that some of the structure rules for language, at least, are indeed the wrong sort to be processing rules. This gives a motive for attributing position (II) rather than (I) or (III) to Chomsky: the speaker "consults" the represented rule but need not actually go through the process specified by the rule.

4.2   CHOMSKY AND POSITION (II)

There is an obvious problem in attributing position (II) to Chomsky: we need to account for all the talk suggesting that linguistic rules govern real processes in the mind. But, perhaps we can explain away this talk by treating it as a metaphor describing the structure of the language.[7] To say that a language consists of a "computational procedure and a lexicon" is a metaphorical way of saying that it consists of a system of structure rules and a lexicon. We can take talk of transformations in a "mathematical" sense,[8] capturing syntactically significant relations between sentences—for example, between actives and passives, and between statements and *yes–no* questions—without supposing that transformations are real processes in the mind.

7. Distinguish actual from merely metaphorical generation, computation, and processing.

The logic machine (2.2) provides a nice analogy. Its derivations are defined over the *wffs* of a formal language. Each *wff* is governed by the formation rules of the language. These rules are the structure rules of the language used by the logic machine. Still, we might describe these rules as a procedure for generating all the *wffs* of the language. In talking in this way, we might have in mind the possibility of a *wff* machine that is governed by these rules and that actually generates these *wffs* by selecting syntactic forms and lexical items, selections that are random except insofar as they are constrained by the rules. But this process is not, of course, something that the *logic* machine does in using the formal language to generate derivations. The talk of the rules of the language generating *wffs* is just a metaphorical way of capturing the way the *wffs* have structures governed by those rules. The generation is mathematical not actual. Analogously, perhaps with the possibility of a sentence machine in mind, we might describe the rules of a natural language as generating all the sentences of the language. But the claim is not that humans are actually machines of this sort. The generation of sentences by the rules of the language is mathematical not actual.

---

[7] I have found that this way of interpreting the process talk appeals to many.

[8] Gilbert Harman confidently interprets Chomsky in this way: "the relevant sort of generation is mathematical, not psychological" (1983: 408); see also Boden 1988: 4; Bock 1995: 207. Chomsky himself remarks: "The term 'generate' is familiar in the sense intended here in logic" (1965: 9).

It is undoubtedly tempting to take the process talk as metaphorical, hence making it possible to adopt position (II) as an interpretation of Chomsky. But there are problems giving in to this temptation. First, the process talk is presented so persistantly as a psychological account and never acknowledged to be metaphorical. Pylyshyn remarks that, despite the difficulties in understanding Chomsky's claims about the place of linguistic rules in the mind,

none of us doubted that what was at stake in all such claims was nothing less than an empirical hypothesis about *how things really were inside the head of a human cognizer.* We knew that we were not speaking metaphorically.   (1991: 233)

Second, some of Chomsky's claims—for example, the allusion to Marr—do not seem open to the metaphorical interpretation.

There is another way to account for the process talk and open the door to (II) as an interpretation. This way is prompted by a certain use/mention sloppiness in Chomsky's discussion.

Influenced by passages like the one quoted earlier (Chomsky 1995b: 15; 200a: 120), we have been working with the idea that *the I-language* does the computing and deriving. Yet the claim is often that *the grammar*, the *theory* of the I-language, does so (e.g., Chomsky 1957: 26–7; 1965: 63–6). And this claim may seem more psychologically appropriate. The idea of derivation within a theory is familiar: it's the idea of inferring particular claims from generalizations. But what is derived from a grammar is not an expression of the language but *a description of* an expression, just as what is derived from an astronomical theory is not, say, a star,[9] but a description of a star. Clearly, the generation of expressions by the I-language would be one thing, the generation of descriptions of expressions by the grammar, another. Yet Chomsky seems uninterested in the difference. Sometimes grammars are said to generate "structural descriptions" (1993a: 36), which is appropriate; othertimes they are said to generate expressions ("strings") (1965: 66), which, initially at least, is not. And often I-languages are said to generate not expressions but structural descriptions (1988: 60; 1991a: 14). Finally consider the following where structural descriptions are *identified with* expressions:

One component of the language faculty is a generative procedure (an *I-language*, hence-forth language) that generates *structural descriptions* (SDs), each a complex of properties, including those commonly called "semantic" and "phonetic." These SD's are expressions of the language.   (1993b: 1)

In brief, Chomsky seems ready to talk of either a grammar or an I-language generating either a structural description or an expression of the language.

The following diagram illustrates what is appropriate and inappropriate if we are strict about the use/mention distinction:

---

⁹ Despite what neo-Kantian worldmakers tell us; see Devitt 1997a: ch. 13. McGilvray 1999 is a neo-Kantian interpretation of Chomsky.

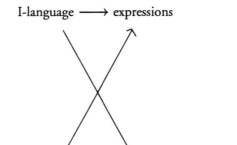

I-language ——→ expressions

Grammar ——→ structural descriptions
of expressions

The lines represent the process of derivation or generation. The horizontal ones are in order according to the use/mention distinction; the diagonal ones are not.

Aside: This use/mention issue is relevant to the interpretation of linguistic texts. For example, the sentence

(1) John hit the boy.

may stimulate something like the following:

(2) [ₛ[ₙₚ[ₙJohn]][ᵥₚ[ᵥhit][ₙₚ[ᴅᴇₜthe][ₙboy]]]]

or a tree with "the same information" (e.g. in Chomsky 1980a and 1995c; and see other essays in Webelhuth 1995). Since 'John', 'hit', 'the' and 'boy' seem to be *used* in (2), it is natural to take (2) as simply a *restatement of* (1) with its syntactic structure made fully explicit, just as 'Cheap (food and wine) can be interesting' is a restatement of 'Cheap food and wine can be interesting' with its structure made partially explicit. Interpreted in this way, (2) is the sort of thing that could be derived from an I-language.

But sometimes (1) will stimulate something like the following, where the words 'John', etc. are italicized:

(3) [ₛ[ₙₚ[ₙ*John*]][ᵥₚ[ᵥ*hit*][ₙₚ[ᴅᴇₜ*the*][ₙ*boy*]]]]

or a tree with "the same information" (e.g. in Chomksy 1957 and 1965). Since the words are italicized and this is the linguistic convention for *mentioning* a word, and since (3) is called "a structural description" (although also "a phrase-marker"), it is natural to take (3) as a brief version of the following *description of* (1):

(4) *John hit the boy* is a sentence made up of a noun phrase consisting of the noun *John* and of a verb phrase consisting of the verb *hit* followed by a noun phrase made up of the determiner *the* followed by the noun *boy*.

(4) is the sort of thing that could be derived from the grammar. (See Baker 1995, pp. 88–92, for explicit examples of outputs like (4).) Another possibility is to

take (3) as a *definite description*—hence *literally* a structural description—of *John hit the boy*: "The sentence made up of a noun phrase ..."

Return now to the main discussion. We have seen that strict observation of the use/mention distinction leaves two candidate stories of generation, the top and bottom lines in the diagram. It is important to distinguish them:

8. Distinguish the generation of expressions by the I-language from the generation of structural descriptions of expressions by the grammar.

What is the bearing of this use/mention issue on the interpretation of Chomsky? If Chomsky required that the generation of expressions by the I-language be psychologically real, then his position would be (i) or (iii), with the implausibilities already noted. If, on the other hand, he required that the generation of structural descriptions by the grammar be psychologically real, then his position might be a version of (ii): the data used in language processing would be not just the structure rules but descriptions that are derived from those rules. Still, this interpretation has its implausibilities. It could hardly be the case that each piece of language processing involves the derivation of all the structural descriptions for the language. So we wonder how it would be determined which ones are derived and how such structural descriptions could be used by the processor (on which more in the next section).

One is left uncertain of Chomsky's position. My best guess is that, in thinking about language use, he *starts* convinced of RT and, on the strength of that alone, convinced of the psychological reality of linguistic rules. This view of the rules needs a powerful psychological assumption—my second methodological point (2.6)—and RT is Chomsky's assumption. He has no worked out opinion about, or even much interest in, *how* that grammar in the head plays a role in language use. What is puzzling about this is that a strong commitment to RT seems inappropriate in the absence of a well-supported theory of language use that gives RT a central role. Even if there are other reasons for believing in RT—and I shall argue later that there are no good ones—these should not be sufficient for commitment. If we can find no place for representations of the rules in language processing, hence no place for them in an account of linguistic competence, we should surely doubt the existence of these representations. We should apply Pylyshyn's Razor (3.1): representations are not to be multiplied beyond necessity.

Finally, this discussion provides another way to draw the earlier distinction between a theory of a language, a grammar, and a theory of competence in that language (2.4). The former is a theory of a metaphorical process of deriving sentences in the language; the latter is a theory of a capacity for actual mental processes of moving from thoughts to sentences of the language and moving from the sentences to thoughts.

The distinctions mentioned in this section are listed in the Glossary, along with much else.

4.3 FODOR, BEVER, AND GARRETT

The Psychology of Language, by Jerry Fodor, Tom Bever, and Merrill Garrett (1974), is rightly regarded as a classic. The authors describe and evaluate research to that time into the psychological reality of language, and make some proposals.

First, Fodor, Bever, and Garrett ("FBG") clearly take RT for granted: a speaker represents the rules of her language and has knowledge about them (p. 7). So we expect their position on the psychological reality of language to be a version of either (i) or (ii). But this is not what it turns out to be.

In section 4.1 I mentioned psycholinguistic attempts to establish the psychological reality of transformations, attempts which are contrary to my third methodological point and which are, I suggested *prima facie* unpromising. FBG make an extensive examination of experiments aimed to confirm this psychological reality. These experiments generally appeared to assume what FBG call "the *derivational theory of complexity* (DTC)": "the complexity of a sentence is measured by the number of grammatical rules employed in its derivation" (p. 319). So, the more transformations there are in the derivation of a sentence the more difficult it should be to understand. In any case, FBG find little direct evidence to confirm the psychological reality of transformations, far too little to convince them of it (pp. 241, 273–4). So they do not hold to (i) (linguistic rules are represented and applied in language use).

FBG have a much more positive view about the psychological reality of structural descriptions:

The parameters of sentences which linguistic descriptions mark enter, one way or another, into a variety of psychological processes concerning language. There seems no serious doubt that *structural descriptions* are, in this sense, psychologically real; they specify at least some of the descriptions under which linguistic messages are interpreted and integrated. (p. 273)

FBG find "a variety of independent experimental evidence" supporting this view (p. 249). This seems to me important and to some degree right. However, from my perspective, the conclusion we should draw from these experiments needs to be put differently: the experiments do not provide evidence that *descriptions* of syntactic properties are psychologically real but rather that the properties themselves are, in some sense.

Here is their account of one experiment, which I shall take as my example:

Fodor and Bever (1965) demonstrated that the patterns of errors in "click location" made by subjects when listening to sentences were related to the constituent structure of the sentences. For example, Fodor and Bever's stimulus material contained recordings of the sentence (5–11) in versions of which a click was located before, after, or in the major constituent break ...

5–11 That he was happy was evident from the the way he smiled.

There was a significantly greater error for location of clicks not objectively placed at the major boundary than for those which objectively occurred at the boundary. There was, moreover, a significant tendency to place mislocated clicks at the major constituent break. (p. 252)

Consider first what this shows about the grammar that ascribes that constituent structure to the language. The experiment provides evidence that, to this extent, the grammar meets the Respect Constraint. For it provides evidence that the rules determining the major constituents are respected by the processing rules that govern the subjects' use of the language. And if the experiment did not provide this, it would be bad news for the grammar. For, we should *hope* to find evidence that subjects respect all the rules ascribed by the grammar and should *expect* to find it for rules that determine something so basic as major constituents. The experiment shows that the subjects' behavior is sensitive to major constituents, thus confirming that part of the grammar's account of linguistic reality. We noted earlier that psycholinguistic evidence can support a grammar (2.5, fifth point). This is an example.

What does the experiment show about the psychological reality of language? At least, it provides evidence that the subjects' linguistic competence, and its processing rules, respect the structure rules ascribed by the grammar to determine major constituents. We knew already, of course, that the competence must respect the language's structure rules—that's the minimal position (M) on the psychological reality of language (3.4)—but we did not know what those rules were. The experiment provides evidence of what they are, as we have just noted. Does it provide any more? Does it support a position on psychological reality stronger than the minimal (M)? It supports the view that there is something within the subjects that respects the rules governing major constituent structure, but does it cast any light on what that something is? I claim not.

I earlier distinguished processing rules that govern rational–causal operations on syntactically structured representations from ones that govern brute–causal operations (3.3), leading to versions (a) and (b) of various positions on the psychological reality issue (3.4). Now to conclude, as FBG do, that the structural description of (5–11) is psychologically real is to side with version (a): the process of understanding (5–11) operates on a metalinguistic representation of its syntactic properties. But this experiment alone provides no evidence for this over the brute–causal alternative of version (b): the process operates directly on the syntactic properties. One might argue, of course, that the process demands a metalinguistic representation, but that argument gets no support from this experiment. I shall later look skeptically at such arguments (11.6–11.8).

Of course, if we assumed RT, then we would have a ready explanation of why the competence respects the structure rules: it respects them because it represents them. And it would then go without saying that the experiment confirms the psychological reality of the structural description of (5.11). For, if representations of the syntactic rules are involved in processing then that processing must operate on metalinguistic representations of syntactic properties. But why should we assume RT? The experiment gives it no support—later I shall argue that it has no significant support—and so gives no support to the psychological reality of structural descriptions.

I think that what goes for this experiment goes for all the others. They provide evidence that the major constituent structure ascribed by the grammar, and even some underlying D-structure, are respected by competent subjects. It is by no means insignificant to have evidence of this, evidence that something-we-know-not-what within speakers respects some pretty subtle rules of language. But the experiments do not show more. They do not show how that respect is achieved. In particular they alone do not support RT and do not show that structural descriptions are psychologically real.

Although FBG endorse RT, they can often be read as expressing a view along these lines, along the lines of the minimal position (M). Thus they say that the experiments I have been discussing

show that linguistic structures engage psychological processes in some way, but they do not seek to explore the character of the interactions.   (p. 264)

And they assess the constraints placed on an ideal sentence recognizer by the optimal grammar in the following terms:

Since the latter device assigns each utterance one of the structural descriptions that the former device generates, the output of the optimal grammar constrains the output of the ideal sentence recognizer. It should be emphasized, however, that the grammar does *not*, in that sense, constrain the operations that the recognizer employs in *computing* its output. It is an open question ... what operations an ideal sentence recognizer must run through in assigning structural descriptions to utterances.   (p. 277)

This is almost a statement of what I have called "the Respect Constraint" on a theory of language comprehension, together with the statement that this is the only constraint that the linguistic rules place on that theory; cf. my third methodological point (2.6). I say "almost" because here, as elsewhere, FBG are committed to the psychological reality of structural descriptions. Even this commitment could be explained away if we overlooked their Representational Thesis. For their discussion, like Chomsky's, has a use/mention sloppiness (see e.g., pp. 18–21). So we could read their commitment as being to the psycho-logical reality of structural *properties* rather than to *descriptions* of those of properties. And then we could read that as a commitment to a psychological reality that respects those properties.

Still, FBG do endorse RT. So we expect RT to feature in their theory of language use. What is their theory?

In discussing language comprehension FBG first reject one version of position (1): "analysis by analysis". This is the earlier-mentioned idea that the parser runs the grammar backwards (pp. 313–16). They then contemplate what is in effect a version of (11) (linguistic rules are represented and used as data in language use) that has attracted many. This is "analysis by synthesis": "the grammar is used to generate a "search space" of candidate structural descriptions which are tested one by one against the input string" (p. 316). But this faces "a serious difficulty": the large size of the space of candidates that will need to be searched. To solve this problem they propose heuristics that "drastically reduce the size of the space to be searched" (p. 317). But, then, the more powerful the heuristic, the less there is for the internalized grammar to do (p. 318). This raises the possibility that heuristics do the whole parsing job leaving nothing for the grammar to do. This is, in effect, the possibility that FBG explore. They offer experimental evidence of two strategies speakers use: one a strategy of clausal analysis (pp. 329–48), and another, of lexical analysis (pp. 348–53). They point to other clues that speakers might use (pp. 353–61). These heuristics "employ the information that is represented by grammatical rules" but not in the form that the grammar presents that information. Indeed, they conclude: "There exist no suggestions about how a generative grammar might be concretely employed as a sentence recognizer in a psychologically plausible model." (p. 368)

This leaves FBG in a rather strange place, as they acknowledge (p. 369). They have not abandoned RT and yet, contrary to expectations, have found no place for its internalized grammar in parsing: the heuristics do all the work. Yet surely if we really do represent the rules of the language the representation must have a central role in language use. That is the presupposition of Chomsky's task (iii) on our first page. As he says, "the rules of the grammar enter into the processing mechanisms" (1980a: 200).

Given the strangeness of their view, FBG contemplate some responses. One of these is, in effect, position (11). They comment on this: "there is, at present, no positive reason for believing it is true" (p. 370). I have already noted that they do not hold (1). So what is their position in my terms? It seems to be

(iv) Some processing rules for language use are represented but they are largely unlike the structure rules of the language and do not use the structure rules as data,

with a large addition. It seems to be (iv) because their explanation of how a speaker's competence and its processing rules respect the structure rules—the explanation in terms of heuristics—does not have a role for the structure rules. The large addition is, of course, RT. So the structure rules are in the mind but they don't parse. In that respect, at least, they are epiphenomenal. Strange indeed! One wonders why FBG do not apply Pylyshyn's Razor and simply abandon RT.

Our discussion of FBG has all been about language comprehension but their line on language production does not alter these conclusions. For the line is similar, as one would expect, but more cautious. They dismiss the version of (1) that has the production system simply running the grammar. Their reason (p. 390) is related to our earlier one for thinking it absurd. They consider a version of (11) which is "analysis by synthesis" again, but find the same problem with it as before: the need for heuristics to cut down the number of candidate analyses to be tested (p. 393). They discuss the experimental studies. They conclude that "practically anything that one can say about speech production must be considered speculative" (p. 434).

The view that the linguistic rules are psychologically real requires a powerful psychological assumption: that is my second methodological point (2.6). FBG make such an assumption, RT. But then they can find no work for RT in explaining language use, thus undermining the assumption. Without the assumption, their investigation makes it seem likely that, for the most part, the rules of the language are not psychologically real: that language processing is handled by a set of heuristic rules that respect the linguistic rules but are mostly different from them: position (iv) (or possibly (v)).

FBG's classic made it clear that the early ideas of psycholinguistics—for example, DTC—had to be abandoned. As Pylyshyn puts it, these ideas were wrong about how a "grammar might be incorporated into a theory of comprehension/production" (1991: 232).

4.4   BRESNAN AND KAPLAN

Joan Bresnan and Ronald Kaplan ("BK"), like FBG, seem to take RT for granted:

A longstanding hope of research in theoretical linguistics has been that linguistic characterizations of formal grammar would shed light on the speaker's mental representation of language.   (1982: xvii)

So we also expect their position to be (i) or (ii). And this time we are not disappointed. Their position is (i).

BK start by embracing "Chomsky's *competence hypothesis*" (p. xvii):

a reasonable model of language use will incorporate, as a basic component, the generative grammar that expresses the speaker-hearer's knowledge of the language ...   (Chomsky 1965: 9)

So they seek a grammar that is not only linguistically motivated but also psychologically motivated (pp. xx–xxii, xxxviii): it must describe real processes in the mind. Indeed, they seem to think that a grammar that is simply linguistically motivated is of no interest (pp. xxiv, xxxviii).[10] This is contrary to what I have argued in Part I and to my first methodological point: a grammar might be simply true of a linguistic reality. Their insistence that the grammar be psychologically motivated is, of course, at odds with my third methodological point. I have argued that there is no reason to suppose in advance that a grammar has any more to do with psychological reality than comes from its meeting the

---

[10] Although elsewhere Bresnan remarks: "Theoretical linguistics has greatly advanced our understanding of the abstract structure of human languages." (1978: 3)

Respect Constraint. Linguistic rules that are accurately described by a grammar may be the wrong sort to govern language use.

BK think that transformational grammars have failed the test of psychological motivation; see our discussion of FBG in the last section. They reject two responses to this failure. The first of these is the response of FBG, which is to reject the competence hypothesis (as we have just seen). The second, is the response of Chomsky, which is to insist on the psychological reality of the transformational grammars even in the absence of psychological motivation, a response that I have also, in effect, criticized (4.1–4.2). Their own response is to seek a different sort of grammar:

a more radical decomposition of competence grammars into an expanded lexical and contracted syntactic component promises to have far greater explanatory power than the current versions of tranformational grammar, permitting a unification of linguistic and psycholinguistic research. (p. xx)

In particular they have in mind "lexical–function grammar" ("LFG"). In this grammar the "information" about a sentence that was previously captured by transformations is captured in lexical entries. Thus the relation between an active and a passive sentence that was captured by transformations involving NP movement is captured by a lexical rule relating active and passive verbs in the lexicon: "apparent NP movement is only an illusion" (p. xxx).

What are the psychological implications of this? BK are committed to "an information-processing model of language use that includes a processor and a component of stored linguistic knowledge K". Part of K "prescribes certain operations that the processor is to perform on linguistic representations". They call this part "the *representational basis*". So, in my terminology, the representational basis represents processing rules which are applied in language use. BK continue: "a model satisfies the *strong competence hypothesis* if and only if its representational basis is isomorphic to the competence grammar" (p. xxxi; see also Bresnan 1978: 3). In my terminology, the processing rules are the structure rules: position (i).

BK think that their LFG is compatible with the strong competence hypothesis, for it has eliminated the transformational derivations that have proved so psychologically elusive. Even lexical rules like the one that derives the lexical entry for the passive verb from that for the active do not have to be actually run by the processor. The passive will have been derived from the active when the active was acquired but after that both active and passive are stored in memory as part of K (pp. xxxiii-xxxiv).

LFG near enough eliminates computations from phrase structure to phrase structure. But it still does have "a single level of phrase structure representing the surface form of a language". This is called "*constituent structure*" ("c-structure") (p. xxviii). Following Chomsky, we found it absurd that producing a sentence involved going through the rewrite processes of building a phrase marker.

Further, we found it equally absurd that parsing a sentence involved running these processes backward (4.1). Do BK think that the processes of building (unbuilding) c-structures are psychologically real? The implication of Bresnan 1978 (pp. 50–2) is that they do.

BK's approach, particularly their enthusiasm for the strong competence hypothesis, stands in nicely clear opposition to my third methodological point. In my view we have no reason to suppose that the strong hypothesis is true. Furthermore, we should have no desire for it to be true: when constructing a grammar we should not be constrained by this hypothesis; when trying to explain the largely unknown processes of language comprehension it is a mistake to suppose a priori that the rules governing these processes are isomorphic to the rules specified by the grammar. The disagreement between a lexical-function and a transformational grammar should be a strictly linguistic one, to be settled according to which gives a better account of linguistic reality. And it could be the case, of course, that they are equivalent and hence equally good.[11]

Bresnan (1978) distinguishes two research objectives. The first is "the grammatical characterization problem" which is "to characterize the grammar that is to represent the language user's knowledge of language". This description reflects her commitment to RT. Without that commitment, we can describe the problem simply as that of characterizing the language. The second is "the grammatical realization problem" which is "to specify the relation between the grammar and the model of language use into which the grammar is to be incorporated as a basic component" (p. 1). She finds too many rival solutions to the first problem: it is "not very well defined". She proposes that "the grammatical realization problem can clarify and delimit the grammatical characterization problem" (p. 59). Her idea is that the story of language use will help us choose a grammar. From the perspective I have argued for, this help can go no further than the Respect Constraint. The rules ascribed by a grammar must be respected by what is psychologically real but we should not expect them to *be* psychologically real. Indeed, it is possible that none of them are thus real. And if some of them are, this gives no extra credit to the grammar, for the grammar's task is to describe the language not the psychology. Finally, the characterization problem is well enough defined in terms of meaning. If two grammars meet the Respect Constraint and give equally good accounts of meaning, they may well be "notational variants" of the same theory and so we do not have to choose between them.

Given their support for RT we must take BK to hold to position (i) but it is worth noting that they do not adduce any considerations in favor of RT and hence in favour of (i), which require the structure rules to be represented, over (iii) which takes them to be simply embodied.

---

[11] "The GB and LFG representations are fairly intertranslatable" (Pinker 1989: 34). "Nontransformational theories ... characterize the same kinds of language facts as movement transformations do, but by various other formal means" (J. D. Fodor 1989: 179). Insofar as this is true, we have only pragmatic reasons for choosing between these theories.

4.5   BERWICK AND WEINBERG

Robert Berwick and Amy Weinberg ("BW") also take RT for granted: "the rules and representations of generative grammar serve as a description of knowledge representation". And they take for granted that this knowledge representation in a speaker provides "the grammatical basis of linguistic performance". These are the powerful psychological assumptions that they make to place linguistic rules in the mind; cf. my second methodological point. They start convinced about these psychological matters despite thinking that "very little is known about the machinery actually governing sentence processing" (1984: 35). This raises the old puzzling question: why be so convinced about RT given this ignorance about its place in a theory of processing? Why not apply Pylyshyn's Razor?

What do BW have to say about sentence processing? They make the undeniable point that the grammar of a speaker's language must be "compatable" with the theory of how the speaker parses that language (p. 35). The question then is: what does this compatability consist in? In my view, it consists in both theories meeting the Respect Constraint and nothing more, my third methodological point. Given their convictions, just described, it is not surprising that BW hanker after something much stronger. They are initially attracted by the Miller and Chomsky (1963) suggestion that "grammars be realized more or less directly as parsing algorithms". This is the earlier-mentioned idea (4.1) that the parser "runs backwards" through the rules, position (I) (or (III) if RT were dropped). BW call this very strong principle "type transparency" (p. 39). However, this principle does not seem to hold for transformational grammars (4.3). BK's response to this, as we have just noted, is to maintain transparency by moving from transformational grammars to LFG (4.4). BW argue that this move is unfounded: "by allowing a rudimentary kind of parallel computation we can bring a transformationally based parser into line with existing psycholinguistic reaction time results" (p. 56). Using a Marcus parser as their example, they point out that if the parser computes in parallel, it may be able to parse sentences that are transformationally complex in the same time as more simple sentences, contrary to DTC (the derivational theory of complexity) which implicitly assumes serial computation. So a transformational grammar can accommodate transparency: the one-to-one correspondence between the rules of the parser and the grammar can remain.

While this may show that we *could* parse like a Marcus parser, and would then have brought the transformation rules into the mind, it does nothing to show that we *do* parse that way.[12] Perhaps we parse the way BK suggest, bringing LFG

---

[12] "it seems virtually certain that neither the human adult nor the human child operates like a Marcus parser" (Howe 1986: 87).

rules into the mind. Indeed, according to BW, these two views of parsing "seem to be empirically indistinguishable" (p. 67).

So far, then, we have seen BW defending transparency and hence position (1). But they are prepared to weaken their position. First, they claim that transformational grammars can follow BK in allowing a "precomputed memory retrieval system" (p. 74): the effects of a transformational rule can be precomputed and stored in the lexicon and so parsing need not involve any processing according to that rule. Second, they appeal to "the notion of grammatical cover": "one grammar is said to *cover* another if the first grammar can be used to easily recover all the parses that the second grammar assigns to input sentences". This "allows us to hold the structural descriptions of a grammar fixed and then consider variations in parsing methods" (p. 78). BW claim that the first of these weakenings is compatible with the view that the transformational grammar is "a central component of the parsing model" (p. 73) and the second with the view that the parser "realize(s)" the grammar (p. 77).

Two comments. (i) With these claims BW seem to imply that the contemplated positions on psychological reality are, in my terms, still versions of (1), albeit very weak ones. But I wonder if this is really so. I wonder if these positions really amount to any more than the minimal (M): for example, perhaps all the covering grammar has to do is respect the grammar covered. (ii) BW claim that "there is a continuum of more to less direct parsing 'realizations' of grammars as parsers". This leads them to the question: "Why not simply dispense with grammar and just look at parsing algorithms instead?" The answer, they think, is "obvious": "we can use competence theory to constrain parsing theory" (p. 76). The context of this claim is, of course, psycholinguistic. Still, it is worth noting that the *only* interest in a grammar that they mention is this psychological one. They do not mention a linguistic interest; cf. my first methodological point. But the main thing to note is that the constraint on parsing that they actually contemplate often seems to amount to my Respect Constraint, suggesting that they may indeed be prepared to settle for (M). Are BW, deep down, and despite appearances and rhetoric to the contrary, in accord with my third methodological point?

Their criticism of FBG's heuristic stategy makes it clear that they are not. The problem they find with this strategy for passives is that "it does not crucially depend on the assumptions of either" LFG or a tranformational grammar; "it can be made compatible with either". In contrast, they claim that the Marcus parser "realizes a transformational theory" (p. 77). This realization, it has to be said, is extremely subtle. Although the Marcus parser does not actually run the rules for passive transformation, the parser is alleged to realize the transformational theory because the theory explains why the parser drops "a trace after a verb with passive morphology" (p. 76). So BW seem to be aiming for a very weak version of position (1). In brief, according to BW, the view that we parse like a Marcus parser has an advantage over the view that we parse using FBG's heuristic simply in virtue of being tied in this way to the transformational theory. This advantage is enjoyed quite independent of any empirical evidence about how we do in fact parse. This is contrary to my third methodological point.

Finally, I follow Stabler (1983: 401) in noting that nothing in BW's discussion of the relation between the grammar and parsing theory warrants commitment to RT and so nothing motivates a very weak version of (i) rather than (iii).

4.6 MATTHEWS

Finally, let us consider the position of Robert Matthews, a philosopher who is close to generative grammar. His position (1991) is similar to BW's. But it differs from theirs, and all the other actual positions we have considered, in a striking way: Matthews does not embrace RT. Indeed, he can find no evidence for RT (p. 187; Demopoulos and Matthews 1983: 405). He even doubts that Chomsky subscribes to it (p. 192).

Matthews' position starts from the assumption that "realist scruples ... dictate that we take the grammar ... to have the speaker/hearer as a model" (p. 188). This runs counter to my first methodological point according to which realist scruples require us to take the grammar to be true of *linguistic* reality. Despite this, the grammar does dictate something about psychological reality: the competence of the speaker/hearer must respect the rules ascribed to linguistic reality by the grammar. Matthews clearly has in mind a closer relation than is demanded by this Respect Constraint. He seeks a way "in which a speaker/hearer might realize a grammar (or, equivalently, the grammar be true of that speaker/hearer)" (p. 188). Since he rejects RT, his position must be a version of (iii). His demand for the closer relation between the grammar and psychological reality runs counter to my third methodological point.

Despite this demand, it is hard to see how the theory he offers differs from the minimal position (M). Consider what he has to say about the Marcus parser. He claims that although it

does not incorporate ... an EST [Extended Standard Theory] grammar for English, EST does bear an explanatorily transparent relation to the parsing theory that would have this parser as one of its models. By this I mean that the syntactic generalizations that are captured by means of the theoretical constructs of EST ... are *explained* in terms of the organization and operation of the mechanisms postulated by the parsing theory ... in the straightforward sense ... that the generalizations stated in an EST grammar for English would be true of a speaker who incorporated a Marcus parser. (p. 189)

Yet these generalizations seem to be "true of a speaker" only in the sense that they are true of the *inputs* of the speaker: the Marcus parser interprets sentences that comply with the structure rules specified by EST; the parser respects those rules.

But those rules are not the ones that are actually realized in the parser: so EST does not describe the parser. The relation of the rules of EST to the psychological reality of the speaker seems to be only that of the minimal position (M): EST describes the language that the speaker is competent in. And "the explanatorily transparent relation" between the parsing theory and EST does not seem to add any more psychological reality to EST because the theory's explanation of how the speaker respects the rules of EST does not ascribe any of those rules to the speaker. If a speaker understands a language, it is trivially the case that the true theory of her parser will stand in that same explanatorily transparent relation to the grammar of the language. For the parser must respect the rules of the language. That is why position (M) should be uncontroversial.

Clearly Matthews wants something stronger than (M). Wherein does the extra strength lie? In attempting to discover how a position differs from (M), we must once again look to criticism of FBG for clues. If Matthews understood "explanatory transparency" in the weak sense I have just described, he should hold that EST might also stand in an explanatorily transparent relation to a theory of "a parser that incorporates heuristic procedures of the sort hypothesized by" FBG. For, the theory of this parser would equally explain how the speaker respects the rules of the grammar: the speaker does so because those heuristic procedures do so. Yet, according to Matthews, FBG's heuristic theory does not do the explanatory job: "the relation of parser to grammar would be explanatorily opaque". Why? Because although "the generalizations stated in the linguistic theory of the grammar would be *satisfied* by models of this heuristic theory ... they would not be explained by these models" (p. 191). The way in which the Marcus parser unlike the heuristic parser is alleged to realize EST rests on this subtle point. So too does the way in which Matthews' position differs from (M). If the subtle point can be be made good, Matthews' position will be a very weak version of (III). I confess that the subtle point is too subtle for me.[13]

In sum, there are signs in Matthews, as in others we have considered, of position (M). This is what we should expect and hope for because this minimal

---

[13] A position Matthews contemplates in a later paper seems even less distinguishable from (M). On the basis solely of a competent speaker's capacity to map utterances of English sentences onto beliefs about what was said with them, he is prepared to speak of the mapping process as a computational implementation of the semantic and syntactic theory of English (2003: 200–2). But all the mapping requires is that the speaker processes sentences with the semantic and syntactic properties of English; i.e., it requires only the uncontroversial (M). It does not require that *the theory of* the semantic and syntactic properties of English has any role in that mental process other than as the theorist's account of the sentences that are processed. The process is "semantic-involving" and "syntax-involving" (Matthews' terms), in the sense that it involves those semantic and syntactic properties, not necessarily in the sense that it involves a theory of those properties.

Radford's position seems also to be indistinguishable from (M). He offers an analogy to help with the psychological reality issue: "Municipal regulations specify certain structural conditions that houses must meet ... What they do not do is tell you *how* to go about building a house ... Phrase Structure Rules should be thought of as analogous to municipal building regulations: they lay down certain structural conditions which sentences must meet" (1988: 132).

position should be uncontroversial. But the view that linguistics is part of psychology demands more than (M) and so Matthews and others are not satisfied with (M). Yet it is hard to mount a case for the robust positions (I), (II), or (III) on the psychological reality issue. So less robust positions are sought: the grammar is descriptive of competence in a way stronger than simply positing rules that are respected by competence but weaker than positing rules that govern processing or are used as data in processing. According to my third methodological point, it is a mistake to *seek* such an intermediate position. Still, perhaps one can be found and I shall not be arguing that it cannot. I shall be concerned with the robust positions. If an intermediate position could be found, then the challenge would be to show that it was *theoretically interesting* that the grammar was descriptive of competence in that way.

4.7 CONCLUSION

We have seen that all the writers considered in this chapter apart from Matthews seem to subscribe to RT. So, *that* is the powerful psychological assumption which, according to my second methodological point, they need in taking the grammar to be true of psychological reality. A commitment to RT strongly suggests position (I) according to which linguistic rules are represented and applied in processing, or (II) according to which the rules are represented and used as data in processing. And (I) does seem to be the position of BK. But the others do not give RT a clear enough place in a theory of language use to justify a confident attribution of (I) or (II) to them. Indeed, FBG seem to hold (IV), which gives no role to the represented rules in language use. And BW's version of (I) is so weak as to be scarcely distinguishable from the minimal position (M) according to which the linguistic rules are simply respected by the processing rules. Since Matthews rejects RT, (I) and (II) are not open to him. He seems to be urging a version of (III) according to which the linguistic rules are embodied and govern processing but his position on psychological reality is so weak as to be also scarcely distinguishable from (M).

RT is so taken for granted by most of these writers that they do not contemplate that the grammar might simply be true of linguistic reality, as urged in my first methodological point. Finally, most of these writers are strikingly at odds with my third methodological point. They do not take the grammar and the theory of competence to be largely independent of each other. Rather, they take them to place heavy constraints on each other, far heavier than the Respect Constraint.

FBG made it clear that early theories of how a grammar should be incorporated into a theory of language use were wrong. As a result grammatical rules were given less role in that theory in the years that followed: "During the past fifteen years, the role of grammatical theory within models of natural language process-

ing has been continually reduced" (Pritchett 1988: 539). Still, the belief that
grammatical rules play a central role in the theory of language use remained, as
Pylyshyn pointed out (1991: 232) and BK, BW, and Matthews demonstrate.
Later work on language processing, to be considered in Chapter 11, indicate that
this belief has weakened in subsequent years. Indeed, this work suggests that
researchers are now pretty much in accord with the methodological points I am
urging.

We have seen no sign of (T), the idea that the grammatical rules have their
place in the mind not as processing rules governing language use but as structure
rules of thought. Indeed, I can find no basis for a confident attribution of (T) to
any of these writers. I shall consider Chomsky's relation to (T) in Part (IV).

Part I of this book argued that linguistics is primarily a study of linguistic
reality. Contrary to received opinion, linguistics is not part of psychology. That
was my first major conclusion. So the great advances in linguistics in recent times
leave the question of the psychological reality of language largely open. The main
concern of this book is to throw light on how this question might be closed. We
have started on this task in Part II by describing some possible positions on the
question, and some historically interesting actual positions on it. We turn next to
the assessment of evidence from various quarters on these positions. In Part III, I
begin with what we might call "philosophical" arguments for RT and hence for
positions (I) or (II): evidence from the rejection of behaviorism in Chapter 5;
evidence from folk psychology in Chapter 6; and evidence from the role of
intuitions in Chapter 7. I find all this evidence wanting. This is the first step in
establishing my *second major conclusion*: there is no significant evidence for RT
and, given what else we know, it is implausible. In Part IV we consider what light
the relation of language to thought can throw on the psychological reality
question. Finally, in Part V, against this background about thought, I shall
consider the evidence from language use and language acquisition. This consideration provides the main evidence for my second major conclusion.

All major conclusions are listed at the end of the Glossary.

PART III

"PHILOSOPHICAL" ARGUMENTS FOR THE REPRESENTATIONAL THESIS

5

The Rejection of Behaviorism

In calling the arguments in this part "philosophical", I do not mean to suggest that they are not empirical. Indeed, in my Quinean view (1998b), all arguments are empirical. Still, some arguments have a distinctly philosophical flavor, particularly in their *distance* from the empirical evidence to which all arguments must ultimately answer.

The first philosophical argument for the Representational Thesis (RT) that I shall consider is the argument from the rejection of behaviorism. The argument can be put briefly: RT, the view that competence in a language involves representing its rules, follows from the rejection of behaviorism, particularly from Chomsky's famous critique (1959) of B. F. Skinner. And my response can be put just as briefly: it doesn't follow; there is a vast amount of logical space between the rejection of behaviorism and RT.

I do not attribute this argument to any linguist. Indeed, perhaps none holds it, particularly in the bald form in which I have just stated it. Still, the literature sometimes seems to suggest the argument; it seems to suggest that once we have seen the failures of behaviorism, RT is obvious. Fiona Cowie (1999: 159–62) attributes the argument to Chomsky and, surprisingly, endorses it. All in all, it is worth a brief consideration.

Behaviorists deny anything to the mind beyond dispositions to behave in certain ways in response to certain external stimuli. For them the mind, linguistic competence included, is just a set of input/output functions. This reflects the crude empiricist dislike of things unseen; an unwillingness to posit theoretical entities that explain the observed phenomena. Behaviorism seems powerless to explain our linguistic abilities, as Chomsky points out. Most strikingly, it founders on the *stimulus independence* of language: most things we say are not tied closely to particular stimuli; indeed the link between stimulus and utterance may be extremely indirect. Furthermore, behaviorism cannot account for the *novelty* of language use: right from the beginning of acquiring a language, the child shows a capacity to produce novel utterances, hence ones that could not have been learned from association with particular stimuli. To explain our linguistic competence, we need to ascribe complicated inner states *interacting with each other*, as well as with various stimuli, to produce our responses: "there are, behind the overtly expressed sequences, a multiplicity of integrative processes" (Chomsky 1959: 55).

I very much agree with this rejection of behaviorism. But our discussion has already shown that the acceptance of a rich mental life underlying language is a long way from RT. Perhaps the rules governing our linguistic performance are embodied without being represented. Perhaps these rules are heuristic rules that are quite different from the rules ascribed by the grammar. Perhaps competence consists in a set of dispositions that mostly involve internal stimuli and internal responses and so mostly involve the fairly brute–causal processing of versions (b) of positions on psychological reality in section 3.4. There is room for a lot of mental complication without RT. The rejection of behaviorism shows that the story of linguistic competence must be a mentalistic one. To establish *which* mentalistic story it is requires a lot more. It requires evidence about *what* precisely is going on in the mind.

I turn now to the argument from folk psychology.

6

Folk Psychology

6.1 PHILOSOPHERS VS. CHOMSKY

The folk say that a person competent in a language "knows" the language. We have noted that the knowledge attributed might be of two very different sorts. It might be knowledge-that, propositional knowledge, or it might be knowledge-how, in the same family as skills, abilities, and capacities. If it is knowledge-how, it might still involve some propositional knowledge about the rules but it might not. And if it is *mere* knowledge-how then the implication seems to be that it does not (3.1). Some philosophers, including me,[1] have argued against the knowledge-that view and, largely for that reason, have claimed that competence is mere knowledge-how.[2] Chomsky is dismissive of the knowledge-how view, arguing that it is "entirely untenable" (1988: 9). He usually writes as if he endorses the knowledge-that view.

We should note first that linguistic competence could not be simply knowledge-that. The competence is a capacity to use language. If that competence

---

[1] 1981: 95–103; Devitt and Sterelny 1989.

[2] Jason Stanley and Timothy Williamson (2001) deny that "there is a fundamental distinction between knowledge-how and knowledge-that. Knowledge-how is simply a species of knowledge-that" (p. 411). On the basis of this they reject my claim in a previous book (1996) that competence in a language does not require any propositional knowledge about the meanings of expressions. And, on the same basis, they would surely reject my claim in this book that competence does not require any propositional knowledge about the syntax of expressions: they would reject my claim that the competent can be ignorant of language. Their ingenious argument starts from the linguistic claim that ascriptions of knowing-how in English contain embedded questions. They then argue that, according to the best semantic theories, such ascriptions attribute propositional knowledge. From this they arrive at their conclusion that knowing-how is a species of knowing-that. So, on the basis of assumptions about language, they draw an unlikely metaphysical conclusion. (Just how unlikely is nicely demonstrated by Schiffer 2002.) I think that we should always be suspicious of this way of proceeding: our linguistics should be guided by our metaphysics rather than *vice versa* because we know far less about our ways of talking about the world than we do about the world talked about (1996, 1997a, 1998a). And I think that Ian Rumfitt (2003) shows that such suspicions about Stanley and Williamson's argument are well founded. Rumfitt attends to ascriptions of knowing-how in other languages and shows that the argument does not hold up. Thus, although some ascriptions of knowing-how in French may fit Stanley and Williamson's analysis, those ascribing knowing how to swim, ride a bicycle, and the like do not. These ascriptions seem to attribute a relation to an activity not to a proposition, just as those who emphasize the distinction between knowing-how and knowing-that would hope.

involved some knowedge-that it would also have to involve some knowledge-how: it would have to involve *knowing how to apply* the knowledge-that in language comprehension and production. (This point is related, of course, to the earlier one that where a rule governs a process by being represented and applied there must be another rule that governs the application; 3.1.) So we should take the knowledge-that view to be that linguistic competence is constituted largely, although not entirely, by propositional knowledge of the rules of the language.

What hangs on this dispute? Briefly, the initial credibility a view gets from siding with the folk. The folk think that the competent person knows the language. One could take the high-handed line that this is just a piece of "folk psychology", one of a set of unscientific folk opinions, and so we need not worry about it. Certainly folk opinions have often been wrong, but they have very often been right too. Opinions that have stood up to the experiences of many lifetimes should not be lightly set aside: the "wisdom of the ages" has often been wise. The parties to the present dispute think, rightly in my view, that the folk opinion of linguistic competence is one we should try hard to accommodate. Now suppose, on the one hand, that this knowledge of language is construed as knowledge-that. Suppose, further, that we accept the Representational Theory of the Mind (RTM) as many do (although perhaps not Chomsky). Then the folk view yields the conclusion that the competent person represents the rules of her language: RT. So positions like (i) or (ii) on the psychological reality of language are supported: the represented rules are applied or used as data in language processing (3.4). I don't claim that this line of argument is explicit in the literature but it often seems to me to be implicit. Next suppose, on the other hand, that the knowledge is construed as knowledge-how. Then the folk view gives no support to RT. And if the knowledge is construed as *mere* knowledge-how, hence not involving any knowledge-that, then *prima facie* RT should be rejected. So, in arguing against the knowledge-that construal, the philosophers are undermining positions (i) and (ii). And in arguing against the knowledge-how construal, Chomsky is undermining the view that linguistic competence is like a skill or ability, a view required by position (iii) according to which linguistic rules are processing rules, and encouraged (as we shall see in Part IV) by position (t) according to which linguistic rules are similar to the structure rules of thought.

Of course, even if arguments in this dispute are persuasive, they leave plenty of room for manoeuver. For example, one could claim, as Chomsky sometimes does, that a speaker's knowledge of a language is *neither* knowledge-that nor knowledge-how (1969a: 86–7; 1969b: 153).[3] Certainly, the ordinary uses of

---

[3] Some phonologists sum up this view mysteriously as follows: "Rather than being *relational* [in the senses of knowledge-how, knowledge-of, or knowledge-that], 'knowledge of language' is for Chomsky *constitutive*, in the sense that there is no distinction between what is known and the knowing of it." (Burton-Roberts *et al.* 2000: 3)

'know' are so many and various that this possibility cannot be dismissed out of hand. Still, a lot of work then has to be done to establish that there is this other sort of knowledge *and* that it supports RT. The *immediate* support that RT gets from identifying linguistic competence with knowledge-that is lost. Or one could accept that the competence is mere knowledge-how but reject the *prima facie* consequence that this rules out RT: one could argue that, *at some level*, this knowledge-how involves representation of the rules. But, once again, the immediate support for RT is lost.

6.2 THE PHILOSOPHERS

Let us start with the philosophers' side of the dispute. The philosophers are mostly influenced by the view that a speaker's knowledge of her language is so unlike uncontroversial cases of propositional knowledge.[4] Stephen Stich (1971, 1978b) made the point nicely. If a person knows that *p*, we expect him to be aware of *p*, or at least to be able to become aware of it when given a suitable prompt; and we expect him to understand expressions of *p*. The ordinary speaker quite clearly lacks this awareness and understanding for most of the grammar. If a person knows that *p*, his knowledge should join up with other knowledge and beliefs to generate more beliefs. If a speaker has knowledge of the grammar it is clearly not inferentially integrated in this way. Consider an example. Without tuition, a speaker is unlikely to have the conceptual recourses to understand even the relatively simple claim that 'NP −> Det + Adj + N' is a rule of English. If she knows that this is a rule, her knowledge is largely inferentially isolated from her other beliefs.

Of course, Chomsky's view is that speakers' knowledge of the rules of the language is only *tacit*. But this is no help to the knowledge-that view because our knowledge of the language is very different also from ordinary tacit propositional knowledge. For, such knowledge is knowledge that a person has not entertained but which he would acknowledge in suitable circumstances; thus, Ron tacitly knows that rabbits don't lay eggs, even though the thought has never crossed his mind, because he would readily acknowledge that they don't lay eggs if the question were ever to arise. Clearly, the typical speaker does not have this relation to claims about the rules of her language. First, she lacks many of the concepts necessary even to understand such claims. Second, even if she had the necessary concepts, the truth of the claims would seem far from obvious to her.

---

[4] Dwyer and Pietroski (1996) argue in the opposite direction. They think that we have such good reasons (of the sort criticized in Chs. 7 and 10 to 12 below) for the view that speakers believe linguistic theory that this view should constrain our theory of belief.

In the face of this one might attempt to define a technical sense of "tacit knowledge" that covered a speaker's relation to the rules of her language.[5] But if that sense *does not* require that a person who tacitly knows the rules of her language represents those rules then this knowledge will clearly do nothing to support RT. And if that sense *does* require that she represents those rules then we need an independent argument to establish that she represents those rules. We need independent evidence that she tacitly knows the rules in a sense requiring that they be represented. So, either way, the definition can do nothing to support RT.

In sum, a person's knowledge of her language is very unlike what we ordinarily think of as propositional knowledge, or even tacit propositional knowledge. So the indubitable fact that speakers do know their language gives no support to RT.

Philosophers have also been influenced by a neat argument proposed by Gilbert Harman (1967). If a speaker's competence in a language consists in having knowledge-that of its rules then, assuming RTM, she must represent those rules. That representation must itself be in a language. What is it to be competent in that more basic language? If we suppose the more basic language is the same as the original language then we are caught in a vicious circle. If we suppose that it is some other language ("Mentalese" perhaps), then its rules also have to be represented. This requires a still more basic language. And so on. The only way to avoid a vicious circle or an infinite regress is to allow that we can be competent in at least one language directly, without representing its rules. Why not then allow this of the original language, the one spoken?

6.3   CHOMSKY

Turn now to Chomsky's side of the dispute. Chomsky takes the knowledge-how view of linguistic competence to be that competence is a "practical ability" to *use* the language in understanding and speech. He objects:

Two people may share exactly the same knowledge of language but differ markedly in their ability to put this knowledge to use. Ability to use language may improve or decline without any change in knowledge. This ability may also be impaired, selectively or in general, with no loss of knowledge, a fact that would become clear if injury leading to impairment recedes and lost ability is recovered.   (1986: 9)

Let us start with the differences in ability to speak. Chomsky gives two examples of the sort of difference that he has in mind. The first is the difference brought about by "a public speaking course" (p. 10). But this is beside the point. The know-how for public speaking *requires* ordinary linguistic know-how but *is*

---

[5] Thus, in an early paper, Fodor counts an organism that knows how to X as tacitly knowing that S if S specifies a sequence of operations that the organism runs through in X-ing (1981: 75). As Graves *et al.* point out, this "liberal" proposal has the consequence that a bicyclist tacitly knows the differential equations that determine how he maintains balance (1973: 324). Martin Davies (1987; 1989) makes an heroic attempt to define a technical sense of "tacit knowledge".

different from that know-how, as the folk plainly acknowledge. The fact that a person competent in a language can gain another competence as a result of a public speaking course or, for that matter, an elocution course or a calligraphy course, does nothing to show that *all* of these competences are not mere know-hows. A point made in the earlier discussion about the concerns of the theory of linguistic outputs—the theory of language—is relevant. The point was that the theory, like the theory of the outputs of the logic machine (2.2), abstracts from a range of properties of the outputs—like form of script and pitch of sound—focusing simply on syntactic properties. It follows that the theory of the competence to produce those outputs must make the same abstraction.

Chomsky's second example is of the difference between "a great poet" and "an utterly pedestrian language user who speaks in cliches" (1988: 10). But, once again, the difference is in another know-how—presumably, largely, a difference in thought—and does not show that knowledge of the language is not know-how. To suppose that it is know-how is not to suppose that there are no other skills that depend on it.

Consider next Chomsky's claim that a person's ability to use a language can be impaired by brain damage even though her knowledge of the language remains relatively stable. There can be no argument with this. But it does not show that the stable knowledge is not know-how because the same can be said of clear cases of know-how. A person knows how to ride a bicycle but cannot do so because his leg is broken; a person knows how to catch but cannot do so because she has blisters; a person knows how to touch type but cannot do so because he has a migraine. Indeed, it is presumably the case that exercising any know-how requires the satisfaction of some internal background conditions.

Chomsky rightly insists that "to know a language ... is to be in a certain mental state, which persists as a relatively steady component of transitory mental states" (1980b: 5). But he writes as if taking this knowledge as mere know-how must saddle it with a whole lot of irrelevant features of performance (1986: 10) and must make behavior "criterial" for the possession of the knowledge not merely evidential (1980b: 5). This is not so. A person's know-how can be an underlying steady state abstracted from features of performance. It can be, as Chomsky insists our knowledge of language is, "a *cognitive system* of the mind/brain"(1988: 10) and yet still be akin to a skill or ability. Usually, such an ability gives rise to certain behavior which then counts as evidence for the ability. But the ability may not give rise to the behavior. The behavior is not "criterial".

6.4 CONCLUSION

It seems to me that Chomsky's tactic in this dispute with the philosophers—roughly, "Don't give an inch"—is a mistake. Chomsky thinks that the cognitive system for language is to be found in a module of the mind, a distinct mental "organ", the "language faculty". This faculty is largely inaccessible to the operations of the "central processor" which does what we would ordinarily think of as thinking; hence the ordinary speaker's inability to state the rules of the language.[6] I think that Chomsky would best accommodate folk talk of "knowing a language" to this view by *accepting* the philosophers' claim that this knowledge is not knowledge-that but knowledge-how, and then arguing that knowledge-how in this case, if not others, requires the representation of rules in a module.[7] This tactic has a disadvantage, of course. If RT is understood in this way it gets no support from the folk talk of knowledge: the argument for RT must start from scratch. But doubtless this is not a disadvantage that would concern Chomsky.

In sum, I do not think that the folk view that we know the language we speak gives any evidential support to RT and hence to positions (i) or (ii). The case for those positions must be developed elsewhere.

---

[6] Some hold to the thesis that the mind is so massively modular that there is little or nothing for the central processor to do (Barkow, Cosmides, and Tooby 1992; Baron-Cohen 1995; Smith and Tsimpli 1995; Sperber 1996). I share Kim Sterelny's skepticism about this thesis (2003: ch. 10); see also Atkinson and Wheeler 2004. So far as I can see, it would take an extreme, hence highly implausible, version of the thesis to count against my arguments. In any case, I shall continue to write as if the thesis were false.

[7] This is what Stich recommends in his peer commentary (1980) but Chomsky does not accept the recommendation (1980c: 57).

7

Intuitions

7.1 INTRODUCTION

So far then we have found no support for the Representational Thesis (RT) in the rejection of behaviorism nor in the folk view that speakers "know" the language they speak. We turn now to a story that linguists tell about linguistic intuitions as a possible source of another argument for RT.

We should start by clarifying what we mean by "linguistic intuitions". We mean *fairly immediate unreflective judgments* about the syntactic and semantic properties of linguistic expressions, metalinguistic judgments about acceptability, grammaticality, ambiguity, coreference/binding, and the like. These judgments are frequently expressed in utterances; for example, " 'Visiting relatives can be boring' is ambiguous" or "In 'Tom thinks Dick loves himself' 'himself' must refer to the same person as 'Dick'." Such metalinguistic utterances are not to be confused, of course, with the vastly more numerous utterances we make about the nonlinguistic world. Nor are they to be confused with behavioral responses that are not metalinguistic utterances; for example, looking baffled by an ungrammatical utterance, or behaving in a way that clearly takes a pronoun to corefer with a certain name. The intuitions in question are *judgments about* linguistic performances not the performances themselves.

So, what story do linguists tell about these intuitive judgments of competent speakers? The story starts with the claim that the intuitions of competent speakers provide the main evidence for linguistic theories. As Chomsky puts it "linguistics ... is characterized by attention to certain kinds of evidence ... largely, the judgments of native speakers" (1986: 36). Indeed, the emphasis on these intuitions is sometimes so great as to imply that they are the *only* evidence the linguist has. Thus, Liliane Haegeman, in a popular textbook, says that "all the linguist has to go by ... is the native speaker's intuitions" (1994: 8).[1] But this is not the approved position. Evidence is also to be found in linguistic usage, at least.

---

[1] But two pages later Haegeman allows, somewhat grudgingly, an evidential role for usage. Andrew Radford opens a book (1988) with an extensive discussion of the evidential role of intuitions. The first mention of the use of the "corpus of utterances" as data does not come until p. 24. Robert Fiengo starts an interesting paper on linguistic intuitions: "Intuitions, with the contents that they have, are the data of Linguistics" (2003: 253).

In the next section I shall argue that speakers' intuitions are not the main evidence for linguistic theories. Still, I agree that they *are* evidence. Why are they? The standard linguistic answer, noted at the beginning of the book (1.1), rests on RT. These intuitions are thought to be good evidence because the speaker derives them from a representation of the rules of the language, a representation that constitutes the speaker's linguistic competence. The derivation is a causal and rational process like a deduction:

it seems reasonably clear, both in principle and in many specific cases, how unconscious knowledge issues in conscious knowledge ... it follows by computations similar to straight deduction. (Chomsky 1986: 270; see also Pateman 1987: 100; Dwyer and Pietroski 1996: 342)

we cognize the system of mentally represented rules from which [linguistic] facts follow. (Chomsky 1980b: 9; the facts are expressed in intuitive judgments)

We can use intuitions to confirm grammars because grammars are internally represented and actually contribute to the etiology of the speaker/hearer's intuitive judgments. (J. A. Fodor 1981: 200–1)

[A speaker's judgments about the grammatical properties of sentences are the result of] a tacit deduction from tacitly known principles. (Graves *et al.* 1973: 325)

Our ability to make linguistic judgments clearly follows from our knowing the languages that we know. (Larson and Segal 1995: 10; see also Pylyshyn 1984: 122; Baker 1995: 20)

So, on this explanation, linguistic competence alone provides information about the linguistic facts; the intuitive judgments are, as I put it, "the voice of competence". So these judgments are not arrived at by the sort of empirical investigation that judgments about the world usually require. Rather, a speaker has a privileged access to facts about the language, facts captured by the intuitions, simply in virtue of being competent and thus embodying representations of its rules in her language faculty, a module of the mind. I need a word for such special access to facts. I shall call it "Cartesian". We would like the details of this Cartesian explanation spelt out, of course. We would like to know about the causal–rational route from an unconscious representation of rules in the language faculty to a conscious judgment about linguistic facts in the central processor. Still, the idea of one sort of representation leading to another is familiar and so this standard Cartesian explanation may seem promising.[2]

We can see in this story an *argument* for RT and hence for positions (i) or (ii) on the psychological reality of language (the represented rules are applied or used as data in language processing; 3.4). For, the standard explanation can be used as the basis for the following abduction: RT is the core of a good explanation of why the intuitions are evidence, and there is no other explanation; so RT is

---

[2] Note that the explanation does not suppose that the speaker has Cartesian access to the linguistic rules, just to the linguistic facts captured by the intuitions.

probably true. If the intuitions are really derived from representations of the grammatical rules then they must be true and hence good evidence for the nature of those rules. But if they are not so derived, how could they be good evidence? How could they have this evidential status unless they really were the voice of competence?[3]

Various things are required for this abduction to be good. One is that RT has to be independently plausible given what else we know. If my second major conclusion can be established, then RT fails this test very badly. But that is not the concern of this chapter. Here I shall be arguing that there are reasons for doubting the standard Cartesian explanation quite apart from doubts about RT. More importantly, I shall be arguing that another explanation of the evidential role of linguistic intuitions, an explanation that does not rest on RT, is better. So the abduction fails anyway. My main concern in this chapter is to show this and hence that RT gets no support from evidential role of intuitions.

I am, of course, understanding the standard explanation and RT in light of the sense of 'represent' illustrated in section 1.1. Although this is the natural way to interpret the linguists' talk, I noted that it may not be the right way. 'Represent' (and its cognates) is used so widely and loosely in cognitive science that it is hard to be confident about what it means on any one occasion. This is not the place to try to analyze these uses and come up with other interpretations. However, I take it that linguists who talk in this way but reject my interpretation, and hence the standard explanation (as I am understanding it), will nonetheless hold that the rules are *embodied somehow* in a speaker without being represented (in the above sense), and govern processing: position (iii). And these linguists are still committed to the Cartesian view that intuitions are the voice of competence, the view that speakers, simply in virtue of being competent, have information about the linguistic facts. How could this be so if the rules are not represented? The linguists need what I shall call "a nonstandard Cartesian explanation" of why linguistic intuitions are good evidence for linguistic theories, an explanation of how unrepresented rules provide the privileged access to linguistic facts.

---

[3] Against the background of the standard Cartesian explanation, we can see the following as a statement of the argument:

Linguists normally take the intuitions of speaker/hearers to be the data to which structural descriptions are required to correspond. But this practice would be quite unwarranted unless it were assumed that speaker/hearers do have access to internal representations of sentences and that these provide a reliable source of information about the character of the abstract object (the language) which, on any view, the grammar is ultimately intended to describe. (Fodor, Fodor, and Garrett 1975: 244)

Graves *et al.* claim that the only plausible explanation of a speaker's explicit knowledge of grammatical facts is that she has tacitly deduced that knowledge from tacitly known principles of the language (1973: 324–9). The argument is implicit in Laurence 2003 (pp. 89–91).

In sections 7.3 to 7.6 I shall argue that the standard Cartesian explanation is not the best: the evidential role of linguistic intuitions can be better explained otherwise. This other explanation does not suppose that the intuitions are the product of embodied linguistic rules, whether represented or not; they are not the voice of competence. Rather, they are opinions resulting from ordinary empirical investigation, theory-laden in the way all such opinions are. If this is right, then the abduction to RT fails. In section 7.7 I shall consider the possibility of a nonstandard Cartesian explanation. As we have just noted, a linguist who rejects the view that linguistic rules are represented (in the above sense) in speakers needs such an explanation. And if he had one, it might, of course, be the basis for an abduction to position (iii). So far as I know, no such explanation has ever been proposed. I shall argue that none is likely to be forthcoming. Finally, in section 8, I shall look critically at the view that it is a task of linguistics to *explain* linguistic intuitions.

I turn now to consider briefly what sorts of evidence we do have for linguistic theories.

7.2   EVIDENCE FOR LINGUISTIC THEORIES

I began the chapter by noting the received view in linguistics that the intuitions of competent speakers provide the main evidence for linguistic theories; indeed, the view is often that these intuitions are near enough the only evidence. These views greatly exaggerate the evidential role of the intuitions. As recent experimenters who did actually test the intuitions of naïve subjects remark, this testing is "in contrast to common linguistic practice" (Gordon and Hendrick 1997: 326). I suggest that, as a matter of fact, only a small proportion of the evidence used in grammar construction consists in the canvassed opinions of the ordinary competent speaker.

So what else constitutes the evidence? (i) One possible source of direct evidence is "the corpus", the linguistic sounds and inscriptions that the folk have produced and are producing as they go about their lives without any interference from linguists. We can observe people and seek answers to questions like: "Do people ever say *x*?"; "How do they respond to *y*?"; "In what circumstances do they say *z*?" The role such observations have played, particularly in the beginnings of linguistics, is insufficiently acknowledged. Linguists may well rely extensively on intuitions now that generative grammars are in an advanced stage (even though not complete, of course). But think back to the beginning, perhaps just to the dark days before there were any generative grammars. Surely a lot of the early knowledge about languages, still captured by generative grammars, was derived from simply observing linguistic usage, much as the field linguist does. Even now, it is hard to believe that *L*-speaking linguists surrounded by other *L*-speakers are uninfluenced by the data they are immersed in. One would expect them, given their training, to be peculiarly sensitive to these data. Anecdotal evidence suggests that they are indeed so sensitive; that they are continually on the watch and noting linguistic oddities. Consider the theory of 'wanna' constructions, for example. We can surely be confident that the linguists' observations of the use of 'wanna' have played a considerable role in building this theory.

(ii) Another possible source of direct evidence in grammar construction, as I have emphasized (2.5), is psycholinguistic evidence of what syntactic rules speakers respect. The actual role of this evidence is small, largely confirming what is already fairly well established, because our knowledge of linguistic reality is so much more advanced than our knowledge of psychological reality. Still, if psycholinguistic evidence showed that a syntactic rule was not respected, that would be very bad news for the rule.

(iii) Interference by linguists can yield further direct evidence: we can contrive situations and see what subjects say or understand. Consider, for example, this description of "the technique of *elicited production*":

This technique involves children in a game, typically one in which children pose questions to a puppet. The game orchestrates experimental situations that are designed to be uniquely felicitous for production of the target structure. In this way, children are called on to produce structures that might otherwise not appear in their spontaneous speech. (Thornton 1995: 140)

Although this sort of technique is frequently used on children,[4] analogous ones are doubtless seldom used on adults because contriving these situations is likely to be laborious. But, clearly, much evidence could be gathered in this way.

We might aptly describe a person's responses in these contrived situations as "intuitive," but those responses are very different from the intuitions that are the main concern of this chapter. They differ in not being judgments about the syntactic and semantic properties of expressions and hence not needing to deploy linguistic concepts.

(iv) Another sort of interference can yield evidence that is less direct: we can *describe* situations and ask people what they would say or understand in those situations. This evidence is less direct because it depends on people's reflections on these situations. Once again, we might aptly describe a person's response as "intuitive" but it is not an intuitive judgment about linguistic properties. Such responses are another source of evidence that is insufficiently acknowledged. Linguists ask themselves, and sometimes ordinary speakers, what they would say or understand in various situations.

(v) Further less direct evidence can be obtained from language acquisition: evidence about what sorts of languages we could learn is evidence about what

---

[4] See Crain *et al.* 2005, section 4, for a nice summary.

language we have learnt. This sort of evidence is, of course, frequently acknowledged.

(vi) Finally, I suggest that a good deal of less direct evidence comes from the
intuitive opinions *of linguists* about the languages they speak. As an entry in
the *Encyclopedia of Cognitive Science* points out, partly because it is sometimes
"difficult to replicate relatively agreed-upon judgments of linguists while testing
naive subjects ... and partly for sheer convenience, linguists rely increasingly
on other linguists for judgment data on some languages" (Schutze 2003: 913).
The intuitions of ordinary speakers may seem to be more present than they really
are because linguists take their own intuitions to be representative.

There are surely many other ways to get evidence of linguistic reality apart
from consulting intuitions, just as there are to get evidence of any other
reality.

In sum, the main evidence for grammars is not found in the intuitions of
ordinary speakers but rather in a combination of the corpus, the evidence of what
we would say and understand, and the intuitions of linguists. Still, it cannot be
denied that ordinary competent speakers do have largely reliable intuitions which
do play an evidential role in linguistics, even if that role is greatly exaggerated. So
we still need to explain that role. And the abduction still stands: RT is the best
explanation of this role.

I shall be developing the theory that linguistic intuitions are theory-laden
empirical opinions. But I begin by noting a tension in linguistic discussions of
these intuitions arising, it seems to me, from the attraction of this theory.

7.3 TENSION IN THE LINGUISTS' VIEW OF INTUITIONS

A simplistic version of the standard Cartesian explanation would be that since
linguistic intuitions are derived from the rules of the language they must always
be true and so are as good as any evidence could be. Although there are signs of
this version in the literature,[5] it is not the approved version. The approved
version allows for errors arising from "noise" (1.1). So, just as there can be
performance errors in using our competence to produce and understand the
sentences of our language, there can be performance errors in producing judgments about such sentences. The explanation is Cartesian in supposing that we
have a nonempirical privileged access to linguistic facts not in supposing that this
access yields infallible judgments.

This retreat from reliance on intuitions seems clearly appropriate on the
standard view. Other retreats are not so clearly so. (i) Although there has been
reliance on intuitions about *grammaticality* the tendency in recent times has been

---

[5] Fodor, Bever, and Garrett 1974: 82; Baker 1978: 4–5.

to emphasize ones about *acceptability, goodness,* and the like,[6] and to offer explanations of these intuitions that are often syntactic but sometimes semantic or pragmatic. Yet *grammaticality* is the notion from linguistic theory and so if the intuitions are really derived from a representation of that theory, shouldn't we be relying on intuitions about grammaticality? If, in our intuitive judgments, competence is really speaking, why doesn't it *use its own language*? What is the causal–rational route from an unconscious representation of something's "grammaticality" to a conscious judgment of its "acceptability"? (ii) Ordinary speakers have many intuitions about grammaticality, coreference, and ambiguity, but few about transitivity, heads, A-positions, c-command, cases, transformations, and so on. Why is that? Why doesn't linguistics have a much wider range of intuitions to rely on? Linguistic theory is very rich. If our competence consists in representing this theory and our competence speaks to us at all, how come it *says so little*? Once again, we wonder how the details of the causal–rational route could be spelt out to account for this.

The clue to what underlies these retreats from reliance on intuitions is to be found in many passages like the following:

it is hardly surprising that informants should not be able to tell you whether a sentence is pragmatically, semantically, or syntactically ill-formed: for these very notions are terms borrowed from linguistic theory: and like all theoretical terms, they are meaningless to those not familiar with the theory.   (Radford 1988: 13)

Such passages reflect a sensitivity to the highly theoretical nature of linguistic terms. And they reflect the attractive thought that these terms have their place in empirical theories that are hard-won by linguists with the result that judgments involving them are not plausibly attributed to people *simply in virtue of being competent speakers*.[7] The retreat to acceptability may seem to escape this thought because 'acceptable' is a very ordinary term and not in linguistic theory.

I see linguists as pulled two ways in their treatment of the intuitive judgments of speakers. On the one hand, the standard view is that speakers represent the true linguistic theory of their language and derive their intuitive judgments from those representations. So, those intuitive judgments, deploying terms drawn from that theory, should be the primary data for the linguist's theory. On the other hand, there is the attractive thought that all judgments deploying those terms are laden with an empirical linguistic theory. Where the judgments are those of the ordinary speaker, that theory will be folk linguistics. We do not

---

[6] For example, Higginbotham 1987: 123; Radford 1988: 10; Hornstein 1989: 26, 38n; Haegeman 1994: 7; Baker 1995: 8, 38. Dwyer and Pietroski do not exemplify this tendency (1996: 346).

[7] In this respect it is interesting to note Chomsky's skepticism about "contemporary philosophy of language" and its practice of "exploring intuitions about the technical notions 'denote', 'refer', 'true of', etc." He claims that "there can be no intuitions about these notions, just as there can be none about 'angular velocity' or 'protein'. These are technical terms of philosophical discourse with a stipulated sense that has no counterpart in ordinary language". (1995: 24; 2000: 130)

generally take theory-laden folk judgments as primary data for a theory. So we should not do so in linguistics.

The emphasis on intuitions about acceptability (also goodness and the like) may seem to remove this tension, but it doesn't really. First, intuitions about acceptability are not the only ones playing an evidential role. There are also intuitions about coreference/binding, ambiguity, and so on, involving terms that are straightforwardly linguistic. Whatever we say about 'acceptable' is no help with the tension associated with these intuitions. Second, 'acceptable' (also 'good' and the like) is a highly context-relative term: it might mean *acceptable in polite society, acceptable in a philosophical argument*, and so on. What a linguist is aiming to elicit from an ordinary speaker is, of course, an intuition about what is *acceptable grammatically in her language*; he wants the voice of her competence. He may attempt to make this explicit; for example, "Is this expression acceptable in your language?" Or it may be implicit; "Is this expression acceptable?" asked in the right context by someone known to be a linguist. In these situations the speaker *may* naturally take 'acceptable' to express her notion of grammaticality (even if she lacks the term 'grammatical' for that notion). If she does take it that way, 'acceptable' in these situations acts as a synonym for 'grammatical'. So we are still pulled toward seeing her intuitive responses as judgments laden with folk linguistics. So the tension remains.

In other linguistic contexts 'acceptable' (and 'good') is likely to be taken in different ways. Thus the question "Is this expression acceptable in your community?" would invite the speaker to consider not only grammatical facts of her language but also pragmatic ones about etiquette, appropriateness, interest, and so on. And there is a considerable risk that the simple "Is this expression acceptable?" and even "Is this expression acceptable in your language?" will also bring in pragmatic considerations. Yet, clearly, the linguist is concerned to ask questions that minimize the intrusion of pragmatics into intuitions that he hopes are the voice of competence.[8] In any case, insofar as pragmatic considerations do intrude, the attractive thought encourages the view that the intuitions are still theory laden: they are laden not only with folk linguistics but also with pragmatic theories about what is good etiquette, socially appropriate, interesting enough to be worth saying, and so on. So there is still a tension.

The discussion in this section is the first step in undermining the standard Cartesian explanation. On the one hand attention to the language in which competence allegedly speaks and to how little it says raises concern about the details of the causal–rational route from representations in the language faculty to a judgment in the central processor. On the other hand, we have begun to see

---

[8] This being so, one wonders why linguists would ever use such a vague, pragmatic, context-relative term as 'acceptable' to seek grammatical intuitions unless pragmatic factors are controlled for (as in "minimal-pair" experiments; see section 7.5).

why the thought that ordinary linguistic intuitions are laden with empirical folk linguistics is attractive.

In section 7.4 I shall present a view of intuitions in general. In section 7.5 I shall apply this view to linguistic intuitions, yielding a view of them along the lines of the attractive thought. This view removes the tension by abandoning the received idea that the intuitions are derived from a representation of the rules: competence has no voice. And it yields an explanation of the evidential role of linguistic intuitions which, I shall argue in section 7.6, is better than the standard one.

7.4   INTUITIONS IN GENERAL

Questions about the status of intuitions do not arise only in linguistics, of course; intuitions play a role in ordinary life and science, and seem to dominate philosophy. What are we to say of them in general? In *Coming to Our Senses* (1996: 72–85) I argue for a naturalistic, and nonCartesian, view of intuitions in general.[9] On this view, intuitive judgments are empirical theory-laden central-processor responses to phenomena, differing from many other such responses only in being fairly immediate and unreflective, based on little if any conscious reasoning. These intuitions are surely partly innate in origin[10] but are usually and largely the result of past reflection on a lifetime of worldly experience".[11]

A clarification. It may be that there are many unreflective empirical responses that we would not ordinarily call intuitions: one thinks immediately of perceptual judgments like "That grass is brown" made on observing some scorched grass, or "That person is angry" made on observing someone exhibiting many signs of rage. Perhaps we count something as an intuitive judgment only if it is *not really obvious*. I shall not be concerned with this. My claim is that intuitions are empirical unreflective judgments, *at least*. Should more be required to be an intuition, so be it.

In considering intuitions and their role in science, it is helpful to distinguish the most basic intuitions from richer ones. Suppose that we are investigating the nature of a kind *F*—for example, the kind *gene*, *pain* or *echidna*. The most basic intuitions are ones that *identify Fs* and non-*Fs*; for example, "This is an echidna but that isn't." It is important to note that to have even these most basic intuitions a person must have the appropriate concepts: you cannot identify an

---

[9] And in 1994: 561–71. See also Kornblith 1998.

[10] In calling the intuitions "empirical" I am claiming simply that they must be *justified* "by experience". Should any justified belief be entirely innate, which I doubt, then beliefs of that sort must have been justified somehow by the experiences (broadly construed) of our distant ancestors, and we must have inherited that justification via natural selection.

[11] "intuition is the condensation of vast prior analytic experience; it is analysis compressed and crystallized …. It is the product of analytic processes being condensed to such a degree that its internal structure may elude even the person benefiting from it …" (Goldberg 2005: 150)

F if you do not have the concept of an *F*. The richer intuitions go on to tell us something about *F*s already identified; for example, "Echidnas look like porcupines". The richer ones may be much less dependable than the basic ones: a person may be good at recognizing *F*s without having much reliable to say about them; this is very likely the situation of the folk with pains.

Identifying uncontroversial cases of *F*s and non-*F*s is only the first stage of an investigation into the nature of *F*s: the second stage is to examine those cases to see what is common and peculiar to *F*s. Sometimes we have a well-established theory to help with the first stage; thus we had Mendelian genetics to identify the genes that were examined by molecular genetics in the second stage. But sometimes we do not have such help: we start pretty much from scratch; we are at the stage of *proto*-science. At that stage, the most basic intuitions are particularly important. In the absence of reliable theory, we must start by consulting the people who are most expert about *F*s to see what *they* identify as *F*s and non-*F*s: we elicit their most basic intuitions about *being an F* in "identification experiments". We are then in a position to begin our investigation. Until recently, at least, this was our position with pains.

When we are starting from scratch, we need the basic intuitions, but we do not need the richer ones. This is not to say that we should not use them. They may well be a useful guide to what our investigation will discover about *F*s; they are "a source of empirical hypotheses" (Gopnik and Schwitzgebel 1998: 78).

We should trust a person's intuitions, whether basic ones or richer ones, to the degree that we have confidence in her empirically based expertise about the kinds under investigation. Sometimes the folk may be as expert as anyone: intuitions laden with "folk theory" are the best we have to go on. Perhaps this is the case for a range of psychological kinds. For most kinds, it clearly is not: we should trust intuitions laden with established scientific theories. Consider, for example, a paleontologist in the field searching for fossils. She sees a bit of white stone sticking through grey rock, and thinks "a pig's jawbone". This intuitive judgment is quick and unreflective. She may be quite sure but unable to explain just how she knows.[12] We trust her judgment in a way that we would not trust folk judgments because we know that it is the result of years of study and experience of old bones; she has become a *reliable indicator* of the properties of fossils. Similarly we trust the intuitions of the physicist over those of the folk about many aspects of the physical world where the folk have proved notoriously unreliable. And recent experiments have shown that we should have a similar attitude to many psychological intuitions. Thus, the cognitive psychologist, Edward Wisniewski, points out that "researchers who study behavior and thought within an experimental framework develop *better* intuitions about these phenomena than

---

[12] I owe this nice example to Kim Sterelny. Gladwell 2005 has other nice examples: of art experts correctly judging an allegedly sixth-century Greek marble statue to be a fake; of the tennis coach, Vic Braden, correctly judging a serve to be a fault before the ball hits the ground.

those of the intuition researchers or lay people who do not study these phenomena within such a framework. The intuitions are better in the sense that they are more likely to be correct when subjected to experimental testing" (1998: 45).

Even where we are right to trust an intuition in the short run, nothing rests on it in the long run. We can look for more direct evidence in scientific tests. In such a scientific test we examine the reality the intuition is *about*; for example, we examine the paleontologist's white stone. These scientific examinations of reality, not intuitions about reality, are the primary source of evidence. The examinations may lead us to revise some of our initial intuitions. They will surely show us that the intuitions are far from a complete account of the relevant bit of reality.

Intuitions often play a role in "thought experiments". Instead of real experiments that confront the expert with phenomena and ask her whether they are *F*s, we confront her with *descriptions* of phenomena and ask her whether she *would say* that they were *F*s.[13] These thought experiments provide valuable clues to what the expert would identify as an *F* or a non-*F*. They can do more: the descriptions that elicit the expert's response indicate the richer intuitions that, as we have already noted, can be a useful guide to the nature of *F*s. Some experiments may be difficult, perhaps impossible, to perform other than in thought. Valuable and useful as thought experiments may be in practice, they are dispensable in principle: we can make do with real experiments. And thought experiments call on the same empirically-based beliefs about the world as real experiments, and their results have the same empirical status.

Aside. This account of thought experiments provides a naturalistic explanation of the characteristic "armchair" method of philosophy. The traditional explanation of this method is that philosophers are conducting thought experiments that probe their *concepts* to yield a priori *rational* intuitions; they are doing "conceptual analysis".[14] The naturalistic explanation accepts that philosophers are conducting thought experiments but construes these differently. The philosophers are not probing concepts but rather *intuitions about kinds*. This is just as well because knowledge of concepts, being a species of semantic knowledge, is very hard to come by. In contrast, philosophers have acquired considerable knowledge of many kinds over a lifetime of acquaintance with them. The philosophers' intuitions that draw on this knowledge, draw on these theories of the world, are not a priori but empirical. The philosophers are conducting thought experiments of the sort described in the last paragraph, counting themselves as experts about the kind in question. Thus, in a famous example of the method, "the analysis of knowledge",

---

[13] There are other things we might ask—for example, "What would happen?"—but these are beside our concerns. Gendler 2003 is a nice summary of views about thought experiments.

[14] The best reason for being dubious of the traditional explanation is that we do not, I have argued (1996, 1998b), have even the beginnings of an account of what a priori knowledge *is*. We are simply told what it *isn't*, namely empirical knowledge. Bealer (1998) and BonJour (1998) are vigorous defenders of rational intuitions; see also Sosa 1998. For an exchange on the subject, see BonJour 2005a, b, c and Devitt 2005a, b.

the philosopher, as expert as anyone in identifying cases of knowledge, confronts descriptions of epistemic situations and considers whether the situations are cases of knowledge. On the basis of these empirical intuitions about cases she constructs an empirical theory about the nature of knowledge. The naturalist does not deny armchair intuitions a role in philosophy but does deny that their role has to be seen as a priori: the intuitions reflect an empirically based expertise in the identification of kinds.

The view I have presented of the limited and theory-laden role of intuitions does not need to be modified for the situation where what we are investigating are the products of a human skill or competence (which is the situation in the philosophy of language and linguistics, of course). This situation would arise if we were (for whatever reason) investigating the nature of horseshoes, chess moves, touch typing, or thinking. Someone who has the relevant competence has ready access to a great deal of data that are to be explained. She does not have to go out and look for data because her competence produces them. Not only that, she is surrounded by similarly competent people who also produce them. As a result, she is in a good position to go in for some central-processor reflection upon the data produced by herself and her associates. This reflection, often aided by appropriate education, can yield concepts and a theory about the data. And it can yield the capacity for sound intuitions, basic and richer, about the data. In brief, she can become an expert. But this is not to say that she *will* become an expert. A person can be competent and yet reflect little on the output of that competence. Or she can reflect a lot but make little progress. Bicycle riders typically fall into one of these two categories. It is a truism in sport that great players do not always make great coaches. The fact that they possess a competence to a superlative degree does not imply that they can articulate and communicate the elements of that competence. Knowledge-how may not lead to knowledge-that. In brief, a person competent in an activity may remain ignorant about it.[15] And even if she does become an expert, we should not assume that her opinions carry special authority simply because she is competent; her competence does not give her Cartesian access to *the truth*. She is privileged in *her ready access to* data, not in *the conclusions she draws from* the data; conclusions of the competent, just like those of the incompetent, are empirical responses to the phenomena and open to question; they arise from the empirical observation of data.

Touch-typing provides a nice example of reflecting on the output of one's own competence. Ask a touch-typist whether a 'k' should be typed with a middle finger and, very likely, he will think to himself, "How would I type a 'k'?" He will attend as he goes through the actual or mental motions of doing so and respond immediately, "Yes". Consider also this report:

---

[15] "Highly skilled performers are often unable to reflect on or talk about how they achieve their skilled performance." (Carlson 2003: 38)

If a skilled typist is asked to type the alphabet, he can do so in a few seconds and with very low probability of error. If, however, he is given a diagram of his keyboard and asked to fill in the letters in alphabet order, he finds the task difficult. It requires several minutes to perform and the likelihood of error is high. Moreover, the typist often reports that he can only obtain the visual location of some letters by trying to type the letter and then determining where his finger would be. (Posner 1973: 25)[16]

The only privilege enjoyed by the typist's judgment about which finger should be used to type a 'k', or about where a letter is placed on the keyboard diagram, is the privilege of being based on what is surely a good datum: on how he, a good touch-typist, types.

Although these typist's judgments are slow relative to his typing, they would probably be fast enough for us to count them as intuitive. And they are likely to be sound, for it is fairly easy to think about typing. Contrast this with thinking about the outputs of another, much more important, human competence, the competence to think, to move in a somewhat rational way from one thought to another. We all have this competence to some degree or other. (Part IV discusses thoughts.) Most of us reflect a bit on this and have some intuitions about what follows from what. Still, these intuitions are likely to be sparse and many of them are surely not sound. Thinking about thinking is so hard.

Now it is, of course, possible that the typist has somewhere in his mind a prior representation of the keyboard which controls his typing and leads to his sound judgment about how to type a 'k'. *But why believe this?* Set aside (until section 11.5) whether we need to posit this representation to explain his typing. We surely do not need the posit to explain his judgment. The much more modest explanation I have just given, making do with cognitive states and processes that we are *already* committed to, seems perfectly adequate for the job. Positing the prior representation is explanatorily unnecessary. Applying Pylyshyn's Razor (3.1)—representations are not to be multiplied beyond necessity—we should not make the posit. Finally, when we turn to the case of thinkers, such positing would seem worse than unnecessary. The idea would have to be that the thinker's mind contains a representation of the "laws of thought" which controls her thinking and which leads her to, say, the *modus ponens* intuition that '*q*' follows from 'if *p* then *q*' and '*p*'. But, as Lewis Carroll's famous dialogue between Achilles and the Tortoise demonstrates (1895), this view of thinking would lead

---

[16] And consider this report (Sun *et al.* 2001). Subjects were placed in front of a computer with the task of navigating a submarine through a minefield using sonar. After some episodes, "subjects were asked to step through slow replays of selected episodes and to verbalize what they were thinking during the episode" (p. 219). The experimenters sum up the results as follows: "The subject at first performed the task on an "instinctual" basis, without conscious awareness of any particular rules or strategies. Gradually, through 'doing it' and then looking at the results, the subject was able to figure out the action rules explicitly. The segment suggested implicit procedural learning at the bottom level and the gradual explication of implicitly learned knowledge" (p. 226). (I discuss implicit learning in section 11.5.)

to an infinite regress.[17] The modest explanation is the only plausible one: a person's thinking is governed by rules that she does not represent and her few intuitive judgments about thinking are the result of reflecting on the performances of herself and others.

On the picture of intuitions I am presenting, what should we make of linguistic intuitions? And whose intuitions should we most trust?

7.5   LINGUISTIC INTUITIONS

The focus in *Coming to Our Senses* is on the explanation of meanings. I claim that the folk are as expert as anyone at identifying *meanings*, expressing the most basic linguistic intuition of all. They do this in the ubiquitous practice of ascribing thoughts and utterances to people; the folk say things like "Ruth believes that Clinton is sexy" and "Adam said that Bush does not speak a natural language". The 'that'-clauses of these ascriptions specify meanings (or "contents"). Because these folk ascriptions are generally successful at serving their purposes—particularly, the purposes of explaining behavior and guiding us to reality—we have reason to think that they are generally true; see the argument for "intentional realism" later (8.1). And note that although part of what is ascribed is a meaning, no semantic term need be deployed: the 'that'-clauses above do not contain such terms and that is normal; a meaning is ascribed by using, in the 'that'-clause, a sentence with that very meaning, or something close. Not only are the folk good at identifying meanings but the poor state of semantic theory gives no reason to think that the theorists will do significantly better.

The situation is different when it comes to deploying the vocabulary of the philosophy of language and linguistics to make intuitive semantic and syntactic judgments about an utterance that has the identified meaning. Let us now apply the modest explanation of intuitions in general to the special case of these linguistic intuitions.

The competent speaker has ready access to a great deal of linguistic data just as the competent typist has to a great deal of typing data and the competent thinker has to a great deal of thinking data: the competent speaker and her competent fellows produce linguistic data day in and day out.[18] So she is surrounded by tokens that may, *as a matter of fact*, be grammatical, be ambiguous, have to co-

---

[17] Suppose that the inference from the two premises, (A) 'if p then q', and (B) 'p', to the conclusion, (Z) 'q' had to be accompanied by a third premise, (C) 'if (A) and (B) then (Z)', which captures the "law of thought" that *modus ponens* is a good inference. Then in order to infer (Z) from these three premises, we would similarly need a fourth, (D) 'if (A) and (B) and (C) then (Z)'. And so on *ad infinitum*.

[18] As Chomsky says, competent speakers "can easily construct masses of relevant data and in fact are immersed in such data" (1988: 46).

refer with a certain noun phrase, and so on.[19] So she is in a position to have well-based opinions about language by reflecting on these tokens. This is not to say that she will reflect. Indeed, a totally uneducated person may reflect very little and hence have few if any intuitive judgments about her language. She may be ignorant of her language.[20] Still it is clear that the normal competent speaker with even a little education *does* reflect on linguistic reality just as she reflects on many other striking aspects of the world she lives in. And this education will usually provide the terms and concepts of folk linguistics, at least. As a result she is likely to be able to judge in a fairly immediate and unreflective way that a token *is* grammatical, *is* ambiguous, *does* have to corefer with a certain noun phrase, and so on. Such intuitive opinions are empirical central-processor responses to linguistic phenomena.[21] They have no special authority: although the speaker's competence gives her ready access to data it does not give her Cartesian access to the truth about the data.[22]

So, on this modest account, how does a normal competent speaker make a grammaticality judgment about a novel expression? As a result of education and reflection, she already has the folk linguistic concept of grammaticality in her language. And she appreciates the connection between this grammaticality and competence in the language: roughly, errors aside, competent speakers produce and understand grammatical sentences. She knows that she is a competent speaker and so uses herself as a guide to what the competent speaker *would do*. So she asks herself whether this expression is something she would say and what she would make of it if someone else said it. Her answer is the datum. Clearly her linguistic competence plays a central role in causing this datum about her behavior. *That* is its contribution to the judgment that she must then go on to

---

[19] This presupposes a realism about linguistic entities that, as noted in section 2.4, is curiously denied by some. I discuss this denial in section 10.6.

[20] This point is nicely illustrated by the following report: "As a graduate student I spent a summer in the Pyrenees (Andorra, Perpignon, etc.) doing field research on the phonology of various dialects of Catalan. Many of our native informants were illiterate peasants. I was forcefully struck how difficult it was to elicit linguistic judgments from them regarding their language, which of course they spoke perfectly well. Just getting the plurals of certain nouns was tough. These folks seemed to be very hard of hearing when it came to hearing the voice of competence! Their difficulty, it seemed, was that their native language was largely transparent to them—they had never thought of it as an object for observation and hence were largely unable to form even the most rudimentary judgments about its character. Catalan speakers with only a modicum of grade school education, by contrast, were good informants, presumably because they had learned through their grammar lessons to think of language as an object with various properties, even if they had no sophisticated knowledge of what those properties might be, theoretically speaking." (Bob Matthews, in correspondence)

[21] Ilkka Niiniluoto urges a similar view: "Linguistic intuition is ... largely observational knowledge about language" (1981: 182).

[22] I emphasize that this is a modest explanation of the origins of a speaker's intuitions about her language. It is emphatically not an explanation of the origins of her linguistic competence and is neutral about the extent to which that competence is innate.

make. She does some central-processor reflection upon the datum to decide whether to apply her concept of grammaticality to the expression, just as she might reflect upon any other relevant data supplied by the behavior of her fellow speakers. If the datum shows that she would have no problem producing or understanding the expression, she is likely to deem it grammatical. If the datum shows that she has a problem, she will diagnose the problem in light of her background theories, linguistic and others, perhaps judging the expression un-grammatical, perhaps judging it grammatical but infelicitous or whatever. Often these judgments will be immediate and unreflective enough to count as intu-itions. Even when they do count, they are still laden with such background theory as she acquired in getting her concept of grammaticality.

What goes for intuitions about grammaticality will obviously go for intuitions about acceptability insofar as these are nothing but intuitions about grammat-icality, insofar as 'acceptable' in the context is simply expressing the speaker's notion of grammaticality (and hence not expressing pragmatic notions like ones about etiquette).[23] And it will go for intuitions about ambiguity and coreference/ binding. Furthermore, we can often be confident that such intuitions of normal educated speakers are right. We often have good reason to suppose that these core judgments of folk linguistics, partly reflecting "the linguistic wisdom of the ages", are good, though not of course infallible, evidence for linguistic theories.

Finally, what about intuitions elicited in ingenious "minimal-pair" experi-ments?[24] In these experiments, ordinary speakers are asked to say which of two word strings is "worse". Since the two strings differ only in that one fails a certain hypothesized syntactic constraint, the experiments control for pragmatic factors. So we can be fairly confident that these comparative judgments, in contrast to simple judgments of acceptability (goodness), are responding only to grammat-ical facts. And the judgments have another nice feature: they are as close to theory free as one could get. Still they are lightly laden with a theory, even if only with a theory constructed during the experiment (see Reply to Objection 2 in section 7.6); they are judgments of which string is worse *grammatically*. And the judg-ments are likely to be right.

In sum, it is obvious that a speaker's own linguistic competence plays some role in the intuitive judgments she makes about the grammatical properties of expressions in her language. On the received linguistic view, the competence supplies *information* about those properties. On the modest view I am urging, it supplies *behavioral data for a central-processor judgment* about those properties. In particular, the grammatical (sometimes partly grammatical) notions that feature

---

[23] Much the same will go also for acceptability intuitions that are not of this sort and are partly pragmatic: they are central-processor responses to the data, laden with pragmatic theories as well as a linguistic one (7.3). And these intuitions may well be reliable, albeit not nearly as useful because of the pragmatic intrusion.

[24] See Crain and Thornton 1998 for a helpful discussion of experiments of this sort.

in these judgments are not supplied by the competence but by the central processor as a result of thought about language. Similarly, the notion of *following from* that may feature in intuitive judgments about thinking is not supplied by the competence to think but by the central processor as a result of thought about thinking. In neither case does competence have a voice.

Although the intuitions discussed are likely to be right, the intuitions that linguistics should mostly rely on are those of the linguists themselves because the linguists are the most expert. This is particularly so when we get beyond the simple cases to theoretically interesting ones like 'The horse raced past the barn fell' and 'Who do you wanna kiss you this time?' The linguists' skill at identifying items with and without a syntactic property like, say, the biologists' skill at identifying items with and without a biological property, is likely to be better than the folk's because their theories are better. Thus linguists have firm, and surely correct, intuitions about the acceptability of many sentences, and about some matters of co-reference, that the folk do not.[25] Linguistic theory is, as linguists are fond of pointing out, in good shape, far better shape than semantic theory. As a result of their incessant observation of language, guided by a good theory, linguists are reliable indicators of syntactic reality; analogously, biologists are reliable indicators of biological reality. So it is appropriate that linguists do tend to rely on the intuitions of other linguists, as we have already noted (7.2).[26]

To say that intuitions, whether those of the linguists or the folk, are good evidence is not to say that they are the only, or even the primary, evidence. Indeed, we can look for more direct, less theory-laden, evidence by studying what the intuitions are *about*, the linguistic reality itself. In fact, there are many other sources of evidence, as I have pointed out in section 7.2. If this is right, theory construction in linguistics *could proceed without any appeal to intuitions at all*. This is not to say, of course, that it *should* so proceed. I have accepted that these intuitions, particularly those of the linguists, are often good evidence. So, they should be used. Intuitions are often a very convenient shortcut in theorizing.

It is time to compare my modest explanation of the evidential role of linguistic intuitions with the standard linguistic one and hence to assess the abduction to RT.

---

[25] Subjects in an experiment (Spencer 1973) considered 150 sentences that linguists had categorized as clearly acceptable or unacceptable. The subjects disagreed with the linguists over 73 of these, either finding them unclear or giving them an opposite categorization. In another experiment (Gordon and Hendrick 1997), naive subjects found co-reference between a name and a pronoun that preceded it unacceptable even where the pronoun did not c-command the name. This is one of several experiments where folk intuitions were discovered to be at odds with the linguists' and with Binding Theory.

[26] Still, as my student Francesco Pupa has pointed out to me, we might prefer the intuitions of the folk to those of the linguists about "peripheral" rather than "core" language (see Chomksy 1986, p. 147, on this distinction). Pupa used the example, "How come you left?" A linguist may find this sentence intuitively ungrammatical because it offends against the rule of Subject–Auxiliary Inversion for wh-questions. Yet it is clearly acceptable as any member of the English-speaking folk will insist.

7.6   COMPARISON OF THE MODEST EXPLANATION
WITH THE STANDARD CARTESIAN EXPLANATION

I shall start by replying to two objections to the modest explanation. I shall then give some considerations against the standard one. I shall conclude by claiming that the modest one is better.

Objection 1.[27] Intuitions about touch-typing, thinking, and the like are not the right analogies for linguistics intuitions. Rather, the right analogy is with intuitions about perceptual experiences, for example, the intuitions aired in illusory situations: "It looks like there is water on the road" when experiencing a mirage; "The moon looks larger when it is close to the horizon" when experiencing the moon illusion; and so on. These intuitions are immediately based on the outputs of a module (Fodor 1983) and throw an interesting light on the nature of that module. They are not covered by the modest theory. No more are linguistic intuitions.

Reply. (i) Perceptual judgments are not good analogues of linguistic intuitions. Consider the visual module. Its task is to deliver information to the central processor of *what is seen*,[28] information that is indeed the immediate and main basis for judging what is seen; our earlier "That grass is brown", "That person is angry", "This is an echidna but that isn't", and "a pig's jawbone" are examples of such judgments. Sometimes what is delivered is misinformation; for example, "There is water on the road" when experiencing a mirage. Locutions like 'looks like' enable us to allow for the possibility of misinformation in reporting these deliverances, as Objection 1 illustrates. The language module has the tasks of language production and comprehension. The task of production is clearly not analogous to the task of the visual module but the task of comprehension is: it is to deliver information to the central processor of *what is said*, information that is the immediate and main basis for judging what is said, for judging "the message".[29] So, intuitions about what the message is are analogous to intuitions about what is seen. But the former intuitions are not the ones that concern us: for, they are not intuitions *about the syntactic and semantic properties of expressions*. (The contrast is between the intuition that the message is that Tom thinks that John loves himself and the intuition that in 'Tom thinks Dick loves himself' 'himself' must refer to the same person as 'Dick'.) If the objection is to be effective, it would have to be the case that the language module *also* delivers

---

[27] An objection along these lines has been pressed on me vigorously by Georges Rey.

[28] As Fodor says, "information about the 'layout' ... of distal stimuli" (1983: 45). He later speculates that it "delivers basic categorizations" (p. 97), categories like *dog* rather than *poodle* or *animal*.

[29] Some "pragmatic" abilities supply bases too, of course, determining the reference of indexicals, removing ambiguities, making Gricean derivations, and so on; see sections 8.3 and 11.8 for more on this.

information of those syntactic and semantic properties, information that would be the immediate basis for the intuitions that concern us. But the view that the module does deliver this information is, of course, precisely what is at issue and so it needs an independent argument. Indeed if the language module did deliver this information it would be *dis*analogous to a perceptual module, as we shall soon see (Further Consideration 1). (ii) The outputs of the language module do indeed throw an interesting light on the nature of that module; consider, for example, the significance of garden-path phenomena in comprehension and slips of the tongue in production. But these phenomena are examples of language usage; they are not intuitions about the linguistic properties of the expressions that result from that usage. (iii) Although perceptual judgments are not good analogues of linguistic intuitions they are covered by the modest theory. I see them as paradigms of fairly immediate and unreflective empirical responses to phenomena, as my discussion showed (7.4).

Objection 2.[30] The claim that the intuitions of the ordinary competent speaker are empirical observations deploying theory-laden linguistic vocabulary is at odds with the following phenomena. (i) Take an English speaker with near enough no education in linguistics and give her two lists, one of twenty clearly grammatical sentences of English and the other of twenty clearly ungrammatical word strings. The first group is labeled '*A*' and the second '*B*'. Now give her a set of strings, some grammatical some not and ask her to classify each one as an *A* or a *B*. She is likely to classify them near enough perfectly. (ii) Next we give her a list of twenty pairs of sentences that are related as active to passive and a list of twenty pairs of sentences that are not so related. We tell her that pairs in the first group are related as *X* to *Y*, those in the second are not. We give her many more pairs, some active–passive related, some not and ask her whether they are related as *X* to *Y*. Once again she is likely to classify them near enough perfectly. These intuitive judgments are not laden with any theory and deploy no linguistic vocabulary.[31]

Reply. What happens in these experiments is that the speaker either *learns* to use the terms '*A*' and '*B*' for her concepts <grammatical-in-English> and <ungrammatical-in-English>, and the terms '*X*' and '*Y*' for her concepts <active> and <passive>; or, more likely, she acquires these linguistic concepts

---

[30] Based on an objection Stephen Stich made in correspondence on Devitt and Sterelny 1989.

[31] I assume that Fodor has something like experiments (i) and (ii) in mind in claiming:

Normal human children are, as far as we know, quite extraordinarily good at answering questions of the form: "What grammar underlies the language of which the following corpus is a sample (*insert PLD here*)?"

Yet, he claims, the children "exhibit no corresponding capacity for answering questions about bagels" (2001: 129). I would have thought they would do just as well in experimental analogues of (i) and (ii) for bagels. (The questions about both language and bagels would surely have to be much less sophisticated than Fodor's.)

while she is learning to use the terms for them.[32] These experiments are analogous to the classic concept learning experiments in psychology and to solving many puzzles in IQ tests. It is not part of my modest view of intuitive linguistic judgments that an ignorant person cannot easily learn to make them. Indeed, most of us *do* easily learn to make many of them in primary school. These judgments are typically about basic linguistic facts that are very epistemically accessible. The judgments are theory-laden, but probably not much more so than many 'observation' judgments; for example, 'Grass is green'; 'Rocks are hard'; 'Elephants are bigger than mice'. Once one has acquired the necessary concepts, these judgments are easy to make; and the concepts are easy to acquire. On the Duhem–Quine Thesis, all judgments are theory-laden, but they are not all laden to the same degree.

So the modest explanation is still in good shape. Turn now to the standard one.

According to the standard Cartesian explanation, the intuitions of someone competent in a language are good evidence for a theory of that language because they are derived from her representation of the rules of the language in her language faculty. The explanation is appealing because the idea of one sort of representation leading to another is familiar. Still, attention to the language in which competence allegedly speaks and to how little it says raised concern about the details of the causal-rational route from an unconscious representation in the language faculty to a conscious judgment in the central processor (7.3). I shall now give three further considerations against the standard explanation.

Further Consideration 1.[33] According to the standard explanation, the language module delivers syntactic and semantic information about expressions to the central processor. If it did this it would be disanalogous to perceptual modules (as noted in Reply to Objection 1). For, if it did, the central processor would have direct access to information that the language module allegedly uses to fulfill its task of processing language.[34] But nobody supposes that the central processor has direct access to analogous information used by perceptual modules to fulfill their processing tasks.[35] Thus, the visual module simply tells the central processor what is seen: something along the lines of brown grass, angry person, an echidna, a pig's jawbone, water on the road, and so on. It does not deliver whatever information the module may use to arrive at such conclusions; it does not deliver "Marr's 'primal', '2.5 D', and '3 D' sketch" (Fodor 1983: 94).

[32] Similarly, I would say, subjects in "artificial grammar (AG)" tasks in psychology (Reber 1967) acquire the concept <grammatical-in-AL> where AL is the artificial language.
[33] I am indebted to my student, David Pereplyotchik, for this point.
[34] I later raise doubts that language processing typically involves this information in the sense of involving representations of syntactic and semantic information (11.6).
[35] "central processors should have free access only to the *outputs* of perceptual processes, interlevels of perceptual processing being correspondingly opaque to higher cognitive systems." (Fodor 1983: 60)

Further Consideration 2. I have noted in the last section that the intuitions of linguists often differ from those of the folk. This should be an embarrassment for the official line. First, why would the intuitions be different if they were the voices of competencies in the one language? An easy answer would be that, to the extent of the differences in intuitions, the linguists do not speak the same language as the folk. But this is very implausible. It is also belied by evidence, both anecdotal and experimental, that linguistic intuitions change with a linguistic education.[36] It is odd that this education should interfere with the causal–rational process by which intuitions are allegedly derived from the underlying representation of linguistic rules. Second, and more serious, from the Cartesian perspective it seems that we should see this interference as the *contamination* of the pure voice of competence with theoretical bias. Therefore, rather than relying on this contaminated evidence linguists should be seeking the intuitions of the most uneducated folk. So, the actual practice of linguists is mistaken. In contrast, if my proposal about the place of intuitions is correct, the change of linguistic intuitions with education is just what we should expect. And the actual practice of linguists is fine. The educated intuitions are contaminated only in the way that all evidence is and must be: it is all theory-laden. Linguistic education should make a person a better indicator of linguistic reality just as biological education makes a person a better indicator of biological reality. Of course a person educated into a false theory may end up with distorted intuitions.[37] But that is an unavoidable risk of epistemic life, in linguistics as everywhere else. We have no unsullied access to any reality.

Further Consideration 3. If a speaker represents the rules of her language then that representation must surely control her language use, whether or not her linguistic intuitions are derived from the representation. And, of course, the received linguistic view is that the representation does both control use and yield intuitions. Yet there is persuasive evidence that it does not play both these roles. If it does not then the intuitions clearly cannot be derived from the representation (because if they were the representation would have to play both roles). The evidence is to be found in the study of "implicit learning", learning that takes place "largely without awareness of either the process or the products of learning" (Reber 2003: 486). I shall later suggest, contrary to a common view in linguistics, language seems to be a paradigm of such learning (11.5). Suppose that it is. Now, if implicit learning were largely a matter of acquiring representations of rules that both govern the performance of a task and yield intuitions about the task, we would expect improvement in performance to be matched by improvement in

---

[36] In one experiment cited in note 25, subjects with at least one course in generative grammar agreed more with the linguists than did "naive" subjects (Spencer 1973). In another, subjects who were encouraged to reflect on a sentence rather than give an immediate reaction agreed more with the linguists (Gordon and Hendrick 1997). Consider also Matthews' report in note 20.

[37] This is not to say that there is no limit to the distortions that education can bring. Here, as everywhere else, reality constrains theories and hence distortions.

intuitions. Yet that is not what we find at all: improvement in task performance is dissociated from improvement in the capacity to verbalize about the task. Consider this summary by Broadbent *et al.* 1986:

> Broadbent (1977) showed that people controlling a model of a city transportation system gave more correct decisions when they had practiced the task than when they had not. However, they did not improve in their ability to answer questions about the relationships within the system. Broadbent & Aston (1978) found that teams of managers taking decisions on a model of the British economy showed a similar improvement in performance after practice. Yet the individuals making up the team did not improve on multiple choice questions about the principles governing the economic model.   (p. 34)

The paper reports further experiments that confirm these results (and go beyond them). Thus, one experiment found "no increase in verbalizable knowledge associated with [a] sudden increase in performance" (Stanly *et al.* 1989: 569).[38] So there is good evidence for thinking that what we implicitly learn in acquiring a language is not a representation of the rules from which we derive our intuitions. So we have good evidence against the standard explanation. Of course, these experiments leave open the possibility that, nonetheless, what we learn is a representation of the rules that controls our language use (without yielding the intuitions), a possibility I shall consider in Chapter 11.

   None of these considerations against the standard Cartesian explanation is decisive, of course. Still, taken together, they do seem to me to undermine its plausibility considerably. Furthermore, I think that these considerations together with the case for the modest explanation are sufficient to establish that the modest explanation is better than the standard one.

   But there is one more important reason for preferring the modest explanation. It arises from the extreme *im*modesty of the standard explanation. The standard explanation rests on RT, a very powerful assumption about the mind. And the important reason is this: we do not need this powerful assumption to explain the reliability of linguistic intuitions. We can explain that reliability without positing representations of linguistic rules in the minds of competent speakers. Consider the analogous phenomena for typing and thinking. We can explain the reliability of intuitions about those processes without positing representations of the rules that govern the processes. Our explanations of these intuitions make do with cognitive states and processes that we are *already* committed to. These modest explanations seemed perfectly adequate for the job and, indeed, much more plausible than their representational rivals. Similarly, I am urging, the modest

---

[38] The evidence does not, of course, show a *total* dissociation of verbalizable knowledge and performance, just a far greater one than would be expected if the knowledge and the performance stemmed from the one representation of rules. Less dissociation was found in some other experiments (Mathews *et al.* 1988) in which the verbalizations were largely descriptions of prior sequences of events in performing the task rather than expressions of knowledge of the rules governing the task. See also Mathews *et al.* 1989.

explanation in the linguistics case. Language is a very striking and important part of the human environment. It is not surprising that empirical reflection on linguistic data, aided by some education, should make people fairly reliable detectors of the most obvious facts about language. We are surely similarly reliable about other striking and important parts of the environment, for example, the physical, biological, and psychological parts. If we can explain the reliability without positing representations of the rules, Pylyshyn's Razor says we should do so.

In conclusion, the modest explanation is better than the standard linguistic one. So the standard one cannot be the basis for a successful abduction to RT. The evidential role of linguistic intuitions does not support RT.

7.7 A NONSTANDARD CARTESIAN EXPLANATION OF THE ROLE OF INTUITIONS?

The standard explanation that I have rejected relies on RT, a thesis that would support position (i) or (ii) on the psychological reality of language: the represented rules are applied or used as data in language processing (3.4). Because of that reliance, I allowed that some linguists may not endorse this explanation (7.1). Some may believe that the syntactic rules of a language are embodied somehow in its competent speakers without being represented, and govern processing: position (iii) on psychological reality. Yet they are still committed to the Cartesian view that linguistic intuitions are the voice of competence, the view that competence alone provides information about the linguistic facts. How could this be so? Can we find what I called a "nonstandard Cartesian explanation" of the evidential role of intuitions (and hence the basis for an abduction to the thesis that the rules are embodied without being represented)? I know of no such explanation and I don't think that any one will be forthcoming.

It helps to note first that even if (iii) were right and the syntactic rules were embodied without being represented this would make no contribution to the *modest* explanation. According to this explanation linguistic intuitions arise from mostly reliable central-processor reflection on linguistic data. If the rules of the language were embodied and governed language processing they would have a role in producing the data that are thus reflected upon (abstracting from performance error). But this would not be a contribution to the explanation. There must, after all, be *some* embodied processing rules that produce the data; that's a consequence of the minimal position (M) that a competence in a language must respect its structure rules (3.4). But, so far as the modest explanation is concerned, it does not matter what rules produce the data. All that matters to the explanation is that the data are the product of competent speakers, whatever their competence consists in and however those data are produced. One might claim, of course, that only by embodying the structure rules could a speaker produce data that is governed by those rules. And if that claim were right it would clearly support position (III). But it remains to be argued that it is right (Ch. 2). More to the point, even if this was successfully argued, the support for (III) would come from that argument not from the modest explanation of intuitions. That explanation does not depend on any assumptions about what produces the data beyond that they are produced by a competent speaker. It does not require that the psychological processing rules involve the syntactic rules of the language.

Any nonstandard Cartesian explanation must of course be different from the modest one. To be different it must give the embodied but unrepresented rules a role in linguistic intuitions other than simply producing data for central-processor reflection. And it must do this in a way that explains the Cartesian view that speakers have privileged access to linguistic facts. It is hard to see what shape such an explanation could take.[39] The explanation would require a relatively direct cognitive path from the embodied rules of the language to beliefs about expressions of that language, a path that does not go via central-processor reflection on the data. What could that path be? The earlier Further Consideration 1 (7.6) comes into play again. Perceptual modules may well be governed by embodied but unrepresented rules. And the operation of those rules may yield information that guides the module in arriving at its message to the central processor about what is perceived. Yet the central processor has direct access only to the message, not to any intermediate information involved in arriving at it. Why suppose that the language module is any different? Consider some other examples. It is very likely that rules that are embodied but not represented govern our swimming, bicycle riding, catching, typing, and thinking. Yet there does not seem to be any direct path from these rules to relevant beliefs. Why suppose that there is such a path for linguistic beliefs? Why suppose that we can have privileged access to linguistic facts when we cannot to facts about these other activities? We do not have the beginnings of a positive answer to these questions and it seems unlikely that the future will bring answers. Even if we could answer the questions and come up with the required explanation, we would still need a persuasive reason to prefer that explanation to my modest one if the abduction to position (III) is to be good.

The standard Cartesian explanation of the evidential role of linguistic intuitions rests on RT. I have earlier produced reasons for rejecting it in favor of the modest explanation. So the abduction to RT fails. A nonstandard Cartesian explanation will rest on the idea that the rules of the language are embodied without being represented, (III). I know of no such explanation. I have just given some reasons for thinking that there is unlikely to be one. So the abduction to (III) fails. And we have found no support for the idea that linguistic intuitions

---

[39] Graves *et al.* dismiss the possibility of such an explanation (1973: 326–7).

reflect information supplied by linguistic competence, no support for the idea that they are the voice of competence.

7.8 MUST LINGUISTICS EXPLAIN INTUITIONS?

The Cartesian view of a speaker's intuitive judgments leads to the view that linguistics should *explain* speakers' intuitive judgments: "If a theory of language failed to account for these judgments, it would plainly be a failure" (Chomsky 1986: 37).[40] In thinking about this we need to make a distinction.

The distinction is between *what the intuitions express* and *the fact that speakers have these intuitions* (Devitt and Sterelny 1989: 520–1). Now, it is obvious that linguistic theory must explain linguistic facts. Insofar as intuitions are *right*, and linguistically relevant, they express linguistic facts and so the theory must explain what they express. But insofar as intuitions are wrong or irrelevant, the theory has no concern with what they express and no need to explain them.[41] Linguists assume that the intuitions are largely right and relevant. I have agreed. It follows that linguistic theory must indeed explain what these intuitions express.

What about the explanation of how speakers' come to have the intuitions? It is no more the concern of linguistics to explain this than it is the concern of biology to explain how folk come to have their biological intuitions or physics to explain how folk come to have their physical intuitions. These explanations may well be worthwhile and interesting but they would be part of *descriptive epistemology* (and hence part of psychology). And, if an intuition is right, there is no *special* epistemological interest in explaining a person's having it: we expect the folk to be fairly reliable detectors of facts about their environment, particularly where the facts are rather obvious. (The need for an explanation is greater when people have *false* intuitions; for example, religious ones.) In this chapter, I have offered the beginnings of an epistemological explanation of linguistic intuitions along these lines.

Although the explanation of speakers having correct linguistic intuitions is part of epistemology not linguistics, it may be *epistemically relevant* to linguistics. For, the abduction that we have considered (but rejected) finds evidence for RT in an explanation of speakers' having those intuitions. But then it is no surprise to

---

[40] See also, Lees 1957: 36; Chomsky 1969a: 81–2; Baker 1978: 4–5; Dwyer and Pietroski 1996: 340. Consider also these analogous claim about semantics: "accounting for our ordinary judgments about truth-conditions of various sentences is the central aim of semantics" (Stanley and Szabo 2000: 240); "Our intuitive judgments about what A meant, said, and implied, and judgments about whether what A said was true or false in specified situations constitute the primary data for a theory of interpretation, the data it is the theory's business to explain." (Neale 2004: 79)

[41] This is not to say, of course, that the theory has no need to explain performance errors like the failure to parse centrally embedded relatives. False intuitions about a language are one thing, errors in using it, another.

find that an epistemological view can be epistemically relevant to linguistics. *Anything* can be epistemically relevant to linguistics. That is a consequence of the Duhem–Quine thesis.

7.9 CONCLUSION

Linguists greatly exaggerate the evidential role of the intuitive judgments of ordinary speakers. Still these intuitions are good evidence for a grammar. Why are they? The Chomskian answer is that they are derived by a rational process from a representation of linguistic rules in the language faculty. I have argued for a different view that has the great advantage of being theoretically modest. Linguistic intuitions do not reflect information supplied by represented, or even unrepresented, rules in the language faculty. Linguistic competence supplies data for these intuitions but the intuitions are not its voice. Rather, linguistic intuitions are like intuitions in general. I have arrived at my *third major conclusion*: Speakers' linguistic intuitions do not reflect information supplied by the language faculty. They are immediate and fairly unreflective empirical central-processor responses to linguistic phenomena. They are not the main evidence for grammars. This conclusion accommodates the evidential role that intuitions play in linguistics without any appeal to embodied rules of the language.

Earlier we found no support for RT in the rejection of behaviorism nor in folk psychology. No support is to be found either in the evidential role of linguistic intuitions. So, I am on my way to establishing my second major conclusion: there is no significant evidence for RT and, given what else we know, it is implausible. Furthermore, the evidential role of linguistic intuitions does not support *any* robust thesis about the psychological reality of the linguistic rules: a competent person has ready access to the output of her competence *whatever* rules produce that output. So the role does not support positions (i) or (ii) according to which the represented rules are applied or used as data in language processing, nor position (iii) according to which the rules govern by being simply embodied (3.4). If there is to be any support for these positions on psychological reality, it must be found elsewhere.

In what way, if at all, is person's language psychologically real in her mind? That is the main concern of this book. According to the argument in Part I, linguistics is not primarily about the mind—first major conclusion—and so the idea that the language is psychologically real does not "come for nothing": it needs, as my second methodological point emphasized (2.6), a powerful psychological assumption to establish it. In the next part, I shall argue for such an assumption, position (T): a language is largely psychologically real in a speaker in that its rules are similar to the structure rules of her thought. In general, I shall urge that the psychological reality issue is best approached from a perspective on thought. Finally, in Part V, against the background of this discussion of thought,

I shall consider the evidence from language use and language acquisition. This will provide the main case for my second major conclusion.

All named or numbered major conclusions, methodological points, and positions on psychological reality are listed in the Glossary.

PART IV

THE RELATION OF LANGUAGE
TO THOUGHT

8

Thought Before Language

8.1 INTENTIONAL REALISM

My aim in this chapter is to argue for various ways in which thought is prior to language. The assumptions of this argument are, it seems to me, relatively uncontroversial and yet their repercussions for the issue of the psychological reality of language are both considerable and strangely unnoticed.

This discussion will lay the groundwork for Chapter 9 which will present an argument for the bold position (T): the structure rules of a speaker's language are similar to the structure rules of her thought. The assumptions of that argument, particularly the Language-of-Thought Hypothesis that thoughts involve language-like mental representations (LOTH), are certainly not uncontroversial.

The discussion in these two chapters, particularly the priority claims, seems in sharp conflict with Chomsky's commitment to thought and language being largely independent of one another, with language residing in a distinct language faculty. I shall set aside addressing this apparent conflict until Chapter 10.

Discussions of the relation between thought and language is often framed around a distinction between the "communicative" and the "cognitive" conceptions of language; see many papers in the helpful collection, *Language and Thought* (Carruthers and Boucher 1998a). I do not follow this practice for reasons that I will make clear in section 9.6.

What are thoughts? In the sense that concerns us, the first step in an answer takes them to be propositional attitudes, mental states like beliefs, desires, hopes, and wondering whethers. Further steps in the answer will follow, particularly in Chapter 9.

Clearly, the view that thought is in some way prior to language is committed to there *really being* thoughts; it is committed to "intentional realism". This realism is my first assumption. It is relatively uncontroversial but still some people reject it: they are *eliminativists*, regarding thoughts as posits of a discredited folk theory. Famously, this was the attitude of the behaviorists. More recently, it has been the attitude of Patricia Churchland (1986) and Paul Churchland (1981, 1989), and some others drawn to connectionism.[1] Many philosophers have responded to

---

[1] I think that Donald Davidson (1980, 1984), under the influence of Quinean behaviorism, is at bottom an antirealist about the mind. However, his views are very hard to discern. I shall not be discussing Davidson's views on mind and meaning here. I have argued against them at length elsewhere (1981: ch. 4; 1996: 66–7, 139–40; 1997a: ch. 10; Devitt and Sterelny 1999: ch. 15).

this eliminativism with "transcendental arguments" to show that it is "incoherent", "unstable", and so forth. I think that such arguments are very misguided.[2] Still, I think that we have a very good reason for supposing that we do indeed have thoughts.

Begin by considering why we ascribe thoughts. Doubtless we have many purposes, but I think we should focus on two very important ones:[3] first, we ascribe thoughts to explain and predict the behavior of the subject; and, second, to use the thoughts and utterances of a subject as guides to a reality largely external to the subject. I shall consider these in turn.

1. Consider this explanation of behavior:

Why did Granny board the bus? She wants to buy a bottle of scotch. She believes that she has her pension check in her pocket. She believes that the bus goes to her favorite liquor store.

Such "intentional" explanations of "intentional" behavior are familiar and central parts of ordinary life, of history, of economics, and of the social sciences in general. They all ascribe thoughts. With the decline of behaviorism, psychological explanations along these lines are even offered for much animal behavior; for example, a rat's maze running.

2. Ascribing beliefs serves another remarkably valuable purpose. If a person believes that the world is such and such, and if the person is reliable, then we have good reason to believe that the world is such and such. Thus, attributing the property of meaning *IT IS RAINING* to Mark's belief not only helps to explain his rain-avoidance behavior—putting on a coat and picking up an umbrella— but also gives us evidence about the weather. We can even learn from someone who is a reliable guide to the way some area of the world is *not*.

We have a wide range of interests in learning about the world. The direct way to serve these interests is to examine the world. The indirect way is to use reliable indicators. Sometimes these indicators are "natural" ones like tree rings. Sometimes they are artifacts like thermometers. Very often they are the beliefs of others. Some belief ascriptions serve our *theoretical* interest in explanation. Many, however, are like ascriptions of desires, hopes, and so on in serving interests that are not really theoretical at all. We have the most immediate *practical* interest in finding out quite humdrum facts about the world to satisfy our needs for food, shelter, a mate, and so on. So it helps to know what is on sale at the supermarket,

---

[2] For examples of transcendental arguments, see Baker 1987: 113–48; Malcolm 1968; Gasper 1986. Barbara Hannan points out how common such arguments are. She discusses one sympathetically but does not endorse it (1993: 171–2). I discuss such arguments briefly in my 1996, section 4.2, drawing on my 1990c, which is mostly a critique of an extremely complicated transcendentalist argument in Boghossian 1990a. Boghossian 1990b is a response to the critique. Devitt and Rey 1991 is a response to that response. Taylor 1994 is a nice critique of transcendental arguments. Such arguments find sympathy in surprising places; see e.g., Fodor and Lepore 1992: 207.

[3] I draw on my 1996: 2.5.

where there is a hotel, who is available, and so on. Ascribing beliefs is a very good way of finding out about anything at all.

We note next that this practice of ascribing thoughts is generally *successful* at serving these two purposes. Day in and day out we explain people's behaviors with these ascriptions. Almost everything we know about the world—what we learn at mother's knee, in classrooms, and from books—we get from ascribing beliefs to people and assessing them for reliability. If there really were not any thoughts, this success would be very hard to explain.

That is an argument *for* thoughts and intentional realism. There are, of course, arguments *against* thoughts and for eliminativism. These arguments do not strike me as persuasive for reasons I have set out elsewhere (1996: 5.3).

So, what is a thought? It is a mental state with a meaning or content (henceforth I will usually talk simply of meanings). There must be more to a thought than its meaning, of course: we must distinguish believing that *s* from hoping that *s*, thoughts that have the same meanings but are nonetheless different. But we need not be concerned with the extra.

8.2 LANGUAGE EXPRESSES THOUGHT

Intentional realism is my first relatively uncontroversial assumption. The next is the folk view that "language expresses thought" ("LET"). As Fodor, Bever, and Garrett say, "there is much to be said for the old-fashioned view that speech expresses thought, and very little to be said against it" (1974: 375). Although relatively uncontroversial, this view has, or should have, significant repercussions on our view of language. It demands that we give a prominent place to thoughts in theorizing about the place of language in the mind and it undermines the view that language and thought are independent.

Once intentional realism is accepted, LET becomes irresistible. LET is reflected in intentional explanations of linguistic behavior. Consider an example:

Why did Granny say "I need a drink"? She believes that she needs a drink. She wants to express her belief to her audience. In her language 'I need a drink' expresses that belief.

What does LET amount to? Roughly, it is the view that language production is a matter of uttering a sentence of the language to express a thought with the meaning that the sentence has in that language: the sentence conveys a "message" that is the meaning of the underlying thought. Related to this is the view that language comprehension is a matter of assigning to a sentence a thought with the meaning that the sentence has in the language. The utterance's message is thus received. Once one has accepted the reality of thoughts and noted that they are essentially things with meanings, it is hard to see any alternative view of the relation between meaningful thoughts and meaningful language.

This is rough in two important ways. (1) The meaning of a sentence that has to be matched with the thought's meaning is its meaning *in the context of utterance*. Thus suppose that my observation of a particular person leads me to a thought with the meaning *HE IS ON FIRE* and I then express this thought by uttering the sentence 'He is on fire.' Because this sentence contains the indexical, 'he', its meaning in English alone does not match the meaning of my thought: we must add in that my use of 'he' refers to the person I am observing. What matches the thought for meaning is not the sentence *type* but the sentence *token*. That token gets its meaning partly from the meaning of the sentence type in English and partly from the token's context of utterance.[4] (2) Sometimes the meaning (in the context) of the sentence that a person uses to express her thought is not the meaning of her thought, it is not what she *means by* uttering the sentence. In the terms of the distinction that Paul Grice (1989) has made famous, her "speaker meaning" is not the *literal* or *conventional* meaning of the utterance.[5] Metaphors provide clear examples of this distinction. Thus I may mean by my utterance of 'He is on fire' not that the person is literally on fire but that he is ebullient. Grice's distinction is important, and I shall return to it soon (8.4), but we can afford to set it aside as we move to our first two priority claims.

8.3   ONTOLOGICAL PRIORITY OF CONCEPTUAL COMPETENCE

I have argued that speakers have meaningful thoughts. I have argued further that their language expresses thoughts. This relatively uncontroversial assumption, LET, has serious consequences for our view of linguistic competence and processing.

The most theory-neutral view of competence in a spoken language comes with position (M), the minimal position on the psychological reality of language (3.4). It is the view that this competence is the ability to produce and understand sentences with the sounds and meanings of that language (analogously, of course, competence in a language in another medium but, for convenience, I will talk only of a spoken language).[6] This view is so neutral that even an eliminativist about thoughts could adopt it. Our relatively uncontroversial assumption leads

---

[4] Sperber and Wilson object to the view that "the communication of a thought is achieved by uttering a sentence identical to it in content"—part of what they call "the code theory of verbal communication"—on the ground that "sentences with pronouns are obvious exceptions" (1998: 187–8).

[5] I am not inclined to think that a mismatch between speaker and conventional meaning (in the context) is as common as some think (Sperber and Wilson 1995, 1998; Bach 1987) but, so far as I can see, nothing I say hinges on this.

[6] In certain circumstances we might say of someone who loses this ability in an accident that she still "knows" the language? The circumstances are ones where we take central parts of the ability to be still intact (6.3). The competence I am describing encompasses more. (Aphasias are discussed in sections 10.1 and 10.2.)

to a more theory-laden view: the competence is the ability to use a sound of the language to express a thought with the meaning that the sound has in the language in the context of utterance; and the ability to assign to a sound a thought with the meaning that the sound has in the language in the context of utterance.[7] In brief, the competence is the ability that matches token sounds and thoughts for meaning.

A qualification is called for: the process from a sound to a thought must involve abilities other than linguistic competence. Linguistic competence provides the process only with those aspects of a token's meaning that come simply from its being of a certain type that is in the language. The process must also involve some "pragmatic" abilities; in particular, it must involve the ability to determine the reference of indexicals and the ability to remove ambiguities. We shall have to say more about these pragmatic abilities later (11.8). Meanwhile, we should modify the second half of our account of linguistic competence to read: an ability, *together with certain pragmatic abilities*, to assign to a sound a thought with the meaning that the sound has in the language in the context of utterance.

LET has led to the view that linguistic competence is an ability to match sounds and thoughts for meaning. If this is right then it is immediately apparent that any theory of linguistic competence, and of the processes of language comprehension and production, should be heavily influenced by our view of the nature of thoughts. So, the psychological reality of language should be investigated from a perspective on thought. That is my *fourth major conclusion*. We will be exploring the nature of thought further in Chapter 9. The results of the exploration will guide my own investigation of the psychological reality of language in the rest of this book.

According to the view that we are presenting, competence in a language *requires* a certain conceptual competence, the competence to have thoughts with the meanings expressible in the language. For, clearly, a person cannot match a sound to a thought for meaning unless she can have the thought with that meaning. The conceptual competence partly *constitutes* the linguistic competence. What more is there to linguistic competence? What is the *other* part? That other part must be a "processing competence", a competence to match for meaning the thoughts that stem from the conceptual competence with certain sounds. The linguistic competence is a combination of the conceptual competence to think certain thoughts together with this processing competence. So our relatively uncontroversial assumption leads to the interesting conclusion that a certain conceptual competence is part of the very nature of a linguistic competence.[8] Since the processing competence is surely not part of the very nature of

---

[7] Thus, consider the following: the language understander "must recognize each of the words in the sentence and determine the syntactic (and semantic) relationship among them ... determine the propositional content or 'message' " (Tanenhaus and Trueswell 1995: 218).

[8] But couldn't someone who had only the processing competence be linguistically competent? It is metaphysically possible for a person to lose her conceptual competence in an accident but retain

the conceptual competence, the conceptual competence has an "ontological priority"[9] over the linguistic competence: it is metaphysically possible to have the conceptual competence without the linguistic competence, but not vice versa.

This ontological priority has temporal consequences. First, a person could not acquire competence in a language before she had acquired the competence to think the thoughts expressible in the language. The acquisition of the conceptual competence must either precede the acquisition of the linguistic one or the acquisitions must occur together.[10]

Second, the ontological priority has consequences for our innate capacities. Wherever one stands on Chomskian nativism, it is obvious that humans, unlike, say, dogs, have an innate capacity to acquire a competence in a natural language. And humans also obviously have an innate capacity to acquire the competence to have the thoughts that such a language can express. There are three points to be made about the temporal relations between these capacities. (a) The ontological priority of the conceptual competence over the linguistic has the consequence that the capacity to acquire a linguistic competence could not have evolved before the capacity to acquire the conceptual one.[11] (b) In light of the constitution of a linguistic competence, the capacity to acquire one must be constituted by the conceptual capacity together with the capacity to acquire a processing competence. The conceptual capacity and the processing capacity might have evolved separately, of course. But, if the processing capacity was an adaptation, something that was selected *for*,[12] it must have evolved at the same time as, or after, the conceptual capacity. For, the processing capacity could only be an aid to fitness by being a tool of thought.[13] And it follows from this that if the linguistic capacity as

her processing competence. Clearly if she were to regain her conceptual competence she would be linguistically competent. But isn't she linguistically competent anyway, simply on the strength of her processing competence? I think not. First, it is rather obvious that she is not competent to understand the spoken language if she cannot think the thoughts that the language expresses. It may not be so obvious that the failure to think these thoughts entails that she is not competent to speak the language. Still, I think we would not count her as being competent. And I am not counting her as being so. (I am indebted to Alex Barber for prompting this note.)

    [9] Adopting Martin Davies' term (1998: 226–7).

    [10] So I think that Pinker is being too cautious in the following passage: "Conceptual development . . . too, might affect language development: if a child has not yet mastered a difficult semantic distinction, such as the complex temporal relations involved in *John will have gone*, he or she may be unable to master the syntax of the construction dedicated to expressing it" (Pinker 1995b: 146).

    [11] Derek Bickerton (1990, 1995) argues that the capacities evolved together. Indeed, he identifies the evolution of the linguistic capacity with the evolution of a cognitive capacity that covers not simply the conceptual competence to have the thoughts but also the competence to reason with them as we do. I think that the identification with the evolution of the conceptual capacity is plausible—see section 12.5 below—but, as Carruthers points out (1998: 108–9), it is hard to see why the reasoning capacity should have come with the linguistic capacity. It is irresistible to speculate about the origins of language but such speculations are inevitably very short of evidence; see Botha 2003 for a helpful discussion.

    [12] Pinker and Bloom (1990) argue persuasively for the adaptationist view but many, including Chomsky, reject it; see, for example, Hauser *et al.* 2002.

    [13] See the papers in Hurford *et al.* 1998, part I.

a whole was an adaptation, it must have evolved at the same time as, or after, the conceptual capacity. (c) On the other hand, if the processing capacity was not an adaptation, hence the linguistic capacity as a whole was not an adaptation, the processing capacity could have been strangely present but unused until the conceptual capacity evolved to exploit it.

An objection to the view I am presenting springs immediately to mind. There is considerable evidence that cognitive impairment and linguistic impairment do not go hand in hand. So how could the conceptual competence be constitutive of linguistic competence? I shall respond to this objection in some detail in Chapter 10, along with discussing the apparently conflicting views of Chomsky. Meanwhile, note that the conceptual competence in question is a competence to think certain thoughts but it is not a competence to *reason well* with those thoughts. So the view allows a linguistically competent person to be stupid.

Finally, here is a consideration in favor of the ontological priority of conceptual competence over linguistic. A consequence of that priority is that an organism *could*, logically, have the conceptual competence to think certain thoughts without having the linguistic competence to express them. But there are persuasive reasons for thinking that some organisms *do, as a matter of fact*, have a primitive sort of conceptual competence, at least, without any corresponding linguistic competence. First, consider apes, dogs, even sheep. The best explanation of their behaviors attributes thoughts to these animals, mostly rather primitive thoughts perhaps, but thoughts nonetheless (Allen and Bekoff 1997). And yet these animals do not have languages in which they could express these thoughts.

A wide variety of studies indicate that nonhuman mammals and birds have conceptual representations. Surprisingly, however, there is a mismatch between the conceptual capacities of animals and the communicative content of their vocal and visual signals … animals acquire and use a wide range of abstract concepts, including tool, color, geometric relationships, food, and number.   (Hauser *et al.* 2002: 1575)

Second, consider our human ancestors. If we go back far enough we will finally reach some ancestors who spoke no language. Yet they surely had thoughts (Bickerton 1990, 1995). Third, consider immature humans. Developmental psychologists have produced persuasive evidence that babies have a rich mental life. Thus, babies show early signs of having such basic concepts as that of a physical object (Carey 1985). (A concept is, of course, a part of a thought.) And a study of deaf children who had not been exposed to any conventional sign language showed ample signs of thought (Goldin-Meadow and Zheng 1998). Despite their lack of a language, the children communicated using gestures that revealed "thought that has not yet been filtered through a language model" (p. 28), "untainted manifestations of child 'thought' " (p. 50). The authors conclude: "Our data suggest that there are indeed thoughts that children themselves bring to the language-learning situation … conceptual starting points for grammatical notions" (p. 52).

So we have very good reason to believe that organisms can have thoughts without having a language to express them. Yet organisms surely cannot have a language capable of expressing thoughts without having the competence to have those thoughts.

In conclusion, the relatively uncontroversial assumption LET undermines the view that language's place in the mind is largely independent of thought: the assumption ties language closely to thought because conceptual competence partly constitutes linguistic competence.

8.4   EXPLANATORY PRIORITY OF THOUGHT

Our next assumption comes from Grice (1989). The Gricean story builds on LET. An utterance has a "speaker meaning" reflecting the meaning of the thought that the speaker is expressing, reflecting its "message". Often that meaning will be the conventional or literal meaning of the utterance in some language in that context. But sometimes it will not be: metaphors are an obvious example where the two meanings come apart (as we noted in section 8.2). Finally, and crucially, speaker meaning is explanatorily prior to conventional meaning: the regular use in a community of a certain form with a certain speaker meaning leads, somehow or other, to that form having that meaning literally or conventionally in the language of that community.[14] So the story is: thought meanings explain speaker meanings; and speaker meanings explain conventional meanings.[15] In this way thought is explanatorily prior to language.[16]

(A conventional meaning can also be established by some influential people agreeing to use a certain form with a certain speaker meaning. Icelanders successfully use this method to keep their language unique and some French would love to use it to keep out English. Still, the method is rare and I shall ignore it. In any case, it also demonstrates the explanatory priority of speaker meaning over conventional meaning.)

This part of the Gricean story is relatively, although certainly not entirely, uncontroversial[17] but other parts are not. (i) Grice and his followers have made

[14] This account would need to be modified along the following lines to deal with indexicals: the regular use of a certain form with speaker meanings dependent on the context leads, somehow or other, to that form having the literal or conventional meaning in the language of yielding such meanings dependent on the context.
    The literal and the conventional meaning of an expression are usually the same, but not always. A person may have an eccentric idiolect: the literal meaning of her expression may not be a meaning it has according to any linguistic convention. I shall ignore this until section 10.5.

[15] This Gricean explanation of the linguistic in terms of the psychological and social is an example of the earlier-mentioned "deep explanation of linguistic reality" (2.7 (iii)).

[16] Davies calls this "analytical priority" (1998: 227). I resist this name because I don't think that the priority involves any a priori analysis of concepts (1996; Devitt and Sterelny 1999).

[17] Michael Dummett (1993) gives a priority to language over thought and Donald Davidson (1984) gives no priority to either. Both these views arise, in my view, from rather behavioristic assumptions about the mind.

many attempts to explain speaker meaning in terms of a baroque structure of communicative intentions. (ii) There have also been attempts to say *how* the regular use leads to a convention.[18] I am not committed to the results of any of these attempts. Indeed, I totally reject the attempts in (i) which strike me as misguided in principle (1981: 80–6; Devitt and Sterelny 1999: 146–51). Furthermore, it is important to note that Gricean explanations of speaker meanings are seriously incomplete because they rest on unexplained thought contents: the speaker means the thought content that he intends to convey but no account is given of the nature of that content. Still, what I do take from the Griceans, the distinction between speaker and conventional meaning and the priority of the former, is sufficient to establish the explanatory priority of language.

The earlier ontological priority had a temporal consequence. A person could not acquire competence in a language before she had acquired the competence to think the thoughts expressible in the language (8.3). The present Gricean explanatory priority also has a temporal consequence. There can be no conventional meanings in a community until there have been the regularities in speaker meanings. And utterances with a certain speaker meaning must be accompanied by thoughts with that meaning. This requires a certain temporal priority of thoughts over language. We shall give some details of this priority later (8.6, 9.5).

We noted in the last section that organisms can have thoughts without having a language to express them and yet cannot have a language capable of expressing thoughts without having the competence to have those thoughts. The part of the Gricean story that I have adopted fits these facts nicely. Furthermore, that part is *prima facie* plausible and has been extensively supported in the literature over the last forty years.[19] All in all, the argument for a general explanatory priority of thought over language seems very persuasive. Indeed, it is hard to think of a plausible alternative. Once one has accepted that there are thoughts which language expresses, this priority seems compelling. Why then might it be resisted?

We shall consider Chomsky's resistance in Chapter 10. And we shall soon consider possible resistance arising from two sources, linguistic relativity and the phenomenon of reference borrowing. But, first, we can use the discussion so far to argue for our theoretical interest in thought being prior to that in language.

---

[18] Schiffer 1972 is an example of particularly valiant attempts at both tasks. Lewis 1969 is the classical attempt to explain conventional meaning, but it is not Gricean. Laurence (1996, 1998) rejects the view that there are any linguistic conventions of the sort Lewis is trying to explain. I shall consider his rejection in section 10.5.

[19] Aside from Grice 1989 and Schiffer 1972, see for example Armstrong 1971, Bennett 1976, Avramides 1989, and Neale 1989. (These works include, of course, parts of the Gricean story that I am not adopting.)

8.5 PRIORITY OF THEORETICAL INTEREST IN THOUGHT

My earlier argument that the linguistic task is to explain the nature of sentence tokens raised the important question: What is our theoretical interest in this task? Why is the task worthwhile? I gave four reasons for thinking it worthwhile (2.4). First, it must be worthwhile if the study of linguistic competence (Chomsky's task (i)) is worthwhile because that study involves my task. Indeed, my task has a certain epistemic and explanatory priority over the study of competence. Second, I noted the interest of an analogous task, explaining the code of the bee's dance. Third, I claimed that substantial and interesting theories—generative grammars—are fulfilling the task. Fourth, and most importantly, I claimed that the properties of tokens that the task studies—meanings, hence the syntactic properties that partly constitute meanings—play striking roles in our lives. We can now expand on this claim and place the linguistic task in a broader theoretical environment that gives priority to interest in thoughts.[20]

Suppose that Mark produces the sound, /It is raining/. We ascribe to this sound the conventional meaning *IT IS RAINING*. If we assume that Mark literally meant this, then we take that meaning to be its speaker meaning too. As a result, we have evidence of his thoughts. Most straightforwardly, if we assume that he is being sincere, we will take him to have a belief with that meaning. So we ascribe the same meaning to the belief as to the utterance it causes; we take the utterance to express the belief. We saw earlier how ascribing that meaning to a belief can directly explain Mark's behavior and guide us to reality. So, ascribing that meaning to an utterance can serve those same purposes indirectly. An essential part of what makes the utterances that humans produce and react to *language* is that the utterances are the expressions of meaningful thoughts. And an essential part of what makes language theoretically interesting is that these thoughts, hence their expression, can explain behavior and guide us to reality.[21] Language is an extraordinarily effective way of making the thoughts of others accessible to us, thoughts that otherwise would be largely inaccessible; and of making our thoughts accessible to others, often in the hope of changing their thoughts and hence their behavior. So we have a great theoretical interest in explaining the properties of linguistic expressions, including their syntactic properties, that enable the expressions to play this striking role. And just as our interest in the properties of the bees' dance leads to an interest in the bees' competence to produce dances so also does our interest in linguistic expressions lead an interest in our competence to produce them. We have the following

---

[20] I draw, once again, on my 1996, secs. 2.3–2.8.
[21] "This is the essence of the language instinct: language conveys news." (Pinker 1994: 83)

"direction of theoretical interest": from thoughts to language to linguistic competence.

In sum, not only does thought have a certain ontological and explanatory priority over language, our theoretical interest in thoughts has a certain priority over our interest in language. I shall return to this theme later in criticizing Chomsky's view of the importance of idiolects and the unimportance of conventional meanings (10.5), and Georges Rey's view of "the intentional inexistence of language" (10.6).

8.6 LINGUISTIC RELATIVITY[22]

One source of resistance to our Gricean-based claim of explanatory priority might come from the ever-popular thesis of linguistic relativity, due originally to Edward Sapir and Benjamin Lee Whorf. For, this thesis appears to be committed to the opposite priority, the priority of language over thought. So we need to consider linguistic relativity.

We might state the thesis of linguistic relativity somewhat vaguely as follows:

Because languages differ significantly in their representations of reality, speakers of different languages differ in some thoughts.

This can yield several more precise versions differing greatly in power and likely truth. Two extreme versions are certainly powerful enough to warrant the aura of excitement and significance that used to surround the thesis of linguistic relativity. The first, sometimes suggested by the writings of Sapir (1949: 162) and Whorf (1956: 213), takes a language to determine not only thought but *reality itself.* This neo-Kantian idea that we make our world with our concepts or language is sadly popular but has, in my view (1997), absolutely nothing to be said for it. The second extreme version, also sometimes suggested (Sapir 1931: 578; Whorf 1956: 213–14, 256), takes a language to *force* people to think in certain ways and to *constrain* them from thinking in other ways; differences between languages lead to thoughts that are insurmountably incommensurable.[23] This version would certainly be inconsistent with my Gricean priority claim but it is highly implausible (Devitt and Sterelny 1999: ch. 10) and is not part of the current debate.

The current debate is over whether a language *influences* its speakers to think in certain ways, whether it *facilitates* some thoughts and not others. This version of linguistic relativity is surely true to some extent. It is much more difficult to invent concepts than to use ones already available. A language makes many concepts available. Thus, it was once very difficult for anyone to have thoughts

---

[22] This section and the next draw on my 2002.
[23] This is the so-called "strong" form of linguistic relativity. It has been argued that Sapir and Whorf did not really hold this view (Gumperz and Levinson 1996: 33n).

about genes because there was no word for genes. And it is *still* very difficult for the speakers of any language that lacks a word for them. But for the rest of us, it is very easy. Suppose that the legendary story of the many Eskimo words for snow were true.[24] Then it would doubtless be easier for the Eskimo than for us to think a whole lot of thoughts about snow. Every specialist group with its own technical vocabulary illustrates the same point: wine tasters, chess and bridge masters can all think certain thoughts more easily than the rest of us. The adoption by the English language of the foreign words 'kow-tow' and 'kosher' may well have made it easier for English speakers to think certain thoughts about behavior toward "a superior" and about what is according to accepted rules or standards. But such examples, of which there are many, are *not interesting* examples of linguistic relativity.

Whorf made very interesting claims about the influence of the *syntax* of languages on thought. He thought that syntactic differences between the Hopi language and an SAE language like English, including their tense-aspect systems, led to different conceptions of time. But there are serious problems with this line of thought. One is that his gloss on the Hopi language is controversial. Another is that it is far from obvious what our conception of time is, let alone what the Hopi's is. And there are more (Devitt and Sterelny 1999: 10.3).

Alfred Bloom (1981) provided what seemed to be powerful evidence of the influence of a language's syntax. He claimed that the absence of distinct counterfactual markers in Chinese made it difficult for Chinese speakers to think counterfactually. But there were problems with his experiments, and when these were fixed the difficulties disappeared (Au 1983).

In recent times, psychologists have investigated some quite exciting examples of linguistic influences. (i) Languages differ in the way they describe spatial and temporal relations. Do these differences affect the way people think about space and time? (ii) Languages differ in the extent to which they distinguish grammatically between objects (e.g. rabbits) and substances (e.g. gold). Do these differences affect the way people think about what objects are made of and their shapes? (iii) Languages differ in the genders they assign to nouns. Do these differences affect the way people think about the object to which the nouns apply? I gather that the jury is still out on the significance of such investigations but they are certainly suggestive of interesting influences of language on thought.[25]

So what bearing do the established truths, even the possible truths, of linguistic relativity have on the Gricean view that thought is prior to language? Very little. First, the Gricean view that thought is prior to language in the explanation of meaning is quite compatible with any amount of causal influence of language on thought. Thus, we are easily able to have thoughts about genes because we have a

---

[24] Pullum (1991) argues that it is a hoax.
[25] See Boroditsky 2003 for a nice summary.

word 'gene'. But it was because of the pioneering thoughts of Mendel that we have the word 'gene' at all. And we get the benefit of the word 'kow-tow' because long-ago Chinese thoughts led to its introduction. Even if Whorf were right about the different influences of the Hopi language and English on thoughts about time, conceptual differences could have established the linguistic differences.

Second, the fact that the presence of a word in a language makes it easy for a speaker to gain a concept does not show that, contrary to the Gricean view, the word has a role in determining the nature of the concept thus gained; it does not show that language is prior to thought in the explanation of meaning. Consider the concept <kow-tow>, for example. It is very likely that English speakers have this concept as a result of the introduction into English of the Chinese word, 'kow-tow'. Yet it is plausible to think that the concept is *constituted* by its association with the concept <show servile deference>. The story of how an English speaker comes to have the concept of <kow-tow> is beside the point of its nature. What makes it the case that a concept she has is *that* concept and not some other one is its association with <show servile deference>. Indeed, we can say quite generally that the cause of *x* is one thing but the nature of *x* may be a quite different thing; think of a war, for example.

So the likely truths of linguistic relativity are not at odds with the Gricean story. Nor are two other matters. First is the likely fact that those who have no acquaintance with a language during the critical period will be cognitively impaired as well as linguistically so; consider the famous cases of "wolf children" (Malson 1972) and of Genie whose parents deprived her of human contact (Curtis 1981). Second are the interesting proposals of Andy Clark, revolving around the following two themes: "the use of text and/or speech as forms of external memory and workspace"; "the (putative) role of words and sentences ... as transformers of the very shape of the cognitive and computational spaces we inhabit" (1998: 174). So far as the Gricean story is concerned our rich conceptual life could be highly dependent on our having a public language.

This discussion of linguistic relativity enables us to say more about the temporal priority of thought over language. (a) The ontological priority of conceptual over linguistic competence (8.3) leads to the conclusion that a person could not be competent with words—for example, 'gene' or 'kow-tow'—before she had the appropriate concepts. Still, the presence of a word in a language may lead a person to gain the word and the concept in the one moment. (b) According to the Gricean explanatory priority (8.4), this presence requires that people *once* had the concept without the word. For, a word is present in a language when its form is conventionally associated with its meaning by speakers of the language. On the Gricean story, that association arose out of the form being regularly used by speakers with that meaning. And those uses require that the speakers already had the concept that the word expresses. So the concept came before the word's presence.

8.7   REFERENCE BORROWING

A better reason for resisting the Gricean story is that it needs an important modification. The modification is not about syntax, our main concern, but it is important enough to warrant discussion. Despite the claims of the last section, I think that we have very good reason for thinking that the natures of many concepts are *not*, as a matter of fact, very different matters from their causes: the causal story of many a concept is intimately involved in an account of its nature. Although thought is indeed *ultimately* prior to the public language in the order of explanation, the meanings (contents) of many of our concepts are to be partly explained by the conventions of the language. These are concepts that partly depend for their natures on *reference borrowing* (or *deference*).

Saul Kripke (1980) and Keith Donnellan (1972) suggested a theory of reference borrowing as part of an historical–causal theory of proper names. The historical–causal theory starts with reference *fixing*. Initial users of a name fix its reference, usually in face to face "groundings" in an object. The first of these groundings is a dubbing but, as I like to emphasize, it is important to the plausibility of the theory to note that a name is likely to be "multiply grounded" in the object. Now, I doubt that the historical–causal theory alone has the resources to explain reference fixing: very likely we will have to appeal also to ideas from indicator or teleological theories.[26] But we can set the problem of reference fixing aside because our concern here is with reference borrowing. The theory is that, after grounding, the name is passed on from person to person in communication situations: later users who have no acquaintance with the bearer borrow the reference of the name from earlier users. For example, consider our current uses of 'Aristotle' to designate the famous philosopher. These uses designate him in virtue of being causally linked to him via centuries of reference borrowings and the initial groundings.

Kripke extended the historical–causal theory to cover natural kind words like 'tiger' and 'water'. So did Hilary Putnam (1975), who brings out the significance of reference borrowing in his talk of "the linguistic division of labour" (pp. 227–8). Language is a social phenomenon. People are equally able (in principle) to use each term of language in their interactions with the world even though they are not equally able to relate that term to the world. How? Because they each gain the benefit of their linguistic involvement with others. Those on whom everyone ultimately depends are, of course, those who have grounded the term. These grounders may be experts, able to give the identity

---

[26] See Devitt and Sterelny 1999 for a detailed discussion of historical–causal theories (chs. 4 and 5) and for a much briefer assessment of indicator and teleological theories (sec. 7.7). Historical–causal theories need multiple grounding to deal satisfactorily with cases of reference confusion and cases of reference change.

conditions of the referent, but it is not essential that they be. What matters is that they have, as a matter of fact, grounded the term to the world.

Tyler Burge (1979) has gone further, making a plausible case that reference borrowing extends to words like 'arthritis', 'sofa', 'contract', and 'brisket'. If so, reference borrowing is a feature of a significant proportion of the words in the language. This is not, of course, to say that it is a feature of all words.

The theory of reference borrowing shows how a person can be linguistically competent with a word despite being largely ignorant, or even wrong, about its referent. People can be competent with the name 'Catiline' despite knowing very little about Catiline; they can be competent with 'Einstein' despite thinking that Einstein invented the atomic bomb; they can be competent with 'elm' and 'beech' without having any knowledge that would distinguish elms from beeches; they can be competent with 'contract' despite wrongly thinking that contracts have to be written.

How does this theory of words bear on concepts? Linguistic competence with a word is sufficient for conceptual competence with the concept that the word expresses. So the theory of reference borrowing shows how people can have concepts like <Catiline>, <Einstein>, <elm>, <beech>, and <contract> despite being ignorant or wrong about their referents.

In sum, the theory of reference borrowing places very little epistemic burden on the linguistically and conceptually competent. Contrast this with the rich burden of associations demanded by some other theories: for example, what philosophers call "description" theories of words; and what psychologists call "classical" and "prototype" theories of concepts. There is, of course, room for argument about *just how little* an epistemic burden should be placed on the competent, but we need not join this argument. Suffice it to say that the competent may associate with a concept little that is true of its referent.

In light of this, we must modify the earlier Gricean account of the priority of thought over language. Consider the concept <Aristotle>. We all have this concept and as a result are able to think thoughts about the ancient philosopher. According to the theory of reference borrowing, we have the concept largely in virtue of a causal chain stretching back to the philosopher. That is, the fact that one of our mental states is the concept <Aristotle> is largely determined by the fact that this mental state is plugged into an appropriate causal network grounded in the philosopher. Think now of this network. It was established and maintained by a *linguistic* convention of using the word 'Aristotle' in communication situations to refer to the philosopher. Such uses participate in the convention. Thus the nature of our concept <Aristotle> is largely determined by this conventional use of the word 'Aristotle'. The conventional meaning of this word, featuring in generations of reference borrowings, is an essential part of the causal chain that largely constitutes the meaning of our <Aristotle> concept. What makes our concept an <Aristotle> concept is largely its relation to a word that conventionally means *ARISTOTLE*.

There is just the same dependence of a concept on language with any person's concept that is based on reference borrowing. So there is likely to be this dependence with most people's concept <elm>, most people's concept <gene>, some people's concept <kangaroo>, and perhaps a few people's concept <arthritis>.

This does modify the Gricean story but it does not come close to abandoning it, for the following four reasons:

(1) Even where a person's concept is based on reference-borrowing, and hence dependent on an established linguistic convention, we have not claimed that it is *entirely* so. Perhaps there is some small epistemic burden on the person's conceptual competence so that the concept has some non-linguistic determiners; for example, perhaps the concept <Aristotle> has to be associated with the concept <human>.

(2) We have not claimed that *all* concepts can be based on reference-borrowing. It is plausible to think that concepts expressed by proper names, natural kind concepts, and some Burgean concepts can be so based. It is not so plausible to think that others like <pediatrician>, <bachelor>, and <hunter> can. If they cannot, the natures of these concepts have no direct dependence on linguistic conventions.

(3) Even where *some* people have a concept of a certain type based on reference borrowing and linguistic convention, it is not the case that *all* people do. Thus, whereas we now have such an <Aristotle> concept, Aristotle's contemporaries who fixed the name's reference by dubbing him 'Aristotle', did not. Furthermore, all those involved in subsequent groundings of a word have a concept which is, to that extent, dependent for its nature not on linguistic convention but on direct confrontation with the appropriate object(s). Some of us have had such confrontations with Kripke, Putnam, elms, and kangaroos, and so have <Kripke>, <Putnam>, <elm>, and <kangaroo> concepts partly based on those confrontations, partly on linguistic conventions.

(4) On the Gricean picture, it is the regularities of speaker meanings arising out of these convention-independent thoughts that establish the convention in the first place. It is in this way that speaker meaning is prior to conventional meaning. So even the concepts of those who have made no groundings, concepts that are therefore dependent on the convention—for example, *our* <Aristotle> concepts—have natures that are *ultimately* explained in terms of groundings. For, the convention itself is explained in terms of groundings. The *creation* of the linguistic convention requires some people to have concepts that are not dependent on conventions. Once created the convention makes it possible for other people to gain the concept by reference borrowing, thus having a concept that is to be explained partly in terms of that convention. Thought meanings explain the conventions that explain *other* thought meanings.

In conclusion, the fact of reference borrowing forces a modification in the Gricean claim but it leaves intact the view that, ultimately, thought is explanatorily prior to language.

8.8 CONCLUSION

In this chapter I have argued for the relatively uncontroversial views that there really are thoughts (intentional realism) and that our language expresses them: LET (8.1–8.2). This led to my fourth major conclusion: the issue of the psychological reality of language should be investigated from a perspective on thought (8.3). It led also to the view that conceptual competence partly constitutes linguistic competence and so is ontologically prior to it. Following Grice, I next argued that thought is explanatorily prior to language (8.4). These ontological and explanatory priorities have some interesting temporal consequences. And on the basis of these priorities, I argued that our theoretical interest in thought is prior to that in language (8.5). The Gricean claim was shown not to be undermined by such truths as there may be in the thesis of linguistic relativity (8.6). However, the claim did have to be modified in light of the phenomenon of reference borrowing. Still, thought is ultimately prior to language in the order of explanation (8.7).

We might sum up these priority claims roughly as follows: thought has a certain priority to language ontologically, explanatorily, temporally, and in theoretical interest. That is my *fifth major conclusion*.

These priority claims, and the approach that they stem from, are very significant for the investigation of the place of language in the mind, and yet they are strangely unnoticed. We shall be paying a lot of attention to them in Chapter 9 in arguing for position (T) and in Chapter 10 in considering Chomsky's apparently conflicting commitment to the independence of thought and language.

9

A Case for the Psychological Reality of Language

9.1 REPRESENTATIONAL THEORY OF THE MIND (RTM)

According to my fourth major conclusion, the nature of thoughts is central to the issue of the psychological reality of language. We will be exploring that nature in this chapter.

I shall present an argument for (T), the position that the structure rules of a speaker's language are similar to the structure rules of her thought. I pointed out earlier that any view that the language is psychologically real in a robust way requires a powerful psychological assumption (second methodological point; 2.6). Position (T) is certainly powerful. And the case for it rests on controversial views about the nature of thoughts, in particular, on the Language-of-Thought Hypothesis that thoughts involve language-like mental representations (LOTH). The case for (T) is far from conclusive. En route to (T), we shall present, in this section, the Representational Theory of the Mind (RTM)

We have already noted that thoughts are mental states with meanings (8.1). What more can we say about them?

(i) We should start with the popular RTM. A first attempt at stating RTM runs as follows: to have a thought, say the belief that p, is to stand in a certain functional relation to a token mental representation that means that p.[1] So the belief has its meaning in virtue of its vehicle, the representation, having that meaning. In adopting RTM, we have for the first time posited mental representations. Pylyshyn's Razor cautions against making such posits beyond necessity (3.1). Positing thoughts is necessary to explain behavior and to use others as guides to reality (8.1). And RTM is necessary to explain thoughts.

The positing of mental representations is the important part of RTM for our purposes and it is clear. Still, there is another part of RTM that is not clear and that is worth a digression.

What exactly does RTM claim about *believing*?[2] The above statement gives the impression that RTM *identifies* believing with a certain functional relation, one

---

[1] Strictly speaking this applies only to "core" thoughts not to thoughts that person has but has not entertained.

[2] This discussion draws on my 2001.

that holds between a person and a token mental representation. But do we really want to say that for a person to have that belief is for them to *believe* such a token? That seems a bit odd. The oddness increases if we change the thought. We surely do not want to say that when a person expects that the Yankees will win she expects a mental token. The oddness becomes unbearable if we follow Quine (1960: 151–6) in thinking that ascriptions involving intentional verbs like "hunt" should be treated similarly to thought ascriptions: to hunt Bin Laden is not to hunt a mental token![3] But if we do not identify believing with the functional relation that holds to mental tokens what, according to RTM, do we say about its nature?

At the core of RTM is the view that the psychological reality underlying

(1) Joe believes that the Yankees will win

is that Joe stands in a certain functional relation to a mental token with a certain meaning. Call that relation "*B*" and the meaning "*M*". So if (1) is true,

(2) Joe *B*s an *M* token.

If *believing* is not identified with *B* what exactly has (2) got to do with (1) beyond supplying the meaning of the thought ascribed? More generally, what have the facts according to RTM got to do with what we ordinarily ascribe to the mind with the likes of (1)? I think that we have to choose between three answers.[4]

1. One answer takes *believing* to be a relation to an intentional object that holds *in virtue of* the relation *B* to a mental token. So, (1) asserts that Joe believes a certain intentional object, the proposition *THE YANKEES WILL WIN*. He does so in virtue of (2). This is neat but it raises two worries.

First, the answer is committed to intentional objects. What are they? The usual view is that they are abstract objects outside space and time. But many of us think that such objects are "creatures of darkness". How could we refer to them? How could we know about them? Second it is unclear, to say the least, *how* a person's relation to such an abstract object can hold in virtue of a relation to a mental token.

2. I prefer an answer that denies that 'believing' is simply a relative term and that *believing* is a relation. Rather, we should think of (2) as a paraphrase that demonstrates the dual function of 'believing' (cf. Quine 1960: 154). One function is to specify the appropriate relation, *B*, and is therefore the function of a relative term. But the other function is that of a quantifier, "supplying the

---

[3] The ascriptions, '*a* hunts *b*' and '*a* believes that *b* is *F*' are similar in two respects: (i) they can be true even if *b* does not exist; (ii) if they are true they might not remain so if we substituted '*c*' for '*b*' even though *b* = *c*.

[4] James Tomberlin (1998, 2001) thinks that we should favor another answer, one that posits nonactual entities. I don't think that this is acceptable (1998a, 2001).

indefiniteness" of 'an M token'.[5] The meaning M is, of course, specified by 'that the Yankees will win'.

From this perspective, although it is appropriate enough to ask about the nature of B, it is not appropriate to ask about the nature of *believing*. Asking that reflects the mistaken view that it is a relation.

3. The previous two answers each allow the facts according to RTM to support what we ordinarily ascribe to the mind; so (1) can be true. I conclude by mentioning an answer that removes that support, making (1) false. The answer follows answer 1 in taking *believing* to be a relation to an intentional object. So (1) would be true if Ralph stood in the *believing* relation to *THE YANKEES WILL WIN*. The answer differs from 1 in not supposing that (1) holds in virtue of (2). Rather the answer claims that (1) does not hold because there are no intentional objects. (1) is a convenient manner of speaking but, when the chips are down, must be abandoned in favor of (2).

This is revisionist but it does not seem objectionably so to me. It is an acceptable fall-back if linguistics tells us that answer 2 does not work. So far as I can see, my argument in this book does not depend on which answer is right. I shall talk vaguely of *believing* "involving" the functional relation B.[6]

RTM leads to a further enriching of our view of linguistic competence (8.3). We can replace our talk of thoughts with talk of mental representations. And since competence involves moving back and forth between mental and linguistic representations it is appropriate to describe the moves as *translation*. So the competence is the ability to translate back and forth between mental representations and the sounds of the language. The conceptual competence that, along

---

[5] I aired this idea in my 1996, p. 216. The view that the underlying structure of a sentence might contain a quantifier not visible on the surface is not surprising. There is so much underlying syntax. Thus linguists find an underlying quantifier in 'He ate' (as Georges Rey reminded me) and Lepore and Ludwig (2000) have argued that complex demonstratives (like 'that dog') have underlying quantifiers.

[6] The three answers parallel suggestions made by Eugene Mills in his critical discussion (1997) of my *Coming to Our Senses* (1996). The present discussion shows that my response to his criticism (1997b: 397–8) was far too harsh. He was right to be puzzled by RTM. And I was wrong to say that "nothing much hinges" on whether we call the functional relation that I am here calling "*B*" "believing".

The discussion raises the question: what is the *common* view of where RTM stands on this issue? Hartry Field's account at least *suggests* the identity-of-relation view: "belief and desire are not attitudes toward propositions, but toward meaningful sentences in a system of internal representation" (1978: 98). So too does Fodor's account: "propositional attitudes are relations between organisms and formulae in an internal language" (1981a: 187). And so too does Rey's masterly presentation of RTM under the name "CRTT" (short for "Computational/Representational Theory of Thought"): he talks of CRTT attempting "to analyze propositional attitudes" (1997: 209), and claims that "hoping, imagining, wishing, dreading, believing, and preferring that p consist in different computational relations to a sentence that expresses the proposition [that p]" (p. 210). But perhaps these suggestions are misleading and these authors are like my earlier self in not addressing the issue carefully.

with a processing competence, constitutes competence in the language is the competence to have mental representations with meanings expressible in the language. RTM makes an important contribution to our theory of linguistic competence and hence to our likely position on the psychological reality of language.

9.2 LANGUAGE-OF-THOUGHT HYPOTHESIS (LOTH)

In the last section we have enriched our view of thoughts by adding RTM, in (i), to the view that thoughts are mental states with meanings. There are more additions to be made.

(ii) I make the relatively uncontroversial assumption that the meaning of this representation involved in thought is complex.[7] An examination of thought ascriptions would confirm this assumption; thus the meanings *ORTCUTT* and *SPY* are parts of the meaning *ORCUTT IS A SPY* ascribed to Ralph's thought by "Ralph believes that Ortcutt is a spy".

(iii) Controversy may begin with the assumption that the mental representation that has this complex meaning is itself complex: it has its meaning in virtue of its parts having meanings. This is clearly a further step because simple things can have complex properties. Consider a nonsemantic example: The property *being a bachelor* may well be complex, consisting partly of *being unmarried*, but it is not the case that part of a bachelor is unmarried. And, in semantics, a simple thing like a flag can have a complex meaning; for example, the meaning *THIS SHIP HAS YELLOW FEVER.*[8]

This further step does not quite take us to LOTH, as we shall see, but the familiar arguments offered by Jerry Fodor for that hypothesis count in favor of the step. The first of these arguments is a "methodological" one, inferring the complexity of the mental representation that causes a behavior from the complexity of the behavior (1987: 141–3). The second argument claims that we need to see mental representations as complex in order to explain *thinking*, the process of inferring one thought from another (pp. 143–7). The third is the classical argument from productivity, based on the potential infinity of a person's thoughts, and its more persuasive recent relative, the argument from systematicity: A person's capacity to think one thought is systematically related to her capacity

---

[7] The assumption is not entirely uncontroversial because it would be rejected, presumably, by those who think that 'that'-clauses name structureless propositions which are sets of "possible worlds". See Richard (1990: 9–37) for a nice critical discussion of this.

[8] For those who prefer to think of sentence meanings as propositions, the point can be put like this: The complexity of a proposition is one thing, whereas the complexity of the tokens that express it is another. See also Fodor (1987: 136–9) on the distinction between the complexity of an intentional object and the complexity of the mental state that has it.

to think many others (pp. 147–53).[9] Set aside for a moment whether these arguments establish that mental representations have *linguistic* complexity and hence establish LOTH. The arguments do seem to make it overwhelmingly plausible that the representations have at least the complexity of our further step: that their complex meanings arise from the meanings of their parts.

This assumption falls short of LOTH because *non*linguistic representations can have this sort of complexity. Thus, part of a map can mean *HUDSON IS CLOSER TO ALBANY THAN TO NEW YORK* and yet the "syntax" of that part—the way its meaning depends on the meanings of its simpler constituents—is very different from that of a sentence.[10] LOTH requires that the simplest meaningful parts of the representation involved in a thought be like words, and that the structure of the representation be like the syntactic structure of a sentence. So the meaning of the mental representation is determined by its words and its syntactic structure just as the meaning of a sentence is determined by its words and its syntactic structure. According to this hypothesis we think in a mental language.

We may seem to have a simple reason for preferring LOTH to the mental-map view. Map-like representations can obviously capture meanings that concern spacial relations but how could they capture the vast variety of other meanings? At first sight, meanings that concern other relations—for example, *NEW YORK IS MORE LIVELY THAN ALBANY*— seem to be no problem. But one wonders how a map could distinguish among the indefinitely large number of relations. And could it capture meanings that concern nonrelational situations like *FELIX IS A TIGER* and *CLINTON IS SEXY*? And what about *TURTLES MAKE POOR LOVERS* and *HIGH INTEREST RATES MAY CAUSE A BANKING COLLAPSE*? And how could it capture quantification, counterfactual conditionals, and other complex thoughts? These meanings seem totally beyond maps. However, David Braddon-Mitchell and Frank Jackson, who favor a mental-map view, have a neat response to such worries: "We can be certain that something map-like can serve to represent any empirical fact about our world. The world itself is map-like" (1996: 172). So I shall suspend judgment on the representational capacities of maps.

(iv) Nevertheless, I think that we should prefer LOTH. Perhaps the view that a mental representation has some nonlinguistic complexity—for example, the complexity of a map—could meet the requirement of Fodor's first methodological argument and could account for the systematicity that is the concern of his third argument, but it is difficult to see how it could account for the mental process of thinking that is the concern of his second argument. Formal logic gives

---

[9] This systematicity seems sort of obvious and yet Kent Johnson (2004) has done an excellent job of casting doubt on it.

[10] Armstrong 1973 proposes a mental-map view. Lewis 1994 entertains the idea that thoughts are map-like; see also Cummins 1996.

us a very good idea of how thinking might proceed if thoughts are represented linguistically. From its very beginning, computer science has used this idea to build machines that do process linguistic representations. In recent years, computer science has developed "connectionist" machines that use representations of a very different sort, if they use representations at all.[11] Despite the striking success of these machines with some forms of problem solving, connectionist processes seem rather far from capturing anything like human inference. We still have very little idea how thinking could proceed if thoughts were not language-like but, say, map-like.[12]

The task of *explaining* the meanings of mental representations provides further support for LOTH. According to the thesis that these representations are complex, the thought that Clinton is sexy, like the utterance "Clinton is sexy", has a part that means *CLINTON*. How are we to explain the contribution that parts like this make to the meanings of wholes? When we are concerned with the analogous problem for sentences, we seek explanations in terms of syntactic structures. We are a long way from having all the details, of course, but the approach seems promising. If LOTH is correct then the same approach is just as promising for thoughts; for, on that view, the meanings of thoughts are the meanings of *mental* sentences. And, once again, we have very little idea of a satisfactory alternative explanation.[13]

Finally, we shall see later (9.5) that the relation of language to thought provides further support for LOTH.

9.3   LINGUISTIC COMPETENCE

Consider the consequences of the discussion so far for our view of competence in a spoken language. We started with the most theory-neutral view of this competence: it is the ability to produce and understand sentences with the

---

[11] Ramsey (1997) argues that they should not be thought to use representations.

[12] Braddon-Mitchell and Jackson rightly point out that maps can evolve over time. They go on: "When cartographers ... put two maps together to make one that incorporates all the information in a single map, these operations are governed in part by the structures of the maps they are working on" (1996: 173). But it is hard to see how this could be a model for thinking which would seem to require that the one map evolve as the result of different parts interacting with each other.

[13] Braddon-Mitchell and Jackson propose a functional-role semantics for their mental-maps view: the explanation of meaning/content is "in terms of how the belief controls behaviour" (1996: 181). We might expect this to lead to meaning holism—the meaning of any belief depends on the meaning of every belief—and indeed it does: "the approach to content via behaviour is one that first yields the content of a rich system of belief, and then give the content of individual beliefs only inasmuch as they are part of this rich system of belief" (pp. 183–4). In my view, the case against meaning holism is overwhelming (1996: ch. 3). It is worth noting that whether the representations involved in thoughts are language-like, map-like, or whatever, their structure rules will be very different from the processing rules governing thinking; cf. the formation and transformation rules of a logic machine (2.2).

sounds and meanings of that language (similarly for a written language, etc.). We then moved from this minimal view to increasingly theory-laden views. (a) Intentional realism (8.1), together with the view that language expresses thought—LET (8.2)—led us to the following view (8.3): the competence is the ability to use a sound of the language to express a thought with the meaning that the sound has in the language in the context of utterance; and the ability (together with some pragmatic abilities) to assign to a sound a thought with the meaning that the sound has in the language in the context of utterance (similarly for inscriptions, etc.). Hence, a certain conceptual competence has an ontological priority over the linguistic competence. (But, remember, the conceptual competence is to have certain thoughts, not to think well with them; sec. 8.3.) It became apparent immediately that a view of the nature of thoughts should be central to our theory of linguistic competence, and hence to our stance on the psychological reality issue; the fourth major conclusion. (b) RTM was the first, fairly modest, step toward a theory of thoughts (9.1). It yielded the view that competence is the ability to *translate* back and forth between mental representations and the sounds of the language. (c) Acceptance of LOTH is a further, fairly huge, step. It yielded the very theory-laden view that competence is the ability to translate back and forth between mental *sentences* and the sounds of the language. So the conceptual competence that, along with a processing competence, constitutes competence in the language is the competence to think mental sentences with meanings expressible in the language.

If LOTH is correct, the process of language production and comprehension is a *translation* process between the language of thought and the speaker's public natural language. This raises the question: *Which* language is thought in? It is tempting to suppose that a person's language of thought is *the same* as the public language in which she expresses her thought. According to this thesis, "Public-LOTH", her language of thought is her language of talk. Something even stronger than (T) would be true: the rules of the speaker's language would be *the same as* the structure rules of her thought. And the translation process in language use should be very easy, like that from spoken to written English. An alternative hypothesis is that a person's thought is in a distinct mental language, "Mentalese". If this is right, the question arises: *How similar* is a person's Mentalese to her public language? We can anticipate difficulties answering these questions because we lack strong evidence about the nature of Mentalese.[14]

The significance of the questions for our concern with psychological reality can be made vivid by considering the logic machine again (2.2). This machine takes *wffs* as inputs, processes them according to rules for valid deductions and

---

[14] Note that the issue here concerns the language that is involved in beliefs, desires, expectations, and other such central-processor states. It does not concern any other languages there may be in modules of the mind.

yields *wffs* as outputs. So, not only are the machine's inputs and outputs *wffs* but all steps of its derivations are *wffs*. The language over which its computations are defined is the formal language that determines the syntactic properties of any *wff*. So, although the rules of that language are not internally real *processing rules* of the machine they are still internally real in a very robust way: they are *structure rules* of the language the machine "thinks in". Similarly, if a person's language of thought were the same as her public language, then the structure rules of her public language would be psychologically real in a very robust way *whether or not any of them were processing rules for language use*: they would be structure rules for her language of thought. And even if the language of thought were a distinct Mentalese, then the structure rules of her public language would still be largely psychologically real provided that her Mentalese was syntactically similar to her public language. That is position (T) on psychological reality.

It is important to note that the possibility that the rules of a speaker's public language might be psychologically real in this way depends on LOTH. If thoughts are, say, map-like, then the rules governing them will be nothing like the rules of a natural language. But once we adopt LOTH, we raise the possibility that the rules of the language we think in will be like those of our natural language. This is an illustration of what I have been emphasizing: that our view on the psychological reality of language depends very much on our view of thoughts.

I once (1981) followed Harman (1973) in arguing for the Public-LOTH. This hypothesis now seems to me mistaken. But I still think it plausible that there is a great deal of similarity between the syntactic rules of Mentalese and the speaker's public language. In the next section I shall consider what can be said for and against the Public-LOTH. In the one after, I shall argue for the syntactic similarity.

9.4 THE PUBLIC-LOTH

One objection to the Public-LOTH can be dismissed quickly. When the living brain of an English speaker is examined, we find no cerebral blackboard on which English sentences are written. Nothing inside the head *looks like* an English sentence. This objection is confused. What *does* an English sentence look like? Practical problems aside, a sentence might look like anything: it can be physically realized as a sequence of acoustic vibrations, as gestures in a sign language, as marks on paper, as a sequence of flags, as electric pulses of various kinds, and so on. So there is nothing incoherent in the idea that sentences could be realized in a neural medium as well. Perhaps tokens of thought, just like tokens of speech or braille, are sentences of a public language.

It is generally agreed that the Public-LOTH must be qualified, at least: *all* thinking could not be in a public language. Our earlier discussion of animals, human ancestors, immature humans, and deaf children not exposed to a conventional sign language indicated that the best explanation of their behaviors often attributes thoughts to them (8.3). Yet these organisms do not have languages in which they could express these thoughts. And some mature human thought is surely not in a public language either: consider our thought about music or chess, for example. So the thesis must be that *most mature* human thought consists in having attitudes of believing, desiring, hoping, etc., to mental sentences in a public language.

This hypothesis has intuitive appeal because our cognitive capacities seem closely correlated with our linguistic capacities. The general development of the two capacities goes hand in hand. Further, it is very plausible to suppose that our ability to think certain thoughts depends on language. There is evidence that we could not reason about large numbers without having a language (Dehaene 1997). And could we have had beliefs about aircraft, or desires about nuclear bombs before we had words for aircrafts and bombs?

The hypothesis also has some introspective support. Speech often *seems* to be thinking out loud; thought often *seems* to be talking to oneself, "inner speech" (Sokolov 1972). Moreover, consider a familiar barrier a person must break through in learning a foreign language: learning to "think in the language". Until she crashes through this barrier, she uses the foreign language by translating back and forth to the familiar home language. Or, so it seems to introspection.

These considerations are far from decisive in support of the Public-LOTH, for the alternative Mentalese hypothesis may well be able to accommodate them. A variety of *causal* stories can explain the simultaneous development in a person of a language and thought without requiring that the thought be in the language: the language might play a causal role in developing thought; or thought, along with environmental features, might play a causal role in developing a language; or both may have the one independent cause, part nature and part nurture.

It seems fairly straightforward for the Mentalese hypothesis to account for the introspective data. First, the phenomenology of inner speech does not dictate that we are actually *thinking in* the language rather than simply using the language as *an aid* to thinking (Clark 1998). Second, perhaps the person's translation of Mentalese into the foreign language takes two steps before breaking through the barrier: she first translates into her native language and then translates that language into the foreign one. Whereas the translation into the foreign language is labored and conscious, the translation into the native language is practiced and unconscious. Hence her initial sense of translating the foreign language but not her native one. She breaks through the barrier when she collapses the two steps into the one unconscious one. Hence her later sense of thinking in the foreign language.

Furthermore, there is introspective and experimental evidence that seems to count against the Public-LOTH. We often seem to have a thought and yet have trouble expressing it, the "tip of the tongue" phenomenon ("TOT"): "Speakers experiencing TOTs know the meaning they want to express, and often have particular information about the word's sound (e.g. it starts with a 't') although they cannot retrieve the full word form" (Vigliocco and Vinson 2003: 184). Yet if the thought were in the very words that express it why would we have the trouble? The phenomenon suggests, rather, that we are struggling to translate our thought from Mentalese into English. But perhaps not. Perhaps we are struggling to form the thought, a thought which once formed is in English and can be easily expressed.

Experiments show that when we read a passage, we tend to remember "the message" rather than the precise wording (Wanner 1977). Thus, take some English sentence that did *not* appear in the passage we read. If we are asked whether that sentence appeared, we are likely to say that it did if it has much the same meaning as one that did. This suggests that we have stored a representation in Mentalese and do not remember which of several English translations of it appeared in the passage. But, again, perhaps not. Perhaps we stored a representation in English but, given our primary interest in the message not the particular form of words that presented it, we were not concerned to store it in the form that presented it: we chose a form that is most "natural" for us, perhaps the one most suitable for retrieval. When asked the question we do not remember whether that sentence or an equivalent one appeared in the passage.

Finally, we can understand a string of words that is not in our language and, indeed, could not be in any human language; for example, "Who do you think that loves Mary?" So it seems as if we can think thoughts that have a syntax unlike any sentence in our language.[15] But does it really seem like that? Perhaps we understand the string not by carrying its syntax into our thought but by translating it into a thought with a syntax that is like a sentence in our language. After all, we often understand the signs and gestures of someone with whom we share no public language. If LOTH is correct, we do not carry the "syntax" of these signs and gestures into our thought but rather translate them into a thought with a linguistic syntax. This syntax might be that of a sentence in our natural language.

So far we have found nothing decisive one way or the other on whether the language of thought is largely a public language or Mentalese. However, I rather doubt that this is a theoretically meaningful issue. What precisely would be required for a mental sentence to be a sentence of, say, English? It must at least have the same syntactic and semantic properties as an English sentence. Our acceptance of LET, the folk idea that language expresses thought, yields the sameness of semantic properties. In the next section I shall argue that sense can be made of the sameness of syntactic properties. The problem with the issue is that this sameness of syntax and semantics is not enough to make the mental sentence

---

15 Thanks to Georges Rey for this point.

English. We can see this by reflecting on the inscriptions 'Nana is a cat' and 'Nana est un chat'. These sentences have the same syntax and semantics but the first is English and the second is French. What makes them so is that the former inscription is an English "vehicle" of meaning and the latter is a French "vehicle". So if the mental sentence that expresses 'Nana is a cat' is to be English rather than French or whatever, *it has to be an English vehicle*. What would make it so?. We could, of course, answer that the mental sentence is English simply *because* it is expressed by an English sentence, but that trivializes the question. There seems to be no possibility of a theoretically interesting answer. English or French vehicles can be found in many media, as we noted at the beginning of this section: in sounds, inscriptions, signs, flags, and so on. But I doubt that that any sense can be made of these vehicles being found in thought.[16]

So I propose to set aside the public vs. Mentalese issue. I shall treat the language of thought as if it were a distinct Mentalese and focus instead on what seems a more theoretically productive issue: How similar is a person's Mentalese to her public language? In particular, how *syntactically* similar is it? If the Public-LOTH had been true then Mentalese would have been syntactically identical to the public language, a position even stronger than (T). But if Mentalese is syntactically similar to the public language, then (T) is true. My *first tentative proposal* is that it is true and so the public language is largely psychologically real in its speakers. I shall now argue for this.

9.5 THE SYNTAX OF MENTALESE

We should start with a qualification. Our earlier discussion of animals, ancestors, and immature humans (8.4) shows that (T) must be taken as applying only to language speakers. An organism that does not speak a language capable of expressing its thoughts can obviously not have thoughts with structures similar to the language that it speaks. So, the daring proposal that we are considering is that the Mentalese syntax of mature humans speaking a natural language is similar to the syntax of that language.

Let us fill out the proposal a bit. If it is correct then the Mentalese syntax for an English speaker is similar to the syntax of English (which is not, as we have just noted, to say that the Mentalese is English). Any Mentalese sentence, like any other sentence, has its particular syntactic structure in virtue of the particular rules that govern it. According to the proposal those rules are similar to those for English sentences. If this were so, the situation would be analogous to the logic machine. The rules of English would be largely psychologically real in the most robust way: they would be similar to the rules of the language that the person

---

[16] Defenders of the public language-of-thought hypothesis, like Devitt 1981 and Carruthers 1996, do not seem to have noticed this problem.

thinks in. The processing rules for translating back and forth between Mentalese and English would be largely defined over the syntactic properties determined by those structure rules even if, as would seem likely, none of the structure rules were processing rules as required by positions (i) and (iii) (3.4).

What about a person who speaks another language, for example Japanese? According to this proposal, the syntax of this person's Mentalese would be similar to the syntax of Japanese and so the rules of Japanese would be largely psychologically real in her. What about someone who is bilingual in English and Japanese? She would be bilingual in Mentalese too, some of her thoughts would have a syntax similar to English, some to Japanese.

Why should we believe this daring proposal? I shall begin my attempt to answer this question by confronting an appealing objection, nicely stated by Stephen Pinker (1994: 78–80).

The crux of this objection is that whereas a public language like English is ambiguous, Mentalese cannot be; and whereas Mentalese is fully explicit, a public language is not. So Mentalese could not be syntactically similar to English.

Consider the English sentence:

(1) Tex likes exciting sheep.

This is clearly syntactically ambiguous. It could mean that Tex enjoys causing sheep to become excited or that he enjoys the company of exciting sheep. In contrast, the mental sentence involved in any thought that (1) expresses cannot be ambiguous if the person's thinking is to proceed in the appropriate rational manner: the central processor can only operate on a mental sentence that makes explicit whether it has the syntax appropriate to the one meaning or the other. Although (1) does not mark, in its brute–physical form, the differences between these two syntactic structures, mental sentences must do so, for only thus can the central processor operate appropriately on these sentences in the process of thinking. So the two mental sentences that might underlie (1) might "look somewhat like":

(2) $[_S[_{NP}[_N\text{Tex}]][_{VP}[_V\text{likes}][_{VP}[_V\text{exciting}][_N\text{sheep}]]]]$

(3) $[_S[_{NP}[_N\text{Tex}]][_{VP}[_V\text{likes}][_{NP}[_A\text{exciting}][_N\text{sheep}]]]]$.

(2) and (3) differ syntactically from each other and so it seems from (1), the English sentence that expresses them both. Consider next the phenomena of pronouns. A passage of English can contain pronouns that might be deictic or anaphoric. If they are anaphoric they might depend for their reference on this or that other expression in the passage. These differences are not explicitly marked in English but they must be in Mentalese.

The differences between Mentalese and English in ambiguity and explicitness seem clear enough. But do these differences really show that Mentalese is not syntactically similar to English? There is persuasive reason for thinking that they do not. A triumph of generative grammar has been to make us appreciate how much of the syntax of a sentence is not explicit, "how unrevealing surface structure may be as to underlying deep structure"; "surface similarities may hide underlying distinctions of a fundamental nature" (Chomsky 1965: 24). Consider empty categories, for example: "An empty category ... is a constituent that has no phonological substance associated with it; it is inaudible in speech, and invisible in the standard orthography" (J. D. Fodor 1989: 156). Consider also the scope of quantifiers. This scope is often not explicit on the surface and yet is revealed at the level of logical form or LF, the level of syntactic structure that most concerns us here (1.3). As Gennaro Chierchia points out: "in the inter-pretation of sentences with quantified NPs, we apply scoping to such NPs. Scoping of quantifiers in English is a covert movement, part of the mental computation of meaning .... The result of scoping ... is what gets semantic-ally interpreted and is called Logical Form". It "provides an explicit representa-tion of scope, anaphoric links, and the relevant lexical information" (1999: c). Considerations of this sort lead Stephen Neale to go further: "rather than saying that (30) ["Every poet respects some sculptor"] is an ambiguous sentence, really we should say that (30) is the surface representation of two distinct senten-ces ... that share an S-Structure representation and in fact look and sound alike" (1993: 119). In sum, once one takes note of the implicit structure of an English sentence it is far from obvious that this structure differs from that of the Mentalese sentence it expresses. Indeed, Cherchia goes on to say: "It is highly tempting to speculate that logical form actually *is* the language of thought" (1999: ci).

In light of this, we can see that the objection moves far too swiftly from a difference in explicitness and ambiguity to a difference in syntax. There are two further considerations which enhance this response to the objection. And the second gives substantial support to (T).

First of all, it is important to distinguish a representation's brute–physical formal properties from its syntactic properties.[17] Whereas the formal properties are *intrinsic* to the representation, the latter are *relational*.

A formal property of the inscription 'Tex likes exciting sheep', in the intended brute–physical sense of 'formal',[18] is that of beginning with an inscription shaped such and such (replace 'such and such' with a description of the shape of 'Tex'). A formal relation between 'Tex likes exciting sheep' and 'Tex loves Mary-Lou' is that of both beginning with an inscription of the same shape. A formal property of a symbol in a computer is that of being a certain pattern of on-off switches. A formal property of a symbol in the brain is that of being a certain array of neurons. Manifestly, the written token of (1) above shares very

---

[17] There is an unfortunate tendency in the literature to confuse these two sorts of properties. For more on this, see my 1996: 258–65.

[18] Confusingly, there is another sense of 'formal' arising out of discussions of "formal languages." Formal properties in this other sense are very similar to syntactic properties.

few formal properties with any spoken token of (1). Similarly, it shares very few with a mental token that (1) expresses.

Syntactic properties and relations are ones that bear on the construction of sentences in a language. A syntactic property of 'Tex' is that of being a noun; of 'likes', that of being a verb; of 'Tex likes exciting sheep', that of being a sentence. A syntactic relation between one interpretation of that sentence and the sentence, 'Exciting sheep are liked by Tex', is that of the latter sentence being the passive of the former. Syntactic properties are ones that reflect a token's relations to other tokens in the language; they are functional properties and *extrinsic* to the representation. Although formally so different, a written and spoken token of (1) might share all their syntactic properties. Sentences that "look different" can be syntactically alike. Formal differences are one thing, syntactic differences, another. In assessing (T), we are considering the extent to which tokens of (1) might share syntactic properties with the formally very different mental token that they express.

Consider next the following question: in virtue of what does a sentence have its syntactic structure, whether explicit or not? What makes it the case that a particular token, for example a token of (1), has the structure it has, perhaps the structure revealed by (2) or (3)? This question does not seek a *description* of the structure that the sentence has—a description that linguists have been so successful at providing—but rather an *explanation* of its having that structure. Since this structure along with the sentence's word meanings determines the sentence's meaning, this explanation is part of an explanation of the sentence's meaning. It is part of an explanation of in virtue of what the sentence has whatever meaning it has.

One of our earlier priority claims points the way to an answer. This was the Gricean claim that thought meanings explain speaker meanings; and speaker meanings explain conventional meanings. In this way, thought is prior to language (8.4).[19] We now wed this Gricean story to LOTH, the hypothesis that is central to the case for (T). So we should answer questions about public language meanings by first addressing questions about Mentalese meanings.[20] The meaning of a mental sentence is determined by the meanings of its words and the syntactic structure that contains them. In virtue of what do the words have their meanings? For basic words, probably including the mental correlates of proper names and natural kind terms, this must be a matter of some sort of direct, presumably causal, relation to their referents.[21] In explaining these relations we

---

[19] It will be remembered that thought meanings are left unexplained in Gricean stories.

[20] Questions about Mentalese meaning are not questions about competence in Mentalese. Just as a theory of a system of linguistic representations—a language—should not be conflated with the theory of competence in that system (Ch. 2), a theory of a system of mental representations should not be conflated with the theory of competence in that system.

[21] What about "empty" terms like 'Pegasus' that lack a referent? This is a tricky question that must be set aside. (My 1981, chapter 6, is an attempt at it.)

are likely to have to appeal to ideas from historical–causal, teleological, and indicator theories of reference. I think, though Fodor (1987) does not, that some words will surely not be basic but rather covered by a description theory; <bachelor> is a likely example. Meanings for these words will come from inferential associations with others; for example, <bachelor>'s association with <adult>, <unmarried>, and <male>.[22] But our concern is more with mental syntax. In virtue of what does a mental sentence have its syntax? Presumably, in virtue of the way in which its meaning depends on the meanings of its parts and in virtue of the structure's role in determining a sentence's possible inferential interactions with other sentences. Thus, the mental sentences <Reagan is wrinkled> and <Thatcher is tough> share a syntactic structure in virtue of a similarity in these respects. Similarly, <All politicians are rich> and <All police are corrupt>, which share a different structure in virtue of their similarities.

In light of this, in virtue of what does a public-language sentence have its meaning? There are two steps to the answer, reflecting the distinction between the speaker meaning of a sentence on an occasion of utterance and its literal or conventional meaning on that occasion. (i) The speaker meaning of a sentence on an occasion of utterance must be determined by the causal story of its production. Thus the speaker meaning of a word in that sentence is determined by the meaning of the mental word it expresses on that occasion. The "speaker syntax" of a sentence on an occasion of utterance is determined by the structure of the underlying mental sentence that the utterance expresses on that occasion and by the way in which the utterance was produced from that mental sentence.[23] (ii) The conventional meaning of a sentence on an occasion of utterance—what it conventionally means in a language given the context—is explained somehow in terms of regularities in speaker meanings: Speakers of the language regularly use one linguistic word to express one mental word, another, another; they regularly use linguistic sentences with one speaker syntax to express one mental syntactic structure, another, another.[24]

Wedding the Gricean story of the general explanatory priority of thought over language to LOTH has yielded a sketch of an explanation of the syntactic properties of public-language sentences. What bearing does this sketch have on (T) and the objection? (i) Suppose that a public sentence was not ambiguous either in word or structure and was produced as directly as could be from a mental sentence. Then surely the speaker syntax of that public sentence would be the same as that of the mental sentence. But perhaps there is no such public sentence. So now suppose that the public sentence is ambiguous in word and structure and that the production process simply reduces the explicitness of the

---

[22] See Devitt and Sterelny 1999, particularly section 7.7, for a discussion of these various theories of word meaning and reference.

[23] In my 1996 (p. 158) I failed to note the importance of the way in which the utterance was produced to its syntax.

[24] I have argued for this view before: 1981a: 80–6; Devitt and Sterelny 1999: 7.5–7.6.

mental sentence it expresses. Consider (1), for example. (a) We have noted that the mental sentence underlying a particular token of (1) must make explicit whether the structure is of the sort captured by (2) or (3). So, what happens in production is that this explicitness is lost. (b) The speaker may know several people named 'Tex' and so that name is ambiguous for him. The mental correlates of this name will explicitly mark the distinction between these various uses of the name: for example, <Tex1>, <Tex2>, and so on. This explicitness is also lost in production. Now if the only effect of the production of a public-language sentence on the syntax of a mental sentence is to reduce its explicitness, it seems as if we must say that it has the same syntax as the mental sentence, albeit less explicitly.[25] How indeed could the speaker syntax of the public sentence differ from the syntax of the mental sentence it expresses? Perhaps it could do so if production does more than reduce explicitness. Thus suppose that a mental sentence has an SOV syntax and production transforms this into what appears to be an SVO public sentence; or that the mental sentence is active and production transforms this into what appears to be a passive sentence. It seems rather unlikely to me that production *would* make these sorts of changes but if it did then perhaps we should say that the syntax of the mental and the public differ. But even that isn't obvious. Perhaps we should say the sentences are implicitly SOV and active, respectively, and so they really have the same underlying syntax as the mental sentence they express.

What I think we can conclude from all this is that if LOTH is correct, the speaker syntax of public-language sentences will be the same as, or similar to, the syntax of the mental sentences they express. So let us be cautious and say that they are similar. Turn now to the conventional syntax. Insofar as the regularly used speaker syntax is similar to the syntax of the mental sentence it expresses, so also will be the conventional syntax that is determined by that regular use. So the syntax of a speaker's language is similar to the syntax of her thought. We have arrived at my first tentative proposal based on (T): a language is largely psychologically real in a speaker in that its rules are similar to the structure rules of her thought.[26] And the objection to this proposal, pointing to differences in ambiguity and explicitness, fails.[27]

How did we reach these conclusions? First, we adopted the controversial LOTH. Second, we noted, what seems scarcely deniable, that public language sentences can have syntactic properties that are not explicit. Third, we pointed to the role of mental sentences in explaining the implicit and explicit syntactic

---

[25] There is a worry about this. Suppose that a sailor starts with the mental sentence <This ship has yellow fever> and expresses it by flying a yellow flag from the mast. Intuitively, the yellow flag has no syntax. Yet it seems to have been produced by a process that simply removed all the explicit syntax of the mental sentence. So why does the flag not have implicitly the syntax of that mental sentence? I don't have a good answer but I'm sure there must be one.

[26] We could, of course, be much less tentative about the conditional proposal that if LOTH then (T).

[27] My previous response to this objection (Devitt and Sterelny 1999: 143) now strikes me as rather inadequate.

properties of the public sentences that express them. These three assumptions seem to make (T) inevitable.

The importance of LOTH to this argument is enormous. Thus, suppose that we dropped it, committing ourselves only to RTM instead. RTM is neutral on the nature of the mental representations involved in thought. So the representations might be map-like. If they were it would still be the case that the syntactic properties of public sentences would have to be explained by the map-like syntax of those representations and by the production processes from those representations to the public sentences that express them. But the explanation could not yield the conclusion that the sentences are syntactically similar to the representations because, of course, the sentences have a linguistic syntax whereas the representations have a map-like one; languages differ from maps.

This prompts an aside. We might well wonder how the syntax of a public language *could* be explained by map-like mental representations and the production processes from these to language. It is unclear how a map-like representation could yield an utterance with a linguistic structure. We noted earlier (9.2) that the view that mental representations are map-like rather than language-like seemed to promise no explanation of the meaning of those representations. We can add now that the view also seems to promise no explanation of in virtue of what a public-language sentence has its syntactic structure. Once one has accepted intentional realism and RTM, we seem to need LOTH to explain the relation of language to thought.

The argument we have presented is the main argument for (T). But there are other considerations that might be thought to give (T) some support.

1. Let us start with linguistic relativity. In our earlier discussion we pointed to obvious examples of the influence of language on thought: the word 'gene' makes it easy for us to have thoughts about genes; the word 'kow-tow' makes it easy for us to have thoughts about showing servile deference. And there is the possibility that there may be more exciting examples of linguistic influence. However, none of these possibilities seemed likely to provide evidence of the influence of the *syntax* of language on the syntax of thought. And that, of course, is our particular interest.

So, the investigation of linguistic relativity does not seem yet to have provided any clear evidence of the influence of language on Mentalese syntax. What is the bearing of this on (T)? Even if there were clear evidence of the influence, that would not *establish* (T): for the syntax of public language to *influence* the syntax of Mentalese is one thing, for them to be *similar* is another. Still, the influence would be significant evidence for the similarity. (Whorf embraced the Public-LOTH and so, for him, the influence leads to Mentalese syntax being identical to the public one; 1956: 252.)

So if linguistic relativity could be established it would support (T). What about the reverse? Would the establishment of (T) support linguistic relativity? No.

A similarity in the syntax of the public language and Mentalese might be the result of the influence of the public language on Mentalese but it also might be the result of the influence of Mentalese on the public language or the influence of something else on both languages.

2. This discussion leads naturally to a question about the origins of a person's Mentalese. Mentalese might be innate, as Fodor famously thinks it largely is, or it might be acquired through experience, or it might be a bit of both. Suppose that some part of the structure of Mentalese is innate. Then it is plausible to think that this part will constrain the structure of any learned natural language in ways that will make its syntax to that extent the same as that of Mentalese. Indeed, I will later consider the idea that all human languages are governed by the rules of Universal Grammar (UG) because those rules are largely if not entirely the innate structure rules of thought (12.4). Suppose, next, that some part of the structure of Mentalese is acquired through experience. Then it is plausible to think that this part is indeed influenced, as the linguisitic relativists think, by the structure of the natural language that the person also acquires. So, either way, whether Mentalese is innate or acquired, it is plausible to think that it is structurely similar to the natural language.

3. An argument along the following lines might seem to show that the syntax of the two languages must be fairly similar. (a) The translation process of production and comprehension must preserve meanings: when a thought is expressed by an utterance, the utterance must mean the same as the Mentalese sentence involved in the thought; when an utterance is understood, it must be assigned to a Mentalese sentence that means the same. (b) The meaning of an expression is a function of its syntax. So, the syntax of the speaker's Mentalese token has to be close enough to that of its expression in her public language to make them mean the same.

The problem with this argument is that the requirement that the meanings of the two tokens be the same is rather vague and thus leaves room for a lot of difference in the syntax of the two tokens. After all, there is a sense in which an active English sentence means the same as its passive, despite their syntactic differences; and there is a sense in which an English sentence means the same as its Japanese translation, despite their syntactic differences. So this requirement does not justify the claim that the two languages are closely similar.

4. Fodor has given a reason for thinking that the syntax of a person's Mentalese is like that of her language: we have to account for the great *speed* of language processing: "the more structural similarity there is between what gets uttered and its internal representation, the less computing the sentence understander will have to do" (1975: 152). And the less the computing the less the time needed to compute. Indeed, if the Mentalese and the language had the *same* structures, we

can imagine a very direct, very speedy, process from English utterance to Mentalese interpretation. But, even if the structures are *similar*, the process could be fairly direct and speedy.

In sum, LOTH opens up the possibility that the rules of a speaker's public language might be psychologically real because they are similar to the structure rules governing the language of thought. In this section I have presented a case for their being indeed fairly similar, hence a case for position (T) on psychological reality. This case is far from overwhelming, particularly as it rests on the controversial LOTH, but it does seem to me to have a lot of plausibility.

Finally, we should add a word to our earlier discussion of the temporal priority of thought over language (8.3, 8.4, 8.6). If Mentalese is not entirely innate, then it is likely that the presence of certain syntactic structures in a natural language will lead a person to gain the related structures in Mentalese. So, for that person, there is no temporal precedence of the structure in Mentalese over the structure in the natural language. But the structure is present in the language at all only because people once had the related mental structure without benefit of that linguistic structure.

As I noted (8.1), the discussion of the relation between thought and language is often framed around a distinction between the "communicative" and the "cognitive" conceptions of language. I have not followed this practice. Before concluding this chapter I shall say why.

9.6 "COMMUNICATIVE" VS. "COGNITIVE" CONCEPTIONS

Peter Carruthers and Jill Boucher describe the distinction between these two conceptions as follows. According to the communicative conception, language is "a mere adjunct to belief and thought"; its "exclusive function and purpose" is "the communication of thought"; "thought itself is largely independent". According to the cognitive conception, on the other hand, language is "crucially implicated in human thinking"; "we think *in* natural language"; language is "*constitutively involved in*", or is "the medium" of thoughts (1998b: 1); "inner verbalization ["inner speech"] is constitutive of our thinking" (2002: 657). In my view, this distinction is too vague to be helpful, conflating many fairly distinct questions.

First there is the question of how similar the language of thought is to the public language. This splits into three. How similar are they in their vehicles, in their syntactic properties, and in their semantic properties? I have argued that they are very similar in their syntactic and semantic properties but that little sense can be made of the question of a similarity of vehicle (8.2, 9.4, 9.5). This conclusion seems to accord more with the cognitive than the communicative conception.

Next there is a question about whether thought or language is prior. This splits into as many questions as there are ways in which one might be prior. I have argued that thought has a certain priority to language ontologically, explanatorily, temporally, and in theoretical interest. That's my fifth major conclusion. The priorities are quite compatible with a great deal of causal influence of thought on language (ch. 8; 9.5). The ontological priority seems to accord more with the cognitive conception than the communicative, the explanatory, more with the communicative than the cognitive.

Finally, there is a question about the function of language. This splits into two. The first concerns the use we actually make of language. I have gone along with the folk idea that we use it to express thoughts. But I think Clark's "supra-communicative" view (1998) that we also use it in various ways as an aid to thinking is very plausible. The second question concerns the *biological* function of the *capacity* for language. Now to suppose that this capacity *has* a biological function is to suppose that it is an adaptation rather than, say, a spandrel.[28] I think that this is an appealing supposition but I have not made it. If the capacity is indeed an adaptation and hence has a function, that function must surely be to express or aid thought (8.3). Perhaps this leans toward the communicative conception.

9.7 CONCLUSION

I started the last chapter by arguing for intentional realism and for LET, the view that our language expresses thoughts (8.1–8.2). These views led to my fourth major conclusion: the issue of the psychological reality of language should be investigated from a perspective on thought. The views, together with some Gricean claims, also led to my fifth major conclusion: thought has a certain priority to language ontologically, explanatorily, temporally, and in theoretical interest (8.3–8.7).

In the present chapter, I have adopted the popular RTM, the view that having a thought involves standing in a certain functional relation to a mental representation (9.1). I went on to argue for the controversial LOTH, the hypothesis that mental representations posited by RTM are language-like. I have emphasized the support for LOTH that comes from its role in explaining think*ing* and in explaining the meanings of mental representations (9.2). LOTH yields view (c) of competence in a language: competence is the ability to translate back and forth between mental sentences and the sounds (etc.) of the language (9.3). If LOTH is correct, what language do we think in? I do not favor Public-LOTH,

---

[28] This is implied by what Searle takes to be a common-sense assumption about language: "The purpose of language is communication in much the same sense that the purpose of the heart is to pump blood." (1972: 16)

according to which a person largely thinks in her public language (9.4). However, I have argued that her language of thought, her Mentalese, is syntactically similar to her public language. I arrived at my first tentative proposal based on (T): a language is largely psychologically real in a speaker in that its rules are similar to the structure rules of her thought. Once LOTH is assumed, various considerations count in favor of this proposal but I give most weight to the following one: the explanation of in virtue of what expressions of a public language have their implicit and explicit syntactic properties yields the view that the structure of Mentalese is similar to, if not the same as, the structure of the public language (9.5). If we are to conclude that language is psychologically real in a robust way, we need a powerful psychological assumption. Mine is (T).

We turn now to consider the bearing of these views of thought on the issue of the language faculty, and to a comparison with the apparently very different Chomskian views of thought and its relation to language.

10

Thought and the Language Faculty

10.1 BRAIN IMPAIRMENT AND THE INDEPENDENCE OF LANGUAGE

The positions I have been presenting in this part of the book, climaxing with (T)—the structure rules of a speaker's language are similar to the structure rules of her thought—seem to conflict with received Chomskian views. I shall consider these apparent conflicts in this chapter. I start, in this section, with my view that conceptual competence partly constitutes linguistic competence, which seems at odds with the Chomskian idea of language being largely independent of thought. There is an objection to my view which I noted earlier (8.3): the view is undermined by the well-known dissociation of cognitive impairment and linguistic impairment. In this section I confront this objection, arguing that my view of linguistic competence is not undermined. In section 10.2, I shall argue that, contrary to received opinion, the evidence from brain impairment does not support the existence of a language faculty. The evidence suggests, rather, that there may not be such a faculty. Aside from that, I shall argue in section 10.3 that, if we accept (T), we should not expect there to be a substantial language faculty because there would not be much for that faculty to do. In sections 10.4 and 10.5, I shall turn to the apparently contrary views of Chomsky. I shall finish in section 10.6 by considering recent claims by Georges Rey that are strikingly at odds with the views I have presented.

The relatively uncontroversial folk idea, LET, that speakers have meaningful thoughts which their language expresses, yields view (a) of competence in that language (8.3): the competence is an ability to use a sound of the language to express a thought with the meaning that the sound has in the language in the context of utterance; and an ability (together with some pragmatic abilities) to assign to a sound a thought with the meaning that the sound has in the language in the context of utterance. This yielded an ontological priority of thought over language. Competence in the language *requires* a certain conceptual competence, the competence to have thoughts with the meanings expressible in the language. But how could this be right? There is considerable evidence that cognitive impairment and linguistic impairment do not go hand in hand. As Pinker puts it: "There are several kinds of neurological and genetic impairments that compromise language while sparing cognition and vice versa" (1994: 46). This seems to demand that the linguistic and the conceptual be independent.

Let us start with cases of linguistic impairment without cognitive impairment. (1) Broca's aphasia provides a famous example. People who suffer damage to Broca's area in the frontal lobe of the left hemisphere of the brain often cannot talk properly; in particular, they have problems with grammar. Yet, their intellectual functions that are not closely tied to language are all preserved (Pinker 1994: 48). (2) Next, some children who do not develop language on schedule are diagnosed with "Specific Language Impairment (SLI)". SLI runs in families and it is plausible to think that it is hereditary. Indeed, the work of Myrna Gopnik on SLI was hyped in the press as the discovery of "the grammar gene" (pp. 297–8). People with SLI "speak somewhat slowly and deliberately .... They report that ordinary conversation is strenuous mental work.... Their speech contains frequent grammatical errors". Yet SLI "does not seem to impair overall intelligence" (p. 49).

Let us assume that these cases really do demonstrate linguistic impairment without cognitive impairment.[1] It is easy to see that this alone does not undermine the story I have been telling. On my view, linguistic competence consists in conceptual competence *together with processing competence*: the thoughts that are the products of the conceptual competence have to be matched for meaning with sentences in the language (8.3). So the linguistic impairment in question here might be simply an impairment of processing competence leaving the conceptual competence unaffected. In this way, a clever person could be linguistically incompetent. The evidence of Broca's aphasia and SLI does not show that the impairment is not simply in processing competence. Indeed, given that these are cases of people who are not, in general, cognitively impaired, where else could the impairment be but in processing competence?

We turn next to cases of cognitive impairment without linguistic impairment, to "linguistic idiot savants" (p. 50). Striking examples are provided by people suffering from the genetically-based Williams syndrome. These people have an unusual elfin-faced appearance and are "significantly retarded, with an IQ of about 50". Yet despite this they are "fluent, if somewhat prim conversationalists" with a fondness for unusual words (pp. 52–3). A wonderful example of a savant is provided by the brain-damaged Christopher who, despite severe mental handicaps, has superb linguistic skills, mastering foreign languages with ease (Smith and Tsimpli 1995). Laura is another example: she has "complex linguistic abilities" and yet "a testable IQ in the low 40s" (Yamada 1990: 3).

---

[1] There is some controversy about this with SLI. Indeed, Cowie (1999) points out that "almost nothing about SLI is uncontroversial" (p. 290) and goes on to give a nice summary of the controversies (pp. 290–3).

Let us assume that these cases really do demonstrate cognitive impairment without linguistic impairment.[2] Once again, it is easy to see that the story I have been telling is not undermined. On my view, the conceptual competence that partly constitutes linguistic competence is a competence to *have* certain thoughts, the thoughts expressible in the language. The competence is not one to *reason well* with those thoughts, it is not a competence at think*ing*. So a linguistically competent person could be stupid. To count against my view, we would need to establish *both* (a), that the savants cannot think thoughts with certain meanings, *and* (b), that sentences out of their mouths really have those meanings. The cases provide no evidence of (a). Indeed, it would be hard to provide it. Our usual best evidence of a person's thoughts is what she says, and that clearly cannot be used as evidence here. And it is not going to be easy to find other behavioral evidence: her failure to act on a putative thought may often arise from a failure of practical reasoning. The evidence that we do have that the subjects are retarded shows only that they are very poor at putting thoughts together in a rational manner, not that they do not have thoughts. Of course, as Eric Margolis has pointed out to me, if we assume a conceptual-role semantics certain failures of rationality will entail a lack of certain concepts and hence an inability to have thoughts involving those concepts. But then we need evidence that this semantics is right[3] and also evidence that the subject's failures of rationality are ones that, according to this semantics, entail a lack of concepts. Suppose, nonetheless, that we did have evidence of (a). Then that would seem to undermine (b). For if a subject lacks the concept $<F>$ and hence has no thoughts about Fs then 'F' out of her mouth will not be about Fs and will not have the meaning it has in the language she seems to speak; it will be "mere noise". To that extent she will not be competent in that language.

In sum, the dissociations demonstrated by cases of impairment are the wrong sort to count against the view that the competence to have thoughts with the meanings expressible in a language is a considerable part of competence in that language.

I turn now to the bearing of this view of linguistic competence, and of the brain impairment evidence, on the established view that there is a language faculty.

10.2 BRAIN IMPAIRMENT AND THE LANGUAGE FACULTY

That language expresses thought (LET) yields the view that conceptual competence partly constitutes linguistic competence. This conceptual competence is in the central processor, the "general learning device" that does the thinking. So, an

---

[2] Although, once again, there is a controversy nicely summarized by Cowie (1999: 293–7).

[3] My 1996 takes a dim view of conceptual-role semantics, arguing that only such conceptual roles as may determine reference constitute meanings.

important part of linguistic competence is in the central processor. Of course, the conceptual competence is not sufficient for the linguistic competence: the thoughts that are the products of the conceptual competence have to be matched for meaning with sentences in the language. So linguistic competence requires a processing competence as well as the conceptual one. That processing competence is surely not in the central processor and so might well be found largely in a language faculty, a mental "organ" that is a relatively central module of the mind distinct from the central processor, and that functions as the cognitive system for language. But, clearly, by removing a large part of linguistic competence from the language faculty we are downplaying its role. So even LET, a view committed to thoughts but noncommittal about their nature, has an important consequence for our view of the place of language in the mind.

Attention to the fact that a person typically has many competencies in a language, not just one, leads to a further downplaying. Indeed, it raises a radical possibility: there may not be a language faculty at all! An English speaker is typically able not only to speak English but to understand it spoken, to write it, and to read it. She may even be able to send it in Morse, understand it in Braille, sign it in naval flags, and so on. Each of these competencies requires that conceptual competence be linked by an appropriate processing competence to a symbolic input or output; each processing competence matches thoughts for meaning with appropriate inputs or outputs. It is, of course, obvious that each processing competence must differ from the others in some respects; thus, the competence to write must differ from the competence to speak simply in virtue of their different outputs. But now suppose that each processing competence differed *totally* from all others. Each one is related to the same conceptual competence, of course, but other than that it has nothing in common with the others. Then there would be no language faculty. For, if there is a language faculty it must be much more than a mere set of unrelated modality-specific processing competencies. It must be a modality-neutral, relatively central, module of the mind, a cognitive system partly responsible for all language processing.[4] It must be a "knowledge system" specific to language, somehow respecting the rules of a language; indeed, on the favored view, the Representational Thesis (RT), the language faculty respects the rules by representing them. On our supposition of a variety of distinct processing competencies (perhaps distinct modules) there would be no place for such a language faculty. The only central modality-neutral competence underlying all of the particular linguistic competencies, the competence that all of these exemplify, would be the conceptual competence that resides in the central processor. *There would be nothing for a distinct, central, modality-neutral, language-specific faculty to do.*

This supposition is sure to seem too extreme. Speaking and understanding spoken English obviously have *something* in common besides conceptual

---

[4] "the language faculty is not tied to specific sensory modalities" (Chomsky 2000a: 121).

competence: they both involve the one linguistic modality, that of phones. But, if we are to save the language faculty, we need something more significant in common than that. In particular, we need to find something in common among linguistic competencies that do not share a modality. For example, does the competence to understand spoken English have anything in common with the competence to read English (beyond the competence to think thoughts expressible in English)? If we could find something in common among all processing competencies then that would play up the language faculty.

The main argument for the existence of a language faculty comes from linguistic nativism, to be discussed in Chapter 12. Still, received opinion is that the evidence from brain impairment supports that existence. And, at first sight, the evidence does indeed seem to provide this support. For, when damage to an area of the brain impairs one processing competence it tends to impair many. This suggests that those competencies are all located in that area. This would seem to be evidence of the commonality we seek. So, let us consider the impairment evidence.

Patients with Broca's aphasia not only have trouble speaking they have trouble understanding speech. Their comprehension impairment is less sweeping but is noticeable when understanding requires "grammatical analysis" (Pinker 1994: 48). Furthermore, "their written communication follows this same production-comprehension dissociation, with impaired writing but often less severe disturbance to reading" (Swinney 1999: 31). Wernicke's aphasia is also multi-modal. In this aphasia "patients utter fluent streams of more-or-less grammatical phrases, but their speech makes no sense" (Pinker 1994: 310–11). Patients also have "a profound comprehension deficit. Furthermore, both writing and (particularly) reading are standardly highly impaired" (Swinney 1999: 31). Finally, Argye Hillis and Alfonso Caramazza generalize as follows about a wide range of aphasias, including Broca's and Wernicke's: "reading comprehension is generally impaired at least to the degree of auditory comprehension, and written output is typically impaired at least as much as spoken output, often mirroring the content of speech" (2003: 177).

Deaf users of a sign language (like ASL) seem to provide further evidence of areas of the brain devoted to language in a modality-neutral way. For, the effect of aphasias on the deaf is analogous to that on hearers:

right-handed deaf signers like hearing persons, exhibit aphasia when critical left-hemisphere areas are damaged ... language impairments following stroke in deaf signers follow the characteristic pattern of left frontal damage leading to nonfluent output with spared comprehension, whereas left posterior lesions yield fluent output with impaired language comprehension...the presence of strong biases that left inferior frontal and posterior temporal parietal regions of the left hemisphere are well suited to process a natural language independent of the the form of the language. (Corina 1999: 756–7)

So, at first sight, brain impairments suggest that the various processing competencies are located in Wernicke's area and Broca's area (and the arcuate fasciculus that joins those areas). This is known as "the Wernicke–Geschwind model". And this classical model may seem to support the idea that there is a commonality between linguistic processing competencies and hence support the existence of a language faculty. However, this first sight is misleading in at least three ways.

First, it has proved impossible to come up with generalizations that really tie one brain function, let alone many, to a particular area of the brain. "The Wernicke-Geschwind model ... is now seen as oversimplified. Areas all over the brain are recruited for language processing; some are involved in lexical retrieval, some in grammatical processing, some in the production of speech, some in attention and memory" (Dronkers 1999: 450). The introduction to a recent state-of-the-art collection on language-brain research notes that "no paper in the present collection focuses on or attributes any special role to Broca's area or Wernicke's area .... There is a dramatic increase in attention to cortical areas outside the traditional perisylvian language zone .... The right hemisphere ... is being rehabilitated" (Poeppel and Hickok 2004: 9–10). Findings from a range of very different studies "do not allow the conclusion that Wernicke's area (or any other brain region) is alone responsible for a given cognitive process. For example, although Wernick's area appears to be important for the understanding of words, it is unclear what—if any—semantic information is represented in this area" (Hillis and Caramazza 2003: 181); "the lexical processing system is distributed over a large area of the left hemisphere" (Caramazza 1999: 470); "the syntactic capacities are not implemented in a single area ... they constitute an integrated system which involve both left and right neocortical areas, as well as other portions of the brain, such as the basil ganglia and the cerebellum" (Moro *et al.* 2001: 117). Ultimately, even the location of aphasias has proved difficult: "despite early reports documenting a close relationship between aphasia classification and site of lesion in chronic stroke, the correlation of aphasia type with location of lesion has not withstood recent attempts at replication" (Hillis and Caramazza 2003: 180). Pinker expresses his frustration at the situation: "the role of Broca's area in language is maddeningly unclear" (1994: 310); "no one really knows what either Broca's or Wernicke's area is for" (p. 311); "pinning brain areas to mental functions has been frustrating" (p. 314).

Of course, there could still be a language faculty even if the various linguistic processing competencies are located in one person in one brain area, in another, another, even if they are located in a person at one time in one area, at another time, another, or even if each of them is located across many parts of the brain. Mental processes are one thing, the physical sites at which they are located in the brain, another. Nonetheless, it would have seemed nice evidence for the language faculty if the various competencies had been, for the most part, located in all people at all times in the one brain area; that would have been nice evidence that there really was a language *module*. Furthermore, if there is to be a language faculty it should be the case that in each person at each time the various competencies are, to a significant extent, located together. But there is no evidence that they are.

The second way in which the first sight is misleading is that even if the various processing competencies could be located in one area according to, say, the Wernicke–Geschwind model, their common impairment when that area is damaged would still not establish that they have the commonality required for a language faculty. For, they might all be totally distinct and yet damaged together. Perhaps their locations are causally related in ways that explain the common impairment. Hillis and Caramazza are interesting on this score. Considering Broca's aphasia in stroke victims, they respond skeptically to the idea that damage to "a central syntactic processor" might be responsible for the range of impairment symptoms. "Rather, it is likely that the frequent co-occurrence of these various symptoms reflects the fact that large, consistent regions of the brain are typically supplied by distinct cerebral arteries, the occlusion of which results in stroke. Suppose the larger area supplied by a vessel such as the superior division of the left middle cerebral artery (MCA) consists of a number of smaller regions each responsible for a specific language function (e.g. grammatical sentence formulation, computation of syntactic relations, and articulation); occlusion of this vessel would typically result in impairment of all three functions." (2003: 179)

The third, and perhaps most important, way in which the first sight is misleading is that even if a particular processing competence is typically impaired along with others in an aphasia, the fact that it often is not suggests that there is no commonality among processing competencies and hence no language faculty. The tell-tale sign of this fact is that claims in the literature about one linguistic impairment being accompanied by another nearly always include qualifying expressions like "tend to", "standardly", "often", "generally", or "typically"; see above for some examples. The literature does not even clearly support the intuitive view that the production and comprehension of speech have much in common.

The evidence on overlap between the production and recognition systems is inconclusive. If there are to be shared resources, the constraints of the two processes entail that the sharing must be at a central level; however, while the evidence outlined [in this paper] is compatible with a shared-resource account, it also does not rule out separation of the two systems.   (Cutler 1995: 124)

The cognitive processing systems responsible for comprehension and production may nonetheless be distinct. Research on language disorders suggests a degree of independence between them, because people with disorders of production can display near-normal comprehension abilities, and vice versa.   (Bock 1999: 456; see also Bock 1995: 205–6)

Not surprisingly, then, competencies involving different modalities have been found to be independent. Thus, the earlier-quoted passage from Hillis and Caramazza, noting that aphasias affecting the spoken language "generally" affect reading and writing, goes on as follows:

However, there are cases of pure (auditory) word deafness, in which comprehension of spoken language is severely impaired, but comprehension of written language is intact ... There have also been reported cases in which written naming accuracy far exceeds spoken naming accuracy. There are also a variety of patterns of pure reading impairment (alexia), writing impairment (agraphia) or both (alexia with agraphia), associated with different lesion sites. (2003: 177)

In another work, Caramazza, notes other selective impairments:

Some brain-damaged patients are selectively impaired in retrieving only the orthographic from (e.g., the spelling of the word *chair*) or only the phonological form of words (e.g. the sound of the word *chair*). Patients of this type can be entirely normal in their ability to understand and define words, but fail to retrieve the correct word form in one, but not the other, modality of output .... there are patients who are impaired in producing verbs only in speaking (they can write verbs and can produce nouns both in speaking and in writing) and patients who are impaired in producing nouns only in speaking; and there are patients who fail to understand written but not spoken verbs. (1999: 469–70)

Caramazza rightly sees this account of highly selective impairments as a challenge to "the view that there exists a modality-neutral lexical node mediating between modality-specific lexical representations and word meaning" (p. 470). Indeed, the account encourages the idea that there is a direct route between thoughts and modality-specific inputs/outputs, a route that does not go though a modality-neutral language faculty; i.e., it encourages our earlier supposition that there is no such faculty.

More encouragement comes from the case of J.B.N.,

who spoke in fluent jargon and failed to comprehend spoken words or sentences, despite normal hearing and "early" auditory processing. Nevertheless, J.B.N had intact writing and comprehension of written language. Thus, this patient did not have impaired semantics, or word meanings, but was impaired in linking spoken words to their meanings and vice versa, owing to poor blood flow in the sylvian branch of the anterior temporal artery, supplying Wernicke's area. (Hillis and Caramazza 2003: 182)

Again this suggests fairly direct routes between thoughts and inputs/outputs, routes that in J.B.N. have been damaged for spoken inputs/outputs but not for written ones. It suggests that there is no place for a language faculty.

Objection.[5] It is not appropriate to consider competencies in a written language, let alone in Morse and so on, in looking for evidence of the language

---

[5] I have heard this sort of objection a few times but have not come across it in the literature.

faculty. These competencies are ones that the child can only acquire by some clearly central process; she cannot acquire them "naturally", under the constraints of Universal Grammar (UG), as she can competencies in a spoken English and ASL. So these written competencies are not the business of the language faculty.

Reply. (i) If there was a language faculty then it would be odd indeed if it was not involved in our competencies in the written language. For if there was one it would play a vital central role in processing the spoken communication of thoughts. Yet the written language can, with one exception, serve to communicate thoughts as effectively as the spoken language. The exception is, of course, that it is a rather slow method of communication. But it is hard to see why this lack of speed would remove the need for the language faculty to play the same vital central role in processing the written communication of thoughts. (ii) Let us accept that competencies in a written language cannot be acquired naturally, although one wonders whether and how this inability has really been established. It is not clear why this difference between the written and spoken languages should be relevant to the nature of the competencies in them. Certainly, if there was a language faculty, our inability to naturally acquire the written competencies would not alone show that the language faculty did not play that vital role in written communication. For, the inability might be explained not by the lack of involvement of the language faculty but rather by some incidental practical problems. Perhaps, the slowness of written communications is what causes the inability. At least, more work has to be done on the objection if it is to undermine the view that if there was a language faculty it would be involved in written communication.

In sum, the evidence from brain impairment seemed, at first sight, to support the idea of a language faculty. Where brain damage impairs one processing competence it tends to impair many, suggesting the commonality among competencies that is necessary for there to be a modality-neutral language faculty. But this first sight is misleading. First, a particular area of the brain cannot be tied tightly to one brain function, let alone to many. Second, even if the various processing competencies could be located in one area, their common impairment when that area is damaged is quite compatible with their being distinct. Their functioning might depend, for example, on a particular cerebral artery that has been damaged. Third, even if a particular processing competence is typically impaired along with others, the fact that it often is not suggests that there is no commonality among processing competences. So it turns out that the evidence from brain impairment provides no persuasive evidence in favor of the existence of a language faculty. Furthermore, the highly selective nature of some impairments suggests that there is a direct route between thoughts and modality-specific inputs/outputs that does not go though a modality-neutral language faculty. All in all, the evidence from brain impairment counts much more against the existence of a language faculty than for it.

10.3 THOUGHTS AND THE LANGUAGE FACULTY

The evidence against the language faculty that we have been considering is only suggestive, of course: it is very far from conclusive.[6] So in this section, I want to consider the *likeliness* of there being a substantial language faculty, given certain assumptions about the nature of thoughts. Given these assumptions, should we *expect* to find substantial commonalities among processing competencies?

Suppose that we move beyond LET, which has governed the discussion so far, and adopt the minimal RTM view of thought: having a thought involves standing in a relation to a mental representation. With RTM goes view (b) of competence: competence is the ability to *translate* back and forth between mental representations and the sounds etc. of the language (9.1). RTM takes thoughts to involve representations but is noncommittal about the nature of those representations. So the representations might be map-like. If they were, the various processing competencies would have the job of translating between map-like structures and very different linguistic structures. This job seems rather formidable. Perhaps then we should expect that there would be a modality-neutral linguistic "knowledge system" that each of the processing competencies could call on to perform the job. Perhaps we should expect that there would be substantial commonalities constituting a substantial language faculty. For, there would seem to be a lot for a language faculty to do.

However, the likeliness of a substantial language faculty seems to disappear if we move beyond LET in two further ways, as I have argued we should. LET yielded an ontological priority of thought over language. The first move is to follow Grice in accepting the relatively, although certainly not entirely, uncontroversial explanatory priority of thought over language (8.4, 8.6–8.7). The second move weds this acceptance to the decidedly controversial Language-of-Thought Hypothesis (LOTH) and view (c) of linguistic competence: competence is the ability to translate back and forth between mental *sentences* and the sounds etc. of the language (9.3). This wedding yields the following version of the Gricean explanatory priority: the meanings of words in a language are ultimately explained by the meanings of the mental words that they express; and the syntactic structures of sentences in the language are explained by the structures of mental sentences that the sentences express. If this is so, I argued (9.5), we have good reason to think that a speaker thinks in a Mentalese that has a syntax very like that of her natural language; we have good reason to accept (T) and hence my first tentative proposal. That greatly affects the job that processing competencies have to do. Instead of the formidable job of translating between, say, map-like structures and linguistic

---

[6] One piece of evidence that may count in favor of a language faculty is evidence that visual word recognition is not "direct" but "phonologically mediated". But the evidence is not conclusive, the whole issue being "a source of seemingly endless controversy" (Seidenberg 1995: 151).

structures, the competencies have the job of translating between similar language-like structures. Intricate as this job doubtless is for each competence, it does not seem that it would be helped by a modality-neutral linguistic "knowledge system"; it is hard to see what a substantial language faculty would have to do.

In the last section, I described evidence suggesting that there are not the commonalities between the various processing competencies required for there to be a language faculty. In this section, I have argued that, if we accept (T), we should not expect to find commonalities that would constitute a substantial language faculty. For, given (T), it is likely that there is not much to an English speaker's syntactic competence in her language beyond her competence in her Mentalese, her conceptual competence. This conceptual competence can carry all this linguistic weight because it is an *English-oriented* competence. We have arrived at my *second tentative proposal*: there is little or nothing to the language faculty.

Let me summarize the key steps to this proposal. First, LET alone downplays the language faculty because according to LET a certain conceptual competence is an important part of a person's competence in a language. That part is in the central processor not a language faculty. If there is a language faculty it must be found in the other part of a linguistic competence, a processing competence. Second, finding this depends on the various processing competencies having a substantial part in common. Yet the evidence from brain impairments suggests that they do not have this commonality and hence that there is no language faculty. Third, if we wed the Gricean explanatory priority of thought over language to LOTH yielding (T), we should not expect there to be a substantial language faculty because there is nothing much for the language faculty to do. This case for the second tentative proposal rests a bit on LOTH but does not totally depend on it as does the case for the first (9.5).

The proposal that there is not a substantial language faculty has to be tentative because the case for it is far from overwhelming. Still, if my line of reasoning is correct, the contrary view that there *is* a substantial language faculty should be even more tentative because the case for it is even weaker. That contrary view requires that there be a substantial commonality among processing competencies. Yet, the evidence from brain impairment does not support this commonality. And if (T) is true the commonality seems unlikely. Even the fairly innocuous LET leads to a downplaying of the language faculty.

Chomsky's nativist discussion of language acquisition may seem to provide a powerful objection to this downplaying, for Chomsky argues against placing our linguistic competence anywhere but in a distinct language faculty. He argues that the rules (principles) of language are so peculiar that we would not expect to find them anywhere but in a distinct language faculty, in particular not in the central processor. Furthermore, no general learning device of the sort found in the central processor could explain the acquisition of a language, a point that seems to be supported by Ray Jackendoff's neat "Paradox of Language Acquisition". I shall later consider and reject these arguments (12.5). Indeed, I shall argue that the discussion of the last two chapters has important consequences for nativism and language acquisition that count further against there being a substantial language faculty (12.4).[7]

I turn now to consider Chomsky's apparently contrary views on some other matters discussed in this part of the book. In the next section I consider his views on thoughts. In the following section I consider his views on conventions and idiolects.

10.4   CHOMSKY ON THOUGHTS

I have no firm view about the extent of Chomsky's disagreement with the claims made in this part of the book. He does seem to accept LET, the folk idea from which I started: "a language is a particular way of expressing thought and understanding the thought expressed" (1991a: 8). He is highly critical of various aspects of the Gricean story but these are not aspects that I have adopted (8.4). Thus, against attempts to explain meanings in terms of a speaker's communicative intentions he rightly points out:

Under innumerable quite normal circumstances—research, casual conversation, and so on—language is used properly, sentences have their strict meaning, people mean what they say or write, but there is no intent to bring the audience (not assumed to exist, or assumed not to exist, in some cases) to have certain beliefs or to undertake certain actions.   (1975b: 62)

And he emphasizes, as I do, the Gricean reliance on unexplained thought contents (1975b: 65–7). I haven't found in Chomsky any discussion of the part of the Gricean story that I have adopted, the part that yields the explanatory priority of thought over language. Indeed, Chomsky has surprisingly little to say about thoughts at all. What he does say certainly does not suggest that he would accept that thought has the various priorities over language summed up in my fifth major conclusion. Indeed, he is naturally construed as thinking that language is largely independent of thought. And any downplaying of the language faculty is decidedly unChomskian. Finally, the signs are that he does not hold LOTH.[8] If he does not, he could not relate the syntax of language closely to that of thought, as (τ) does.

---

[7] "Cognitive linguistics", which is opposed to generative linguistics, also rejects the language faculty: "language is not an autonomous cognitive faculty ... conceptual structures and processes proposed for language should be essentially the same as those found in nonlinguistic human cognition" (Croft and Cruse 2004: 328). Cognitive linguistics arose out of an opposition to truth-conditional semantics that seems to me very mistaken (1996). However, its idea of a "production grammar", stimulated by the need to accommodate idioms, is certainly interesting.

[8] Although Carruthers and Boucher claim that "Chomsky (1957) argued that thought had to be translated out of language into a 'language of thought' in the process of linguistic understanding" (1998b: 9). Chomsky is certainly dubious of a Fodorian "universal Mentalese" (2000a: 176–8). This is not the sort of Mentalese that I am urging because I accept that there may be a great deal of causal

Any theory of language that accepts the reality of meaningful thoughts must relate those thoughts somehow to meaningful language. Making this connection seems particularly important for a mentalistic theory of language like Chomsky's. For, thoughts are *clearly and indubitably* in the mind.[9] We would expect the relation between thought and language to be at center stage in a discussion of the psychological reality of language. So, it is strange to find that Chomsky does not say much about the connection.[10]

I am talking here of thoughts as *mental states*. Frege talked of thoughts as *abstract objects* that are grasped by people in these mental states. These putative objects are more usually called "propositions". Chomsky clearly doubts that such objects have any place in the study of language.[11] I agree. What is surprising is that he says so little about thoughts as mental states.

Passages like the following indicate a rather different view of the relation between language and thought from the ones we have outlined:

[The language faculty] is internally highly modularized, with separate subsystems of principles governing sound, meaning, structure and interpretation of linguistic expressions. These can be used, to a sufficient degree, in thought and its expression ...   (1991b: 51)

Elsewhere he includes "conceptual–intentional systems", along with "articulatory and perceptual systems", among "performance systems" that use "expressions generated by the I-language". The conceptual–intentional systems use the "meaning" provided by the LF properties of an expression (1995b: 19–20; 2000a: 124–5). A message I take from such passages is that the rules or principles of the I-language are distinct from any structure rules governing thought but they, and the expressions they generate, are nonetheless *used in* thought. But how could they be thus used? We can see, of course, how language is used by thought in the articulatory and perceptual systems, for that use is involved in expressing thoughts and interpreting utterances. So we understand the last "in expression" part of Chomsky's "used ... in thought and its expression". But what *other* uses

influence of language upon thought (9.5). The reasons for Chomsky's doubts do not count, so far as I can see, against my picture of Mentalese and its relation to language.

[9] In claiming this I do not mean to deny, what indeed I believe, that the identity of a thought depends partly on its relations to the world outside the mind.

[10] Nor do others. Fodor remarked some time back that "relatively little attention has been paid the question of how models of language articulate with theories of cognition" (1975: 100). And this has continued: "the relationship between language and thought has been relatively little discussed in recent decades" (Carruthers and Boucher 1998b: 2).

[11] "Such understanding as we have of these matters does not seem to be enhanced by invoking thoughts that we grasp ..." (1994: 25–6). "The notion 'common store of thoughts' has no empirical status, and is unlikely to gain one even if the science of the future discovers a reason, unknown today, to postulate entities that resemble 'what we think (believe, fear, hope, expect, want, etc.)' [The view that there is a common store of thoughts] seems groundless at best, senseless at worst" (1996: 47).

are there that he could have in mind for the distinct conceptual–intentional system? What is the first "in thought" part of this claim? We need to use our grasp of the I-language to express thoughts and understand their expression but what else could we use it for? If the popular RTM is correct, thought must be in a representational system, either a language or a system of some other sort. So thought itself is already governed by a system of structure rules. What use could thought then have for a distinct system of linguistic rules? According to (т), of course, the two systems are similar and so one might perhaps say, on the strength of this, that the linguistic rules are thus used in thought. But that is presumably not what Chomsky has in mind. Even if we do not adopt RTM, we must see thoughts as already having meanings. So what use could thoughts make of meanings generated by the I-language other than the use of expressing them? Finally, we wonder how the picture of one module governing the meaning and another, the structure of a linguistic expression, can yield a plausible view of the way a thought, *which already has a meaning and structure*, leads to that expression?[12]

A different view of the relation between language and thought may also underlie Chomsky's view of the prospects for his task (iii), the psycholinguistic task of explaining language perception and production. "The perception problem has to do with how we interpret what we hear. ... The production problem, which is considerably more obscure, has to do with what we say and why we say it. We might call this latter problem Descartes's Problem" (1988: 4–5). Chomsky's thinks that this problem, unlike the part of the perception problem that concerns the parser, may well be a mystery, "beyond the range of our understanding" (1991b: 41). The difficulty with the problem, pointed out by Descartes, is "that normal human speech is unbounded, free of stimulus control, coherent and appropriate ... what we might call 'the creative aspect of language use' " (p. 40).[13] But it is surely a mistake to identify the production problem of task (iii) with Descartes's problem.

We should start by distinguishing the creativity that Chomsky has in mind from another that he clearly does not, what we might call "the creativity of language". The latter creativity is to be found in the *productivity* of language: someone competent in the language has the capacity to produce any one of an indefinitely large number of novel sentences. Descartes' problem is concerned with a creativity in language *use*: roughly, we might say just about anything at just about any time. But this problem seems to reduce to two other problems, *neither of which are the production problem of task (iii)*. The first of these is the problem of explaining the creativity of *thought*. For our thoughts are indeed, in some sense, "unbounded, free of stimulus control" and, as a result, so too are the sentences

---

[12] Chomsky's modularized picture is, as Larson and Segal say, "broadly assumed in modern linguistic theory" (1995: 72).

[13] On some of this creativity problem, see Kasher 1991b.

that express our thoughts.[14] If we could explain this creativity of thought we would have partly explained "the creative aspect of language use". The creativity of thought may well be mysterious but it surely has nothing to do with psycholinguistics and task (iii). The second problem underlying Descartes' problem is that, whatever we think, we seem free to express it or not to express it. If we could explain this apparent freedom of speech as well as explain the creativity of thought, we would have completed the explanation of the creativity of language use. Yet explaining this apparent freedom of speech is again nothing to do with psycholinguistics. The apparent freedom is just an example of the apparent freedom of action in general; as Chomsky puts it, "our actions are free and undetermined" (1988: 147). So this second part of Descartes' problem is nothing but the famous problem of freewill. This problem may also be beyond us but it is a philosophical problem not a psycholinguistic one. The strictly psycholinguistic problem of task (iii) starts only after the thought to be expressed and the intention to express it have been formed: "the process begins with a communicative intention, a *message*, that stands at the interface between thought and language" (Bock 1999: 453). Descartes' problem, the problem of explaining the formation of the thought and the formation of the communicative intention, are simply not the concern of psycholinguistics. Just as the perception part of task (iii) seeks to explain how we move from hearing an utterance to the thought that is its interpretation, the production part of the task seeks to explain how we move from the intended expression of a thought to the utterance that is its expression. This task may well be very hard, but it does not seem particularly mysterious. And it does not seem to pose any interesting problem of creativity.

If one had anything like the view of the relation of language to thought that I have been urging, even just LET, one would surely give pride of place to the creativity of thought in discussing the creative aspect of language use. Yet Chomsky does not even mention it.[15]

In sum, it is clear that Chomsky would reject position (T) with its dramatic lessening of the role of the language faculty. Even the much less radical claims of ontological and explanatory priority for thought seem at odds with his views. But perhaps this is an illusion, given that his view of thoughts and their relation to language remains obscure.[16]

---

[14] The unboundedness of thought is strangely overlooked by Hauser *et al.* (2002) in arguing that the human recursive capacity to generate an infinite range of expressions, unlike the human conceptual–intentional system, is unique to the species. Yet humans are unique in their recursive capacity to generate an infinite range of *thoughts*, however much else humans may share conceptually with other animals. And if they did not have that conceptual capacity for "discrete infinity" it would be very odd that they had the linguistic capacity for it (8.3).

[15] However, he has this to say later in speculating about the origins of language "this small mutation ... giving us the capacity *to think* creatively and to speak creatively" (1988: 183–4; emphasis added).

[16] In a peer commentary, Roger Schank criticizes Chomsky for divorcing "the conceptual from the language" (1980: 37). Chomsky does not reply to this criticism in his response (1980c: 53–4).

One wonders why Chomsky says so little about thoughts. Perhaps he thinks, reasonably enough, that it is difficult to find anything that can be confidently said. But, as I am arguing, it is also difficult to find anything that should be confidently said about the place of language in the mind. Indeed, if my fourth major conclusion is right, the latter is *more* difficult, because, according to that conclusion, a view of the place of language in the mind should be heavily dependent on a view of thoughts.

10.5 CHOMSKY ON CONVENTIONS AND IDIOLECTS

In this section I shall explore Chomsky's views on four other matters that seem somewhat at odds with the Gricean view of the relation of thought to language that I have urged (8.4, 9.5).

(i) Chomsky seems to doubt that there are regularities of the sort needed for "the norms and conventions of language". "If by 'conventions' we mean something like 'regularities in usage', then we can put the matter aside; these are few and scattered" (1996: 47; see also 1980a: 81–3).

(ii) Furthermore, such conventions as there are, in an ordinary sense, do not have "any interesting bearing on the theory of meaning or knowledge of language" (1996: 48).[17]

(iii) Chomsky says of communication that "it does not require shared 'public meanings'. . . . Nor need we assume that the 'meanings' . . . of one participant be discoverable by the other. Communication is a more-or-less matter, seeking a fair estimate of what the other person said and has in mind" (1994: 21).[18]

(iv) Chomsky emphasizes that linguistics should not be concerned with a language like Chinese or English. A language in that sense has a "sociopolitical dimension" which makes it an unsuitable notion for the science of language (1986: 15–16); "the notion 'common language' has no place in efforts to understand the phenomena of language and to explain them" (1996: 47). Rather our primary concern should be, in effect, with *idiolects* (1986: 16–17; 1996: 48).[19]

---

[17] Fodor does not agree with (i) and (ii); see his1975, ch. 3 and the following: "think of a natural language as a system of conventional vehicles for the expression of thoughts (a view to which I know of no serious objections)" (1981a: 196).

[18] Cf: "we should give up the attempt to illuminate how we communicate by appeal to conventions" (Davidson 1986: 446).

[19] The view that linguistics should be about idiolects is standard in Chomskian circles: "in linguistic theory . . . the object of study is the idiolect. . . . References to community languages, or to dialects of languages, if they are needed at all, are in any case references to derivative things, characterized loosely in terms of the overlapping idiolects of members of groups whose individuals are in frequent serious communication with each other" (Higginbotham 1989: 155); "A linguistic theory is correct exactly to the extent that it is the explicit statement of a body of linguistic knowledge possessed by a designated individual language-user" (Barber 2001: 263); "the proper object of linguistic inquiry is a speaker's *idiolect*" (Barry Smith 2001: 285).

From my perspective these claims are puzzling. To bring out why, I need some more background. On the Gricean story I urged, conventions seemed to come into the picture when we take account of the distinction between the speaker meaning of an utterance—what the speaker means by it—and its conventional meaning on the occasion—what, in the context, it means according to linguistic conventions that the speaker is participating in. Clearly, the speaker meaning is the one that matches the thought meaning. I have said, rather vaguely, that the conventional meaning of an utterance in a language is explained somehow in terms of regularities in speaker meanings (8.4). And I have not bothered to distinguish it from the literal meaning of the utterance. It is time to say a little more about these matters.

Mostly we can identify the conventional meaning of an utterance with its literal meaning, but we cannot always do so. Idiolects are occasionally a bit eccentric: the literal meaning of an expression in a person's idiolect may not be a meaning it has according to any linguistic convention. Donald Davidson brings this out nicely in his discussion of Mrs. Malaprop's "a nice derangement of epitaphs" (1986): what she literally means is "a nice arrangement of epithets" and yet her words do not mean this according to any convention.

What is it for a certain expression to have a certain literal meaning in a person's idiolect? On my view, the expression has that meaning in virtue of that person being disposed to associate the expression with that meaning in the production and comprehension of language: she is disposed to use that expression to express a concept (a part of a thought) with that meaning; and she is disposed to interpret that expression by assigning a concept with that meaning to it.[20] Occasionally a person will not do what she is normally disposed to do; she will deliberately assign another meaning to an expression, as in a metaphor; or she will make a performance error; or she will make an adjustment in understanding Mrs. Malaprop. In these cases, an expression will have a speaker or audience meaning that is different from its literal meaning in the person's idiolect.

How does the conventional meaning of an expression in a community relate to the literal meanings it has for speakers in that community? Suppose that speakers in the community share a disposition to associate the expression with a certain concept meaning, thus generating a regularity of so associating it. Then the speakers share a literal meaning. If this sharing is partly explained by the appropriate causal relations between the speakers' dispositions, then that literal meaning will be the conventional one in the community. It is, of course, hard to say precisely what causal relations are appropriate for the shared literal meaning to be conventional, but the center of what has to be said is that any speaker has

---

[20] This account would need to be modified to deal with an indexical which has a type meaning that yields token meanings that vary with contexts. We might say that the indexical has that type meaning in virtue of the person being disposed to use it to express concepts with token meanings that are thus dependent on the context; and being disposed to interpret indexicals by assigning a concept to it that is thus dependent on context.

her disposition because other speakers have theirs and hence regularly use the expression with that meaning; there is some sort of mutual understanding (Lewis 1969, Schiffer 1972). The norm is for speakers in a community to share a literal meaning because they stand in the required causal relations. As a result, the literal meaning of most expressions for most speakers will be the conventional meaning of those expressions in the speakers' community. Mrs. Malaprop is an exception.

Before considering Chomsky's four claims, we should attend to Stephen Laurence's surprising view of these matters (1996, 1998). He rejects the idea that there are any linguistic conventions of the sort just described and hence rejects "convention-based semantics". He thinks that our semantic theory should be concerned simply with literal meanings in an idiolect. His rejection is largely based on criticisms of Lewis' account of conventions in general and of linguistic conventions in particular. But this is not a good reason for the rejection. Lewis starts by pointing out that it is a "platitude that language is ruled by convention" (1969: 1). Laurence takes the platitude to be that linguistic properties are not *intrinsic* properties: "I completely agree that language is conventional in the trivial sense: it isn't an *intrinsic* property of the noise 'chocolate' that it means *chocolate*" (1996: 272). But this is clearly not the right way to understand the platitude because very many properties that are not intrinsic are not conventional: *being a parent, being a moon*, and so on. And it also clearly not what Lewis has in mind. Lewis does not mention intrinsic properties in describing the platitude, saying rather that "we who use [words] have made them mean what they do because somehow, gradually and informally, we have come to an understanding that this is what we shall use them to mean" (1969: 1). In brief, the platitude is that linguistic conventions are created and sustained by regular practice together with some sort of mutual understanding. (They might also be created by explicit agreement, of course, but they rarely are.) I sympathize with Laurence's criticisms of Lewis' highly intellectualized account of these conventions. And I have just acknowledged the difficulty of coming up with a satisfactory account. But this should not shake our conviction that there are such conventions, not only in language but in many other facets of life. That there are is indeed a platitude, something that should be abandoned only in the face of powerful evidence.

Against this background, I turn to Chomsky's four claims. Consider claim (i): there are few regularities in usage and hence few linguistic conventions. Chomsky thinks that this should be a truism (1996: 48). Yet it is surely astounding. Although it is possible in principle to have an idiolect that is not based on regularities in usage and hence is entirely unconventional, nobody in fact comes close to having such an idiolect. Of course, if Chomsky is right, a great deal of syntax is innate and hence not conventional. (We should note that the innate syntax will *certainly* lead to regularities albeit not conventional ones.) Still, the syntactic differences between public languages show that much syntax is not innate. These differences are captured, on the received Chomskian view, by different settings of "parametric values". Very occasionally an idiolect's parameter settings may be eccentric but almost always they will be conventional. Thus most people in the USA participate in parameter-setting conventions that lead them to speak an SVO language; most people in Japan participate in parameter-setting conventions that lead them to speak an SOV language. The ubiquity of regularities in usage and linguistic conventions is even more apparent when we turn to words. Despite Mrs. Malaprop, almost any word in anyone's idiolect is conventional:[21] if we take any such word, we are almost certain to find that its literal meaning is the meaning it has conventionally among some group of people with whom the person is in touch. This does not, of course, imply that the group will be the same for each expression. Indeed, we can expect to find considerable variation; thus, I share my meaning of 'wowser' with nearly all Australians and hardly any Americans; I share my meaning of 'chutzpah' with many Americans and few Australians; I share a meaning of 'wet' with most English, many Australians, and few Americans; I share my meaning of 'disinterested' with a rapidly diminishing subgroup of Australians, Americans, and English. In brief, I would say, in contrast to (i), that almost all noninnate syntax and almost all the word meanings of anyone's idiolect are conventional.

There is indeed something a little paradoxical about denying the frequency of linguistic conventions. The linguistic method of consulting the intuitions of linguists and other speakers to discover facts about a language, discussed in Chapter 7, presupposes masses of conventional regularities among them, even while allowing for some differences in idiolects. Books are written and papers are given about expressions in this or that language, all of which presuppose a great deal of regularity in usage among speakers.

Turn next to Chomsky's claim (ii): conventions have no interesting bearing on the theory of meaning or knowledge of language. Chomsky thinks that this also should be a truism (1996: 48). Yet, if it were true it would seem to be at odds with what most linguists are actually doing. For, what they are mostly doing is theorizing about the largely conventional syntactic and semantic properties of expressions (Ch. 2). And they are right to be doing so, in my view. Conventional meaning is important to theory in at least four ways.

First, conventional meaning plays a role in explaining the acquisition of a person's idiolect: an expression typically has a certain literal meaning in a person's idiolect as a causal result of its having that meaning conventionally in a local group. Acquiring a language is almost entirely a matter of moving, under the causal influence of primary linguistic data that are (performance errors aside) instances of local linguistic conventions, from an innate "initial state" of readiness for language to a "final state" of participation in those very linguistic conventions.

[21] In claiming this I do not mean to deny that there may be some innate constraints on word meanings. However, for ease of exposition, it will do no harm to ignore this possibility.

Second, as I have argued earlier (8.7), if a person's concept "borrows" its reference—a common occurrence nicely captured by Putnam's talk of "the social division of labor" (1975: 227–8)—then its meaning is partly explained by the conventional meaning of the public word that lends the reference.

Third, and more important, consider why we are theoretically interested in language in the first place. I have argued that we are interested in it because linguistic expressions play a certain extraordinarily important role in our lives (8.5). That role is as a guide to thoughts, thoughts which explain behavior, serve as our main source of information about the world, and perhaps have other functions as well (8.1). *The property of a linguistic expression that enables it to perform its important role is its largely conventional meaning.* It is because it has that meaning that it is so worthwhile to produce and so readily understood. That meaning is constituted by conventional word meanings and a syntax that is conventional to a considerable extent. On hearing an utterance, a person who participates in the conventions it involves can, with the help of pragmatic abilities that determine indexical references and remove ambiguities, immediately grasp the thought or message that the utterance expresses. It is in virtue of those largely conventional properties that the utterance is such a quick and effective guide to the speaker's thought. Our theoretical interest in language is in explaining the nature of these largely conventional properties that enable language to play this guiding role.[22]

Finally, the fourth way in which conventional meaning is important emerges in the discussion of claim (iii) to which I now turn. According to this claim, communication does not require that a person shares a meaning with another nor that the other's meaning is discoverable. The position I argue for in *Coming to Our Senses* (1996) is at odds with this. According to that position it is, *as a matter of fact*, common for people to share thought meanings and utterance meanings. These shared meanings are ascribed by attitude ascriptions for our semantic purposes of explaining behavior and being guided to reality. Because there is an "intimate link", sometimes an identity, between the meaning ascribed and a meaning of the content sentence of the ascription, ascribing meaning in this usual way *requires* the ascriber and the ascribee to, near enough, share a meaning. The efficacy of using thought ascriptions to serve those semantic purposes *requires* that thought meanings be both discoverable and widely shared. The communication of thoughts by language is certainly *possible* without shared utterance meanings—think of many cases where speaker meaning diverges from conventional meaning—but the efficacy of using language as evidence of thought meanings *requires* that utterance meanings be widely shared, as we have in effect noted in the last paragraph. Finally, the importance of shared meanings is nicely demonstrated by a type of misunderstanding: people take themselves to share a meaning but they are wrong, often with disastrous consequences.

---

[22] So "convention-based semantics" does not lack motivation; cf. Laurence 1996: 270.

If all this is right, claim (iv) is largely mistaken. First, linguistics should not be primarily concerned with idiolects. The concern should be, and I think is, with the meanings of linguistic expressions, hence their syntactic properties, that are *shared* in the idiolects of a group of people, shared largely because the meanings are conventional in that group but also, in the case of syntactic properties, perhaps partly because they are innate. Although the idiolects of two members of a group, *X* and *Y*, could in principle be the same, they are obviously in fact always a bit different. But any meaning that *X*'s idiolect does not share with *Y*'s will typically be shared with the idiolect of someone else, *Z*, and many others. The concern of linguistics should be with meanings shared between the idiolects of *X* and *Y*, other meanings shared between the idiolects of *X* and *Z*, and so on. For, it is because of these shared meanings that the expressions play their important role of making people's thoughts accessible to others in communication. And it is because the meanings play this role that explaining them is so theoretically interesting. Insofar as an idiolect does not share meanings with any other idiolect it is of little linguistic interest (although it may be of medical or psychological interest). This yields my *sixth major conclusion*: the primary concern in linguistics should not be with idiolects but with linguistic expressions that share meanings in idiolects.

Second, the dismissal of concern with "a common language" like English seems overblown, at least. The members of any group that share a meaning of one linguistic expression tend to share meanings of a vast number of others and it is convenient, on the basis of this, to follow the custom of classifying sets of these expressions with shared meanings as English, Spanish, and so on. The classification is bound to be a bit vague but no more so than many scientifically appropriate ones. And such classifications *seem* to be useful in linguistics, for linguistics books and articles are replete with them.[23] Are these classifications mere manners of speaking that can be paraphrased away when the serious linguistic work is to be done? I think not: they are necessary for the linguist *to identify what she is talking about, to identify the subject matter.* For, the subject matter is the shared meanings and syntactic properties of linguistic expressions *in a certain group of people.* To identify this subject matter she has to identify the

---

[23] Thus, picking four books almost at random from my shelves I found the following. (i) The first few pages of Haegeman's GB textbook (1994) have many uses of "English" to classify shared meanings. Then "English" is compared with "Italian"; for example, "In Italian a subject of a subordinate clause can be moved to the main clause domain across the overt conjunction *che,* corresponding to *that*; in English this is not possible" (p. 20). And then with Spanish and French (p. 23). And so on throughout the book. (ii) A book following the generative approach is called "English Syntax" (Baker 1995). (iii) A long article, "X-bar Theory and Case Theory" (Webelhuth 1995b) is full of references to various languages (and a language group); for example, "English", "German" (p. 40), "Icelandic" (p. 50), "French" (p. 51), "the Australian aboriginal language Warlpiri" (p. 65), "Japanese" (p. 66), "Arabic" (p. 76), "Welsh" (p. 78), "Breton" (p. 78), "Hindi" (p. 80), and "Romance" (p. 81). (iv) Early in Chomsky's Managua Lectures we find: "These sentences illustrate a certain feature of Spanish not shared with such similar languages as Italian" (Chomsky 1988: 12); "Here we observe a difference between English and Spanish" (p. 13).

group. Mostly the group can be identified well enough with a term like 'English' but sometimes we need a less precise term like 'Romance' and sometimes a more precise one like 'Australian–English' or 'the Somerset dialect of English'. A "sociopolitical dimension" does occasionally intrude into such classifications but the intrusion can be resisted by linguists; for example, a linguist may think that, for almost all expressions, there is no theoretical point to the politically inspired division of Serbo-Croatian into Serbian and Croatian and can simply refuse to go along (unless she is a Serb or a Croat). In any case, the point is not that linguistics should be focusing on expressions in, say, Italian rather than Romance, or in, say, English rather than *x*-English for various values of '*x*'. (And the point is certainly not about "who gets to own" a term like 'English'.) The point is that the primary focus should be on linguistic expressions that share meanings in the idiolects of a group of people and so the groups will have to be identified one way or another. All linguistic generalizations, save those of UG that cover *all* expressions, must make use of these identifications. So these identifications are important.

This concludes my discussion of Chomsky's puzzling claims (i) to (iv). I turn finally to some rather startling claims that have been made recently by Georges Rey. These claims are strikingly at odds with the views I have presented in this section. I will develop my views further by contrasting them with Rey's claims.

10.6   REY ON "THE INTENTIONAL INEXISTENCE OF LANGUAGE"

Rey begins by noting:

It would seem to be a commonplace that people, when they talk, produce tokens of such things as words, sentences, morphemes, phonemes and phones—I'll call tokens of all such types, "Standard Linguistic Entities" ("SLE"s). Part and parcel of this commonplace would be the presumption ... that these entities can be identified with some sorts of *acoustic* phenomena, e.g., wave patterns in space and time.   (Rey 2006: 237)[24]

He correctly observes that this view has been repeatedly challenged by linguists over the years, and undertakes to defend what he takes to be the hypothesis implicit in the challenge, what he calls a "*folie à deux*" view. This view arises out of the following negative picture of SLEs:

the human ability to speak natural languages is based on the existence of a special faculty that includes a system for the intended production and recovery of SLEs. To a first approximation, instructions issue from speakers' phonological systems to produce certain

---

[24] He wrongly cites Devitt and Sterelny (1987: 59) as an example of this view. In the passage cited we are talking about the sounds and inscriptions that *realize* SLE's. We emphatically do not think that SLEs—for example, phones—can be *identified* with a sound type: we do not think that a sound token is an SLE simply in virtue of its overt physical properties. On this see our later discussion (ch. 13) of Saussure.

SLEs, and these instructions cause various motions in their articulatory systems, which in turn produce various wave-forms in the air. These wave-forms turn out, however, not to reliably correspond to the SLEs specified in the instructions. ... Indeed, were SLE tokens actually to exist, it would be something of an accident. Their existence is completely inessential to the success of normal communication and to the needs of linguistic theory.... the apparent objects ... are best regarded as (in Franz Brentano's 1874/1973 phrase) "intentional inexistents": "things" that we *think about*, but that (we often know very well) don't actually exist, such as Santa Claus and Zeus. (pp. 239–40)

So Rey has two conclusions. First, he has the antirealist conclusion that, apart perhaps for a few accidents, the world does not really contain linguistic entities, entities with the usual range of linguistic properties including, of course, conventional meanings in a language.[25] We have encountered this antirealism before: it was the second doubt about my view that the linguistic task concerns linguistic reality not psychological reality (2.4). Second, Rey concludes that language does not need such entities to play its role and hence these entities are irrelevant to the theory of language. For, that theory isn't really about any acoustic phenomena in space-time. This conclusion stands opposed, of course, to my claims about the theoretical interest of explaining the conventional meanings of such acoustic phenomena (8.5, 10.5).

This is not the place to attempt a full response to Rey's arguments for these conclusions. My main concern is to show why I reject the conclusions. Still, I shall briefly indicate the lines of my response to his arguments.

(i) My response to his argument that the various *syntactic* properties of SLEs cannot be regarded as properties of the acoustic stream would build on the following ideas. The argument shows that the linguistic structure of an utterance is not obvious and superficial. But this structural property is relational not intrinsic and relational properties are *typically* not obvious or superficial. Yet objects really have relational properties; for example, some objects really are paperweights, moons, echidnas, Australians, and so on. Sometimes, it is easy to tell that an object has a certain relational property because that property is well correlated with superficial properties. This makes it quite easy to tell an echidna, but not an Australian (if she keeps her mouth shut). And it makes it quite easy to tell many English adverbs, the ones that end in 'ly'. It can also be easy to tell that an object has a certain relational property if learning to identify the object involves learning to identify it as having that property. This makes it quite easy to identify the other English adverbs; identification comes with word recognition. One way or another, it is quite easy to tell the explicit structural properties

[25] Several conversations and the following comment from an anonymous reviewer of Devitt 2006 make me wonder if this sort of antirealism is common among linguists: "The sound waves produced by a speaker, or the gestures of an ASL user, or the ink marks of a text, understood as environmental features, have no linguistic properties whatsoever, not lexical, not phonological, not syntactic, not semantic."

of utterances although sometimes hard to tell the implicit ones. But utterances still really have both (9.5).

(ii) My response to his argument that the various *phonological* properties of SLEs cannot be regarded as properties of the acoustic stream would build on the following ideas. The argument shows that no naïve brute–physical account of the relation between sounds and phonemes is possible. Phonology shows that there are many complicated ways in which sounds can instantiate a phoneme, including relations to other sounds; and that a sound may be able to instantiate more than one phoneme.[26] Similarly, there are many complicated ways in which inscriptions can instantiate a letter; and so on for other linguistic media. But this does not show that the sounds, inscriptions, etc. do not instantiate SLEs. Quite the contrary. The property of being Australian is instantiated by a vast variety of physical forms; for example, the forms of the capitalist Rupert Murdoch, the runner Cathy Freeman, the horse Phar Lap, the city of Sydney, a bottle of Penfolds Grange, and the many forms of the saying "No worries, mate". The property of being the word 'cat' is instantiated by a much smaller variety of physical forms, a variety of sounds, inscriptions in many different fonts and handwritings, and so on. Just as all the former instantiations really are Australian, all the latter really are the word 'cat'. And note that just as some things do not count as Australian, some things do not count as the word 'cat'.[27]

Turn now to Rey's conclusions. He thinks that the intentional inexistents that he identifies with SLEs have the usual linguistic properties but that the actual entities—particular sounds, inscriptions, etc.—that we would ordinarily think of as SLEs lack these properties, including conventional meanings. *From my perspective*, if these entities really lacked conventional meanings they could still have speaker and audience meanings (and perhaps literal meanings). We would then be in a prelinguistic state, a state analogous to that of a foreigner in a country where everyone speaks a language that is totally alien to her. Communication would be possible, but hard and *very* elementary, pretty much limited to conveying the crudest messages about food, drink, sex, and shelter. It would depend on the "natural meaning" of signs—of 'grrhh', play actings, and the like—and a great deal of insight into other minds. (One thinks immediately of the discussion in Bennett 1976.) If that were indeed the situation, there would be no theoretical point to attributing a speaker meaning to the signs produced: we

[26] "In natural speech, properties of the acoustic signal associated with one phoneme often overlap or co-occur with the properties of adjacent segments ... Researchers have been unable to find invariant sets of acoustic features or properties that correspond uniquely to individual linguistic units." (Nygaard and Pisoni 1995: 65–6)

[27] I can't resist noting that worries about the physical realization of phones led to the metaphysical disaster of Saussurian structuralism, hence to the metaphysical catastrophe of post-structuralism (Devitt and Sterelny 1999: ch. 13). Antirealism seems to be an occupational hazard of phonology. Rey is at pains to resist this hazard, distinguishing what he takes to be the unreality of SLEs from the reality of, e.g., automobiles.

might as well simply talk of the contents of the thoughts and the intentions to express them using those signs. Note that this is not to say, as presumably Rey would say, that the signs do not *have* speaker meanings—for we can say that they have speaker meanings *in virtue of* being the expression of those thoughts—but simply that there is no theoretical interest in their having them.

From my perspective, then, if Rey were right we would be in this "primitive" situation for communication and theory. Contrast this situation with the actual situation, considering communication first. The actual situation is obviously very different from the primitive one as, of course, Rey would agree. Rather than being hard and elementary, communication is actually easy and extraordinarily sophisticated, conveying complicated messages about a limitless variety of topics; as Quine says, about "tables, people, molecules, light rays, retinas, air waves, prime numbers, infinite classes, joy and sorrow, good and evil" (1966: 215). So, how does Rey think such communication is possible given that there are no SLEs? On his view, what is going on that saves us from being in the primitive situation? This is where he appeals to his *folie à deux* hypothesis:

> when [the wave-forms] impinge on the auditory system of an appropriate hearer, this hearer's phonological system will be able to make an extremely good guess about *the intentional content* of the speaker's instructions, not about any actual SLEs, which, *ex hypothesi*, never actually got uttered. Indeed, this sort of guessing in general is so good, and the resulting perceptual illusion so vivid, that it goes largely unnoticed, and speakers and hearers alike take themselves to be producing and hearing the SLEs themselves. It is in this way that it's a kind of *folie à deux* (or *à n*, for the n speakers of a common language): the speaker has the illusion of producing an SLE that the hearer has the illusion of hearing, with however the happy result that the hearer is usually able to determine precisely what the speaker intended to utter.   (2006: 239–40)

Despite all this illusion the "happy result" is achieved because the hearer makes "an extremely good guess". Something has gone very wrong here.

On my view, there is only a small need for guesswork in communication because, normally, the conventional meaning of an expression in the linguistic community of the speaker and hearer provides a rich clue to the speaker's thought. That clue is often not sufficient, of course: the hearer has to determine the reference of indexicals and remove ambiguities. These pragmatic skills (about which we shall say more in section 11.8) require insight into other minds but seldom anything that is appropriately called "guesswork" because the conventional meaning gives the hearer such a big start in understanding. That big start is precisely what Rey removes. If the sounds and inscriptions people produce do not have conventional meanings grasped by all parties, how could communication be so effective? We can see, of course, how it can *sometimes* take place without any conventions—consider the primitive situation, for example—but how would the rich and complex communications that dominate our daily lives be possible? On Rey's view, communication seems to rest on *miraculous* guesses.

Rey would surely object that I have overlooked something crucial to communication in the actual situation that distinguishes that situation from the primitive one. On his *folie* view, the "extremely good guess" is made by a hearer who shares "a common langue" with the speaker. This raises a number of questions.

First, what makes the languages of the speaker and hearer a common, or the same, language? For Rey, the answer is that the linguistic objects of thought for speaker and hearer are the same *intentional* objects. We wonder, then, what makes them the same in the absence of any *actual* objects that are the same. This is, of course, another example of the old problem of "intentional identity", the problem of explaining a common focus of thought where there is nothing at the focus; see the delightful Geach 1967 for a discussion. But it would seem to be a particularly difficult example.

Second, consider the significance of the intentional identity of linguistic objects to communication on Rey's view. On anyone's view, successful communication requires that the message intended by the speaker be (near enough) the same as the message understood by the hearer. On my view, this matching of messages is usually and largely achieved because the superficial properties of the physical entities (sounds, inscription, etc.) that make up the message-conveying SLE provide excellent clues to the hearer about the SLE's conventional meaning, a meaning that largely constitutes the message intended by the speaker. The superficial properties provide those clues, of course, because there is a conventional regularity of using such an entity with those properties to express a meaning that is part of the message. So, contrary to Rey's claim (2006: 251), linguistic properties do play a causal role.[28] In contrast, the matching of messages is achieved on Rey's view by the intentional object that is the speaker's SLE being (near enough) the same as the intentional object that is the hearer's. *That* is the significance of the intentional identity. But then how is this happy identity achieved? Clearly the superficial properties of the physical entity—the entity that is the SLE on my view—must provide the hearer with clues to the speaker's intentional object. How could the superficial properties do that? Not by being excellent clues to the conventional meaning of the physical entity, as I think they are, because that entity has no conventional meaning on Rey's view. We are still left with a miracle: the success of hearers at guessing speakers' intentional objects without having the benefit of conventions that relate physical entities to meanings. And we are left with the closely related miracle of all parties to a successful communication being under the *same* illusion about the linguistic properties of a physical entity that has none.

---

[28] This raises two well-known philosophical problems: the problem of properties that are relational not intrinsic having causal powers; and the problem of properties that supervene on others having causal powers. Linguistic properties are both relational and supervening. But then so are almost all properties outside physics and even, I'm told, some in physics. Linguistic properties are in very good company.

Finally, how did speaker and hearer come to speak the same language? Some of a person's language may well be innate but she learns a good deal of it. On my view, this learning is a matter of acquiring conventions of a language as a causal result of experiencing the regular exercise of the conventions in a community. Once again linguistic properties have a causal role. A consequence of this learning process is that a person, more or less, shares a language with others in the community. But this story depends on what Rey denies, the existence of linguistic entities with conventional meanings. Without those entities, language learning becomes a mystery.[29]

Turn finally to the contrast between our theoretical needs in the primitive situation and in the actual one. In the primitive situation there is no interest in, or point to, attributing meanings to the signs that attempt to convey messages. Rey thinks that this is true in the actual situation too. Indeed he thinks that the actual existence of meaningful linguistic entities is irrelevant to linguistic theory. This is not so. The study of the (largely) conventional meanings of actual linguistic entities, meanings constituted by a (partly) conventional syntax and conventional word meanings, is the concern of linguistic theory. Our theoretical interest in language is in explaining the nature of these conventional meanings that enable language to play such an important role in our lives.

In sum, in response to Rey's argument, I would argue that linguistic entities really exist even though they are relational and even though the one expression can appear in a variety of physical forms. In response to his conclusions, I have argued that it is in virtue of the conventional meanings of linguistic entities that the entities play their extraordinarily important role in communicating messages. It is in virtue of those meanings that a language is acquired. Linguistic properties do play causal roles. If there really weren't any linguistic entities, communication would be miraculous and language learning a mystery. Our theoretical interest in language is in conventional meanings.

10.7 CONCLUSION

The piece of folk wisdom that language expresses thought (LET) leads to the view that conceptual competence is a considerable part of linguistic competence. I argued that this view is not undermined by the well-known dissociation of cognitive impairment and linguistic impairment (10.1). Since conceptual

---

[29] These two paragraphs bear on Laurence's claim (aimed at Devitt and Sterelny 1987) that the shared meaning of an expression could arise from a "coincidence in *literal idiolect meaning*" (1998: 208). Indeed it could and would. But it would be a miracle that such shared meanings played the role that they do in communication if the sharing were not a convention that speakers and hearers participate in. And it would be a mystery how people came to share meanings of so many expressions if not by experiencing the conventions of using those expressions with those meanings. These "coincidences" would cry out for explanation.

competence is in the central processor, it follows from LET that a good deal of linguistic competence is too. The rest of linguistic competence consists in processing competencies for spoken language, written language, and so on. If there is to be a modality-neutral, relatively central, language faculty, it must be found in some commonalities between these modality-specific processing competencies. At first sight, the evidence from brain impairment may seem to support the idea that there are these commonalities and hence a language faculty. I argued that this is misleading and that this evidence counts much more against the existence of a language faculty than for it (10.2). Aside from that, if we move beyond LET to (T)—the view that the structure rules of a person's language are similar to the structure rules of her thought—we should not expect to find the commonalities that would constitute a substantial language faculty because there would not be much for the language faculty to do. I arrived at my second tentative proposal: there is little or nothing to the language faculty (10.3).

Where does Chomsky stand on thoughts and their relation to language? It is surprisingly difficult to say. I offered some reasons for thinking that his stance is very different from the one presented in this part of the book (10.4). I went on to look critically at some claims that Chomsky makes against linguistic regularities and conventions, against the need for shared and discoverable meanings in communication, and in favor of idiolects rather than common languages. I emphasize that it is because of shared conventional meanings in a group that language can play its important role of making the thoughts of each member of the group accessible to the others. This yields my sixth major conclusion: the primary concern in linguistics should not be with idiolects but with linguistic expressions that share meanings in idiolects (10.5). Finally, I consider Rey's view that linguistic objects are merely intentional. I argue, in contrast, that these objects are real parts of the world. And the task of linguistics is to explain the nature of their conventional meanings (10.6).

I argued for (T) and my first tentative proposal in Chapter 9: a language is largely psychologically real in a speaker in that its rules are similar to the structure rules of her thought. If that is correct then the rules of the language will be psychologically real in a robust way. Furthermore, position (T) encourages doubts that the language is psychologically real in any *other* robust way described in section 3.4. It particularly encourages doubts that speakers represent the rules of the language, as required by the Representational Thesis (RT) and positions (i) and (ii). According to position (i), the speaker applies those represented rules in language processing; according to (ii), she uses those representations as data in processing. Yet resorting to represented rules in these ways seems an indirect and inefficient way to solve the problem of translating between an English and a Mentalese sentence with very similar structures. (T) also encourages doubts that the rules of the language are simply embodied processing rules, as required by position (iii), because the rules of the language seem to be the wrong sort of rules to govern the translation process. These doubts remain, although they are less pressing, if we have to settle for the less-committal Representational Theory of Mind (RTM). And I don't think they should disappear even if we have to settle for the almost noncommittal view that language expresses thought (LET).

Aside from these doubts about views of the psychological reality of language, I think (т), perhaps even RTM, should make us a little dubious that the processing rules, whatever they may be, operate on metalinguistic representations of the syntactic and semantic properties of linguistic symbols, as versions (a) of positions on psychological reality require, rather than being directly responsive to those syntactic and semantic properties, as versions (b) require (3.4). Perhaps the move to metalinguistic representations is an inefficient way of handling the translation. Perhaps this is a place to apply Pylyshyn's Razor: representations are not to be multiplied beyond necessity (3.1).

Part I argued for my first major conclusion, that linguistics is not part of psychology. It follows that the truth of a grammar alone provides insufficient reason to suppose that the rules it ascribes to a language are psychologically real in speakers of the language. *A fortiori*, it provides insufficient reason to suppose that those rules are *represented (encoded)* in the speakers, and hence insufficient reason to adopt RT as part of a theory of linguistic competence. The supposed truth of the grammar leaves the issue of the psychological reality of language fairly open. In Part III we found no evidence for RT, and hence for positions (ı) and (ıı), in various "philosophical" arguments: the arguments from the rejection of behaviorism, from the folk truism that the competent speaker knows her language, and from the role of linguistic intuitions. We had thus begun the task of establishing my second major conclusion: there is no significant evidence for RT and, given what else we know, it is implausible. And I claimed to have established my third major conclusion: Speakers' linguistic intuitions do not reflect information supplied by the language faculty. They are immediate and fairly unreflective empirical central-processor responses to linguistic phenomena. They are not the main evidence for grammars. The focus of Part IV was on thoughts and led to two more major conclusions: the fourth one that the psychological reality of language should be investigated from a perspective on thought; and the fifth one that thought has a certain priority to language ontologically, explanatorily, temporally, and in theoretical interest. Guided by those conclusions, a case was presented for (т), the view that the structure rules of a speaker's language are similar to the structure rules of her thought. In this way her language is largely psychologically real in her. That was my first tentative proposal. My second was that there is little or nothing to the language faculty.

It is time now to see if there is any evidence for RT and positions (ı) and (ıı) in the psycholinguistic studies of language use and language acquisition. And it is time to see what light those studies cast on other positions on psychological reality. It is clear that the fate of all positions rests heavily on the psycholinguistic evidence. It is interesting to note, in contrast, that the fate of position (т) rests very little on this evidence. The psychological assumptions that do nearly all the work in the case for (T) are the view that language expresses thought (LET), the Language-of-Thought Hypothesis (LOTH), and the Gricean explanatory priority of thought over language. These assumptions are agreeably independent of the details of language use and acquisition. Of course, LET is a theory of what language use consists in—the matching of sentences and thoughts for meaning—but our reason for believing it does not come from psycholinguistic discoveries. Our reason comes from our acceptance of thoughts. And we accept thoughts because they successfully explain behavior and guide us to reality. We are drawn to the Gricean priority because it is the best explanation of the relation of thought to language, and to LOTH because it is part of the most promising explanation of thoughts. Neither of these reasons are matters of language use at all.

Named propositions like RTM and LOTH, and views of competence, are all listed in the Glossary, along with the major conclusions and tentative proposals.

Let us now turn to the psycholinguistic evidence.

PART V

LANGUAGE USE AND AQUISITION

11

Language Use

11.1 INTRODUCTION

The aim in this chapter is to assess a range of positions on language use. In the next chapter we will consider language acquisition.

Let us start by recapitulating the possible positions on language use set out in section 3.4, starting with the uncontroversial minimal position:

(M) A competence in a language, and the processing rules that govern its exercise, respect the structure rules of the language: the processing rules of language comprehension take sentences of the language as inputs; the processing rules of language production yield sentences of the language as outputs.

This position is silent on *how* the competence respects the structure rules of the language. In particular, it does not say whether the competence respects those rules because the rules are psychologically real in some way. The remaining positions are not silent on this matter:

(I) The structure rules of the language are also processing rules that are represented in the speaker and applied in language use.

(II) The structure rules of the language are represented and used as data by the processing rules of language use.

(III) The structure rules of the language are also processing rules for language use but the processing rules are not represented.

(IV) Some processing rules for language use are represented but they are largely unlike the structure rules of the language and do not use the structure rules as data.

(V) The processing rules for language use are unrepresented and largely unlike the structure rules of the language.

In Chapter 4, we considered some historically interesting *actual* positions on language use and related them to these possible positions. We started with some tantalizing, and hard to reconcile, remarks by Chomsky, drawn from several writings. We then moved to more detailed positions proposed by Fodor, Bever, and Garrett (1974); Bresnan and Kaplan (1982); Berwick and Weinberg (1984); and Matthews (1991). All of these writers take the grammar of a language to be somehow true of the psychological reality of its speakers. They do not contemplate that the grammar might simply be true of linguistic reality, as urged by the first of my methodological points in section 2.6. All of the writers except Matthews seem to take the Representational Thesis (RT) for granted. So, *that* is the powerful psychological assumption which, according to my second methodological point, they need in taking the grammar to be true of psychological reality. Finally, most of these writers are strikingly at odds with my third methodological point. They do not take the grammar and the theory of competence to be largely independent of each other. Rather, they take each to place heavy constraints on the other. According to my third point, the only limit on the independence of these two theories arises from "the Respect Constraint": a theory of a linguistic competence must posit processing rules that respect the structure rules of the language, and a grammar must posit structure rules that are respected by the competence and its processing rules. Because of this, the justification of the grammar and the justification of the theory of competence are partly dependent on each other. But in all other ways the two theories are independent.

Fodor, Bever, and Garrett made it clear that early theories of how a grammar should be incorporated into a theory of language use were wrong. As a result, grammatical rules had a reduced role in the theory of language use in the decade or so that followed. Still, as Pylyshyn pointed out (1991: 232), and the above-mentioned writers demonstrate, the orthodox Chomskian belief that grammatical rules play a central role in the theory of language use remained.[1] However, the discussion of language processing in sections 11.7 to 11.8 indicate that this belief has weakened in subsequent years. The psycholinguistic interest in trying to find the rules of the language embodied in a speaker's mind seems to have steadily diminished without, so far as I can see, much explicit acknowledgement that it has;[2] the interest is simply withering away.[3] Psycholinguists mostly now approach the study of language processing as if it were, except for the Respect Constraint, independent of grammars. And so they should.

The question of whether or not the rules of the language are embodied in the mind is one of the two that dominate positions (i) to (v). (i) to (iii) say that they are; (iv) and (v) have no such commitment. Rules might be embodied by being

---

[1] Consider also the following: "Linguistic theory is a theory of native speakers' underlying knowledge of their language ... . The goal of psycholinguistics is to explain how linguistic knowledge is acquired and how it is mentally represented and used to actually produce and perceive language" (Frazier 1995: 2–3).

[2] Kathryn Bock is an exception. She concludes an article with some remarks very much in the spirit of the third methodological point: "It should be clear by now that production theory is a theory of using language, not an account of how language is represented, and that linguistic frameworks whose province is the static organization of language knowledge are unlikely to provide the theoretical machinery for explaining how that knowledge is deployed in time." (1995: 207)

[3] Avery Andrews has drawn my attention to the near disappearance of concern for the psychological reality of rules in discussions of LFG (lexical–function grammar) even though that concern was the initial motivation for this approach to grammars, as noted earlier (4.4).

represented or they might be simply embodied (3.1). This leads to the other dominating question: Are some processing rules represented in the speaker? (i), (ii), and (iv) say that they are; (iii) and (v) say that they are not. A distinction between rules that govern "rational–causal" operations and rules that govern "brute–causal" operations (3.3) led to another question and to two versions of (iii) and (v): Do some processing rules operate on metalinguistic representations of the syntactic and semantic properties of linguistic items? Version (a) says that some do. Version (b) says that none do: the rules are directly responsive to those properties of linguistic items; the process is fairly brute–causal and associationist. These three questions will be the concern of this chapter.

A consequence of positions (i) and (ii) would be that RT was correct. We have so far found no evidence for this thesis. My *first*, and main, goal in this chapter is to argue that language use provides no persuasive evidence for RT and that RT is implausible. This is the most important step in arguing for the second major conclusion of this book: there is no significant evidence for RT and, given what else we know, it is implausible. Hence, (i) and (ii) should be rejected. The final step in arguing for this conclusion is in the next chapter on language acquisition. Much of the argument in the present chapter against RT counts also against position (iv), the view that processing rules other than the structure rules of the language are represented.

The popularity of RT can often seem overwhelming. Still, the following quotes show that I am not alone in my doubts about it. Stabler has this to say about the two positions on language processing that involve this thesis: of (i) he says that it is "not supported by any available evidence"; of (ii), that it is "not supported by available data either" (1983: 395). Roger Schank and Lawrence Birnbaum make a more sweeping claim covering (iii) as well: that among psychologists "even the strongest partisans of generative linguistics" are convinced that "there is no evidence that people make use, in comprehension or generation, of the kinds of rule devised by generative linguistics to describe linguistic phenomena" (1984: 221). Pylyshyn claims that, to his knowledge, "there have been no arguments that the rules of language ... are explicitly encoded" (1991: 247).[4] Matthews says that "nothing, so far as I can see, suggests that ... grammars are internally represented by speaker/hearers, if by this one means explicitly represented or tokened" (1991: 187). My main goal is to add to the case against RT.

Positions (i) and (ii) take the structure rules of the language to be involved in processing by being represented. According to position (iii), the structure rules are otherwise psychologically real: they govern processing without being encoded. I have already raised doubts about this (2.6, 3.2). My *second* goal is to cast further doubts on this and hence give support to (v): the processing rules are largely unlike the structure rules.

---

[4] Pylyshyn seems to have overlooked his own earlier argument to this effect (1980a: 121; 1980b: 163). This argument is address in section 11.4, point 5, below.

To reject (ɪ) to (ɪɪɪ) is not, of course, to deny that the structure rules are embodied in the speaker's mind at all. Indeed, if (т) is true these rules are similar to the structure rules of thought and so, to an extent, obviously embodied. And they will even be relevant to language processing because the processing rules will *operate on* the syntactic properties of thoughts determined by those structure rules. Still the structure rules will not *be* embodied processing rules. The rules will characterize the structure of the thoughts that are involved in the processing, they will not govern the processing from thoughts to language and from language to thoughts. If (ɪ) to (ɪɪɪ) are rejected, and we are to save the orthodox Chomskian view that grammatical rules play a more central role in language use than is provided by the minimal (м), then I think that (т) is the only hope.

My *third* goal concerns the metalinguistic representations of the syntactic and semantic properties of linguistic entities. According to version (a), the processing rules operate on these representations; according to version (b), they do not. If RT is true then version (a) must be but even if RT is false, (a) might be true: processing might be a rational information flow even if the rules governing it are not represented. (a) seems to be the received view even among many who reject, or do not clearly hold, RT.[5] My goal is to cast doubt on this view, trying to make (b) seem plausible. I conclude that we have good, although very far from conclusive, reasons to think that the speedy automatic part of language processing is indeed fairly brute–causal associationist.

My discussion will be guided by the fourth major conclusion: the psychological reality of language should be investigated from a perspective on thought. And it will be guided as always by Pylyshyn's Razor: representations are not to be multiplied beyond necessity (3.1).

11.2 "THE ONLY THEORY IN TOWN"

It seems that many linguists are influenced toward RT by an inference to the best explanation, or abduction, about language use: RT is thought to provide "the only theory in town". The abduction runs along the following lines. We can explain language comprehension if we see it as a rational process of testing hypotheses about a person's speech input. *And there is no other way to explain it.* On this view, if the psycholinguistic evidence to be considered later showed that a certain linguistic rule was playing a role in this process (and so was psychologically real), it would have to be represented. For hypothesis testing *is* a process of testing one representation against others.[6] (Note that this argument concerns language comprehension. It is striking that the analogous argument for production does not have any appeal.)

---

[5] See Frazier 1995 for example.

[6] I have often heard such arguments but have been unable to find a clear case in the literature. For a case that comes close, see J. A. Fodor 2001: 113–15.

In recent years, abduction has come in for considerable criticism from philosophers of science, particularly those who are dubious of scientific realism. This criticism seems to me unwarranted (1997a: 111–13; 2005c). So I think that many abductive inferences are good. But, of course, not all are good. And the inference from the evidence of language use to the conclusion that this use involves representations of the structure rules of the language—RT—seems to me an example of one that is not good. Indeed, I think that it is really rather bad.

My judgment here cannot be supported by appealing to an algorithm for deciding which abductions are good for no such algorithm is available. Still, we do know some factors that should influence our decisions.

One thing that worries people about abductive arguments is that they can seem *too easy*. Whenever we have some previously unexplained phenomena, we can easily come up with *some* putative explanation if we do not operate under any constraints; thus, if we are prepared to tolerate absurdity, we can appeal to gremlins, acts of God, or Martian invaders. So, criterion (A) of a good abduction is that it involves *a good explanation*. As is well known, it is hard to say much about what makes an explanation good. But goodness requires at least two things (A1). The explanation must not only not be absurd but it must be plausible given what else we know, it must be *plausible relative to background knowledge*. A corollary of this requirement is that if none of our candidate explanations meet this requirement, then we should *not* accept an abduction involving the best of this implausible bunch. Rather than such a rush to judgment we should follow a course of action the virtues of which are sadly underappreciated: we should *suspend judgment and keep looking*. (A2) Next, a good explanation must have *an appropriate level of detail*: if the explanation posits x as the cause of y, it must say enough about *the mechanism by which x causes y* to not leave this mysterious; a wave of the hand is not sufficient.[7] If we do not have the details we need, we should, once again, suspend judgment.

Criterion (B) of a good abduction is that the explanation it features must be better than any *actual* alternative or even any alternative that is *likely*, given what we already know. Attention to likely alternatives is important. Even if the featured explanation does not face any worked-out alternatives, we may have some ideas for alternatives that, given our background knowledge, seem promising. Until those ideas have been explored sufficiently to be set aside, we should suspend judgment on the abduction. (This is not to be confused with the extreme skeptical view that we should not embrace an abduction until *all possible* alternative explanations have been set aside. We need wait only to set aside alternatives that are likely, given what we already know.)

---

[7] Berkeley rightly criticizes an abduction for Locke's "representative realism" on this score. The abduction is that the existence of a material world causing and resembling our ideas provides the best explanation of those ideas. Berkeley points out that we do not have any idea of the mechanism by which a material body can cause a resembling spiritual idea (1710: sec. 19).

I shall argue that explanations of language use that appeal to RT do not meet *any* of these criteria. Concerning (A1), these explanations are surely not absurd but I shall argue that they are implausible given what else we know. Concerning (A2), the explanations of language use involving RT that have been provided so far are singularly lacking in details. Fodor, Bever, and Garrett (1974) showed how early attempts to provide such details failed badly (4.3) and the situation has not improved significantly since. Indeed, given the consensus that, at this stage, we know very little about language processing,[8] we are surely not in a position to give a general explanation of this processing, whether involving RT or not, that is sufficiently precise, complete, and successful to be an appropriate candidate for a good abduction. Chomsky has dismissed the view that linguistic competence is "a set of dispositions" as "merely a promissory note" (1980b: 5). But all views, including the view that this competence involves representation of the linguistic rules, are really just promissory notes at this time. Concerning (B), there is a range of likely alternative explanations of language use that need to be investigated before we should embrace an explanation appealing to RT. That explanation takes the processes of language use to be highly "rational". The likely alternatives take it to be less so, perhaps not even rational at all. There is no basis for expecting that the best explanation of language use is likely to involve RT. Indeed, the evidence suggests strongly that the best explanation is unlikely to.

So I will be arguing that positions (i) and (ii) are implausible. What else can we hope to discover at this point about language use? Not that one of the other positions is the conclusion of a persuasive abduction. The best we can hope for, given our present level of ignorance, is an assessment of the likelihood that a position will, or will not, be the conclusion of a persuasive *future* abduction.

Criterion (A1) emphasizes that abductions are judged against a background of what we already know. In the next section I shall summarize what we already know about linguistic competence, which should guide us in seeking a good abduction about language use. In the following three sections, 11.4–11.6, further background will be introduced and *preliminary* assessments will be made of the likelihood of a future abduction supporting each of the various positions. This assessment will be made prior to any consideration of the psycholinguistic evidence from language use itself. The idea is to see what direction seems promising for the explanation of language use given what else we know and don't know about other matters. I shall be mainly concerned to demonstrate

---

[8] Some expressions of this consensus: "Very little is known about how [a device for sentence comprehension] might operate, though I guess that, if we started now and worked very hard, we might be able to build one in five hundred years or so" (J. A. Fodor 1975: 167); "we know so little about the actual machinery engaged in human sentence parsing" (Berwick and Weinberg 1984: 35); the relation between the grammar and the parser "remains to be discovered" (Pritchett 1988: 539); "we know very little about the computational machinery involved in language processing" (Matthews 1991: 190–1).

the *prima facie* unlikelihood of support for positions (i) and (ii) and hence for the idea that RT has a place in the explanation of language use: not only is it not now part of the conclusion of a good abduction it is unlikely to be so in the future. I am also concerned to throw doubt on position (iv) and the idea that language use involves *any* represented rules at all, and on position (iii) and the idea that linguistic rules are also embodied processing rules. These considerations against (i) to (iv) are considerations *for* position (v). In section 11.6 I will present some considerations in favor of version (b) of (v), in favor of a radical brute–causal view of processing. Finally, in sections 11.7 and 11.8, I turn to the psycholinguistic evidence on language use. My discussion of this is inevitably very brief but it is still, I think, enough to show that the evidence at this point does not give any reason to modify these preliminary assessments of how the future is likely to go.

So my focus will be on whether, given our background knowledge, positions are likely to be part of the future. But if they aren't—and I shall be arguing that (i) to (iv) aren't—then they shouldn't be part of the present.

11.3   BACKGROUND ON LINGUISTIC COMPETENCE

Various views of linguistic competence have emerged to form the framework for theorizing about language use. These views vary in the amount of their theoretical commitment. I shall present them in order of increasing commitment.

The most theory-neutral view of competence in a spoken language is that it is the ability to produce and understand sentences with the sounds and meanings of that language. We then moved from this minimal view to increasingly theory-laden views. (a) Acceptance of the folk view that language expresses thought (LET; 8.2), led to the view that the competence is the ability to use a sound of the language to express a thought with the meaning that the sound has in the language in the context of utterance; and the ability (together with some pragmatic abilities) to assign to a sound a thought with the meaning that the sound has in the language in the context of utterance. So competence in the language *requires* a certain conceptual competence, the competence to have thoughts with the meanings expressible in the language (8.3). (b) Acceptance of the Representational Theory of Mind (RTM) led to an even more theory-laden view: competence is the ability to *translate* back and forth between mental representations and the sounds of the language. So competence in the language *requires* the competence to think mental representations with meanings expressible in the language (9.1). (c) Acceptance of the Language-of-Thought Hypothesis (LOTH; 9.2) adds still more theory: competence is the ability to translate back and forth between mental *sentences* and the sounds of the language. So competence in the language *requires* the competence to think mental sentences with meanings expressible in the language (9.3).

On views (a) to (c), conceptual competence is the essential core of linguistic competence and enjoys a certain ontological priority over it. On (b) the required conceptual competence is competence in *some* system of mental representations, perhaps a map-like one, perhaps a language-like one, or perhaps something else altogether; on (c), it is competence in a language-like *Mentalese*. So our view of the nature of thoughts becomes central to our theory of linguistic competence, and hence to our stance on the psychological reality issue. In particular, LOTH makes it plausible that the structure rules of a person's Mentalese are similar to those of her public language, position (τ), and hence that the rules of her public language will be largely present in her mind even if they are not processing rules for language use. The processing rules will *operate on* the syntactic properties of mental and public representations even if the rules that determine the nature of those syntactic properties are not among the processing rules.

We should note that just as the theory of competence in a system of linguistic representations—a language—should not be conflated with the theory of that system, the theory of competence in a system of mental representations should not be conflated with the theory of that system (Ch. 2). Thus the theory of mental representations is the theory of their meanings, of the properties in virtue of which those representations, as parts of thoughts, play a role in explaining behavior and informing us about reality. The theory of the competence is the theory of the ability to produce such representations, the ability to think.

If we assume LOTH and view (c) then we can say something about the nature of Mentalese competence, reflecting what we said earlier about the nature of Mentalese meaning on the same assumption (9.5). First, Mentalese competence is complex. One part is syntactic competence. That consists in an ability to combine Mentalese words of the various syntactic categories into the sentences of Mentalese; for example, the ability to combine <Reagan> and <wrinkled> to form the sentence <Reagan is wrinkled>; and the ability to form a sentence like <All police are corrupt> using the quantifier <all>. The other part of Mentalese competence is lexical competence, a competence with mental words. We need to distinguish basic words, probably including the mental correlates of proper names and natural kind terms, from the nonbasic ones. Competence with a basic word must consist in having thoughts involving that word that are directly linked, presumably causally linked, in the appropriate way to the word's referent. I think (1996), unlike Jerry Fodor (1987), that some words will surely not be basic but rather covered by a description theory; <bachelor> is a likely example. Competence with such a word will consist in associating it inferentially to others; for example, associating <bachelor> with <adult>, <unmarried>, and <male>.

Next, consider competence in the spoken language. Syntactic competence is the ability to translate back and forth between the syntactic structures of the sounds of the language and structures of mental representations. And lexical competence is the ability to translate back and forth between the words of the language and mental words.

If we do not assume LOTH but rather assume that mental representations are map-like then we would, of course, have to give a different account of conceptual competence and, as a result, a different account of linguistic competence. It is hard to see what account we could come up with just as it is hard to see how we could explain the meanings that these map-like representations would be required to have (9.2). And if we remain more neutral altogether, resting with RTM, or even just LET, we can make little further progress at this point in explaining linguistic competence.

It is worth noting that acceptance of the relatively uncontroversial LET alone has a significant consequence for the place of RT. For, according to LET, our linguistic competence is partly, perhaps even largely, constituted by a certain conceptual competence: a person cannot match sounds and thoughts for meaning unless she has the capacity to have thoughts with those meanings (8.3). This downplays the language faculty, as we have already noted (10.2), and thereby downplays the significance of RT. Even if competence in a natural language does partly consist in representing the rules of the language and making use of those representations somehow in language processing, an important part of it consists in something altogether different: the capacity to think certain thoughts.

Finally, consider the task in language *comprehension*. Given LET, the task is to pick up clues of the syntactic and semantic properties of the input so that it can be matched with an appropriate thought. Given RTM, the task is to find clues to a correct translation of the linguistic input. Similarly, given LET, the task in language *production* is to select an appropriate linguistic output for the thought. Given RTM, the task is to produce a correct translation of the thought. So, in theorizing about language use, we should not look for more than seems to be required for these tasks.

In what follows I shall always start from the assumption of LOTH and view (c) of competence; that will be my default background. I shall then consider the consequences of replacing this assumption with other views about the nature of thoughts and linguistic competence.

11.4 IMPLAUSIBILITY OF REPRESENTED RULES IN LINGUISTIC COMPETENCE

Against this background, and more to be introduced, let us now begin a preliminary assessment of the likelihood of persuasive future abductions supporting the various positions, particularly positions (i), (ii), and (iv) that involve representations of rules. We shall see that the prospects of such abductions are not promising, given that background, and given the likelihood of abductions to other less representational conclusions.

The considerations I shall present move from relatively "a priori" ones toward more empirical ones. I put most weight on the most empirical of all, the psychology of skills, discussed in the next section. None of these considerations alone comes close to being decisive but the cumulative effect of them seems to me to be fairly telling. And the only-theory-in-town abduction is left looking totally unpersuasive.

1. It is clear that computers run software programs by representing rules and it is clear that computers can use represented rules as data. There are also uncontroversial examples of humans representing rules. We represent the rules of games like chess and baseball. We represent the rules of etiquette and of processions. We represent some of the rules of a foreign language in trying to learn it. And so on. But these uncontroversial examples do not encompass much of human life. And, we should note, a large part of what makes these examples uncontroversial is that we can, and do, *state* the rules. In this respect, a person's relation to the rules of her native language is very different (6.2). Now, of course, the inability of an English speaker to state the rules of English may simply reflect the fact that her representation of rules is in a language module that is largely inaccessible to consciousness. But is there any reason to believe that this *is* a fact? Indeed, is there *any* uncontroversial example of rules being represented in an inaccessible module?[9] According to Stabler, "no [neurophysiological] evidence has been found ... either for linguistic processing or any other cognitive processing" governed by representations of the rules (Stabler 1983: 399). We have noted before that should a rule govern a cognitive process, it could be the case that it governs by being embodied without being represented (3.1). So, where we have evidence that a certain rule does govern, Pylyshyn's Razor demands *further* evidence before we conclude that it does so by being represented; we need further evidence that the rule plays its role like a softwired rule in a general-purpose computer rather than like a hardwired rule in a special-purpose computer. I suggest that there is a striking lack of this further evidence with human cognitive processing. Indeed, as I shall try to demonstrate, the evidence is much more against represented rules than for them.

---

[9] In recent years "the theory–theory" has become a popular explanation of folk psychological judgments; see, for example, many discussions in Davies and Stone 1995. Our minds are thought to contain a representation of a largely true theory of human psychology which we then apply to yield our psychological judgments about one another. The explicit inspiration for this theory of mind is the standard Cartesian explanation of intuitive linguistic judgments: just as those judgments are derived from a representation of a theory of the language so also are the psychological judgments derived from a true psychological theory. I rejected that explanation of linguistic intuitions in Chapter 7. If I am right in this rejection then the theory–theory loses its inspiration. Without that inspiration, it is unlikely that the theory–theory's explanation of psychological judgments will seem appealing. In any case, I think it should be rejected for a similar reason: a more modest explanation is more plausible. A few platitudes like "If x humiliates y then y is likely to hate x" may well be represented and play a role in psychological judgments. But, according to the more modest explanation, these judgments are largely the result of the folk being "hardwired" by nature and nurture to make them intuitively, without reflection or inference, and fairly accurately.

2. Call the processing rules for Oscar's production of (his idiolect of) English, "*P*". So, according to position (I), *P* includes the structure rules of English which are represented and applied in language production. According to position (II), *P* consults a representation of those rules in production. Either position will, of course, guarantee that P *respects* those rules as it must; see (M) (3.4).

Assume LOTH and consider what must happen in a simple case of language production. Oscar intends to express the thought that water is not good to walk on. As a result he moves a mental sentence <Water is not good to walk on> that means *WATER IS NOT GOOD TO WALK ON* into "the Message-Out box". The task of expressing this message is to "translate" that mental sentence into an English sentence with that meaning; for example, into 'Water is not good to walk on': *P* must function as a translation manual. According to (I) and (II) this translation involves the metalinguistic theory of English. How might that theory be brought to bear? The input for the translation task has to be the mental sentence <Water is not good to walk on>. So we have an immediate problem: this is not something that the metalinguistic theory can do anything with at all. For, that theory is a theory of English not Mentalese. So, it can yield syntactic and semantic information about the likes of 'walk' and 'water' but has nothing to say about the likes of <walk> and <water>.

(i) One proposal might be that Oscar has *another* (tacit) metalinguistic theory, a theory of Mentalese. The idea would be that having this theory largely constitutes his competence in Mentalese just as having the earlier theory largely constituted his competence in English. Indeed, if language use requires that Oscar's English competence involves representing its rules, we might expect that language use would also require that his Mentalese competence involves representing its rules. Now this further metalinguistic theory does yield information about <walk> and <water>. The theory of Mentalese could, of course, handle the input, <Water is not good to walk on>, and we can perhaps then imagine how it might be possible for this theory to work with the theory of English to yield the desired translation. For example, the theory of Mentalese supplies Oscar's processor with the information that <water> means *WATER* and the theory of English, that 'water' does too. We can imagine how the processor could combine these two bits of information to conclude that 'water' is the way to translate <water>.

But, of course, this proposal is outlandish and has surely never been made. (Note that Fodor insists that the rules of Mentalese are *not* represented; 1975: 65–6.) A major problem for the proposal becomes obvious when we remember Harman's argument discussed in section 6.2 and ask the question: What language would these metalinguistic theories be in? Suppose that the language were Mentalese (so, on position (I), *P* would be analogous to an English-French dictionary written in English). But then competence in Mentalese could *not* consist in representing its rules because that representation presupposes the competence; we would be caught in a vicious circle. Suppose next that the language was not Mentalese but, say, Metamentalese (so, on position (i), *P* would be analogous to an English-French dictionary written in German). But then what about the competence in Metamentalese? To avoid a regress we must suppose that this competence does not require representing the rules. But then why not suppose this for competence in Mentalese, thus abandoning the proposal?

(ii) Abandoning this hopeless proposal, a much better one suggests itself: *P* takes the mental sentence as input and yields its meaning in some fairly brute–causal way. For example, it takes <water> and yields *WATER*. The metalinguistic theory of English, represented presumably in Mentalese, can then be brought to bear on this meaning, concluding that 'water' is the way to express it.

According to (i) there are two theoretical "middlemen" between Mentalese and English, between <water> and 'water'. (ii) drops the first, the tacit theory of Mentalese. A further proposal leaps to mind: (iii) we should also drop the second, the tacit theory of English. So in language production we go in a fairly brute-causal way from <water> to 'water' without applying any theory of either; the process is not rational but more like an inner transduction or reflex. Of course, (iii) gives RT no role in explaining language production. Yet (iii) seems *prima facie* more plausible than (ii): representing the rules seems an unlikely way to accomplish what the system needs to do. According to (ii) Oscar does not need a representation of Mentalese rules to go from <water> to *WATER*. Why then suppose that we need a representation of English rules to go from *WATER* to 'water'? Pylyshyn's Razor counts against this supposition. Indeed, the Razor even counts against the supposition that *P* must operate on metalinguistic representations of the properties of 'water', it counts against version (a). What use would it be to *P* to represent the fact that 'water' means *WATER* in going from *WATER* to 'water'? (We shall say more along these lines in section 11.6.) Evidence from language production might, of course, show that we do need these representations but, I shall argue, it does not.

We have been considering language production but the point could also be made for language comprehension. Call the processing rules for Oscar's English comprehension, "*U*". It seems *prima facie* unlikely that *U* will need the help of a representation of the rules of English.

For the sake of argument I have assumed LOTH. But, so far as I can see, the argument would not be affected if we assumed that the representations involved in thoughts are not language-like. Thus, suppose they are map-like, as RTM allows. The metalinguistic theory of English can do no more with a mental map that represents that water is not good to walk on than it can with a mental sentence that does. An analogue of (i) according to which the translation involves a theory of the mental map is just as outlandish as (i) according to which the translation involves a theory of Mentalese. And the analogue is just as open to the Harman argument. Once that "middleman" theory is dropped and we move to an analogue of (ii), the further move to drop the other "middleman" theory, the theory of English, and adopt the analogue of (iii) will seem enticing.

What about if we abandon RTM and hence the idea that thoughts involve mental representations? If we are that noncommittal about the nature of thoughts, we will have difficulty saying anything much about their role in language processing. It is hard to see how this difficulty will make RT more plausible.

3. I suggested earlier that structure rules governing a representational input or output often seem to be *the wrong sort* of rules to be processing rules: they do not seem to be the sort of rules that would govern a process that the system actually goes through (2.4, 2.6, 3.2, 4.1). This is certainly the case with the logic machine and is very likely the case with the bee's waggle dance (2.2). Similarly, I suggested that some linguistic structure rules—for example, the rules for forming D-structure phrase markers and transformation rules—seem to be the wrong sort of rules to be the processing rules governing language use: the computational procedures that Chomsky identifies with an I-language are not plausibly seen as psychologically real processes (4.1). These suggestions become particularly telling given RTM and the view that language use is a translation process: *the structure rules seem particularly unsuitable for the process of translation*. Thus, if (T) is correct, each translation task is between a linguistic representation that has a certain structure and a mental representation that has a similar one. It is hard to see how the rules determining that these representations *have* those structures could govern *the process of matching* the structures. So my *third tentative proposal* is that the structure rules of a language are the wrong sort of rule to govern the process of language use. This proposal counts not only against position (I) according to which the structure rules are represented and applied in processing but also against (III) according to which those rules govern the processing without being represented. It thus gives support to (V) according to which the processing rules are unlike the linguistic rules. The case for the third tentative proposal continues in 4 below and in sections 11.6 to 11.8.

4. A further problem for positions (I), (II), and (III) arises from an old criticism of the claim that a grammar's rules are psychologically real. I expressed the criticism earlier as follows: "If we can come up with one grammar for a language, we can come up with many which, though they posit different syntactic rules, are equivalent in their explanation of meaning: they are equally able to capture all the syntactically determined facts about meaning. We need psycholinguistic evidence to show which grammar's rules are in fact playing the role in linguistic processing, evidence we do not have" (2.6). According to (I), (II) and (III), "the structure rules of the language" are psychologically real. These rules must, of course, be the rules described by a *true* grammar of the particular linguistic reality. Call our preferred grammar, "*G1*". But, as the old criticism points out, there will be other grammars just as true of that linguistic reality. Call one of these

"*G2*". (Perhaps *G1* is a transformational grammar and *G2* is a lexical-function grammar; 4.4–4.5.) This poses a problem additional to those raised in 1 to 3 above. Thus, suppose that we set aside our doubts that a representation of rules plays a role in language processing and our doubts that those rules are the right sort to govern the processing. Why should we suppose, as (ɪ) must, that representations of *G1*'s rules govern processing rather than representations of *G2*'s? Why should we suppose, as (ɪɪ) must, that representations of *G1*'s rules are used as data in processing rather than representations of *G2*'s? Why should we suppose, as (ɪɪɪ) must, that the unrepresented but embodied rules of *G1* govern processing rather than those of *G2*? Psycholinguistic evidence might, of course, support one of these suppositions but we have no reason in advance to choose which one it will support.[10]

5. The next consideration against RT arises in dismissing something that may seem to *support* RT and hence (ɪ) or (ɪɪ). It might be thought that RT gets support from the apparent fact that language comprehension, language production, and intuitive linguistic judgments draw on the same linguistic knowledge. Pylyshyn, for one, once thought so:

> we appear to have multiple access to [grammatical] rules. We appeal to them to account for production, for comprehension, and for linguistic judgments. Since these three functions must be rather thoroughly coordinated . . . , it seems a reasonable view that they are explicitly represented and available as a symbolic code.   (1980a: 121; he seems to have changed his mind later: 1991: 247).

I have argued against this idea of multiple access to the grammatical rules. First, we do not need to see a speaker's intuitive judgments as derived from a representation of those rules. Rather, we should see these judgments as ordinary empirical central-processor responses to linguistic phenomena. That was part of my third major conclusion (Ch. 7). And I have argued that the competencies may share little more than a conceptual competence, the competence to think the thoughts expressible in the language. The evidence from brain impairment suggests that they do indeed share little more (10.2). And if we accept the appealing LOTH and hence position (ᴛ)—the structure rules of a speaker's language are similar to the structure rules of her thought—that is just what we should expect. This led to the second tentative hypothesis: there is little or nothing to the language faculty (10.3). It is hard to see a place for the represented rules in the little of the language faculty that may be left. Indeed, if the fairly brute–causal view of language use to be explored in the sections 11.6–11.8 is correct, there is no place. This brute–causal view yields a ready explanation of the

---

[10] Note that equivalent grammars do not pose a similar problem for my first tentative proposal that the rules of a speaker's language are similar to the structure rules of her thought (9.5). For the purposes of this proposal, the rules of *G1* and *G2* count as the same because they determine the same syntactic properties. What matters to the proposal is that the syntactic properties of the speaker's language are similar to those of her thought.

little shared by the competencies: the association between conceptual content and language "runs both ways": "it may be the case that the lexical network allows activation to spread in both directions because it is used for both production and comprehension" (Dell 1995: 195–6).

6. The discussion in Fodor, Bever, and Garrett 1974, summarized in section 4.3, brings out the implausibility of position (II). How can the represented rules be used as data in language use? Consider language comprehension. Suppose that, somehow or other, the processing rules come up with a preliminary hypothesis about the structure of the input string. In principle, the represented rules might then play a role by determining whether this hypothesis could be correct (assuming that the input is indeed a sentence of the language). The problem in practice is that to play this role the input would have to be tested against the structural descriptions generated by the rules and *there are just too many descriptions*. The "search space" is just too vast for it to be plausible that this testing is really going on in language use. This led Fodor, Bever, and Garrett to explore the idea that heuristic rules not representations of linguistic rules govern language use.

7. What advantage does an object get from having its processing rules represented rather than just embodied? A consideration of the standard general-purpose computer provides one answer. Because the computer represents the rules of software programs it is relatively easy to change what the computer does: we simply change the program; i.e., load the computer up with a program which represents different rules. In contrast, it is relatively hard to change what a machine like a special-purpose Turing Machine, a dedicated wordprocessor, or a calculator does by changing an unrepresented rule, a rule built into its hardware: we have to call on an engineer to do some rebuilding. The flexibility and "plasticity" that comes from representing rules is also apparent in human affairs. Because we represent the rules of games and of etiquette, it is fairly easy to change those rules. Think particularly of the way children's games often proceed: the rules for a game are invented and agreed upon; the game is played for a bit and found wanting in certain ways; a modification of the rules is proposed; there is more play followed by further modifications. These changes are easy because the children represent the rules, indeed, they state them. Now the problem for positions (I), (II), and (IV) is that linguistic competence is singularly lacking in this sort of plasticity. As Stabler points out:

we do not find any evidence of plasticity with regard to linguistic competence that would indicate that an encoding of the grammar influences the operation of any sort of human computing system. (1983: 399; see also Pylyshyn 1991: 243–8)[11]

---

[11] A sign of this lack of plasticity, pointed out to me by my student Francesco Pupa, is that people learning a second language mistakenly import features of their first language into the second. Thus speakers of a Slavic language like Croatian tend to omit the definite and indefinite articles of English; and Italians tend to add vowels to the ends of English words that should end with

8. Language processing is extraordinarily fast. Indeed, as Fodor points out, "it may be that ... the efficiency of language processing comes very close to achieving the theoretical limit" (1983: 61). Representing rules which have to be applied or consulted is an unlikely way to achieve this efficiency. This also counts against (i), (ii), and (iv)

Matthews brings these two considerations together nicely: "the limited plasticity (and lability) of acquired grammatical competence would seem to render explicit representation unnecessary, while the relatively greater efficiency of processors whose programs are 'hardwired' rather than explicitly represented would seem to render it undesirable" (1991: 187).

The final and most important consideration, 9, against the representation of rules in linguistic competence deserves a section of its own. This consideration arises from the psychology of skills in general.

11.5 PSYCHOLOGY OF SKILLS

9. Animals, birds, and insects, exhibit a great range of skills. So too do humans; for example, ball catching, bicycle riding, piano playing, touch typing and adding. Many human skills are motor but some are cognitive. Indeed, it is important to note the large role of cognitive skills: "much of our mental activity can be understood in terms of skill acquisition—we acquire skills for reading, solving problems within a particular domain, recognizing particular patterns, and so on" (Reisberg 1999: 460). Our linguistic competence has all the marks of a cognitive skill. Thus, we have just noted its limited plasticity and its speed. These are typical characteristics of skills (Anderson 1980: 226–30; Logan 1988: 492). Another such characteristic is that the process of exercising a skill is unavailable to consciousness (Logan 1988: 493). This also is a feature of linguistic competence. Finally, once a skill has become established, it is "automatic" with the result that it can be performed whilst attention is elsewhere (Anderson 1980: 230–5; Reisberg 1999: 460).[12] Once again, this is a characteristic of linguistic competence. As Fodor points out (1983: 52–5), we normally cannot help but hear a piece of language as a piece of language with a certain meaning: we cannot simply hear it as a sound and we cannot, for the most part, choose our interpretation of it. All in all, it is very plausible to think that linguistic competence is a cognitive skill. So, we can expect to learn something about its nature from considering the nature of cognitive skills in general. For example, if the rules

---

consonants. This inflexibility would be puzzling if mastery of the second language were a matter of learning to represent its rules. The representation of the first language should be simply set aside whilst representing the second just as one piece of software is set aside whilst using another.

[12] A consideration of "the Stoop effect" demonstrates "that automaticity is not an all-or-none phenomenon" (Palmeri 2003: 300).

that govern the exercise of skills in general are typically embodied without being represented that will count heavily against (i), (ii), and (iv).

Earlier (3.1), in discussing the dancing of the bee, the diving of the kingfisher, the ball catching and thinking of humans, I pointed out how *prima facie* implausible it is to think that such skills involve representations of the rules that govern them. Pylyshyn's Razor lay behind this assessment: if we have good reasons for supposing that a system is governed by a rule, the Razor demands that we produce further reasons before supposing that the rule governs by being represented and applied. So the assessment presumes that this demand has not been met. Does the psychological study of skills support this presumption? I shall argue that it does: there seems to be no persuasive evidence for the representation of the rules. Do we find evidence for a stronger conclusion, evidence that the rules are *not* represented? I think that we do but the evidence is far from decisive. The psychological study is still at an early stage and we simply do not know enough about skills to draw the stronger conclusion. Aside from that, although such progress as the study has made does mostly support the stronger conclusion, one part of the study does not and has to be explained away.

Psychologists agree about several matters. (i) As pointed out earlier (3.1), they distinguish, rather inadequately, between two sorts of "knowledge", "declarative", and "procedural". Where declarative knowledge is explicit, accessible to consciousness, and conceptual, procedural knowledge is implicit, inaccessible to consciousness, and subconceptual. And where declarative knowledge involves explicit or declarative memory, procedural knowledge involves implicit or procedural memory. Declarative memory holds factual knowledge such as that Washington is the capital of America, while implicit memory holds rules that govern processes, "routinized skills, ... priming, and classical and operant conditioning" (Bjorklund *et al.* 2003: 1059). The evidence for the dichotomy between implicit and explicit memory, the dichotomy between procedural and declarative knowledge, and other related dichotomies "lies in experimental data that elucidate various dissociations and differences in performance under different conditions" (Sun 2003: 698).[13] (ii) Although declarative knowledge may play a role in learning a skill, there is consensus that the skill itself is a piece of procedural knowledge. (iii) There is consensus also that cognitive skills are like motor skills: "recent work across a wide range of disciplines now provides evidence for the view that 'skills of mind' and 'skills of eye, ear, and muscle' are fundamentally similar" (Rosenbaum *et al.* 2001: 454; see also Masson 1990; Carlson 2003); motor skills are "set apart by their emphasis on the movement of the limbs and torso as well as on the outcome of the movement in terms of the goal of the act" (Newell 1996: 441).

[13] See also Schacter 1999 (p. 394), the many results cited by Sun *et al.* 2001 (p. 207); Cleeremans 2003 (p. 492); Mulligan 2003 (pp. 1115–17); Reber 2003 (p. 491).

In light of this, our view of the nature of skills depends on our view of the nature of procedural knowledge and implicit memory. Here there are lots of interesting ideas but no consensus. Indeed, our knowledge of this matter is at an early stage: "a great deal remains to be learned about the cognitive and neural mechanisms of implicit memory" (Schacter 1999: 395); "the overall picture that emerges from just over a century of scientific research is that human long-term memory ... is varied, dynamic, and constructive, and quite unlike current human-made memory devices in virtually every important respect" (Richardson-Klavehn and Bjork 2003: 1104); "there is no consensus regarding the details of the dichotomies" mentioned in the last paragraph (Sun 2003: 698).[14] The key issue for us is whether or not such knowledge as we do have gives any support to the view that the rules that govern a skill are represented. This is not the place, of course, for an exhaustive discussion of the literature on skills. Still, we can learn something helpful from a brief discussion.

Consider first what we can learn from the literature attending particularly to motor skills. A recent encyclopedia article describes four challenges facing research on motor control and describes many models proposed to meet these challenges. It is striking that there is no suggestion that the rules involved in these models are represented in the organism. The first challenge is the redundancy problem; there are, for example, a near infinite number of ways to pick up a particular apple. So, "we need to explain how one movement is chosen from the plethora that are possible" (Brown and Rosenbaum 2003: 127). Four types of model have been proposed: "models that emphasize properties of the peripheral neuromotor system; models that emphasize effector interactions; models that emphasize geometric restrictions; and models that emphasize cost reduction" (p. 128). The only mentalistic talk in the discussion of these models is of "desired positions" being "represented as modifiable equilibrium positions". The second challenge is to model relations between movements and their effects. Here there is talk of "predicting sensory outcomes" and "comparing" these to "obtained feedback", "predicting what change in motor commands will correct a mismatch between intended and obtained results". The third challenge is to capture the way an organism, even an insect, anticipates "the perceptual consequences" of actions "(feedforward)" and to capture the "rapid correction for perceived errors (feed-back)" (p. 129). The proposal for feedforward—the "Smith predictor"—is that "a controller not only sends signals to the muscles to bring about immediate perceptual changes; it also preserves a copy of the expected perceptual changes and compares them with actual feedback signals when they arrive". We seek models for feedback that take account of "Fitts' law"[15] in trying to "optimally compensate" for "the inherent variability of motor control" (p. 131). The fourth

---

[14] Axel Cleeremans (2003) refers to "as many as eleven different definitions" of the "implicit learning" that is thought to be involved in skill acquisition (p. 491).

[15] "$MT = a + b \log_2(2A/S)$" where MT is the movement time, S is the size of the target, A is the distance to be moved, and a and b are constant parameters (Mon-Williams *et al.* 2003: 122).

challenge is "movement sequencing" "studied mainly in connection with such tasks as walking, speaking, typewriting, and drawing" (p. 127). There is behavioral evidence of "advance planning"; for example, "performance errors (e.g. slips of the tongue) reveal implicit knowledge of what will be said or done". Heirarchical models have been proposed according to which "serial ordering of behavior is achieved by the unfolding of high-level goals into lower-level constituents" (p. 131). In sum, this article contains some rather mentalistic language (even in talking of insects)—"desired", "represented", "predicting", "comparing", "intended", "anticipates", "planning", etc.—but no talk of represented rules. Similarly, another article (Mon-Williams *et al.* 2003) talks of "the nervous system" having "preplans" (p. 124) and "storing information" (p. 126), and another (Wolpert and Ghahramani 2003) of its mapping, knowing (p. 138), estimating, and predicting (p. 139), but neither talk of its representing the rules by which the system performs these actions.

Turn next to "dynamical systems theories", which "de-emphasize mental representations" altogether whilst attempting to "provide substantial detail concerning how skills are actually performed". These theories have been "prominent among researchers concerned with motor skills" (Carlson 2003: 41); they are "particularly appropriate to account for motor control" (Port 2003: 1028). But theories of this sort aim to cover cognitive skills as well: "a provisional consensus seems to be emerging that some significant range of cognitive phenomena will turn out to be dynamical" (van Gelder 1999: 345); the theories have "a record of success across a wide range of cognitive abilities, including perception, sensorimotor activity, language, attention, decision making, and development" (Garson 2003: 1036). They are also concerned with skill *learning* treating it "as the process of discovering ways of coordinating activity" (Carlson 2003: 41). (So they bear also, as do the theories to follow, on the concerns of the next chapter.) Coordination is, indeed, central to the dynamic approach. Thus, J. A. Scott Kelso, in his influential book, *Dynamic Patterns* (1995), claims that "coordination ... is a fundamental feature of life" (p. xi) and aims to discover "the laws and principles of coordination" that govern it (pp. 287–8). So, what is a dynamical system? It "is a set of quantitative variables changing continually, concurrently, and interdependently over quantitative time in accordance with dynamical laws, described by some set of equations". Modeling it makes "heavy use of calculus and differential or difference equations" (van Gelder 1999: 245). A key feature for our purposes is that these equations have no place for representations of rules and very little for representations at all:

These equations are not ordinarily defined over representations, but instead over the variables for the system's properties. From the [Dynamical Systems] point of view, representations are not essential to an explanation of the mechanisms of cognition, since what matters is the way in which system variables evolve according to the system's equations of motion. Although dynamical explanation may mention representations, these are conceived of as emergent aspects of system activity. (Garson 2003: 1035)

Two other approaches have a lot in common with the dynamical systems approach.[16] First, the Gibson-inspired ecological approach (Fowler and Turvey 1978; Kugler and Turvey 1987) "seeks the solution to motor skills through the mapping of perception to action with minimal appeal to representational processes .... Rather the movement form may reflect emergent properties of the self-organizing biological system, in a fashion that is consistent with pattern formation principles of complex physical systems that drive, for example cloud formations, sand-dune formations, and vortices in streams" (Newell 1996: 442). Second, connectionist networks (Rumelhart and McClelland 1986) have had some of their most conspicuous successes in accounting for skills. As is well known, these networks store information not in represented rules but in patterns of connection weights among units. "Neural network models are capable of learning complex sets of input-output patterns, including those in which some logical rule governs the transformation of input to output patterns ... they are able to do so without developing an explicit representation of the rule" (Masson 1990: 233–4). Many think that a general account of skills might be based on a connectionist architecture (see, for example, Sun *et al.* 2001).

Next, consider the influential "instance theory" proposed by Gordon Logan. This theory is friendly to representations but makes no mention of the representation of rules. On this theory, the final "automatization" stage of learning a skill is "the acquisition of a domain-specific knowledge base, formed of separate representations called '*instances*' of each exposure to the task". Processing at that stage "relies on retrieval of stored instances which will occur only after practice in a consistent environment" (1988: 492). "Attending to a stimulus is sufficient to retrieve from memory whatever has been associated with it in the past" (p. 493). Crudely, you perform the action appropriate to the stimulus because you remember doing so before.

So far, then, we have found no sign in discussions of skills of rules being represented. That changes when we consider theories proposing "production systems". I shall take John Anderson's "adaptive control of thought" ("ACT") theories as my example (1983; 1993; Anderson and Lebiere 1998).[17] The basic idea for skill acquisition, which has gone through several developments, is that declarative knowledge in working-memory, and practice, leads over time to the accumulation in long-term memory of representations of production rules, rules that if a certain condition obtains then a certain action is to be performed (an IF–THEN rule), and to speeding up the application of these rules. Consider

---

[16] Tim van Gelder sees ecological psychology as an example of "dynamical work" (1999: 244) and Kelso expresses sympathy for it (1995: 34–7). Van Gelder thinks that the dynamical and connectionist approaches "overlap": "Connectionism is best seen as straddling a more fundamental opposition between dynamical and classical cognitive science" (1999: 245); "neural networks are examples of dynamical systems" (Garson 2003: 1038; see also Port 2003: 1029).

[17] SOAR theories (Laird *et al.* 1987) provides another example. Jones 2003 is a helpful account of production systems.

learning to change gears in a stick-shift car, for example. You start with declarative knowledge acquired from a set of instructions: "First, take your foot off the accelerator, then disengage the clutch", and so on. With practice, "procedularization" occurs and all these processes become automatic. What then is the skill itself, on this view? It is the accumulated representations of production rules, and the capacity to apply the represented rules speedily in performance without calling on working-memory. Indeed, procedularization may well be accompanied by the loss of the declarative knowledge in working-memory. This theory "de-emphasized the perceptual-motor details of how skills are performed" (Carlson 2003: 41). In this respect, and in its emphasis on representations, it is the opposite of the dynamical systems theory.

ACT theory does a nice job of accounting for many of the phenomena of skill learning including the transfer of training from one skill to another (Singley and Anderson 1989; Masson 1990: 222–8; Sun *et al.* 2001: 205–6). ACT-R theory, the most recent ACT theory, "accounts for a wide range of cognitive phenomena, including perceptual-motor tasks, memory, and problem-solving" (Johnson *et al.* 2003: 32).[18] The key question for us is whether this achievement requires that the production rules that are learnt be represented. Descriptions of ACT are often vague on this matter but the received view is that the rules are represented: "in ACT both declarative and procedural knowledge are represented in an explicit, symbolic form (i.e. semantic networks plus productions)" (Sun *et al.* 2001: 235; see also Masson 1990: 223). Yet it is notable that Christian Lebiere, one of the developers of ACT, does not list this view of production rules among ACT's "three theoretical assumptions" (2003: 8) nor among its "four claims related to production rules" (p. 9). And since the production rules constitute procedural not declarative knowledge there seems to be no immediate and pressing need to take them as represented. Because ACT theories are based on general-purpose computer models (Anderson 1983: 2) it is perhaps not surprising that the cognitive architecture they propose involves the representation of production rules. Still, we wonder whether we should take this aspect of the model seriously if we are looking for a simulation of skills that exist in real organisms. Is there any reason to think that the IF–THEN rules that become embodied in an organism as a result of practice are represented rather than merely embodied? Perhaps we can suppose that the organism has simply learnt to respond to the working-memory representation of a certain condition with the appropriate action. Is there any explanatory gain in supposing further that it does this by representing the rule governing this response and applying it? Anderson himself remarks that "the production is very much like the stimulus-response bond" (Anderson 1983: 6). And Pinker calls it "a knee-jerk reflex" which is "triggered" (1997: 69). Should

---

[18] It also seems to explain skill at chess. The idea is that this skill consists in acquiring production rules each of which specifies an action given a certain chess position. Chess masters may have as many as 50,000 such rules (Newell and Simon 1972). However this picture of chess playing is controversial (Holding 1992).

we then apply Pylyshyn's Razor and take the rule to be simply "fired" when the representation of the condition matches the rule's IF-component?[19]

The general-purpose computer may mislead here by encouraging the idea that learning a skill is a matter of *reprogramming*, a matter of changing the rules represented in the software. Yet it seems more likely that this learning is a matter of *rebuilding*, a matter of building new rules into the hardware; a new special-purpose computer is acquired. Experience may do for us what the engineer does for the computer.

So, I am doubting that we should be led by the production-systems approach to conclude that a skill must involve representations of production rules. This doubt is supported by the following considerations. (i) I have often harped on the fact that the human skill of thinking, the most cognitive skill of all, could not consist generally in applying representations of the "laws of thought" (3.1, 7.3, 7.5). So, this skill, at least, need not involve represented rules. (ii) The focus of the production-systems approach is on skill *learning*. But many skills seem to be largely, if not entirely, innate. One thinks immediately of the skills of insects—the bee's dance is an elaborate example—and of animals. The primitive motor skills of humans—grasping objects, walking, etc.—also seem to be of this sort. And, once again, there is our skill at thinking, which is surely largely innate. The motivation for represented production rules that comes from the production-systems approach to learning is absent with these largely innate skills. (One might insist that skills are learned *by definition*,[20] but this would be a pointless maneuver. Something with the nature of a skill that is, as a matter of fact, learnt, could, in another possible world, be innate. Its nature does not depend on its source. And we expect what I am calling "largely innate skills" to have natures importantly similar to acquired skills. A general theory of skills should be interested in that similarity.) (iii) The production-systems approach yields a totally "top-down" picture of skill learning: it all starts from declarative knowledge. Yet, intuitively, a lot of skill learning seems to be "bottom-up": rather than starting with declarative knowledge, we observe, practice, and "just pick the skill up". Even when we start with declarative knowledge, it often seems, intuitively, as if that knowledge plays a relatively small part in the acquisition of the skill; think, for example, of learning to throw a frisbee or ride a bicycle. These intuitions are confirmed by the literature on *implicit learning*, to which we now turn.

A. S. Reber defines implicit learning as follows: "the capacity to pick up information about complex stimulus displays largely without awareness of either the process or the products of learning" (2003: 486). There is much evidence that a lot of skill learning is of this bottom-up sort. Classical conditioning is an

---

[19] Note that this claim has no bearing on whether the mind is unitary as Anderson (1983) holds or modular as Fodor (1983) holds.

[20] "*Skill* refers to an acquired ability that has improved as a consequence of practice." (Carlson 2003: 36)

example. And implicit learning has been famously exemplified in sequential (or serial) reaction time ("SRT") and artificial grammar (AG) tasks. In SRT tasks, subjects presented with a sequence of target stimuli learn to exploit the structure in the sequence even though generally unaware of that structure (p. 487). In AG tasks, subjects memorize "exemplary strings" and are then asked to classify novel strings for well-formedness. Their performance at this task shows that they have "a considerable amount of knowledge about the underlying structure of the symbol strings. The learning appears to be taking place largely independent of awareness, and subjects find it particularly difficult to communicate to others the knowledge they are applying" (p. 488; see also Reber 1989). Sun *et al.* (2001) cite a great deal of evidence that "individuals may learn complex skills without first obtaining a large amount of explicit declarative knowledge ... and without being able to verbalize the rules they use" (p. 207).

What are the implications of the study of implicit learning? In particular, what does the study add to our understanding of the nature of skills? According to Axel Cleeremans, computer models show that "elementary, associative learning processes (as opposed to rule-based learning) are in fact often sufficient to account for the data" of implicit learning (2003: 496). "it is clear that the knowledge acquired in typical implicit learning situations need not be based on the unconscious acquisition of symbolic rules" (p. 497). Stanley *et al.* suggest that the knowledge that is exploited in performing a task is a "memory for past sequence of events related to the task" (1989: 571). Mathews *et al.* suggest that it is "memory-based processing, which automatically abstracts patterns of family resemblance through individual experiences with the task" (1989: 1098). Reber notes that the bottom-up systems of implicit learning "are rather easily simulated by connectionist architectures" (2003: 487). Mathews *et al.* (1988) assume something like a connectionist model. Reber points out that even a sea slug can exhibit implicit learning in Pavlovian conditioning (2003: 489). These discussions clearly count heavily against the idea that skills are governed by represented rules. Finally, if implicit learning were largely a matter of acquiring representations of rules that govern the performance of a task *and that yield verbal reports about the task*—which, it will be remembered, is the received view of language learning—we would expect improvement in performance to be matched by improvement in verbal reports. Yet that is not what we find at all, as we pointed out earlier in discussing the source of linguistic intuitions (7.5).

Consider, finally, the following thoughts on how implicit learning is *implemented* in the nervous system. Reber thinks that this learning is "probably supported by neurological systems that are old evolutionarily and antedate those 'top-down' systems that are dependent on complex encoding and conscious control, the hallmarks of explicit systems" (2003: 486). He airs the hypothesis that "implicit learning and memory occur within the cortical areas involved in processing the stimuli for which the learning is occurring, and hence will be found virtually throughout the brain" (p. 491). Yamadori *et al.* report as follows:

"In recent years it has been made clear that neurological substrata of skill acquisition is different from those engaged in data-related information acquisition .... The former is named procedural memory and the latter declarative memory" (1996: 49). "Unlike declarative memory which related mainly with the thalamus, hippocampus, and neocortical structures, this perceptual-verbal skill [mirror reading] acquisition is very likely related with the subcortical structures" (p. 51). Finally, consider the following summary of the findings of Posner *et al.* (1997) based on brain imaging:

there are four mechanisms that work together to generate skill acquisition. Firstly, automaticity is a result of an increase in the links between previously isolated subsystems. Secondly, when skills are acquired, the size or the number of brain areas involved increases. As a result, the computation within modules is improved. Thirdly, skill acquisition could be due to the replacement of the initial components by other more efficient components. Finally, certain brain areas can start performing tasks formerly implemented by different areas, indicating circuit change.   (Johnson *et al.* 2003: 34)

These findings about the implementation of skills do not, of course, rule out that the rules governing skills are represented in the mind, but they certainly do not encourage that view. And they are congenial to the earlier idea that skill learning involves "rebuilding the hardware" rather than "reprogramming the software".

So what conclusions should we draw about the nature of skills from these psychological studies? The studies yield a range of interesting ideas but no very confident conclusion about this nature. First, the ideas are seriously incomplete in their details. Second, it is hard to see a rational basis at this time for a sweeping acceptance or rejection of the ideas of one or other theoretical camp. Rather, we should entertain many ideas whilst often suspending judgment on their truth. We are clearly at an early stage in our understanding of skills. Nonetheless, we can say confidently that the studies have not provided persuasive evidence that skills typically involve represented rules. This is not to say, of course, that the evidence shows definitively that the skills do *not* involve represented rules. Still, the literature on motor skills, on dynamical systems theories, on connectionist theories, on instance theories, on implicit learning, and on the implementation of skills counts heavily against the idea that skills do.[21] The only support for the idea that they do may come from production-systems theories. But, as I have noted, there are reasons for doubting the appropriateness of these theories' apparent commitment to represented rules in a general theory of skills.

What is the bearing of all this on the matter of linguistic competence? Well, we are surely right in assuming that linguistic competence is a skill. So we should expect to form conclusions from the study of that competence that are similar to

---

[21] So does the literature on the related issue of animal navigation and cognitive maps; see, for example, Gallistel 1990. In an article on this topic, Bruno Poucet claims that "our understanding of memory has considerably improved in recent years ... largely due to the use of animal models" (2003: 150). So one wonders why the literature discussed in this section contains no references to these models.

those from the study of skills in general. So, we should expect to discover that it is early days in our understanding of the nature of linguistic competence, as indeed we have discovered (11.2), with the result that we should mostly suspend judgment about the matter. And rather than finding persuasive evidence for RT we should expect to find a weight of evidence against it. Perhaps our study of language in particular confounds these expectations. But I shall argue later that it does not (11.7–11.8).

Finally, the psychological study suggests that if learning a first language is implicit learning then we should be particularly dubious of RT. And language learning seems to be a paradigm of implicit learning: "Natural languages are acquired with substantial contributions from implicit acquisitional mechanisms" (Reber 2003: 486; see also Cleeremans 2003: 492).[22] In support of this, we note that linguists are fond of emphasizing how little explicit instruction the child gets whilst acquiring a language at a remarkable rate. Of course, acquisition could still begin with declarative knowledge if the child, all on its own, arrived at sufficiently many explicit hypotheses about the language. Anderson assumes that the child does (1983: ch. 7) but this seems rather dubious. Finally, although competent speakers typically show some capacity to describe this knowledge in their intuitive linguistic judgments, this capacity is very limited (ch. 7).

All in all, the psychological study of skills—of their nature and of how they are acquired—is bad news for the view that language processing rules are represented. This adds to the bad news for various positions presented in the last section. That evidence was briefly as follows: should we find evidence of a processing rule, there is always the possibility that it is hardwired rather than represented; it is implausible that the translation task of language processing will involve a theoretical middleman; the linguistic rules are the wrong sort of rules to be processing rules; we have no reason to suppose that the rules of our preferred grammar are represented rather than those of another meaning-equivalent grammar; it is hard to see a place for the represented rules in the little that competencies may share; it is unclear how represented rules could be used as data; language processing is not plastic enough and is too fast for it to involve represented rules. In light of these considerations, it seems unlikely that positions (i), (ii), or (iv) will be the conclusion of a persuasive future abduction; such an abduction is unlikely to seem plausible given what else we know. And the only-theory-in-town abduction (11.2) seems totally unpersuasive.

In my initial discussion of this abduction I noted the consensus that we know very little about language processing at this stage. In particular, we do not have a worked out and persuasive theory of this processing that includes RT. So the issue with that thesis is whether it is likely to be part of the best worked out and

---

[22] Many linguists would doubtless disagree: "There has been something like a consensus in linguistics for about twenty years that [language acquisition is not a case of implicit learning]" (Anonomous referee of Devitt 2006).

persuasive future theory (11.2). In pondering this, mindful of criterion (B)'s requirement that a good abduction should feature an explanation that is better than any that is *likely* given what we already know, we should note that if we knew more about how the processes underlying other skills worked without representing rules we could likely explain how language processing worked similarly. It would be rational to accept RT if we had a good worked-out theory of language use involving RT and little prospect of a good theory that does not involve it. This is very far from our present situation.

11.6 BRUTE–CAUSAL PROCESSING

The main focus of our preliminary assessment in the last two sections has been on positions (i), (ii), and (iv) and the issue of the representation of rules. We have also attended briefly to position (iii) and the issue of linguistic rules governing processing without being represented. We have barely touched on the idea, arising from the distinction drawn in section 3.3, that language use may be a fairly brute–causal associationist process—version (b)—rather than a process involving metalinguistic representations of the syntactic and semantic properties of linguistic expressions—version (a). We turn now to that idea. My *fourth tentative proposal* is that version (b) is correct.

First, a clarification. Some parts of language use involve abilities other than those strictly of linguistic competence, abilities that we have been calling "pragmatic". Thus, as we have already noted (8.2), language comprehension involves assigning referents to indexicals. It also involves using contextual clues to remove ambiguities. And language use in general involves Gricean processes: in production, the process of tailoring the expression of thought to the hearers and circumstances; in comprehension, the process of figuring out what thought the speaker is likely to be expressing. Some of these processes may well involve central-processor reflections on linguistic items. Version (b) is not concerned with any such process. The processes that are brute–causal according to version (b) are the *speedy automatic* ones which may arise solely from a person's linguistic competence, from her ability to speak and understand her language, or may arise partly from that ability and partly from pragmatic abilities like that of assigning referents. My tentative proposal is that these processes are fairly brute–causal.

Any position that is committed to the representation of rules playing a role in language processing must be committed also to the version (a) view that metalinguistic representations of the syntactic and semantic properties of linguistic inputs and outputs play a role. So, positions (i), (ii), and (iv) have this commitment automatically. Positions (iii) and (v) do not hold that rules are represented and so leave the brute–causal alternative of version (b) as a possibility. Nevertheless (b) does not seem to have much popularity even among those who may hold (iii) or (v). Indeed, the *received* view in linguistics and psycholinguistics seems to be the version (a) view that processing operates on metalinguistic representations. Thus Fodor, Bever, and Garret describe language "perception as the matching of *stimuli* to *descriptions*" (1974: xvi). Fodor claims that "a representation of a message must have, among, its inputs, a representation of the grammatical relations exhibited by the sentence to which the message is assigned" (1975: 167). And, according to Matthews, "language understanding, it is widely assumed, involves the recovery and representation for later use of the syntactic structural descriptions associated with the uttered sentence (or phrase)" (2003: 198). In this section, arguing for my fourth tentative proposal, I shall present some reasons for doubting this received view and for favoring a brute–causal alternative, particularly version (b) of position (v). The point is not, of course, to offer the alternative as a complete explanation of language use. Like the received view, it is far far too lacking in details for that. The point is rather to suggest that the best explanation is more likely to comply with the brute–causal alternative than the received view. And the considerations favoring the alternative are, it goes without saying, far from decisive. The fourth proposal really is tentative.

I mentioned earlier (3.1) that we cannot look into the mind and simply "see" if there are representations of this or that. We don't even know enough about what to look for. So we should only posit such representations if we can find some serious causal work that they have to do: Pylyshyn's Razor. Sadly, it is often difficult to tell when we have found causal work for representations: the issue is simply not that clear. Still, I am inclined to doubt that there is causal work for representations of syntactic and semantic properties in the speedy automatic part of language processing.

We have just noted that the psychological literature on skills, particularly that on motor skills, dynamic systems theories, connectionist theories, instance theories, implicit learning, and the implementation of skills, counts against the view that the rules that govern language use are represented. I think this literature should also make us doubt that language use involves representing syntactic and semantic properties; it makes such a view of language use seem too intellectualist. Those doubts are particularly encouraged by the sheer *speed* of language processing. This is not to say that the literature on skills is hostile to talk of representation in general. There is indeed plenty of such talk. It is not obvious, of course, whether we should take this talk to be about representations *in the sense that concerns us here*, as explained in section 1.1. As I noted there, 'represent' and its cognates are often used fairly indiscriminately in psychology.[23] Aside from the

---

[23] One wonders, for example, about the uses in Sun *et al.* 2001 (p. 208); Reber 2003 (p. 489); Cleeremans 2003 (p. 493); and Taatgen 2003 (p. 822). Gallistel remarks: "Few other concepts generate such heated discussion among psychologists as the concept of representation" (1990: 15). He is careful in explaining his own concept: "I use the term *representation* in its mathematical sense. The brain is said to represent an aspect of the environment when there is a functioning isomorphism between an aspect of the environment and a brain process that adapts the animal's behavior to it" (p. 3). But isomorphism alone will not do the job for him: it misses that each point in the cognitive map represents a particular aspect of the environment; and that the map represents the environment but not vice versa.

explicit talk of representations, we noted that even the literature on motor skills includes a deal of mentalistic talk that seems to demand representations. Perhaps we should not take this talk too seriously. Much of the literature suggests that skills have fairly brute–causal associationist natures and so does not encourage the idea that language use involves representations of the syntactic and semantic properties of language.

It is worth noting that the positions of Bresnan and Kaplan and Berwich and Weinberg discussed earlier (4.4–4.5) have a place for a fairly brute–causal process in language parsing. Thus, Bresnan and Kaplan, in arguing for their lexical-function grammar, allow that the derivation of the passive lexical entry from the active can be stored in memory so that it does not have to be actually run in language processing (1982: xxxiii–xxxiv). And Berwick and Weinberg, in defending transformational grammars, allow for a "precomputed memory re-trieval system" (1984: 74) so that transformations do not have to be run in processing.

I now want to present a relatively "a priori" reason for favoring a brute–causal view of language processing. But I start with a *caveat*. My concern is with whether language use involves representation of the syntactic and semantic properties of the sounds, inscriptions, etc., of the language (which I will often briefly call "the linguistic properties"). For convenience, let us set aside inscriptions, etc., taking sounds to be representative of linguistic items. My concern is not with whether language use involves representation of the phonetic and phonological properties of the sounds. Clearly, these properties have to be recovered somehow from the acoustic signal at the beginning of speech perception and bestowed somehow on the signal by the end of speech production.[24] I assume that this must involve, at least, representations of the phonetic properties, the "physical" properties of the sound, as a result of a transduction. Beyond that I shall (wisely) have nothing to say on the vexed question of what else it involves,[25] including on the influence of lexical knowledge on the recovery process.[26] I suppose, although I shall not argue,

---

[24] "Speech perception processes ... require a transformation of the auditory input from the peripheral auditory system to a spectral representation based on more generalized auditory patterns or properties, followed by the conversion of this spectral representation to a more abstract feature (phonological) representation, and ultimately the mapping of this sound structure onto its lexical representation" (Blumstein 1999: 644).

[25] Burton-Roberts *et al.* 2000 paint a nice picture of just how vexed phonological theory is: "There seems to be almost no conceptual assumption in the foundations of phonological theory that is not controversial." There is conflict "even about what kind of entity phonological entities are" (p. 1), about whether they are "grounded in phonetic substance" or "mental objects" (pp. 8–9). Even on the assumption that the entities are so grounded, "there is scope for disagreement as to what phonetic content consists in ... , the exact nature of the relation between the phonological and the phonetic, and how we are to draw the boundary between them" (p. 9). Some of these problems arise, in my view, from trying to accommodate phonology to the Chomskian internalist view of language; see note 23 in section 2.5.

[26] "phonetic perception is itself influenced by input from higher-order linguistic levels, most notably information from the lexicon" (Miller 1999: 788).

that my reasons for doubting that syntactic and semantic properties are represented would carry over to phonological properties.

In considering the brute–causal alternative, I shall assume the Language-of-Thought Hypothesis (LOTH) and hence (т): the structure rules of a speaker's language are similar to the structure rules of her thought. Some of the case for the alternative may survive if we assume only RTM, the minimal theory of thoughts that allows that thoughts might be map-like. But the alternative certainly seems most plausible assuming LOTH because that assumption lessens what has to be done in language processing (10.3). So the case for the fourth tentative proposal, like that for the second (10.3), rests a bit on LOTH.

What, given LOTH, does the brute–causal alternative add to the background assumption about linguistic competence (11.3)? The alternative yields a view of competence that is like the earlier theory of intuitions (Ch. 7) in its modesty. It does not posit any representations of linguistic properties. So, competence in a language does not involve the speaker in propositional knowledge about the syntax and semantics of the language. Linguistic competence consists in a *conceptual competence*, grounded in the external world, together with *a set of translation skills* that are *mere dispositions* (cf. Chomsky 1980b: 5), although not of course *behaviorist* dispositions.

This modest view stands opposed to the received view that language processing involves representing the syntactic and semantic properties of linguistic inputs and outputs. Thus, on the received view, in understanding

(1) John hit the boy

the processor deploys a whole lot of syntactic vocabulary—like "NP" and "DET"—to arrive at *a mental metalinguistic statement about* the input along the lines of the structural description:

(2) $[_S[_{NP}[_N John]][_{VP}[_V hit][_{NP}[_{DET} the][_N boy]]]]$.

Translated into ordinary English, this statement amounts to something like:

(3) *John hit the boy* is a sentence made up of a noun phrase consisting of the noun *John* and of a verb phrase consisting of the verb *hit* followed by a noun phrase made up of the determiner *the* followed by the noun *boy*.

And, in understanding (1), the processor deploys some semantic vocabulary to arrive at statements like

(4) *hit* means *HIT*

where '*hit*' refers to a word and '*HIT*' refers to a meaning.

Now this received view cannot be the *whole* story of understanding. For what we have to end up with in "the message-in box" is not a mental metalinguistic statement *about* the linguistic input, however detailed, but a mental statement that *means the same as* the input. That is, on hearing (1), what we end up with is a *translation* of (1), something that means *JOHN HIT THE BOY.* That is what understanding the sentence amounts to. Understanding does not amount to metalinguistic analyses like (3) and (4), which tell us *about* the syntactic and semantic properties of (1). The *task* is not to generate a *theory* of the linguistic input but to generate a synonymous mental representation. Of course, generating (3) and (4) might be *a way to* the synonymous representation. But in that case we need a further story about the final *transition* from the metalinguistic (3) and (4) to the synonymous representation. How do we get from a theory of the input sentence to a mental representation that is synonymous with the sentence?

Presumably, the final transition would have to be some brute–causal process: once a person has this full analysis of the input, she just goes straight to the synonymous representation. And, presumably, the *initial* steps in forming the analysis have to be brute–causal too: thus, hearing the sound of *hit* and forming a representation of its phonetic properties simply prompts the analysis (4) (or perhaps a representation of phonological properties that leads to (4)). But this raises the idea: perhaps we never ascend into a mental metalanguage to make this analysis but rather go brute–causal from the beginning so there does not have to be any such transitions. The language processor assigns syntactic and semantic properties not in the sense that it *describes* the linguistic input using terms for those properties but in that it *transforms* the input into mental expressions having those properties. Analogously, a certain key stroke is processed by a calculator as a '4' without being described as a '4': that stroke simply and brute–causally yields a representation of 4. So the idea is that the processor receives a phonetic representation of (1) as input, a representation of a sound that represents John hitting the boy, and transforms it through however many stages, governed by some hard-wired rules, into a mental representation of John hitting the boy. It doesn't "think about" the input provided by *hit*, describing it as a V and as something that means *HIT*, it simply responds to it with something that is a V and means *HIT*. There are no representations of the linguistic properties of the sentence. There are simply representations of what it represents, John hitting the boy.

Suppose that the received view is true of some processor. So, the processor ascends into a metalanguage, goes through several stages of theorizing about the input before finally descending into a mental representation that is synonymous with the input. Then presumably another processor could go through "the same stages" without the ascent and descent. We should wonder then if there is any psycholinguistic evidence favoring the received view over this brute–causal idea. If not, Pylyshyn's Razor favors the brute–causal idea.

Consider analysis (4). The brute–causal idea makes us wonder whether any explanatory work is done by supposing that this analysis takes place. What work does it do to suppose that the processor represents this semantic property of *hit*? It seems more plausible that in processing that word we simply come up with a representation that *has* the property of meaning *HIT*. And if that is what we do, presumably that representation will also have the property of being a verb. So we have no need to come up with a representation *of* its being a verb, as in (3). The simpler story is surely that hearing the word *hit* does not prompt a person to come up with a mental representation *about* the word but rather with a representation, <hit>, that is a verb and means *HIT.* The natural and efficient design for translating *hit* into <hit> surely accords with this simple story.

This point about language comprehension becomes more vivid if we consider the analogous point about language production. If we are to suppose that comprehension starts with analysis of the properties of *linguistic* inputs, shouldn't we also suppose that production starts with the analysis of the properties of *mental* inputs? Consider someone saying (1). The person had a thought, <John hit the boy>, and expressed it by producing (1). The analogous first step to (4) would be

<hit> means *HIT.*

But the supposition that we go through this first step is almost as outlandish as the earlier one that language production starts with an application of a metalinguistic theory of Mentalese (11.4, point 2). For one thing, what language would this representation be in? Presumably it could not be in the language of <hit> itself, Mentalese. It would have to be in some meta-Mentalese. If we can get from the mental <hit> to the linguistic *hit* in production without analyzing <hit>, we wonder why we cannot get from the linguistic *hit* to the mental <hit> in comprehension without analyzing *hit*?

Objection: The way a word should be processed depends on its syntactic category, on whether it is a verb, noun, adjective, or whatever. What the processor must have then are rules for each syntactic category. It surely does not have a rule for each word of that category. So, it has rules for processing all adjectives, not a rule for each adjective. And such a general rule must operate on a representation of a word as a member of that category, on a representation like <That is an adjective>. **Response:** Why must the general rule operate on a representation? To represent a word as an adjective, the processor must first recognize that it is an adjective. Whatever clue enables this recognition could simply trigger rules appropriate for adjectives: the processor responds to it as an adjective without representing it as one. Being an adjective is not a local physical property of a word, as Rey likes to emphasize (1997: 128; 2003b: 178–9), and so recognizing a word as having that property may not always be an easy matter (although it mostly is; see 10.6). But it is not made any easier by supposing that it involves representing the word as an adjective rather than simply responding to it as an adjective.

Let me fill out the brute–causal view a bit more, starting with words. The view is that there is a simple association stored in memory between a linguistic word—more accurately, a representation of its phonetic properties—and the corresponding mental word with the result that the one leads straight to the other without any analysis. This association is established by the regular use in the community of the linguistic word to express the mental word, a regularity that also establishes the conventional meaning of that linguistic word (9.5). The same story also applies to familiar sentences—for example, 'What's the time?' and 'How are you?'—and familiar expressions, including idioms—for example, 'kick the bucket', 'butterflies in the stomach'.[27] The view is not, of course, that these simple associations are all there is to the use of these expressions. Thus, pragmatic abilities will be called on in language comprehension to determine the reference of 'you', to remove ambiguities, and so on (see the clarification that began this section). But the view is that simple associations are at the core of the processes. This story for words and familiar expressions seems very plausible. And there seems to be no reason why it cannot be extended to syntax. The basic idea again is of simple associations stored in memory, in this case of syntactic structures in thought with similar (implicit and explicit) syntactic structures in language so the presence of the one prompts the other. Each of the structural features of any linguistic sentence—the features captured by structural descriptions like (2) or by phrase-structure trees—is associated with a similar structural feature of mental sentences. This association is established by the regular use in the community of that linguistic structure to express the mental structure, a regularity that also establishes the conventional syntax of that linguistic structure (9.5). In comprehension, a person must identify the structure from clues provided by the syntactic category of words (which comes with word recognition), word order, and the like.[28]

I have frequently remarked that the structure rules of a language seem the wrong sort to govern processing (2.6, 3.2, 4.1, 11.4). This is certainly so on the brute–causal picture I am presenting. The translation task requires that a mental syntactic structure be associated with a linguistic one. The rules governing such associations—along the lines of structure x causing structure y—are nothing like linguistic structure rules. This supports my third tentative proposal and counts against positions (i) and (iii). There is more support in the next two sections.

This brute–causal associationist picture of language processing risks the fury of Fodor. For, Fodor has a *very* dim view of associationism: "associationism ... is, and always has been, an intellectual disaster" (2001: 104; see also 1975: 173). Its return makes him feel old and depressed (2001: 100). But it is important to note that, although I am suggesting that there may be a place for associationist processes in language use, I am obviously not embracing associationism in general.[29] For, influenced by Fodor himself, I favor LOTH and with it a highly

---

[27] "Idioms must be stored in the mental lexicon" for language production. They "do not require simultaneous selection of several lexemes." (Wheeldon *et al.* 2003: 761)

[28] Kintsch 1984 gives some examples of potential clues (113–15).

[29] Gallistel (1990) makes telling criticisms of associationist models of classical conditioning. He offers a rival representational model which "assumes that the animal has a record of what occurred when, that it can segment this record into the temporal intervals over which a given CS was present, that it can sum these intervals, that it can count the number of occurrences of the US in each such interval, and that it can sum the number of occurrences of the US during different intervals of CS presence to obtain the total number of USs observed in the presence of a given CSs" (p. 424). He produces some impressive evidence for these assumptions.

rational–causal view of thinking. So the suggestion is that we need a hybrid architecture for the mind, a rational–causal part for the higher functions like thinking and a brute–causal associationist one for lower functions like language processing. There is, of course, nothing novel about such a proposal:

I will argue for the plausibility of a particular kind of hybrid architecture, whose abstract levels are classical . . . I assume that connectionist networks, or close variants thereof, provide adequate models of moderately low level cognitive processes, which may include pattern recognition and some motor control.   (Hadley 1999: 200; see also Johnson *et al.* 2003; Sun 2003; and Cleeremans 2003)

Despite his contempt for associationism, even Fodor allows a place for associationist connections in his account of word recognition: "these connections have a real, if modest, role to play in the facilitation of the perceptual analysis of speech" (1983: 82). But one wonders why the role has to be so modest. Why could it not extend to syntax recognition? In an earlier work, he follows the claim that "English speakers *can* infer messages from representations of grammatical relations" with the following: "But though they presumably can, they presumably don't. What apparently happens is that grammatical relations are computed only when all else fails. There exist heuristic procedures for sentence recognition which, in effect, ignore grammatical relations and infer messages directly from lexical content, accepting, thereby, the penalties of fallibility" (1975: 167–8). One wonders why these heuristic procedures could not be associative and why they could not be all there is to the *speedy automatic* process of language processing.

I emphasize that in entertaining the brute–causal associationist view of language use I am not entertaining the return of empiricism as a general theory of mental processes. I would not contemplate for a moment that thinking, for example, was an associationist process (Part IV). Still some processes surely are associationist, as even Fodor allows. The issue is whether the processes of language use are among them. Can associationism be extended that far?

We are not concerned here with what seem intuitively to be performance failures. Thus, there will be sentences of the language that a person cannot translate satisfactorily into thought in the brute–causal way. And there will be sentences she cannot produce because she cannot think the corresponding thought. (But will there be any thoughts that she *can* think but cannot translate into sentences of the language?) Presumably the central processor helps deal with the sentences that she cannot immediately translate. If the "message-in box" receives an unacceptable message, then the central processor orders a rerun: using memory of the starting point, another attempt at translation is made. If even this fails to yield a satisfactory message in comprehension, then the central processor may have to take a serious hand. Perhaps this will involve deploying such declarative linguistic knowledge as the person has acquired at school and elsewhere to try to analyze the input. But it may mostly consist in trying several times to get "a feel" for the troublesome sentence by comparing it to others until the syntactic structure is recognized by the associative memory. And this may fail: there may be sentences of the language that a speaker simply cannot translate into Mentalese or, at least, cannot without a great deal of help from a teacher. Thus, I haven't yet managed to parse Fodor's example, 'Bulldogs bulldogs bulldogs fight fight fight' as a sentence despite the clue "Take the first two verbs as transitive" (1975: 168).

Despite these limitations in what a person can produce and understand, there is a sense, of course, in which a person is competent with any of the infinite number of sentences in her language; her competence is *productive*. In what sense? To answer, we must draw on our earlier discussion of competence (11.3). We note, first, that her capacity to think thoughts, her conceptual competence, is productive: if it weren't for resource limitations in her memory, time, computational power, and so on, she could think any of an infinite number of thoughts. LOTH has a ready explanation of this: the structure rules governing her Mentalese allow, by multiple embeddings, connectives, and so on, the generation of an infinite number of thoughts; there are a finite number of rules for combining a finite number of mental words—concepts—into mental sentences but no limit on the number of rule applications that might govern a sentence. And *any* successful theory of thought must pass the test of explaining the productivity of thought.[30] Turn next to her language. It is productive, of course, in just the same way as her thought is according to LOTH: its structure rules can yield an infinite number of sentences. The productivity of her linguistic competence is then easily explained: each of the structure-determining rules for thought is associated with a structure-determining rule for language. If it weren't for resource limitations she could think any of the infinite number of thoughts and exploit those associations to express them, and she could exploit those resources to understand any of the infinite number of sentences of the language. *Given the productivity of thought and language* the brute–causal story of language processing is quite compatible with the productivity of linguistic competence.

Finally, Pylyshyn may have a problem with the brute–causal story. At the beginning of this chapter I quoted his doubts about RT. He is, nonetheless, somewhat tentatively committed to the view that the syntactic properties of expressions are represented in parsing:

Although there may be some doubt as to whether grammatical rules are explicitly encoded, there appears to be good evidence that both the output of the analysis (i.e. LF) and certain intermediate steps in the parsing *are* so encoded. These have to do with the fact that certain universal properties of the language faculty appear to be stateable only in terms of certain properties of the parse tree. For example, the various constraints on movement are stated in relation to certain properties of the analysis of the sentence, and thus imply that such an analysis is actually available to the system in the course of parsing

---

[30] This is a test that connectionism seems to fail as Fodor and Pylyshyn (1988) emphasize.

and/or generation. Attempts to design parsing systems have also suggested that not only the logical form itself, but also various intermediate stages of the grammatical analysis may be explicitly encoded. In other words it is likely that parts of the analyzed structure of the sentence appears as a symbolic code, although the rules themselves may not appear in such a form. In computer jargon, although the rules may simply be compiled into the functional architecture of the system and not accessed in interpreted mode, the data structures to which these rules apply are explicitly represented and their form is empirically significant. (Pylyshyn 1991: 247–8)

But one wonders why the fact that movement constraints and the like have to be stated in relation to syntactic properties requires an encoded analysis of the sentences. And one wonders whether the parsing systems designed so far can plausibly be seen as throwing much light on how humans actually parse.

This completes our preliminary assessment of positions on language use, an assessment made prior to considering the psycholinguistic evidence from language use itself. In this section, I have argued for my fourth tentative proposal: the speedy automatic language processes arising wholly or, at least, partly from linguistic competence are fairly brute–causal associationist processes that do not operate on metalinguistic representations of the syntactic and semantic properties of linguistic expressions. So the persuasive future abduction on language processing is likely to support version (b) not (a). I think that this view is plausible although the case for it is very far from decisive, of course. If the view is indeed plausible, this adds to the already powerful case, presented in the previous two sections, against positions (i), (ii), and (iv). For, if processing involved representations of the rules, as those positions claim, then it would have to operate on representations of the syntactic and semantic properties adverted to in those rules rather than brute–causally. I conclude that the likelihood of a future abduction supporting any of these three positions is remote. I have urged also that the structure rules of a language are the wrong sort of rule to govern what is, given RTM, the translation process of language use; my third tentative proposal. This counts against (iii). So I think that we can predict with a fair amount of confidence that the explanation of language use will support (v): the processing rules are unrepresented and largely unlike the structure rules of the language. And I think that we can predict with some small confidence that language processing will not operate on metalinguistic properties of the linguistic expressions but will be more brute–causal.

What about the-only-theory-in-town abduction (11.2)? It should be dismissed. It fails every criterion of a good abduction. The discussion of the last three sections shows that its appeal to RT to explain language use is very implausible given what we already know. So it fails (A1). We noted at the beginning that the explanation fails (A2) because of a serious lack of details. Finally, it fails (B). The discussion of skills in the last section makes it seem likely that the future will yield a good alternative explanation that does not involve the representation of rules. The discussion in this section suggests that this alternative may be brute–causal. Such alternatives are much more promising than explanations appealing to RT.

We turn now to an inevitably brief consideration of the psycholinguistic evidence on language use. I think that this evidence should not persuade us to modify these preliminary assessments.

11.7 PSYCHOLOGY OF LANGUAGE PRODUCTION

We shall see that a good deal of day-by-day work on language processing does not address the architecture questions that most concern us: whether this processing involves the rules of the language, either represented or otherwise embodied. There seems to be little interest in this issue that was once so pressing. Psycholinguists mostly now approach the study of language processing as if it were, except for the Respect Constraint (2.4–2.6), independent of grammars. There is not even much focus on whether processing involves representations of syntactic and semantic properties. However, the favored models of this processing mostly seem to support a fairly brute–causal view of the processing; they seem to support the fourth tentative proposal.

I shall discuss language production before language comprehension for two reasons. First, our focus is on processes arising from linguistic competence. All language use involves processes, including central processes, arising wholly or partly from pragmatic abilities, but such processes are more prominent with language comprehension. For, language comprehension requires the assignment of referents to indexicals and the removal of ambiguities. Language production does not face these problem and so the role of factors other than competence is not so important: "The direct apprehension of the message sets speakers apart from their listeners, for whom ambiguity is rife" (Bock 1999: 456). Second, I think that work on language production speaks more clearly to the architectural issues that concern us than does the work on language comprehension: it not only allows our preliminary assessments to stand, it strengthens them.

I shall begin by describing, in broad terms, some fairly uncontroversial facts about language production. I shall then go into some details. Finally, I will describe the main areas of controversy.

Language production consists in processes "from mind to mouth". These processes start with intentions to communicate messages, intentions to express thoughts. The processes go from these intentions to the articulation of linguistic expressions: "the cognitive processes that convert nonverbal communicative intentions into verbal actions. These processes must translate perceptions or thoughts into sounds, using the patterns and elements of a code that constitutes the grammar of a language." There are two steps in language production, a grammatical one (producing a "lemma") and a phonological one (producing a "lexeme"). "Grammatical encoding refers to the cognitive mechanisms for retrieving, ordering, and adjusting words for their grammatical environments, and phonological encoding refers to the mechanisms for retrieving, ordering, and adjusting sounds for their phonological environments" (Bock 1999: 453). At the grammatical stage words with the appropriate meanings have to be retrieved and put into a syntactically appropriate frame. It is "generally assumed that syntactic properties of words are retrieved as a consequence" of word retrieval. The retrieval of a word is "competitive" and occasionally leads to errors because "other words similar in meaning are also activated" (Vigliocco and Vinson 2003: 184). Similarly, the phonological stage may produce a word similar in sound to the desired one. "When words exchange, they exchange almost exclusively with other words from the same syntactic class.... When sounds exchange, they exchange almost exclusively with other sounds from the same phonological class" (Bock 1999: 455). Two sorts of evidence have been adduced in theorizing about language production: spontaneously occurring errors, slips of the tongue and dysfluencies ('um's, 'ah's, repetitions, etc.); and the results of laboratory experimentation.

Let us now consider some more details of the first step, grammatical encoding:

Assuming that the speaker wants to express the event 'The ferocious dog bites the boy', the stored meaning-based representations for 'ferocious', 'dog', 'to bite', and 'boy' are retrieved. These representations would further specify that 'dog' and 'boy' are nouns (hence usable as subject and object), 'to bite' is a verb (hence specifying a relation between the nouns), and 'ferocious' is an adjective (hence it can modify a noun). These representations also specify that 'dog' and 'boy' are common, countable nouns, and may be pluralized, and that 'to bite' may be used to refer to the past, present, or future, depending on the speaker's intentions. The message-level information controls the assignment of the different lexical elements to their intended grammatical functions (e.g. 'dog' is assigned to be the subject, and 'boy' as the object and not vice versa, which would result in the unintended sentence: 'The boy bites the ferocious dog'). Message-level information also ensures that the appropriate specification of number for the noun 'dog' (singular) and tense for the verb 'to bite' (present) are passed along.   (Vigliocco and Vinson 2003: 185)

This account exemplifies just what we would expect: the message, what the speaker intends to convey, controls the process (4.1). Thus, the speaker's thought involving <dog> meaning DOG leads to the retrieval of the word 'dog' with that same meaning. The message also determines that the word appears as subject and not object and comes in the singular. What goes on in this retrieval process? There is no suggestion that the process is governed by represented rules. Does it even involve representations of syntactic and semantic properties? Researchers talk of the process retrieving "stored information" (p. 184; see also Levelt *et al.* 1999: 2), but this storage may be in the form of implicit memory, about which much remains to be learnt (11.5). There seems to be nothing here that requires the representation of syntactic or semantic properties of 'dog'. Indeed, what would be the use of retrieving the information *that* 'dog' means DOG? The account is compatible with the following brute–causal picture: 'dog' is selected because it is associated with <dog>; its subject position is associated with the place of <dog> in the message; its singularity is associated with the singularity of <dog>. What about the syntax of the sentence? The retrieval of 'dog' is the retrieval of something that *is* a noun and hence something that must be fitted into the sentence in the way appropriate for a noun. But this does not require a representation *that* it is a noun. Of course, more has to be done to fix the syntax of the sentence; for example, the singularity of the subject demands the singularity of the verb. But researchers see this sort of grammatical constraint as "procedural knowledge concerning how words can be used in sentences" (Vigliocco and Vinson 2003: 185) and so there is no clear need for these constraints to be represented.

The dominant role of connectionist models in psycholinguistic research into language production supports a brute–causal picture. Thus, in a survey article, Joseph Stemberger (2003) discusses three sorts of model. Two are overtly connectionist, "Network Models: Local Models" and "Network Models: Distributed Models", and he has this to say about third, "Symbolic Models": they have not been accompanied by "detailed proposals about processing" but "the spirit of their proposals has been instantiated in network models" (p. 158). Consider also the talk of "activation" in the work of some leading researchers. Gary Dell explains production errors as follows: "semantically and phonologically similar words become activated in the process of retrieving a target word; thus, these have some chance of erroneously replacing the target"; "the phonological effects on word slips reflect the spreading of activation from a target word to the target word's phonemes, and from there to other nontarget words that share those sounds." "But why should we want to propose that activation moves from sounds to words during language production?. ... It may be the case that the lexical network allows activation to spread in both directions because it is used for both production and comprehension" (1995: 195–6). William Levelt, Ardi Roelofs, and Antje Meyer explain lexical selection in the following way. "An active lexical concept spreads some of its activation to 'its' lemma node, and lemma selection is a statistical mechanism, which favors the selection of the highest activated lemma" (1999: 4). Their "theory is modeled in terms of an essentially feed-forward activation-spreading network" (p. 6). Dell, Franklin Chang, and Zenzi Griffin conclude that "the PDP approach offers the best chance to explain production as a skill. ... Perhaps most importantly, a PDP approach to language production expresses its commonalities with other linguistic, and even nonlinguistic, skills" (1999: 539–40).

Finally, consider where there is controversy in the theory of language production. Bock mentions three controversial areas. (a) There is a dispute over whether "regularly inflected words are stored and retrieved from memory in the same way as uninflected words ... or require a separable set of specifically inflectional operations" (1999: 455; see also Vigliocco and Vinson 2003: 184). (b) Theories diverge over "the relationship between phonological encoding and the higher level processes of lexical selection and retrieval. The *discrete-stage view* [Levelt *et al.* 1999] argues that each step is completed before the next is begun". So there is no feedback, just feedforward. "In contrast, *interactive* views (Dell *et al.* 1997) embrace the possibilities of partial information from one stage affecting the next (*cascaded* processing) and of information from lower levels affecting higher levels of processing". There is feedback as well feedforward (Bock 1999: 455; see also Vigliocco and Vinson 2003: 185). (c) Finally, there is controversy over whether language production and comprehension involve distinct cognitive systems. The fact that they seem to draw on the same linguistic knowledge suggests that they are not distinct although, as we noted (10.2–10.3), there may be little overlap beyond the sharing of a conceptual competence. We have just seen that some further overlap is supported by the interactive view of Dell according to which activation moves from sounds to words even in production just as it must do in comprehension.[31]

It is noticeable that these areas of controversy do not concern RT at all, nor do they even talk of representations. They do not seem to bear on any of the positions on language use that we have described.

In sum, the psycholinguistic study of language production that I have summarized does not undermine our preliminary assessment that there is no place for RT in the explanation of language use. Indeed, the study gives further support to that assessment. The study, particularly the prominence of connectionist models, also supports our preliminary assessment in favor of the brute–causal view, version (b), over the view that production involves representations of syntactic and semantic properties, version (a); it supports my fourth tentative proposal. Still, it is clearly far too early to be confident about either view. Finally, the rules governing the retrieval processes of language production look nothing like the language's structure rules. This supports my third tentative proposal that the structure rules are the wrong sort to govern processing, a proposal that stands opposed to position (III). The case for the third proposal concludes in the next section.

Our focus here has been on processes arising from linguistic competence. Still we should acknowledge the role of other abilities in language production. Deciding how to convey a message is a surprisingly complicated pragmatic process: "the tailoring requirements are legion" (Bock 1999: 456). In tailoring an utterance, "production accommodates its processing to the needs of comprehension" (Ferreira 2003: 747). Thus, we have to choose what language to speak, whether to whisper or shout, whether to speak fast or slow, which referential expression to use for an object in mind, and so on. We take into account our relationship with the listeners, what we think they are capable of understanding,

---

[31] Levelt *et al.* (1999: 7) remain largely neutral on the issue but their peer commentators, Anne Cutler and Dennis Norris (1999) urge a common architecture for production and comprehension.

what we think they will find interesting, and what we suppose to be mutually known. We follow the Gricean cooperative principle. Some of these tailoring processes seem to be brute–causal—some "specific modifications occur unintentionally and automatically" (p. 749)—but some are surely central and rational. This does not demand any revision in the view that the speedy automatic processes of language production, whether arising from linguistic competence alone or partly from pragmatic abilities, are brute–causal, involving no metalinguistic representations.

This concludes our discussion of language production. We turn now to the other half of language use, language comprehension.

11.8   PSYCHOLOGY OF LANGUAGE COMPREHENSION

Work on language comprehension, like that on language production is not mostly addressing the architecture problems that concern us. There seems little interest in finding the rules of the language somehow embodied in the mind. Although the work on comprehension does not undermine our preliminary assessments, we shall see that it does not give them quite the support provided by the work on production.

We have just acknowledged the role in language production of abilities other than linguistic competence. There are very many of these "pragmatic" abilities involved in language comprehension and it will be helpful to start our discussion by mentioning some of them. The ultimate task in language comprehension is to grasp the thought that the speaker means to convey by a sentence. Part of this task is (typically) understanding the literal meaning of the sentence uttered. Parts of this are obviously not fulfilled simply by exercising lexical and syntactic competence. Thus, a person's lexical competence explains why she processes a sound /he/ as a pronoun but it does not explain why she assigns it one referent rather than another. Her lexical competence will explain why she might assign one of the two meanings of an ambiguous word like 'bank' but it will not explain which one she assigns; similarly, her syntactic competence, and an ambiguous structure like 'Visiting relatives can be boring'. Processing indexicals and ambiguous expressions requires abilities other than those that constitute mastery of the language. And much else that goes on in comprehension does too: "sentence processing necessarily involves the efficient use of many different types of information" (Gorrell 1999: 749). It is common to call the other abilities, "world knowledge", in distinction from the "linguistic knowledge" of lexical and syntactic competence (Gernsbacher and Kaschak 2003: 723). Some of this world knowledge is surely to be found in the central processor.

The world knowledge that plays a role in comprehension needs to be construed broadly to include not only general knowledge about the world but also knowledge of the discourse. As an example of the influence of discourse, consider how we often fix the referent of a pronoun: we take it as anaphoric on some noun phrase that was prominent in prior discourse. As an example of the influence of general knowledge, consider how we would understand, "Fiona poured wine into Alex's favorite glasses". Our knowledge that drinking glasses rather than eye glasses are appropriate receptacles for wine will determine our choice of interpretation. Part of our worldly knowledge is our knowledge of other minds. This plays an obvious role in our interpretation of deictic pronouns. We use our understanding of a speaker who says, "He is crazy", to determine the referent of 'he': given what she is looking at, gesturing at, or what is otherwise salient, given what we know about her, we figure out who she is likely to be referring to. We go through a similar process to interpret ambiguous names.[32] In general, in interpreting a speaker's utterance we take account of what we know of the speaker's interests and knowledge, what we think she would think interesting and appropriate to say, and so on. The Gricean cooperative principle plays a role in comprehension as in production.[33] Finally, we should note that we tend to favor the most frequent meaning in interpreting an ambiguous word or structure.

Although there is general agreement that comprehension involves all this world knowledge—what I have been picking out with my talk of "pragmatic abilities"—as well as strictly linguistic competence, there is not of course agreement about how it does. It is clear that linguistic competence alone can only match linguistic words and structures with concepts and thought structures that are parts of *possible* interpretations, given the language. We must look to pragmatic abilities to complete the interpretation where there are indexicals and to choose between possible interpretations where there is ambiguity. A key disagreement is over whether pragmatic abilities play a role in determining choice of structure *from the beginning* or whether there are some initial processes governed solely by syntactic competence. We shall consider this disagreement in a moment. But first we should continue with some further uncontroversial views about the role of linguistic competence in comprehension.

Our linguistic competence is deployed in word recognition and parsing: "the comprehender must recognize each of the words in the sentence and determine the syntactic (and semantic) relationship among them, as defined by the grammar of the language" (Tanenhaus 2003: 1142). Parsing assigns a syntactic analysis to the sentence. That together with the assignment of meanings in the process

---

[32] See Pietroski 2003 for some nice examples of the pragmatics of reference determination and related matters. It is worth noting that worldly knowledge plays a similar role with motor skills. Thus, given the state of a baseball game and beliefs about the pitcher, a batter expects a fastball and so "interprets" a pitch as a fastball unless presented with evidence, probably too late, that it is not.

[33] This is not to say that we should embrace the standard Gricean account of how people understand figurative language. Edward Wisniewski cites much evidence against this account. Thus, "given an appropriate discourse context, people do not take longer to understand figurative utterances". And it is not the case that "people seek nonliteral meanings if and only if the literal meaning makes no sense in context". "Just exactly how people understand figurative language is not resolved" (1998: 52).

of recognizing words yields a semantic interpretation. The sentence is not presented all at once: in speech, there is a stream of sounds; in reading (English), the eye focuses on the beginning of the sentence at its left and moves in jumps to the end of the sentence at its right. How soon does processing begin? "One thing that we can now be certain of is that sentence comprehension begins almost immediately" (Pickering 2003: 463). Thus, consider our processing of the spoken sentence. *The student spotted by the proctor was expelled.* "By the middle of the first vowel in *student*, potential lexical candidates, such as student, stool, and stoop are becoming active in memory, along with their associated syntactic and semantic representations." The choice between these candidates is made almost immediately: "convergence on the most likely lexical candidate occurs shortly after enough phonetic input is received to distinguish the input from other likely alternatives—often well before the word ends" (Tanenhaus 2003: 1143). Consider also the processing of the highly ambiguous word *bug*. "Research has shown that multiple meanings of *bug* are often initially activated by the language comprehension system. Then, within milliseconds, the appropriate meaning is selected, and the other meanings are discarded." Often this process involves the enhancement of some meaning by, for example, prior discourse: "by selectively suppressing and enhancing information, comprehenders can select the appropriate meanings of the words they encounter" (Gernsbacher and Kaschak 2003: 724). These examples illustrate the problem of word recognition. An analogous problem faces the parser. The presentation of a sentence often leads to temporary structural ambiguities. Thus, the initial fragment, *The student spotted,* in the sentence above is ambiguous until the sentence continues. The continuation makes it clear that the fragment is a relative clause but up to that point it could have been a main clause, as in *The student spotted the proctor and hid his crib sheet*; *spotted* could have been "attached" into the structure of the fragment in more than one way. Several models have been proposed of how speakers resolve such temporary ambiguities. "The assumption common to these models is that syntactic analysis is accomplished by a special computational device that makes direct use of grammatical information" (Tanenhaus and Trueswell 1995: 228). Finally, "working memory is important in language comprehension because words and syntactic structures need to be held in memory until a sentence has been processed fully" (Gernsbacher and Kaschak 2003: 725).

Turn now to disagreements. The one already mentioned has been the main focus of research: "researchers in sentence processing have been primarily concerned with how readers and listeners resolve the structural ambiguity that arises in assigning grammatical relationships to words and phrases as a sentence unfolds" (Tanenhaus 2003: 1143). "But can information such as semantic plausibility be used to 'guide' parsing in cases of ambiguity? This has been the dominant question in parsing research" (Pickering 2003: 463). To think that parsing is not guided in this way is to favor the modular view of parsing: the parser is autonomous. This view has the consequence that some comprehension processes arise wholly from syntactic competence. The view is the basis for the "*garden-path* model", one of "three broad theoretical frameworks" for research in this area. The other frameworks are "*referential theory*" and "*constraint-based* approaches" (Tanenhaus and Trueswell 1995: 229). I shall say a brief word about each.

The garden-path model is a serial one with two stages. The initial stage is guided by two principles. Lyn Frazier and Janet Fodor describe the first of these, "Minimal Attachment," as follows: "each lexical item (or other node) is to be attached into the phrase marker with the fewest possible number of nonterminal nodes linking it with the nodes which are already present" (1978: 320; see also Frazier and Rayner 1982). In following this rule "the parser chooses to do whatever costs it the least effort" (p. 295); it builds the simplest grammatical structure.[34] The other principle is "Late Closure": "make an attachment into the phrase that is currently being processed as long as the alternative attachments are equally simple" (Tanenhaus and Trueswell 1995: 230). The second stage of parsing is one of combination and revision. Only there can information about the discourse context and general knowledge of the world play a role; the first stage is governed by linguistic knowledge alone.

The referential theory has a different view. Stephen Crain and Mark Steedman argue that "the primary responsibility for the resolution of local syntactic ambiguities in natural language processing rests not with structural mechanisms", as in the garden-path model, "but rather with immediate, almost word-by-word interaction with semantics and reference to the context" (1985: 321; see also Ni *et al.* 1996). Interpretations are constructed in parallel and the parsing route is determined by whichever interpretation is the most plausible in the context (p. 328). So world knowledge and pragmatic factors are involved from the start. There are three principles for this. "The Principle of A Priori Plausibility" states: "If a reading is more plausible in terms either of general knowledge about the world, or of specific knowledge about the universe of discourse, then, other things being equal, it will be favored over one that is not" (p. 330). "The Principle of Referential Success" states: "If there is a reading that succeeds in referring to an entity already established in the hearer's mental model of the domain of discourse, then it is favored over one that does not" (p. 331). Finally there is "A Principle of Parsimony" to deal with a situation where "there are two or more possible senses neither of which succeeds in referring in the hearer's model" (p. 333).

Constraint-based models are similar to referential ones in some respects. They allow parallelism and multiple interactive sources of constraint on parsing, including general knowledge of the world. They do not require an initial stage guided simply be syntax. "Ambiguity resolution is viewed as a constraint-satisfaction

---

[34] The more recent "dependency locality theory" uses a similar principle (Gibson 2003: 1138–40).

process, involving competition among incompatible alternatives (Tanenhaus and Trueswell 1995: 232). "Models incorporating constraint-based ideas are increasingly realized within connectionist architectures" (Tanenhaus 2003: 1145).

Not surprisingly, connectionists make some bold claims about what they can accomplish with language. Thus, James McClelland claims that "a class of connectionist networks known as the simple recurrent net [SRN] ... could learn to become sensitive to long-distance dependencies characteristic of sentences with embedded clauses, suggesting that there may not be a need to posit explicit, inaccessible rules to account for human knowledge of syntax" (1999: 139). However, Steedman thinks that "claims to model human language acquisition using SRNs must be treated with some caution" (2003: 767). Anne Cutler has this to say about the state of play with word recognition: "The currently most explicit models are TRACE ... and SHORTLIST ..., both implemented as connectionist networks.... They both propose that the incoming signal activates potential candidate words that actively compete with one another by a process of interactive activation" (1999: 797).

There is no consensus on which of the models for comprehension should guide us to the future. Martin Pickering sums up the evidence as follows: "Overall, there is good evidence that people use many relevant sources of information rapidly, but it is unclear precisely which model of comprehension is correct" (2003: 464). According to Edward Gibson, "the details of the relative timing and strengths of the resource and informational constraints are currently not known" (2003: 1140). Steedman has this to say in a judicious comparison of the strengths and weaknesses of connectionist and symbolic approaches to language: "Neurocomputational mechanisms have proved their worth in the field of pattern recognition and classification, where they can extract structure latent in inputs such as images of faces, handwritten letters, and speech, and embody that structure in recognizers that would be impossible to specify by hand, or that are orders of magnitude more efficient than rule-based mechanisms, even when these are statistically optimized." But they have "been much less successful at demonstrating the kind of recursive productivity that rule-based systems are good at .... However, it has proven very difficult to build rule-based linguistic or computational-linguistic systems with coverage on the scale characteristic of human linguistic and reasoning abilities" (2003: 765). (The recursive productivity of linguistic competence may not be as big a problem for connectionism if I am right in section 11.6 in attributing this productivity to the productivity of thought.)

What are the implications of each model for our architectural concerns? The main debate in the literature we have been summarizing is about the interpretative clues that the hearer gets and the order in which they are used. There is much talk about knowledge and information but little attention to the way in which this knowledge and information is embodied in a hearer; see, for example, Tanenhaus and Trueswell 1995 and Pickering 2003. And, we should note, that there is much about the choice between interpretations that are possible given the language, but little about how linguistic competence makes those interpretations available for choice in the first place. Before there can be a resolution of a lexical or syntactic ambiguity, competence must generate some candidate interpretations. The literature seems to take it for granted that this step, at least, is brute–causal. Indeed, what else could it be? We can go further down this brute–causal path if we set aside garden-path models for a moment. Constraint-based theories, with their links to connectionism, certainly give support to a brute–causal associationist picture of the contribution of linguistic competence to speedy automatic language comprehension. And that picture also seems suitable for the rather similar referential theory, even though the theory is not presented in those terms. On all these theories, we can see an ambiguous word of an utterance as activating the several concepts with which it is linguistically associated, and an ambiguous structure as activating the several conceptual structures with which it is linguistically associated. At the same time multiple factors arising from general knowledge and context suppress some associations and enhance others, all in a fairly brute–causal way.

These considerations push us toward a brute–causal picture and my fourth tentative proposal, but a feature of the garden-path model may push us away from this. Frazier and Fodor take their theory to support the view that a hearer mentally represents the well-formedness conditions of her language:

> when making its subsequent decisions, the executive unit of the parser refers to the geometric arrangement of nodes in the partial phrase marker that it has already constructed. It then seems unavoidable that the well-formedness conditions on phrase markers are stored independently of the executive unit, and are accessed by it as needed. That is, the range of syntactically legitimate attachments at each point in a sentence must be determined by a survey of the syntactic rules for the language, rather than being incorporated into a fixed ranking of the moves the parser should make at that particular point... (1978: 322n)

So they are proposing a version of position (11): rules of the language are represented and used as data.[35] But it is unclear why the well-formedness conditions have to be represented and surveyed. Why could not the rules governing the "subsequent decisions" be embodied but unrepresented rules that *respect* (in my technical sense) the well-formedness conditions? It is hard to see what "pay off" there is in having the conditions represented. Pylyshyn's Razor counts against our supposing that they are (11.4).

Even if these conditions need not be represented, we may wonder whether, on this theory, the syntactic properties of the input have to be. The "executive unit"

---

[35] Note also Fodor's later commitment to the processor being "transparent" in the following sense: it "makes use of information about linguistic structure in the form in which the mental ("competence") grammar provides it, so that statements from the grammar do not have to be modified, translated, or 'pre-compiled' before they can be applied to sentences" (1989: 177).

has to take account of earlier parsing decisions which have been held in working memory (Gernsbacher and Kaschak 2003: 723). Could this be a brute–causal process? The answer to this must depend in part on the nature of working memory. This is another place where there are many models but it is far too early to draw conclusions. Thus Barbara Dosher summarizes three of these models, "the feature model", "the primacy model", and "the distributed associative memory model", noting that each has successes and failures. Yet each "assumes a quite different form of representation and makes quite different assumptions about the nature of memory" (Dosher 2003: 575). This seems to hold also for other models (Lewandowsky and Farrell 2003). Only one these many models, the ACT-R theory of Anderson discussed earlier (11.5), would be clearly committed to the representation of the syntactic properties of linguistic inputs. Still, it may well be that the garden-path model does require such representations.

Where does this brief discussion leave our preliminary assessments? Most importantly, it does not undermine them. And I think that it gives further support to our negative view of RT. Clearly constraint-based connectionist approaches support our assessment that the future will be fairly brute–causal, hence support our fourth tentative proposal. These approaches look promising but it is too early in the study of language comprehension to be confident that they are right. That assessment does not get the boost here that it got with language production. So the fourth proposal must be particularly tentative. Still it remains, in my view, better supported than the contrary view that the speedy automatic part of language processing operates on metalinguistic representations of syntactic and semantic properties.

Finally, in support of my third tentative proposal but contrary to position (III), we have seen no sign of the structure rules of the language governing the process of comprehension. Given the translational nature of the task, if RTM is correct, it would be odd if we had. Whether these rules for comprehension arise simply out of linguistic competence, like Minimal Attachment, or arise partly out of pragmatic world knowledge, like The Principle of A Priori Plausibility and the (implicit) rules governing a connectionist network, they seem nothing like the structure rules of the language. These rules for comprehension help us select among possible interpretations. The rules have to cope with the fact that the sentence is not delivered all at once. There have to be rules about how much to take account of before reacting and how to adjust in light of the next bit, etc. A rule for comprehension will not *be* a grammatical rule although it will, of course, *respect* grammatical rules. Consider, for example, the following proposal for handling empty categories in parsing: "Do not posit a trace at sentence position P if the sentence does not contain a suitable antecedent for a trace at P" (J. D. Fodor 1989: 160).[36] It is not surprising that "few attempts [at establishing

---

[36] See also the grammar-based rules proposed by Bradley Pritchett (1988) to handle garden-path phenomena.

the 'psychological reality' of specific syntactic frameworks] have been convincing" (Tanenhaus and Trueswell 1995: 223). The rules of such frameworks characterize the *structures* of linguistic items and so are the wrong sort to govern the *processes* of translating expressions with those structures into thoughts.[37]

This concludes the case for my third tentative hypothesis, a case that has been developing slowly throughout the book (2.4, 2.6, 3.2, 4.1, 11.4, 11.6, 11.7). The proposal has to be tentative, of course, because we know so little about language processing. Still, the proposal seems much more plausible than the alternative that the structure rules are processing rules. Our brief consideration of language use has provided much more evidence against this alternative than for it. And the alternative seems a priori unlikely given the translational task these rules have to perform.

11.9 CONCLUSION

In earlier chapters I have found no support for the Representational Thesis, the thesis that the structure rules of the language are represented in the mind (RT). My first, and main, goal in this chapter has been to argue that language use provides no persuasive evidence for RT and that RT is implausible. The only-theory-in-town abduction to establish RT is far too lacking in detail to be successful: it fails criterion (A2) of a good abduction (11.2). But its failures are much worse than that. It fails criterion (A1) because it is not plausible given what we already know and it fails criterion (B) in not being better than actual or likely alternatives. Indeed, I have argued that not only is it not now part of a good abduction it is unlikely to be so in the future. The preliminary stage of this argument was prior to addressing evidence from psycholinguistics. First, I presented the following considerations against RT: should we find evidence of a processing rule there is always the possibility that it is hardwired rather than represented; it is implausible that the translation task of language processing will involve a theoretical middleman; the linguistic rules are the wrong sort of rules to be processing rules; we have no reason to suppose that the rules of our preferred grammar are represented rather than those of another meaning-equivalent grammar; it is hard to see a place for the represented rules in the little that competencies may share; it is unclear how represented rules could be used as data; language processing is not plastic enough and is too fast for it to

---

[37] As Fodor notes: "The study of sentence parsing and production is concerned to a large extent with processes and procedures about which 'pure' linguistics makes no claims." However, she continues: "Its closest contact with linguistic theory concerns the properties of mental representation. How are sentence structures mentally represented by speaker/hearers? How is the grammar mentally represented?" (1992: 3). My second major conclusion, aimed at RT, implies that the grammar is not mentally represented by speaker/hearers. My fourth tentative proposal in favor of brute–causal processing implies that sentence structures are not either.

involve represented rules (11.4). I then considered what we can learn from the psychology of skills and their acquisition. For, linguistic competence is a skill and seems to be acquired by implicit learning. That psychology counts heavily against RT (11.5). The final stage of the argument briefly addressed the psycholinguistic evidence on language use. I claim that this evidence does not undermine our preliminary assessment that there is no place for RT in the explanation of language use. Indeed, the study gives further support to that assessment (11.7–11.8).

This argument provides the most important step in the case for my second major conclusion: there is no significant evidence for RT and, given what else we know, it is implausible. The final step in the case is in the next chapter.

According to position (I), the structure rules of the language are also processing rules that are represented and applied in language use. According to position (II), the structure rules are represented and used as data in processing. So both (I) and (II) are committed to RT. So the argument against RT obviously counts against these positions. But much of the argument mostly counts also against position (IV) which is committed to the representation of the processing rules for language use that are unlike the structure rules for the language.

My second goal in this chapter has been to cast doubt on position (III) and the view that the structure rules for the language are unrepresented processing rules. The structure rules are the wrong sort of rule to govern what is, given RTM, the translation process of language use. The rules governing the retrieval processes of language production and the interpretative process of language comprehension look nothing like the language's structure rules: my third tentative hypothesis (11.4, 11.6–11.8).

These arguments against (I) to (IV) count in favor of (V). So I think that we can predict with a fair amount of confidence that the explanation of language use will support (V): the processing rules are unrepresented and largely unlike the structure rules of the language.

My final goal concerned the metalinguistic representations of the syntactic and semantic properties of linguistic items. According to version (a) of (V), the processing rules operate on these representations; according to version (b), they do not. If the Representation Thesis were true then version (a) would be but even if RT is false, (a) might be true: processing is a rational information flow even if the rules governing it are not represented. My goal has been to cast doubt on this view, trying to make (b) seem plausible. I presented a case for the view that the speedy automatic language processes arising wholly or, at least, partly from linguistic competence are fairly brute–causal associationist processes. The case is relatively a priori and far from decisive but I think it is appealing. It gets support from the prominence of connectionist models in the theory of language production and, at least, is not undermined by the state of play in theorizing about language comprehension. I think that we can predict with some small confidence that we will discover that language processing does not operate on metalinguistic properties of the linguistic expressions but is more brute–causal: my fourth tentative proposal (11.6–11.8).

My argument for this proposal, like the argument against RT that dominates this chapter, reflect my commitment to Pylyshyn's Razor. I think that RT is implausible because the speaker's representation of linguistic rules does no explanatory work. And the difficulties in finding explanatory work for representations of linguistic properties leads me to the fourth tentative proposal.

The received Chomskian view is that the rules of a language are psychologically real in a speaker—whether they are represented or not—and play a role in language processing. My fourth major conclusion, arising from the view that language expresses thought (LET), was that this issue of psychological reality should be investigated from a perspective on thought (8.3). This has already yielded some significant results, both positive and negative. On the positive side, I have argued first for the controversial Language-of-Thought Hypothesis (LOTH) and then on that basis for (T) and my first tentative proposal: a language is largely psychologically real in a speaker in that its rules are similar to the structure rules of her thought (9.5). And to the extent of that similarity, the linguistic rules play a role in language processing because the rules governing that processing operate on syntactic properties determined by the structure rules of thoughts. On the negative side, if LOTH and hence (T) are false, the arguments in this chapter against (I) to (III) imply that the rules of the language are not psychologically real in any other robust way. We have arrived at my *fifth tentative proposal*: if LOTH is false, then the rules of a language are not, in a robust way, psychologically real in a speaker.[38]

The fourth major conclusion will yield further results in the next chapter when we consider language acquisition. This consideration does not change the assessment of language use in this chapter.

---

[38] I noted the possibility earlier (4.6) of a less robust "intermediate" view on the psychologically real issue: the grammar is descriptive of competence in a way stronger than simply positing rules that are respected by competence—position (M)—but weaker than positing rules that govern processing—positions (I) and (III)—or are used as data in processing—position (II). I have not argued that there is no such position. But if there were, then the challenge would be to show that it was *theoretically interesting* that the grammar was descriptive of competence in that way.

12

Language Acquisition

12.1 INNATENESS THESES

Chomsky is famous for his strongly nativist answer to his question (ii), "How is knowledge of language acquired?" (1.1). There is a rich innate "initial state" for language acquisition that heavily constrains the languages that humans can acquire in the way we naturally acquire our native language. On the basis of this initial state and "primary linguistic data" ("PLD"), a person's competence in some language "grows" until it reaches a "final state". Because of the innate constraint, there is a certain system of rules (or principles) shared by all natural human languages.

'UG' ('Universal Grammar') is used to refer, at least, to a theory of this shared system of rules. But, because the received view is that the initial state *embodies* these shared rules, 'UG' is often used as if it were *definitive* that it refers also to a theory of the linguistic rules innately embodied in the mind (or, perhaps to the rules themselves innately embodied). For reasons that will quickly become apparent, it suits my purposes not to follow that usage. I shall take it as definitive of 'UG' that it refers to a theory of the shared rules, leaving it as an open question whether or not those rules constitute the initial state.[1]

Our main concern in this book has been with the final state of a person's competence in a language and with the place of the rules, described by the grammar of that language, in that state; our main concern has been with positions on this described in section 3.4. We have so far found no persuasive evidence to support the view that this final state consists in a representation of the rules of the language, no persuasive evidence for the Representational Thesis (RT). So we have found no persuasive evidence for position (i) according to which those rules are represented and applied in processing, nor for position (ii) according to which those are represented and used as data in processing. Indeed,

---

[1] Although there is a lot of agreement about UG, agreement about what rules *are* shared and innately embodied, there is still some disagreement. The disagreement is beside the point of this chapter and so I shall ignore it, writing as if there were a settled UG.

the evidence suggests that the rules are not represented. This evidence includes the evidence on the nature of skills, discussed in section 11.5. For, competence in a language is a skill and the weight of evidence is that skills do not typically involve representations of the rules that govern them. The evidence discussed in that section also included evidence from skill *learning*. Language learning seems to be a paradigm of *implicit* learning and the evidence strongly suggests that implicitly learning a skill does not involve representing the rules that govern it. However, that earlier brief discussion of language learning did not address the very important innateness issue. Perhaps attention to this issue will show that RT is true after all. We shall address that question at the end of the chapter. We shall see that the bearing of the innateness issue on RT, and on other views of the final state, is not as direct as one might have expected.

Aside from considering this bearing, an interest in the psychological reality of language leads to a concern with the innateness issue in its own right. What is the initial state from which the final state of competence arises? In particular, are the rules described by UG embodied, perhaps even represented, in the initial state? Most of this chapter will be concerned with these questions and Chomsky's nativist answer to them.

Chomsky's claims about innateness are thought by him and others to force a reassessment of the traditional debate between empiricists and rationalists over "innate ideas". Rationalists thought that many concepts were innate. Empiricists rejected this. It is thought that Chomsky's nativism strongly supports the rationalist side.

In considering this nativism, it is important to distinguish a range of different theses that are not adequately distinguished in the literature. First, there is a *boring* thesis. This is the thesis that human beings are innately predisposed to learn languages; it is because of some innate initial state that, given linguistic data, almost every human learns a language. The thesis is boring because every informed person, even the crudest empiricist, should believe it and, so far as I know, does believe it. How else, for example, could one explain the fact that humans can, but dogs cannot, learn English? One needs to go further to make an innateness claim interesting, saying something about the innate initial state. Chomsky, of course, typically goes a lot further.[2]

Second, there is a set of three *interesting* theses:

1. The initial state is *a language-specific learning device in a distinct "language faculty" not in the central processor*. The innate state that makes language learning possible is not simply a general learning device that makes all learning possible, it is a special, relatively central, module of the mind.

---

[2] However in one place, amazingly, Chomsky does seem to take the innateness thesis to be the boring one: "To say that 'language is not innate' is to say that there is no difference between my granddaughter, a rock, and a rabbit" (2000b: 50).

This is the minimal interesting nativist thesis. It tells us *where* the initial state is in the mind. But it does not tell us anything about the constraints that this state puts on language learning. The next thesis does.

2. The initial state *constrains humans to learn only languages that conform to UG*. So any language that they can learn naturally will have rules specified by UG. Let us describe this as the initial state "respecting" the rules described by UG—the "UG-rules"—on analogy with our earlier talk of the final state of competence respecting the rules described by the grammar of the language learnt. We pointed out that this thesis about the final state should be uncontroversial (2.4). Not so the thesis about the initial state. For, if it is right, the universality of UG-rules is not a mere accident of human history but is determined by our biological heritage: it is "in our genes".

This seems to me a *more* interesting thesis than 1. Where 1 simply tells us where the initial state is, 2 tells us that this state constrains our languages in a very significant way. But 2 does not tell us *what* innate language-constraining rules in the initial state make this state respect the UG-rules. The next thesis does.

3. The initial state respects the UG-rules *because it embodies the UG-rules*. Not merely do we inherit *some* language-constraining rules that makes us respect the UG-rules, which is all that thesis 2 requires, we inherit the UG-rules themselves.

This addresses the "what" issue and so is clearly an *even more* interesting thesis than 2. I suspect that linguists find the move from 2 to 3 easy because of their conflation of a theory of syntax—a grammar—with a theory of competence. I emphasized that the conflation encourages the view that the psychological reality of grammatical rules "comes for nothing" with the grammar (Ch. 2). Similarly it encourages the view that the psychological reality of UG-rules "comes for nothing" with universal grammar, UG. Suppose that this reality did come for nothing. Then the idea that the initial state respects the UG-rules because the UG-rules are innate would be very inviting, even if not compelling. But the psychological reality does not come for nothing: the conflation is a mistake. The psychological reality of UG-rules is not a "free lunch" but something that requires psychological evidence.[3]

Combining 1 and 3 we get the view that the language-constraining rules are UG-rules and they are in a language faculty. Chomsky certainly embraces theses 1 and 3, at least (1991a: 22). Now it is important to note that neither of these theses entail that speakers have innate representations of linguistic rules or innate propositional knowledge—knowledge-that—about them: the innate rules might be simply embodied and any innate knowledge might be simply knowledge-how (3.1). As a

---

[3] Two nativists inspired by Chomsky recently stated their nativism in a form that entails 2 but not 3: "there are substantive 'universal' principles of human grammar and, as a result of human biology, children can only acquire languages that conform to these principles" (Crain and Pietroski 2002: 163).

result, these theses alone do not entail the existence of any innate *concepts* and so do not seem to bear on the traditional debate over innate ideas. In any case, interesting as these theses undoubtedly are, they are not at the center of the debate. For, Chomsky and his followers seem to go significantly beyond them in claiming that linguistic rules are indeed innately represented and propositionally known.

Third, this move to knowledge and representation turns the interesting thesis 3 into a *very exciting* thesis that clearly involves a commitment to innate ideas. This is a thesis that no empiricist, traditional or contemporary, could allow:

3R. The UG-rules that are innately embodied according to 3 are so *because they are innately represented in Mentalese*: UG itself, the theory of those rules, is innately known. This "initial-state representationalism" is, of course, the ana-logue of the "final-state representationalism" expressed by the Representational Thesis (RT). So, let us call 3R the "I-Representational Thesis".

Combining 3R with 1 yields the view that the language-constraining rules represented in the language faculty in Mentalese are UG-rules: UG itself is innately known and in the language faculty.

There can be no doubt of Chomsky's commitment to a distinct language faculty and so to thesis 1. And it is natural to take him to be committed to 3R and I-Representationalism just as it was natural to take him to be committed to RT (1.1); see Chomsky 1965, pp. 25–33, for example. Certainly, Jerry Fodor takes him to be:

what Chomsky thinks is innate is primarily a certain *body of information*: the child is, so to speak "born knowing" certain facts about universal constraints on possible human languages. (1983: 4)

Indeed, as Fodor points out, only by construing Chomsky's nativism in this way can we see it as in the rationalist tradition of innate ideas:

It's because Chomsky holds that the innate information available in the initial state of language acquisition is *ipso facto* among the intentional object of the learner's proposa-tional attitudes that Chomsky's theory of mind is indeed continuous with the tradition-ally rationalist postulation of innate *ideas*. (2001: 109–10)

Graves *et al.* make the same point in attributing innate tacit knowledge to the child:

In order for rationalists to argue from the existence of innate *structures* to the existence of innate *knowledge*, some notion of tacit knowledge is required so that they can claim that the grammatical structures represented in transformational grammars are objects of knowledge. (1973: 318)

So it seems that Chomsky believes the combination of 1 and 3R, the most exciting thesis of all. A great deal of the attention given to Chomsky's claims about innateness comes from construing them in this very exciting way. So I shall call this combination "Chomskian Nativism".

12.2 EVIDENCE FOR NATIVISM

In this section, I shall briefly consider some arguments, mostly very familiar ones, noting which of the various nativist theses they seem to support.

Sui generis: It is pointed out that language learning is *sui generis*: it is quite unlike the acquisition of other cognitive skills. (i) It is done very young and has to be done before about age twelve, within "the critical period". (ii) The level of achievement is quite uniform by comparison to other intellectual skills: *all* normal children acquire a language. (iii) All children, whatever their language, acquire elements of linguistic capacity in the same order. Acquisition is developmentally uniform across individuals and cultures.[4]

This evidence might well be thought to support thesis 1, the minimal interesting nativist thesis that language learning is controlled by a language-specific faculty, distinct from the central processor. I shall later argue that this evidence is in fact quite compatible with language learning being controlled by the central processor (12.5). What needs to be emphasized now, however, is that this evidence alone gives no support to thesis 2, hence none to 3 or 3R, because it throws no light on the constraints that the initial state places on the languages that we can learn. In particular, it does not show that they must comply with the UG-rules.

I turn to some arguments that, taken as a package, give persuasive support to thesis 2: humans are innately constrained to learn only languages that conform to UG; the initial state respects the UG-rules. This is certainly an interesting nativist thesis, but it is not as strong as 3, let alone 3R. What needs to be emphasized is that these familiar arguments alone do not justify adopting a stronger thesis than 2, because they do not show us what it is about the initial state that makes it respect the UG-rules. Nor do these arguments support thesis 1, for they throw no light on where the initial state is to be located in the mind. In sum, these arguments leave us way short of Chomskian Nativism.

Universality: The first argument is simple. Suppose, as I am prepared to, that the linguists are right in thinking that all human languages are governed by UG-rules. Then this is a very striking universality. UG-rules are quite unobvious and it is not hard to invent a language that is not governed by them; for example, one that does not observe the structure-dependency principle. How come no human language is like this? Thesis 2 provides a plausible explanation: humans are innately constrained to speak only UG languages. Indeed, how else is the universality to be explained? Putnam (1967) has an answer: human languages are all governed by UG-rules because they are all, as Stephen Stich puts it, "descended from a single common ur-language whose details have been lost in pre-history" (1978a: 283). Putnam points out that if nativism were correct

---

[4] See Laurence and Margolis 2001, sec. 4 for a nice summary.

then our language capacity would have come in just one evolutionary leap. Now if there was that one leap, it very likely yielded a single language which was the common ancestor of all human languages. But then having that common ancestor alone explains why all languages share certain rules. So, we have no need to see humans as innately constrained to follow those rules: they follow them because, "by chance", the first language followed them and has passed them on. However, this ingenious explanation has a crucial flaw. Not all human languages *are* descended from a common ancestor: some are created almost from scratch, as we shall see in a moment. So the nativist explanation still seems the best.

Poverty of Stimulus: The nativist argument that receives the most emphasis concerns the poverty of stimulus received by the language learner. The grammatical rules picked up by the child are abstract, subtle, and unobvious. Yet, Chomsky claims, the child learns these rules from data of degenerate quality and limited range (1965: 58). The problem with the quality is that the data include many ungrammatical strings: false starts, slips of tongue, 'um's and 'ah's, and so on. The problem with the range is that the data seem to provide no evidence bearing on many of the rules that the child masters; in particular, they contain little explicit instruction and almost no negative evidence, evidence that something is *not* grammatical. It is hard to see how the child could derive the linguistic rules from these impoverished data available to her. She must have a head start, being tightly constrained to favour UG-rules.

This argument for thesis 2 has a lot of appeal at first sight but that appeal is greatly diminished by a closer look. First, Fiona Cowie (1998: chs 8 and 9) has argued persuasively that the linguists' claims about the data available to the child, plausible as they may seem, are actually rather dubious.[5] For, they are largely based on the intuitions of linguists about the available data rather than on empirical evidence. And where attempts have been made to gather the evidence they suggest that the data available to the child is much richer than Chomskians suppose; for example, that it includes evidence for the structure-dependency principle; and that it includes lots of negative evidence. In sum, we lack evidence about just how impoverished the child's data really is.

Next, I think that the possibility of an alternative nonnativist explanation of learning from impoverished data has been dismissed too quickly. Chomsky tends to restrict his opponents to crude empiricist methods of learning that are hopelessly inadequate to explain learning *in general*. So one possible response to Chomsky is to posit a richer and more sophisticated innate *general* learning

---

[5] Laurence and Margolis (2001) are not convinced. Nor are Crain and Pietroski (2001). See Lewis and Ellman 2001; Pullum and Scholz 2002; and Scholz and Pullum 2002 and 2006, for further criticisms of poverty of stimulus arguments. Lewis and Ellman draw attention to the importance of statistical information available to the language learner: "the statistical structure of language provides for far more sophisticated inferences than those which can be made within a theory that consides only whether or not a particular form appears" (p. 369).

device. In effect, Putnam made a response of this sort (1967: 297–8). Cowie has several interesting further suggestions along these lines. But our earlier discussion of the psychology of skills (11.5) suggests a rather different response. Where Putnam and Cowie follow Chomsky in treating language learning as if it were a largely top-down rational process, we should rather treat it as the largely bottom-up implicit learning of a skill, more brute–causal than rational.[6] Although it is plausible to think that many skills are acquired in the implicit way, we know very little about how they are. In particular, we know next to nothing about how a skill might be thus acquired on the basis of what seems to be impoverished data. (How *do* we learn to throw a frisbee or ride a bicycle?) If we did know more about this in general, we might be able to see how a child could learn a language from impoverished data.

So I think that we should be a bit dubious of the claim that the data available to the child is so impoverished and a bit dubious of the claim that the child could not learn a language from such data as is available. Despite these doubts, the poverty-of-stimulus argument does still seem to me to have some force. For, it does still seem to me *likely* that the data available to the child is too impoverished for her to learn the language unless she is tightly constrained. I just think the poverty-of-stimulus argument we have been considering is some way from having established this. However, the arguments to follow, which one might also label "poverty-of-stimulus arguments", do seem to me to advance the case for nativism considerably.

Language Creation: (i) Some natural languages are sign languages. These are also governed by UG-rules but are nonetheless often very different from the local spoken language: "natural sign languages show all the structural properties of other human languages yet have evolved independently of the spoken languages that surround them" (Newport and Supalla 1999: 758). Thus, ASL, widely used among the deaf in America, is very different from English but similar to some other spoken languages. This strongly suggests that the initial state for human language is innately constrained to respect the UG-rules, as thesis 2 claims. This is further confirmed by the fact that children do not readily acquire *derivative* sign languages, ones intentionally invented, "presumably because [these languages violate] natural structural principles for human languages" (p. 758). (ii) The deaf provide another example of language creation: "isolated deaf children not exposed to signed languages spontaneously generate gestural systems that share many formal and substantive features with received languages" (Gleitman and Bloom 1999: 435). *The New York Times* recently described an example. The al Sayyid Bedouin Sign Language, used by about 150 deaf people in a village in the Negev desert, "developed spontaneously and without outside influence. It is not related to Israeli or Jordanian sign languages, and its word order differs from

---

[6] And this treatment gets some support from studies on early mappings of words to referents; Samuelson and Smith 1998, 2000.

that of the spoken languages of the region". The language "which started only 70 years ago" is still "under development" (Wade 2005: F3). (iii) There is striking evidence, discussed by Pinker (1994: 32–9), that children brought up speaking Pidgin—a simple makeshift language with little grammar—"creolize" that language *in one generation* into a language with the complex grammar of any normal human language. Thus, young Nicaraguan deaf children brought into a school where the older children used a pidgin sign language, LSN, developed a creole sign language, ISN. All of this suggests that "children do not merely learn language; they create it" (Gleitman and Bloom 1999: 436). And the fact that the languages they create all conform to UG-rules is powerful evidence for thesis 2.

The Continuity Hypothesis: Stephen Crain and his colleagues have urged "the continuity hypothesis", maintaining "that child language can differ from the language of the linguistic community only in ways that adult languages can differ from each other" (Crain and Pietroski 2001: 146). Children do not immediately arrive at the language that surrounds them, they make "errors"; for example, many insert " 'extra' Wh-words in their long-distance questions" as in 'What do you think what pigs eat?' This "error" is "presumably not a response to the children's [English-speaking] environment" (p. 179) but it exemplifies a construction found in German and some other languages. This seems to be evidence that "children are trying out grammars with features found in adult languages elsewhere on the globe" (pp. 178–9). If it can be established that children never try out languages that violate principles of Universal Grammar, then this would indeed be further strong evidence for the nativist thesis 2.[7]

In sum, I think that Universality, Poverty of Stimulus, Language Creation, and the Continuity Hypothesis, jointly present a persuasive case for thesis 2.[8] However, it is important to note, they alone are not sufficient to establish anything stronger. They support the view that the initial state respects the UG-rules but tell us nothing about what makes that state respect these rules. Thus, they alone do not establish that the initial state respects the rules by embodying them, thesis 3, and even less that it does so by representing them, thesis 3R. Nor do the arguments tell us that the initial state is in a language faculty, thesis 1. Only Sui Generis seems to give direct support to thesis 1.

---

[7] See Crain and Pietroski 2002, sec. 3 for a summary of further evidence for the continuity hypothesis.

[8] I don't think that the case is conclusive, however: more work needs to be done. And I join with Scholz and Pullum (2006) in being skeptical of recent triumphalist claims for linguistic nativism. A particular cause of concern about 2 arises from the distinction between "core language" and "periphery" where the latter is not "determined by fixing values for the parameters of UG" (Chomsky 1986: 147). On the basis of a study of the hard cases for linguistic theory, "the syntactic nuts", Peter Culicover (1999) has argued that the periphery is so extensive as to cast doubt on the whole idea that there is a core determined by UG; see J. D. Fodor 2001 for a judicious assessment of the argument. (Thanks to my student Francesco Pupa for drawing my attention to this issue.)

In what follows I shall take thesis 2 for granted. So, an interesting nativism will not be in question. I shall be concerned with whether we should go further down the nativist path. I shall start by dismissing the argument that we should go much further to 3R and I-Representationalism because that is "the only theory in town" (12.3). But, on a positive note, I shall present a case for adopting thesis 3, or something close (12.4). I shall then turn negative again, looking skeptically at thesis 1 (12.5). And I shall argue firmly against adopting the I-Representational Thesis (12.6). I shall conclude by considering the bearing of this discussion on the main concern of this book, the nature of the final state (12.7). This will conclude my argument against RT. So I will be concluding that a person in the initial state is totally ignorant of the rules of UG and a person in the final state can be totally ignorant of the rules of her language.

12.3   "THE ONLY THEORY IN TOWN" AND I-REPRESENTATIONALISM (THESIS 3R)

We are assuming that the initial state respects the UG-rules—thesis 2—but why should we take the large step to the "very exciting" I-Representationalist thesis 3R? Even if thesis 3 is correct and humans respect the UG-rules because the initial state embodies them, why suppose that it does so by *representing* them? Why suppose that UG itself is psychologically real?

Once again we face an only-theory-in-town argument (cf. 11.2). Many linguists think that we can explain language learning if we see it as a rational process of hypothesis testing or, recently, of parameter setting, for the language of the child's community. *And there is no other way to explain it.* So, any linguistic rule that plays a role in language learning has to be represented, for that is what the rational process demands.

Fodor has offered the most explicit version of this argument. He characterizes Chomsky's account of language learning as follows:

[It] is the story of how innate endowment and perceptual experience interact *in virtue of their respective contents*: the child is viewed as using his primary linguistic data either to decide among the candidate grammars that an innately represented "General Linguistic Theory" enumerates (Chomsky 1965) or to "calibrate" endogenous rule schemas by fixing parameter values that the innate endowment leaves unspecified (Chomsky 1982). This sort of story makes perfectly good sense so long as what is innate is viewed as *having* propositional content: as expressing linguistic universals, or rule schemas, or whatever. But it makes no sense at all on the opposite assumption.   (1983: 5)

And Fodor emphasizes, with characteristic exhuberance, "that *no* account of language learning which does not thus involve propositional attitudes and mental processes has ever been proposed by anyone, barring only behaviorists" (1981a: 194).

I have earlier (11.2) suggested two criteria for a good abduction. (A) The abduction must involve a *good* explanation. This has at least two parts. (A1) The explanation must be plausible given what we already know. (A2) The explanation must have an appropriate level of detail. (B) The explanation must be *better* than any alternative that is actual or likely given what we already know. With these criteria in mind, it is interesting to consider some of Fodor's responses (2001) to Cowie's critique of Chomskian Nativism, a nativism that she rightly takes to include I-Representationalism.[9]

As Fodor notes, Cowie accepts that Chomskian Nativism "is the best available theory of language acquisition" because rival theories "do not yet exist". Yet she still rejects an abduction along the lines illustrated above (Cowie 1999: 249). Fodor finds this "puzzling": "One might have thought that I *just couldn't have* a better reason for preferring my theory to yours than that yours doesn't exist" (2001: 115n). There is no puzzle. Cowie is prepared to accept that the Chomskian explanation is the best currently available. But she also clearly thinks, for reasons described briefly below, that it is *not good enough*; it is not "sufficiently well articulated at this time" (p. 210); "it provides no real explanation of language acquisition at all" (p. 249). In brief, she thinks that it badly fails my criterion (A). Indeed, she may also think that it fails criterion (B), for she thinks that the development of alternative explanations has been stifled by the dominance of the Chomskian paradigm. So she may not think that the Chomskian explanation is better than any alternative that is *likely* given what we already know. In any case, it is clear that what she is urging is that we *suspend judgment* on Chomskian Nativism.

We might anticipate that Fodor would be unimpressed with the virtues of this course of action. Years ago he claimed that "remotely plausible theories are better than no theories at all" (1975: 27). And he seems never to have met an only-theory-in-town argument he didn't like. So it is no surprise that he is quite unmoved by Cowie's criticism that Chomskian theories do not show *how* a language learner exploits the information allegedly provided by UG. "Cowie needs a *principled* reason for doubting that the problem about how UGs function in language acquisition can be solved" (2001: 117).[10] No she doesn't! Fodor thinks that "all she's got is that, to date, nobody has solved it" (*ibid*). *And that, near enough, is all she needs to suspend judgment.* She would need a principled

---

[9] In his enthusiasm for Cowie's critique, which knows every bound, Fodor strangely misrepresents her as rejecting (what I have called) RT (2001: 111–13). I only wish that she did but she didn't. She takes Chomsky's famous argument against Skinner to have "established" that "language mastery involves a wealth of syntactic, semantic, and pragmatic knowledge . . . . It requires the endorsement of (R)" (1999: 162). (R) is a thesis, "Representationalism", that is similar to my RT.

[10] Consider also the following response: "the entire force of [Cowie's] argument comes down to the observation that specific UG-based accounts of particular aspects of language acquisition are controversial" (Laurence and Margolis 2001: 260).

reason for doubting that an innate UG could explain language acquisition if she were arguing that it couldn't. But she is not. Rather, she is arguing that we have insufficient reason *now* to say that an innate UG *does* explain language acquisition.[11]

It may be better to *entertain* remotely plausible theories rather than entertain none but that does not show that it is better to *believe* those theories rather than believe none. And it is not better *unless there is good evidence for them*. Fodor's abductive standards are too low.

Further confirmation of this emerges later. According to the famous poverty-of-stimulus argument for Chomskian Nativism, the PLD is too impoverished for a person to learn a language from it without the help of rich innate linguistic constraints. Cowie's extensive study of the empirical literature leaves her skeptical about this. Again, Fodor is unimpressed. "What she needs, but clearly doesn't have, is an argument that the available data suggests, even remotely, a PLD so rich that the child can, as it were, squeeze through with lots of room to spare" (2001: 121). And, once again, she doesn't need this. To suspend judgment she does not have to argue that the PLD is that rich. She just has to argue, as she does, that there is a *lack of evidence* that the PLD is as poor as the poverty-of-stimulus argument demands. She is arguing that there has been an unwarranted rush to judgment, not that the judgment is wrong.

Cowie's reasons for having a dim view of the currently available Chomskian nativist explanations of language acquisition are briefly as follows. These explanations come in two sorts, the older hypothesis-testing models and the currently more popular parameter-setting models. She discusses the latter first. She rightly points out that "there is no parameter-setting theory of language acquisition" but really only "theory fragments" (1999: 257). She argues, convincingly in my view, that these fragments have many problems (pp. 257–63). She then considers hypothesis-testing models. Formal learning theory has developed sophisticated versions of these which arguably show how languages might be learn*able* but they are not, and do not claim to be, psychologically plausible. They do not show how a child could learn a language "within some developmentally credible amount of time" (p. 266) and they ascribe assumptions to the learner that cannot plausibily be ascribed to a child (pp. 266–9). Years ago, Pinker gave six conditions that a theory of language acquisition must satisfy and argued that "no current theory of language learning satisfies, or even addresses itself to, all six conditions" (1979: 218). Cowie concludes, I think rightly, that "the situation is little better today" (1999: 270).

---

[11] Collins also misses this point: "Cowie (1999, p. 272) scolds the nativist for 'I'm the only president you've got'-style arguments; this is quite jejune. No-one seriously involved in linguistics and related disciplines is trying to gain any knock-outs" of empiricism (2003: 187). Cowie's main criticism of this style of nativist argument is not that it fails to "knock out" empiricism but that it does not justify Chomskian Nativism.

Fodor's response to Cowie's criticism of Chomskian Nativism is an extreme example of a common response to such criticisms. Time and again the lack of a detailed alternative empiricist explanation of language acquisition is trotted out as if it were a near decisive point in favor of Chomskian Nativism. Consider another three responses to Cowie, for example.[12] (i) Crain and Pietroski have the following plonking response to Cowie's suggestions about the data that may be available to the child and about what the child might be able to extract from the data: "These would be interesting suggestions, were they accompanied by a proposal about how children extract the various kinds of constraints ... from the data available to them. But Cowie does not, in this sense offer an alternative to positing a Universal Grammar" (2001: 159–60). (ii) Stephen Laurence and Eric Margolis clearly give a lot of weight to the following: "*No one* has a fully articulated account of language acquisition to offer and between the two camps nativists clearly have the more detailed theories" (2001: 244). (iii) John Collins defends Chomsky's demand that the empiricist produce an alternative as follows: "It is because empiricism and its behaviourist progeny so grievously underestimated the complexity of what a speaker knows that it is apposite to demand concrete proposals which are sensitive to the many data. Otherwise, there is 'nothing to discuss' " (2003: 187). But, to repeat the methodological point, the defense of Chomskian Nativism requires much more than pointing to the poor state of alternatives. It requires that the nativist explanation be good. And that requires that *it* be worked out in sufficient detail to be convincing. Until that has been done, we should suspend judgment on it even if we had no ideas for an alternative.

Finally, it is worth noting that there are some well-known problems for parameter-setting models. On these models, the language acquisition device has to set twenty to thirty binary switches on the basis of PLD. That's all. This might seem fairly simple at first sight. Yet, in fact, it is very difficult. Here is the problem:

No input sentence ever exhibits the action of one and only one parameter. Even the simplest sentences involve combinations of parameter settings. A simple transitive sentence in English, for example, involves the action of parameters regulating the direction and form of Case assignment, the attachment of verbal morphology, agreement, and theta-role assignment. Thus, sentences look the way they do because principles and parameters form coalitions to derive the language. In order to represent the input stream and properly set parameters to their target values, the learner must untangle these coalitions of parameters. (Clark 1994: 483)

Some ingenious attempts have been made to solve this problem but none has yet succeeded. Janet Fodor sums up the situation as follows:

---

[12] Consider also Lasnik and Uriagereka 2002 (p. 150) and Crain and Pietroski 2002 (pp. 173–6), responding to Pullum and Scholz 2002. Scholz and Pullum aptly reply: "It is possible to evaluate an argument for a view without raising questions of theory comparison" (2002: 187).

Despite years of effort, it has proven extremely difficult to show how the syntax of a natural language could be acquired even if it were completely innate except for 20 to 30 binary choices to be determined by the input sample.   (2001: 368)[13]

In sum, Cowie finds the abductive argument for 3R and I-Representationalism unconvincing. I think that she is right to do so. Still, as noted, she is inclined to think that I-Representationalism yields the best explanation of language acquisition currently available, even though not one that is good enough. I think that this is far too generous. In the next three sections I shall say why: given what we already know, explanations along other lines seem much more promising.

12.4   EMBODIMENT OF UG-RULES (THESIS 3)

In these three sections, I shall be arguing about which way the future may lie in the explanation of language acquisition. I shall certainly *not* be aiming to establish an abduction that is a rival to the only-theory-in-town one. That would be a foolish aim at this time because, so far as I can see, we are *nowhere near* an explanation of language acquisition with sufficient detail and evidential support to be the basis of such an abduction. So, the best we can hope for at this time is an explanation sketch that seems likely to be the basis for a persuasive future abduction. This is not surprising. Linguistic competence is a skill and, as we noted earlier (11.5), it is very early days in our understanding of skills and their acquisition. Given how little we know about the acquisition of skills in general it would indeed be surprising if we *could* explain language acquisition. Not so long ago, Reber bemoaned the fact "that the topic of learning should be so poorly represented in the contemporary literature in cognitive psychology". Indeed, he thought that this may explain the move to nativism. "Failure to explicate how complex knowledge is acquired invites the supposition that 'it was there all the time' " (1989: 219).

Far as we are from an explanation of language acquisition, psycholinguists are of course making steady progress toward one. I want to suggest a place where some other progress can be made. According to thesis 2, which we are assuming, humans are innately predisposed to learn languages that conform to UG; the initial state respects the UG-rules. Clearly this calls for an explanation: What is it about initial state that makes it respect those rules? How do we explain the respect? The answer must form the core of any explanation of language acquisition. So, any light that we can throw on the answer should guide us in seeking an explanation of language acquisition, it should guide us to the future.

---

[13] I am indebted to Janet Fodor for instruction in these matters. She and her colleagues at CUNY think that they are on the way to a solution. The key is the "parametric decoding" of the input sentences: "Sentences must be parsed to discover the properties that select between parameter values." (Fodor 1998: 339)

Thesis 3 provides an answer: the initial state respects UG-rules because it embodies them; those very rules are innate in us. In this section I shall explore the prospects of this explanation from the perspective of views on the nature of thoughts presented in Part IV. I shall also very briefly consider the prospects of some alternative explanations. In the next, section 12.5, I shall consider the consequences of this discussion for the language faculty and thesis 1. None of this discussion suggests that the initial state represents UG-rules as thesis 3R, and hence Chomskian Nativism, requires. I shall continue the case against this I-Representationalist thesis in section 12.6. 3R is not only not now part of a good explanation of language acquisition (12.3) but, given what we already know, it is not likely to be part of a good explanation in the future.

A view of how a competence is acquired needs to be guided by a view of the nature of the competence that is acquired.[14] So, our view of language acquisition should be guided by our view of the final state of linguistic competence. The relatively uncontroversial assumption that language expresses thought (LET) yields the view that linguistic competence is partly constituted by conceptual competence. So our view of the final state depends on our view of the nature of thoughts. This led to my fourth major conclusion: that the psychological reality of language should be investigated from a perspective on thought (8.3). Position (T), based on the Language-of-Thought Hypothesis (LOTH), is the most committed position on this nature presented in Part IV: a person thinks in a Mentalese governed by structure rules that are similar to those of her language. What explanation does this suggest about why the initial state respects the UG-rules? It suggests that the state respects those rules *because they are largely, if not entirely, innate structure rules of Mentalese.* Thus, it suggests something close to a version of thesis 3. This suggestion is my *sixth tentative proposal.*

Why the qualifications in the proposal? Well, part of the explanation of the respect may be found not in the innate structure of thought but in the innate *processing* constraints on the way thoughts can be expressed in language and on how language can be understood in thought. Still, position (T) should make us wonder whether the innate constraints on Mentalese alone explain why the initial state for language acquisition respects the UG-rules. Furthermore, if there were these initial-state processing constraints, they should be reflected in substantial commonalities among *final-state* processing competencies. Yet, our earlier discussion of brain impairment suggests that there are no such commonalities (10.2).[15]

What we are contemplating here is the idea that we are innately disposed to think thoughts that are governed by the structure rules of UG. It is because of the

---

[14] As Mark Singley and John Anderson point out (1989: 1), citing Newell and Simon 1972.

[15] And the evidence from brain injury does not seem to help with the innateness issue. "Absolutely no current theory of brain localization or recovery can accommodate [data on hydrocephalus]. In general, the brain injury data show surprising robustness of language, without giving straightforward answers to questions of language innateness." (Maratsos 2003: 696)

constraints on thought thus imposed that all human languages share certain features. Thus, it is because all structure rules for thought accord with the principle that grammatical rules are structure-dependent ("the structure dependency principle") that all linguistic rules do. It is because of such constraints on thought that language learning has the special features much emphasized by the linguists. On the basis of these innate rules and, according to the usual story, only debased and impoverished experience of her linguistic environment, a person comes to have thoughts largely governed by the rules of a complicated language, rules that underlie her own linguistic performance. Language learning appears to be *sui generis* because the development of thought under the stimulus of language (8.6–8.7) *is sui generis*.

We have good reason to suppose that all the higher animals have innate capacities to think but that these capacities differ; in particular that the human capacity is far greater than that of, say, the dog. What do these innate differences consist in? They consist in differences in the structure and processing rules governing the systems of representation in which animals think. These innate rules constrain an animal's thinking. If the animal has the capacity to learn a language, as the human does, then the innate structure rules of thought must constrain the languages it can learn: it cannot learn a language that expresses thoughts it is innately constrained not to think. So, *some* innate constraints on language, at least, must come from the innate constraints on thought.[16] Now add to this picture the following view of the final state of language learning for a human: the human thinks in a Mentalese with structure rules that are similar to the structure rules of the language learnt, position (T). On this view the innate structure rules that constrain thoughts and hence language are the innate syntactic rules of Mentalese. And a nice explanation of why we are innately constrained to acquire languages that respect the UG-rules is that those rules are largely the innate structure rules of thought: thought constrains language by embodying the UG-rules.

I earlier considered an objection to the thesis that a person's language of thought is her public language (Public-LOTH). The objection pointed to the fact that we can understand a string of words that is not in our language and, indeed, could not be in any human language (9.4). It might be objected now that this fact counts against the view that the innate constraints on language stem from the innate structure rules of Mentalese. For, the fact seems to show that there are greater constraints on human language than on thought. But does it really show this? As I responded before, perhaps we understand the string by "translating" it into a "well-formed" thought with the syntax like that of our natural language. But let us suppose that we sometimes do not, and accept that we can think thoughts that are not "well-formed". This need not undermine the

---

[16] Note that Pinker moves without comment from talk of the "language instinct" to talk of "the instinctive nature of thought" (1994: 20).

proposed view of innateness. The view need not be that a person *cannot* think at odds with the rules of her Mentalese—rules that are largely those of her language—or at odds even with the rules of the initial state. The claim could be that the speaker is *not disposed* to think such thoughts. So it is not "natural" to think them. But perhaps one *can* deliberately think them; and perhaps performance error leads one accidentally to think them from time to time.

In sum, assuming thesis 2—the initial state respects the UG-rules—position (T), based on LOTH, suggests that something close to thesis 3 is right: the state respects the UG-rules because it largely embodies them as structure rules of thought. That's my sixth tentative proposal. Of course, we do not now have anything close to a good explanation of language acquisition along these lines. That's one reason why the proposal is tentative.[17] Still, if thesis 2 and position (T) are right, we can expect something close to thesis 3 to be the core part of a persuasive future explanation of language acquisition.

This sort of proposal is far from novel. As Chomsky himself notes (1966: 52–3), a proposal like this is to be found in the eighteenth-century Port-Royal grammarians. And Michael Maratsos (1989: 122) has aired a similar one more recently.[18] These proposals should surely be attractive to the nativist. So one wonders why they have not been more popular. Perhaps Chomsky's argument to be considered in the next section is the explanation.

(T) arises from a bold conjecture about the nature of thought, LOTH. But, suppose now that we drop LOTH, and hence (T), and have some other view of thoughts. Then this route to thesis 3 is lost. Whatever the nature of thoughts, the innate constraints on thoughts must provide some of the constraints on language, as we emphasized. But if thoughts are not language-like but, say, map-like then the innate structure rules governing them must be very different from UG-rules because UG-rules govern languages not maps. Insofar as the innate structure of thought constrains language that constraint would not arise from embodied UG-rules.

So, without LOTH and (T), we must look elsewhere for a place for thesis 3 in the explanation of why the initial state respects the UG-rules. Even if (T) is correct, we allowed that some constraints on language may come from innate processing rules. And, doubtless, the likelihood increases that some will if (T) is not correct because thoughts are not language-like and LOTH is false. However, as we noted above, these sorts of initial-state processing constraints should yield substantial commonalities among *final-state* processing competencies which our earlier discussion of brain impairment did not reveal (10.2). In any case, it is hard to see how the UG-rules could be these innate processing rules for learning language from PLD: they seem to be the wrong sort of rule; the structure-dependency principle, for example, is simply not that sort of processing rule.

---

[17] We could, of course, be much less tentative about the conditional proposal that if LOTH then the UG-rules are largely, if not entirely, innate structure rules of thought.

[18] I owe these references to Cowie 1999: 276–81.

This point is, of course, analogous to that of my third tentative proposal against explaining language use in terms of embodied structure rules (11.4). In sum, if (τ) is correct then 3 provides an explanation of why we are innately predisposed to learn languages that respect the UG-rules. But if LOTH and hence (τ) are not correct the explanation fails. And it is hard to see how 3 could be otherwise justified. So we would have no good reason for thinking that the UG-rules are innately embodied in a robust way. We have arrived at my *seventh tentative proposal*: if LOTH is false, then the UG-rules are not, in a robust way, innate in a speaker.[19] This is the initial-state analogue of the final-state fifth tentative proposal: if LOTH is false, then the rules of a language are not, in a robust way, psychologically real in a speaker (11.9).

If (τ) is false, what then is the likely shape of a future explanation of why the initial state respects the UG-rules? The explanation must be in terms of the innate structure of thought and innate processing rules for converting thoughts into language and vice versa. That much is clear. But, absent some theory of the nature of thoughts—for example, that they are like maps—we can barely say anything more. Only against a background theory of thought can we assess the plausibility of explanations of why the UG-rules are respected; cf. my fourth major conclusion.

In sum, given thesis 2 and position (τ), we have good reason to suppose that something close to thesis 3 will explain why the UG-rules are respected and hence that something close to thesis 3 will be a core part of a persuasive future explanation of language acquisition: sixth tentative proposal. But (τ), based on LOTH, is highly speculative. Without it, thesis 3 is unlikely to be part of that future: seventh tentative proposal. And without it, we will need an alternative theory of thought to predict that future.

12.5   THE LANGUAGE FACULTY (THESIS 1)

In Part IV I noted that the view that language expresses thought (LET) alone downplays the language faculty because according to LET a certain conceptual competence is an important part of a person's competence in a language. That part is in the central processor not a language faculty. So, if there is a language faculty it must be found in the other part of a linguistic competence, processing competencies. Finding this then depends on the various processing competencies having a substantial part in common. For, a set of modality-specific processing

---

[19] The qualification, "in a robust way", is to allow for the possibility, analogous to the one noted earlier for the grammar (4.6, 11.9), of a less robust intermediate view on this innateness issue: UG might be descriptive of the initial state in a way stronger than simply positing rules that are respected by that state—thesis 2—but weaker than positing rules that are literally embodied in that state – thesis 3.

competencies does not a language faculty make: the faculty must be a relatively central, modality-*neutral*, cognitive system partly responsible for all language processing. Yet the evidence from brain impairments suggests that processing competencies do not have the required commonality and hence that there is no language faculty (10.2). Finally, I argued that if we wed the Gricean explanatory priority of thought over language to LOTH yielding (т), we should not expect the commonality that would constitute a substantial language faculty because there would be nothing much for the language faculty to do. This led to my second tentative proposal: there is little or nothing to the language faculty (10.3).

I shall start this section by showing how the present discussion gives further support to the second tentative proposal by casting doubt on the thesis 1 view that the initial state is a language-specific learning device in a distinct language faculty. I shall then respond to two objections to the second proposal. The first objection arises from the apparently *sui generis* nature of language acquisition. The second is a well-known argument of Chomsky's for placing the initial and final state of linguistic competence in a distinct language faculty.

I have emphasized that, whatever the nature of thoughts, there must be innate constraints on them, and those constraints must provide *some* of the constraints on language acquisition. Insofar as they do, *the initial state for language is not in a language faculty, a language-specific learning device, but in the central processor, the general learning device*. For, the constraints are on thoughts and thoughts are in the central processor. Of course, the language-constraining rules may not be entirely there: some of them may be innate processing rules for language. If these were appropriately central and modality-neutral they would constitute a language faculty. If thoughts were not language-like but rather, say, map-like, then we might expect that there would be such innate constraining rules. For, the task of moving from innate map-like thoughts to language seems formidable enough to need some innate help. So we might expect that innate processing rules, along with the innate constraints on thought, would explain why the initial state respects the UG-rules. So we might expect a good part of the initial state to be in a language faculty. But these expectations are undermined by something we have already noted twice: if there were such innate processing rules, they should give rise to final-state commonalities among processing competencies that the literature on brain impairment does not confirm. Furthermore, the expectations disappear if we adopt LOTH and hence (т). For then, I have just argued, the best explanation of why the initial state respects the UG-rules is that those rules are largely innate structure rules of Mentalese. (т) thus encourages the idea that the initial state is entirely in the central processor.

All in all, I think we have good reason to believe that the main constraints on language will come from the innate structure of thought. Steedman goes a bit further: "the only plausible source for the innate component lies in the conceptual structure with which the child comes to language learning, and which either evolved or was learned for more general cognitive purposes" (2003: 770).[20]

This idea is supported by some recent psycholinguistic research that gives a central role to the central processor in language acquisition. Dedre Gentner and Laura Namy (2005) sum up the situation as follows:

Current theories of word learning, and of language acquisition more generally, have turned increasingly toward domain-general cognitive and social explanations of children's acquisition of language ... There is increasing support for the idea that general learning mechanisms, guided by social-interactional knowledge, operate in encoding and processing both the incoming stream of language and the informational structure of the environment. These mechanisms appear to facilitate all aspects of language learning—speech segmentation, word learning, and perhaps even the acquisition of grammar.   (p. 533)

The emphasis of their research is very much on the acquisition of words. Based on research on analogy and similarity they propose that the process of comparison—structural alignment and mapping—facilitates lexical acquisition. They find persuasive evidence that it does. They wonder whether this process might also "contribute to children's ability to derive grammatical regularities". They claim that "some intriguing lines of evidence suggest that this may be a direction worth pursuing" (p. 557).

It is time now to consider objections to the proposal that there is little or nothing to the language faculty. First, I noted that evidence of the *sui generis* nature of language learning might seem to support thesis 1 and commitment to a language faculty (12.2). Language acquisition is alleged to be quite unlike the acquisition of other cognitive skills: it is done very young in the critical period; all normal children do it; and they acquire elements of linguistic capacity in the same order. But once one has accepted, as I already have (8.6), that the Gricean picture allows any amount of causal influence of language on the capacity to have certain thoughts, this evidence no longer counts in favor of the language faculty. For, the evidence is then quite compatible with the view that not only is competence in a language normally acquired in the critical period in a constrained uniform way under the influence of that language but so also is the competence to think the thoughts expressible in the language. On this view, the acquisition of *one* cognitive skill is *not* unlike the acquisition of language: the skill

---

[20] Steedman does not note, however, that this view lessens the case for a language faculty. Indeed he writes, surprisingly, as if the view is implicit in Chomsky. Steedman is also strikingly noncommittal on the extent to which the structure of thought *is* innate:

The question of how much of [the grounded conceptual structure upon which both reasoning about the world and development of language depend] is actively learned by the individual prelinguistic child, and how much of it has been compiled into heritable 'hard-wired' components during the process of evolution of humans and their animal ancestors, and the question of what further apparatus is needed for the development of language and whether its origins can also be traced to more generally useful cognitive abilities, remain open.   (2003: 770–1)

in question is the skill to think the thoughts the language expresses. Indeed, the acquisition of that cognitive skill normally brings the linguistic skill with it. (Note that the cognitive skill in question is one of *having thoughts* not of *thinking well* with them.)

This view predicts that people who have no acquaintance with a language during the critical period will be cognitively impaired as well as linguistically so. And that is indeed what we find as we have already noted in our discussion of linguistic relativity (8.6), citing the famous cases of "wolf children" (Malson 1972) and of Genie (Curtis 1981).

Now evidence against this view could come from dissociations, during and after the critical period, between the development of a capacity to use sentences of a certain structure and the development of a capacity to think the thoughts that those sentences express. Thus, on the one hand, it would be evidence against the view if those who develop into linguistic idiot savants could not think thoughts that their words seem to express. But there seems to be no evidence of this, although there is of course evidence that they are not good at the process of thin*king* (10.1). On the other hand, it would be evidence against the view if there were people who, in the critical period, learnt neither a language nor the capacity to think the thoughts that language expresses, but *afterwards* learnt to think the thoughts (without, of course, learning the language). But, we should note, it would not be clear evidence against the view if there were people who, in the critical period, did not learn a language but did learn to think thoughts that they could not express. For the failure to learn the language could be attributable to some failure in processing between thought and language. In any case, I know of no evidence of either sort that might be thought to count against the view.[21] And it is hard to know what *is* lost in the critical period by the late learner. "Such 'critical period' or 'sensitive period' effects ... cannot by themselves reveal just what is being lost or diminished in the late learner: This could be some aspects of learning specific to language itself, general capacities for structured cognitive learning, or some combination of the two" (Gleitman and Bloom 1999: 436).

Turn next to Chomsky's well-known argument for placing the initial and final state of linguistic competence in a distinct language faculty. It is to be found in passages like the following, accompanying Chomsky's presentation of nativism:

---

[21] The case of Genie does not supply evidence of the second sort. Genie had no significant experience of language until she was thirteen. She then acquired a "relatively well-developed semantic ability" but "very little syntax or morphology." Her speech consisted in "the stringing together of content words" (Curtis 1981: 21). Despite this she performed quite well on a range of cognitive tasks (pp. 21–2). There is no evidence here that she developed the capacity to think thoughts she could not express nor even that the primitive syntax of her utterances is not replicated in the thoughts those utterances express.

It is hardly conceivable that principles of the sort we have been considering have any general applicability beyond the language faculty, and no general mechanisms or principles have been proposed that shed any light on the questions we have been addressing, to my knowledge.   (Chomsky 1986: 150)

The idea is that the principles of the initial and final states of competence in a language are so peculiar that we would not expect to find them anywhere but in a distinct language faculty, in particular not in the central processor. Furthermore, no general learning device of the sort found in the central processor could explain the acquisition of a language. Ray Jackendoff's neat "Paradox of Language Acquisition" seems to provide support for this latter claim:

If general-purpose intelligence were sufficient to extract the principles of mental grammar, linguists (or psychologists or computer scientists), at least some of whom have more than adequate general intelligence, would have discovered the principles long ago. The fact that we are all still searching and arguing, while every normal child manages to extract the principles unaided, suggest that the normal child is using something other than general-purpose intelligence.   (1997: 5)

If RT were correct, with the result that the final state involved a set of propositions about the language, then these arguments might seem to be based on proper contrasts. For, the propositions about language are indeed very different from others. And the arduous and incomplete central-processor learning of these propositions by linguists would contrast strikingly with the easy and complete learning of the propositions by children. But we have so far found no persuasive reason to believe RT and many reasons to disbelieve it. If we abandon it, then the contrasts are not proper and the arguments collapse.[22]

What are the proper contrasts then? We have noted (11.5) that learning a language is acquiring a skill, the skill, according to the noncommittal position (a) on competence, at matching sounds and thoughts for meaning. So we should think of acquiring it as like acquiring other skills, particularly cognitive skills. These skills are, primarily at least, pieces of procedural knowledge or knowledge-how, not pieces of declarative knowledge, knowledge-that, or theory. So one proper contrast is between the acquisition of *cognitive skills* and the acquisition of *theories*. These acquisitions are surely by different mechanisms. Indeed, many skills, probably including linguistic competence, differ from theories in being acquired by *implicit* learning. But this alone does not show that the mechanism for acquiring a skill is not in the general learning device. We would surely *expect* the mechanism for a *cognitive* skill—for example, playing chess or adding—to be in that device. And, if position (T) is right, that is where the mechanism for language learning may largely be because there may not be much to a speaker's ability with a

---

[22] Similarly Chomsky's contrast between the uniform achievement of knowledge of language and the nonuniform achievement of knowledge of physics (1975: 144) is not proper if RT is incorrect.

language beyond her ability to think thoughts—thoughts about *anything*—in a Mentalese which is governed by the rules similar to those of the language.

The acquisition of theories draws attention to another proper contrast: that between the structure rules for thoughts and the processing rules that govern inference, the rules that take us from thought to thought in the acquisition of knowledge-that. I have made much of this contrast before, using the analogy of the contrast between the formation and transformation rules of logic (2.2). But, we note, both these sorts of rule are embodied in the general learning device.

The upshot of this is that if we do not adopt RT, a thesis for which we have so far found no persuasive support, Chomsky's well-known argument against placing linguistic competence in the central processor collapses. And the central processor is where the competence very likely is if LOTH and hence (T) are correct: there would be little or no truth in thesis 1. Even if some other view of thought is correct there may not be much of our innate capacity for language to be placed in a language faculty; there may not be much truth in 1. It goes without saying that none of this establishes that there is no language faculty, but it does give some reasons for doubting its role and significance. It supports my second tentative proposal.[23] The case for this proposal rests a bit on LOTH but does not totally depend on it.

In first making this proposal I pointed out that the contrary view that there is a substantial language faculty should be even more tentative because the case for it is weaker (10.3). That contrary view required that there be a substantial commonality among processing competencies, something for which we found no evidence. And if (T) is true the commonality seemed unlikely. Now we see that if (T) is true, the best explanation of why the initial state respects the UG-rules is that those rules are largely the innate structure rules of thought and hence in the central processor not a language faculty. Of course (T) might not be true. (T) depends very heavily on LOTH, which is certainly speculative, but I know of no persuasive argument against LOTH. And even if (T) were false, innate constraints on thought in the central processor must be part of the explanation of why the initial state respects the UG-rules (provided that there are are thoughts). All in all, we seem to lack any significant reason *for* believing in the language faculty. Things would look different, of course, were RT true. But we have found no reason to believe that it is.

My fourth major conclusion (8.3) urges us to investigate the psychological reality underlying language from a perspective on thought. It is appropriate now to summarize some significant results of that approach. The approach yielded my first tentative proposal, based on LOTH, that a language is largely psychologically real in a speaker in that its rules are similar to the structure rules of her thought (9.5); and it yielded my fifth tentative proposal that if LOTH is false

---

[23] We should note that innate phonology must be found a place in the mind and that place is surely not in the central processor. But it alone can hardly constitute a language faculty. Indeed, in an important respect, it seems accidental that languages are typically spoken.

then the rules of a language are not, in a robust way, psychologically real in a speaker (11.9). These proposals concerned the final state of linguistic competence. In this chapter, the approach has yielded two analogous proposals about the initial state: my sixth tentative proposal that humans are predisposed to learn languages that conform to the UG-rules because those rules are, largely if not entirely, innate structure rules of thought (12.4); and my seventh tentative proposal that if LOTH is false then the UG-rules are not, in a robust way, innate in a speaker (12.4). Finally, in this section, the approach has yielded the conclusion of the argument for the second tentative proposal, which concerns both the initial and final state: there is little or nothing to the language faculty.

In this section I have cast doubt on thesis 1 which is one half of Chomskian Nativism. In the next section I shall cast doubt on thesis 3R which is the other half.

12.6 IMPLAUSIBILITY OF I-REPRESENTATIONALISM (THESIS 3R)

If we assume thesis 2 and a robust position on thoughts, position (T), I have argued (12.4) that a persuasive future abduction concerning language acquisition is likely to support something close to thesis 3: the initial state embodies the UG-rules because they are largely the innate structure rules of thoughts. But without (T), the prospects for 3 in a future theory of language acquisition seem poor. Insofar as the prospects for 3 are poor, so too are the prospects for the I-Representationalist version of 3, 3R. So, the prospects for 3R also seem to depend on (T). I have earlier gone along with Cowie in rejecting the only-theory-in-town abduction for 3R: the explanation it involves is far too lacking in detail and evidential support. But is 3R likely to be part of a persuasive future explanation? My discussion of 3 so far has made no mention of represented rules. Is that a mistake? In this section I shall argue that it is not. I-Representationalism is not only not now part of a good explanation of language acquisition, it is not part of the best. And it is unlikely to be part of a good future explanation.

A. The final state of linguistic competence is a skill. So we should look to psychological studies of skills, summarized in section 11.5, for guidance about this competence. We have already found no significant support there for RT as an account of the final state. What light do those studies throw on the initial state of competence and on the I-Representational Thesis?

Let us start with I-Representationalism. I have been unable to find any suggestion in the psychological literature on skill acquisition that innate representations of the rules underlie the acquisition of a nonlinguistic skill.[24] On the top-down production-systems view, skill acquisition starts from declarative knowledge but it is not claimed that this knowledge is innate. Quite the

---

[24] See Johnson *et al.* 2003, for example.

contrary.[25] In any case, language acquisition seems to be a paradigm of bottom-up implicit learning. We noted that if it really is a case of implicit learning, then we should be particularly dubious of RT as a view of the final state of linguistic competence. Indeed, the literature on skills suggest that skills have a fairly brute–causal associative nature and so does not encourage the idea that language processing involves representations even of the syntactic and semantic properties of language let alone of the linguistic rules (11.6). If we are right to be thus dubious of RT as a view of the final state, we should be even more dubious of the I-Representational Thesis as a view of the initial state. In sum, innate representations of rules do not seem to underlie nonlinguistic skills. This is bad news for the idea that they underlie linguistic skills and hence bad news for I-Representationalism.

This is not to say, of course, that innate structures play no role in skill acquisition. Indeed, an analogue of the boring innateness thesis for language is obviously true for skills in general: we can only acquire them because of some innate capacities. Perhaps some analogues of thesis 2 are true: perhaps there are some *interesting* innate constraints on the sorts of skills we can learn. Doubtless, these will typically not be *as* interesting as thesis 2. Finally, even if the innate basis for one of these skills is quite rich, it will be like that for a language skill in not being so rich that the skill is totally innate: the skill still has to be learned.[26]

These remarks about the innate structures for skill acquisition do not take us very far, of course. But, at this stage, we simply do not know enough about skill acquisition to go much further. The psychological study of skill acquisition throws little light on the innate structures underlying skills, hence little light on the innateness of language. If the study were advanced enough to provide good detailed theories of the acquisition of skills like typing and adding, we might hope that it would provide a lot of insight into language acquisition. But the study is not that advanced. Still, the insight that the study does provide gives no support to the idea that the acquisition of linguistic competence involves the innate representation of rules, hence no support to the I-Representational Thesis.

I noted earlier (4.6) that Bob Matthews rejects RT as an account of the final state. We might expect that he would also reject its analogue, the I-Representational Thesis, as an account of the initial state. And so he does. Indeed, he urges that we abandon "a rationalist account of language learning" (1980: 25); the constraints "on the form of acceptable grammars ... are so severe as to render grossly inappropriate any characterization of the acquisition process in terms of hypothesis testing. Data serve not so much as evidence for a hypothesized grammar as they serve as a series of triggering events that determine the course of

---

[25] Indeed, it would be preposterous to claim that the declarative knowledge involved in favorite production-systems examples like learning to use a stick shift was innate.

[26] Mons-Williams, Tresilian, and Wann 2003 (p. 125) takes it as *definitive* of a skill that it is learned—a pointless stipulation in my view (11.5)—and Carlson 2003 (p. 36), that it is improved by practice.

grammatical development" (p. 26). I think that the literature on skill acquisition encourages this idea of language learning as a fairly brute–causal matter.[27]

B. Normal mature humans have two very impressive cognitive skills. A consideration of the acquisition of these skills counts further against I-Representationalism and throws more light on the initial state for language acquisition. The skills in question are: (i) the skill of having complicated thoughts covering a limitless range of subjects; (ii) the skill of thinking, of moving in a somewhat rational manner from one thought to another.

(i) Assume LOTH for a moment. Then our skill at having thoughts has the following two parts: the syntactic skill of combining mental words of the various syntactic categories into mental sentences; and the skill of having the mental words, the concepts, that fit into those sentences (11.3). We have very good reason to suppose that some of the syntax of thought is innate (12.4). Still, nobody would suggest that what is innate is a representation of syntactic rules. A version of Harman's objection (6.2) would loom: the suggestion would lead either to a vicious circle or to an infinite regress. And even those who believe, as Jerry Fodor does (1981), that our concepts are largely innate will not hold that we innately represent the rules of the concept; for example, that <echidna> means *ECHIDNA*. So, our skill at having thoughts is an uncontroversial example of one that does not involve any innate representation of its rules.

Now, these remarks assume LOTH. But the conclusion would be just the same if we assumed only the Representational Theory of Mind (RTM) and left the nature of mental representations open. Thus, if those representations are map-like, their structure rules will still not be innately represented.

(ii) Turn next to our skill at thinking, at moving from one thought to another. I think it plausible that some of the rules governing this process are learnt: there is a bit of practice making better. But one thing we can surely be confident about is that many of these rules are innate. How else could we even get started in forming our world view? And another thing we can surely be confident about is that these innate "laws of thought" are not represented. Our initial thinking is not governed by some higher-level thoughts about thinking (3.1, 7.3). Our skill at thinking is another uncontroversial example of one that does not involve innate representations of its rules.

(i) and (ii) then serve as nice examples of cognitive skills without innate representations of rules. But they do more. I have emphasized that, whatever one's view of thoughts, the innate constraints on their structure are one part, at

---

[27] On this score, it is worth noting that whereas Chomsky's early hypothesis-testing theory of language acquisition (1965) may seem to demand the representation of innate rules, the later parameter-setting theory (1982) does not. As Stabler points out, this theory "appears to be particularly amenable to the view that the grammar is not represented" (1983: 398). The theory leads Collins to conclude: "There is nothing *rational* about acquiring language" (2004: 512). Indeed, the idea of parameter setting as "triggering" suggests a fairly brute–causal process.

least, of the innate constraints on language. This leaves open the possibility that innate constraints on language processing may be another part. The literature on brain impairment and position (T) led me to the conclusion that this possibility was not likely (12.5). Still, it remains a possibility and so let us suppose, for the sake of argument, that it is actual. Our discussion of (i) bears on the part of the innate linguistic constraints concerning structure, our discussion of (ii), on the part concerning processing. In discussing (i), we saw that the innate constraints on thought do not involve innate representations of rules. So, to that extent, I-Representationalism is false: to that extent the initial state does not respect the UG-rules because it represents them. It still might be the case, of course, that any further innate constraints that there may be on language processing are in the form of represented rules. Thus, adopting LOTH, it might be the case that there were innate Mentalese representations of these further constraints. But our discussion of (ii) provides a more inviting model: just as our thinking is partly governed by innate processing rules that are embodied without being represented so too is our language use. There seems to be no basis for insisting that the rules governing language use are represented. This is a time to apply Pylyshyn's Razor.

In conclusion, a comparison of linguistic competence with other skills and attention to the nature of thoughts and thinking suggest that we should abandon the I-Representationalist thesis 3R. Assuming position (T) and the interesting nativist thesis 2—the thesis that the initial state respects the UG-rules—we have seen that the prospects for thesis 3—the thesis that the initial state embodies those rules—look good: sixth tentative proposal (12.4). But the evidence counts against going further to 3R. And without (T), the prospects for even 3 look bleak: seventh tentative proposal (12.4). So, whether or not (T) turns out to be true, it is unlikely that I-Representationalism will be part of a persuasive explanation of language acquisition. There is no significant evidence for the I-Representational Thesis and, given what else we know, it is implausible. That is my *seventh major conclusion*. A human does not innately represent the UG-rules nor does she innately know anything about those rules; she is totally ignorant of them. If this is right then the view, much-hyped on the intellectual cocktail circuit, that language acquisition supports the traditional doctrine of innate ideas is mistaken.

Of course, this discussion of the I-Representational Thesis about the initial state has proceeded without assuming RT about the final state. This is appropriate because we have so far found no persuasive reason for believing that thesis and many reasons for disbelieving it. But suppose, despite this, that RT were true: the final state consists in representations of the rules of the language. Then presumably such representations must be involved in all the learning steps between the innate initial state and the final state. This does not, of course, show that the initial state involves such representations: the rules of protocol and of chess are often represented in the mind but surely none of these representations are innate.

Perhaps the view that the initial state involves represented rules gains plausibility if the final state does. But unless we can find another example of innate representations of rules underlying a skill, that gain is not going to be great.

In the last section I cast doubt on thesis 1 and the commitment to a language faculty. In this section I have cast doubt on thesis 3R. So I think that we should accept neither part of Chomskian Nativism.

12.7   BEARING ON THE REPRESENTATIONAL THESIS (RT)

So far in this chapter we have been concerned with the nature of the initial state of linguistic competence. It is time now to return to the main concern of this book, the final state of that competence. What bearing does our discussion of the initial state have on that concern? What else can we conclude about the nature of the final state from a consideration of language acquisition?

The argument in earlier chapters strongly suggests that RT is false. If it is, I have just argued, the I-Representational Thesis is surely false also. And it would quite likely be false even if RT were true. So, I am confident about the falsity of I-Representationalism. Let us now reverse the order of argument. What does the falsity of I-Representationalism show about RT? It surely does not entail the falsity of that thesis: my competence in chess may consist partly in my declarative knowledge of its rules and yet that knowledge was surely not innate. Nonetheless, the falsity of I-Representationalism certainly does nothing to support RT. And it adds to the attractiveness of the view that RT is also false.

But suppose the argument of this chapter were mistaken and I-Representationalism were true. Would that show that RT was true? It seems not. In discussing skills in general (11.5) we noted that the automatic procedural stage of a skill involving no declarative knowledge could arise out of a cognitive stage involving such knowledge. So it seems that a skill involving no representation of its rules can arise out of a representation of its rules. Still, it might be objected that the cognitive stage of that sort of skill was learned not innate. How could a skill involving no representation of its rules in the final state arise out of an innate representation of its rules in the initial state? Could the innate representation just disappear so that it is not part of the final state? Perhaps so. The natural learning of a language has to be achieved before the end of the critical period. So *something* that enables language acquisition is clearly lost by that point. If I-Representationalism were true then presumably what would be lost would be the innate representation of UG-rules. The mind is "programmed" to acquire a language according to these representations during the critical period and then to delete the representations. So even I-Representationalism does not directly support RT. Still, it would surely make RT more attractive.

In sum, although the I-Representationalist Thesis about the initial state of linguistic competence and RT about the final state are natural bed-fellows, neither thesis provides significant evidential support to the other. More importantly, our discussion of the innateness issue counts against the I-Representationalist Thesis and provides the final step in the long-developing argument against RT. My seventh major conclusion is that we should abandon the former, my second, the latter. In abandoning the former we conclude that a person in the initial state is totally ignorant of the rules of UG. In abandoning the latter we conclude that a person in the final state can be totally ignorant of the rules of her language.

Finally, in abandoning RT we are, of course, rejecting positions (I) and (II) on language use. But our discussion of nativism does not seem to have any other significant bearing on positions on language use.

12.8 CONCLUSION

There are some fairly familiar arguments for linguistic nativism: arguments from the *sui generis* nature of language learning, from the universality of UG-rules, from the poverty of stimulus, from language creation, and from the continuity hypothesis. The *sui generis* argument seems to support thesis 1—the innate initial state for language acquisition is in a distinct language faculty—although I argue that the evidence here is actually compatible with the initial state being in the central processor (12.5). I think that the other arguments, taken jointly, present a persuasive case for thesis 2: humans are innately predisposed to learn languages that conform to the UG-rules; the initial state respects the UG-rules (12.2).

Can we then establish any other nativist thesis? At this stage, we are far short of a good explanation of language acquisition that could form the basis for a sound abduction in favor of any other thesis. So, Fodor's only-theory-in-town abduction for the very exciting I-Representationalist thesis 3R should be dismissed, as Cowie argues (12.3). Still, we can make some progress by seeking an explanation of the initial state's respect for the UG-rules. If we assume position (T)—a person thinks in a Mentalese governed by structure rules that are similar to those of her language—we have good reason to suppose that something close to thesis 3 will explain that respect and hence be part of a persuasive future explanation of language acquisition; we have good reason to suppose that the UG-rules are, for the most part, innate structure rules of thought. This is my sixth tentative proposal. But if LOTH and hence (T) are false, then it seems unlikely that thesis 3 will be part of the future. My seventh tentative proposal is that if LOTH is false, then the UG-rules are not, in a robust way, innate in a speaker (12.4).

Is linguistic competence in a language faculty? Without RT, for which we have so far found no significant support, Chomsky's well-known argument for placing linguistic competence in such a distinct language faculty—hence, for thesis 1— collapses. If (T) is correct that competence very likely is in the central processor, and even if (T) is not correct that competence may be largely there. This adds to the earlier case for my second tentative proposal that there is little or nothing to the language faculty (10.3). The contrary view that there is a substantial language faculty seems to lack any significant evidence (12.5).

Assuming (T), we have found a case for thesis 3 as part of the future. Should we go further to 3R? A comparison of linguistic competence with other skills and attention to the nature of thoughts and thinking, suggests that we should not. I-Representationalism is not only not the conclusion of a present good abduction, it is unlikely to be of a future one. My seventh and final major conclusion is that there is no significant evidence for the I-Representational Thesis and, given what else we know, it is implausible. So both parts of Chomskian Nativism, thesis 1 and thesis 3R, are likely false.

Finally, the issue of nativism has less bearing on our view of the final state of linguistic competence than one might have expected. In Part III we found no evidence for RT in the arguments from the rejection of behaviorism, from the folk truism that the competent speaker knows her language, and from the role of linguistic intuitions. Our Chapter 11 discussion of language use provided more evidence against RT than for it. The consideration of language acquisition in this chapter has given no support to RT. My second major conclusion is established: there is no significant evidence for RT and, given what else we know, it is implausible.

In conclusion, in this book I have argued that a number of Chomskian views about the psychological reality of language are ill-supported by evidence and argument and are probably wrong. My major conclusions and tentative proposals are to be found at the end of the following Glossary.

Glossary of Named or Numbered Items

(Parenthetical references are to the section in which an item is best explained)

NAMED THESES

The Representational Thesis (RT) A speaker of a language stands in an unconscious or tacit propositional attitude to the rules or principles of the language which are represented in her language faculty (1.1).

The Respect Constraint A theory of a competence must posit processing rules that respect the structure rules of the outputs. Similarly, a theory of the outputs must posit structure rules that are respected by the competence and its processing rules (2.3).

Pylyshyn's Razor Representations are not to be multiplied beyond necessity (3.1).

Intentional Realism People really have thoughts (8.1).

LET Language expresses thought (8.2).

The Representational Theory of the Mind (RTM) Having a thought involves standing in a certain functional relation to a mental representation (9.1).

The Language-of-Thought Hypothesis (LOTH) Thoughts involve language-like mental representations (9.2).

Public-LOTH A person's language of thought is the same as her public language (9.3).

The I-Representational Thesis The rules specified by UG are innately represented in the mind (12.1).

DISTINCTIONS

(1) Distinguish the theory of a competence from the theory of its outputs/ products or inputs (2.1).

(2) Distinguish the structure rules governing the outputs of a competence from the processing rules governing the exercise of the competence (2.2).

(3) Distinguish the respecting of structure rules by processing rules from the inclusion of structure rules among processing rules (2.3).

(4) Distinguish processing rules that govern by being represented and applied from ones that are simply embodied without being represented (3.1).

(5) Distinguish the representations of structure rules used as data in processing from the representations of structure rules that are applied in processing (3.2).

(6) Distinguish processing rules that govern a "rational-causal" operation on syntactically structured representations (or symbols) from ones that govern "brute-causal" operations that may or may not involve representations (3.3).

(7) Distinguish actual from merely metaphorical generation, computation, and processing (4.2).

(8) Distinguish the generation of expressions by the I-language from the generation of structural descriptions of expressions by the grammar (4.2).

METHODOLOGICAL POINTS

First There is something theoretically interesting for a grammar to be true about other than the psychological reality of speakers: it can be true about a linguistic reality (2.6).

Second The view that a grammar has any more to do with psychological reality than that it must posit structure rules that are respected by the competence requires a powerful psychological assumption about competence (2.6).

Third The Respect Constraint makes the justification of the grammar partly dependent on the justification of the theory of competence, and vice versa. Beyond that, however, the grammar and the theory of competence are independent of each other (2.6).

Fourth A grammar as a theory of a language has a certain epistemic and explanatory priority over a theory of the psychological reality underlying language (2.6).

SOME POSSIBLE POSITIONS ON PSYCHOLOGICAL REALITY

(**M**) A competence in a language, and the processing rules that govern its exercise, respect the structure rules of the language: the processing rules of language comprehension take sentences of the language as inputs; the processing rules of language production yield sentences of the language as outputs (3.4).

(**I**) The structure rules of the language are also processing rules that are represented in the speaker and applied in language use (3.4).

(**II**) The structure rules of the language are represented and used as data by the processing rules of language use (3.4).

(**III**) The structure rules of the language are also processing rules for language use but the processing rules are not represented (3.4).

(**IV**) Some processing rules for language use are represented but they are largely unlike the structure rules of the language and do not use the structure rules as data (3.4).

(v) The processing rules for language use are unrepresented and largely unlike the structure rules of the language (3.4).

Versions (a) Some processing rules operate on metalinguistic representations of the syntactic and semantic properties of linguistic items and there is a rational information flow (3.4).

Versions (b) Processing rules do not operate on metalinguistic representations of the syntactic and semantic properties of linguistic items but are directly responsive, in a fairly brute–causal associationist way, to these properties (3.4).

(τ) The structure rules of a speaker's language are similar to the structure rules of her thought (9.5).

VIEWS OF LINGUISTIC COMPETENCE

(a) Assuming LET: the ability to use a sound of the language to express a thought with the meaning that the sound has in the language in the context of utterance; and the ability (together with some pragmatic abilities) to assign to a sound a thought with the meaning that the sound has in the language in the context of utterance (similarly for inscriptions, etc.) (8.3).

(b) Assuming RTM: the ability to translate back and forth between mental representations and the sounds of the language (9.1).

(c) Assuming LOTH: the ability to translate back and forth between mental sentences and the sounds of the language (9.3).

NUMBERED INNATENESS THESES

1 The initial state is a language-specific learning device in a distinct "language faculty" not in the central processor (12.1).

2 The initial state constrains humans to learn only languages that conform to UG; it respects the UG-rules (12.1).

3 The initial state respects the UG-rules because it embodies the UG-rules (12.1).

3R (The I-Representational Thesis above) The UG-rules are innately represented in the mind (12.1).

Chomskian Nativism Theses 1 and 3R (12.1).

MAJOR CONCLUSIONS

First Linguistics is not part of psychology (2.8).

Second There is no significant evidence for the Representational Thesis (RT) and, given what else we know, it is implausible (4.7).

Third Speakers' linguistic intuitions do not reflect information supplied by the language faculty. They are immediate and fairly unreflective empirical central-processor responses to linguistic phenomena. They are not the main evidence for grammars (7.8).

Fourth The psychological reality of language should be investigated from a perspective on thought (8.3).

Fifth Thought has a certain priority to language ontologically, explanatorily, temporally, and in theoretical interest (8.8).

Sixth The primary concern in linguistics should not be with idiolects but with linguistic expressions that share meanings in idiolects (10.5).

Seventh There is no significant evidence for the I-Representational Thesis and, given what else we know, it is implausible (12.6).

TENTATIVE PROPOSALS

First (based on position (T) above) A language is largely psychologically real in a speaker in that its rules are similar to the structure rules of her thought (9.5).

Second There is little or nothing to the language faculty (10.3).

Third The structure rules of a language are the wrong sort of rule to govern the process of language use (11.4).

Fourth The speedy automatic language processes arising wholly, or at least partly, from linguistic competence are fairly brute–causal associationist processes that do not operate on metalinguistic representations of the syntactic and semantic properties of linguistic expressions (11.6).

Fifth If LOTH is false, then the rules of a language are not, in a robust way, psychologically real in a speaker (11.9).

Sixth Humans are predisposed to learn languages that conform to the rules specified by UG because those rules are, largely if not entirely, innate structure rules of thought (12.4).

Seventh If LOTH is false, then the rules specified by UG are not, in a robust way, innate in a speaker (12.4).

References

Allen, C., and M. Bekoff. 1997. *Species of Mind: The Philosophy and Biology of Cognitive Ethology.* Cambridge, MA: MIT Press.

Anderson, John R. 1980. *Cognitive Psychology and its Implications.* San Francisco: W. H. Freeman and Company.

—— 1983. *The Architecture of Cognition.* Cambridge, MA: Harvard University Press.

—— 1993. *Rules of the Mind.* Hillsdale, NJ: Lawrence Erlbaum Associates.

—— and Christian Lebiere. 1998. *The Atomic Components of Thought.* Mahwah, NJ: Lawrence Erlbaum Associates.

Antony, Louise. 2003. "Rabbit Pots and Supernovas: On the Relevance of Psychological Data to Linguistic Theory". In Barber 2003a: 47–68.

—— and Norbert Hornstein, eds. 2003. *Chomsky and His Critics.* Oxford: Blackwell Publishers.

Armstrong, D.M. 1971. "Meaning and Communication". *Philosophical Review* 80: 427–47.

—— 1973. *Belief, Truth and Knowledge.* Cambridge: Cambridge University Press.

Atkinson, Antony P., and Michael Wheeler, 2004. "The Grain of Domains: The Evolutionary–Psychological Case against Domain-General Cognition". *Mind and Language* 19: 147–76.

Au, T. K. 1983. "Chinese and English Counterfactuals: The Sapir–Whorf Hypothesis Revisited". *Cognition* 15: 155–87.

Avramides, A. 1989. *Meaning and Mind, An Examination of a Gricean Account of Language.* Cambridge, MA: MIT Press.

Bach, Kent. 1987. *Thought and Reference.* Oxford: Clarendon Press.

Baker, C. L. 1978. *Introduction to Generative–Transformational Syntax.* Englewood Cliffs, NJ: Prentice-Hall, Inc.

—— 1995. *English Syntax*, 2nd edn. Cambridge, MA: MIT Press. 1st edn, 1989.

—— and J. J. McCarthy, eds. 1981. *The Logical Problem of Language Acquisition.* Cambridge, MA.: MIT Press.

Baker, Lynne Rudder. 1987. *Saving Belief: A Critique of Physicalism.* Princeton: Princeton University Press.

Barber, Alex. 2001. "Idiolectal Error". *Mind and Language* 16: 263–83.

—— (ed.). 2003a. *Epistemology of Language.* Oxford: Oxford University Press.

—— 2003b. "Introduction". In Barber 2003a: 1–43.

Barkow, J., L. Cosmides, and J. Tooby, eds. 1992. *The Adapted Mind.* Oxford: Oxford University Press.

Baron-Cohen, S. 1995. *Mindblindness: An Essay on Autism and Theory of Mind.* Cambridge, MA: MIT Press.

Bealer, George. 1998. "Intuition and the Autonomy of Philosophy". In DePaul and Ramsey 1998: 201–39.

Bennett, J. 1976. *Linguistic Behaviour.* Cambridge: Cambridge University Press.

Berkeley, George. 1710. *Principles of Human Knowledge*

Berwick, R. C. 1983. "Using What You Know: A Computer-Science Perspective". *Behavioral and Brain Sciences* 3: 402–3.

—— and A. S. Weinberg. 1984. *The Grammatical Basis of Linguistic Performance: Language use and Acquisition.* Cambridge, MA.: MIT Press.

Bever, T. G., J. M. Carroll, and L. A. Miller, eds. 1984. *Talking Minds: The Study of Language in Cognitive Science.* Cambridge, MA.: MIT Press.

Bickerton, Derek. 1990. *Language and Species.* Chicago: University of Chicago Press.

—— 1995. *Language and Human Behaviour.* Seattle: University of Washington Press.

Bjorklund, David F., Wolfgang Sneider, and Carlos Hernandez Blasi. 2003. "Memory". In Nadel 2003, vol. 2: 1059–65.

Block, Ned, ed. 1981. *Readings in Philosophy of Psychology, Volume 2.* Cambridge, MA.: Harvard University Press.

Bloom, A. H. 1981. *The Linguistic Shaping of Thought: A Study of the Impact of Language on Thinking in China and the West.* Hillsdale, NJ: Erlbaum.

Blumstein, Sheila E. 1999. "Phonology, Neural Basis of". In Wilson and Keil 1999: 643–5.

Bock, Kathryn. 1995. "Sentence Production: From Mind to Mouth". In Miller and Eimas 1995: 181–216.

—— 1999. "Language Production". In Wilson and Keil 1999: 453–6.

Boden, M. A. 1984. "Animal Perception from an Artificial Intelligence Viewpoint". In *Minds, Machines and Evolution,* ed. C. Hookway. Cambridge: Cambridge University Press.

—— 1988. *Computational Models of the Mind.* New York: Cambridge University Press.

Boghossian, Paul A. 1990a. "The Status of Content". *Philosophical Review* 99: 157–84.

—— 1990b. "The Status of Content Revisited". *Pacific Philosophical Quarterly* 71: 264–78.

BonJour, Laurence. 1998. *In Defense of Pure Reason: A Rationalist Account of A Priori Justification.* Cambridge: Cambridge University Press.

—— 2005a. "In Defense of A Priori Reasons". In Steup and Sosa 2005: 98–105.

—— 2005b. "Reply to Devitt". In Steup and Sosa 2005: 115–18.

—— 2005c. "Last Rejoinder". In Steup and Sosa 2005: 120–2.

Boroditsky, Lera. 2003. "Linguistic Relativity". In Nadel 2003, vol. 2: 917–21.

Botha, Rudolf P. 2003. *Unravelling the Evolution of Language.* Amsterdam: Elsevier.

Braddon-Mitchell, David, and Frank Jackson. 1996. *Philosophy of Mind and Cognition.* Oxford: Blackwell Publishers.

Bresnan, Joan. 1978. "A Realistic Transformational Grammar". In Halle, Bresnan, and Miller 1978: 1–59.

—— ed. 1982. *The Mental Representation of Grammatical Relations.* Cambridge, MA: MIT Press.

—— and Ronald Kaplan. 1982. "Introduction: Grammars as Mental Representations of Language". In Bresnan 1982: xvii–lii.

Broadbent, Donald E. 1977. "Levels, Hierarchies, and the Locus of Control". *Quarterly Journal of Experimental Psychology* 29: 181–201.

—— and B. Aston. 1978. "Human Control of a Simulated Economic System". *Ergonomics* 21: 1035–43.

—— Peter FitzGerald, and Margaret H. P. Broadbent. 1986. "Implicit and Explicit Knowledge in the Control of Complex Systems". *British Journal of Psychology* 77: 33–50.

Brown, Liana E., and David A. Rosenbaum. 2003. "Motor Control: Models". In Nadel 2003, vol. 3: 127–33.

Burge, Tyler. 1979. "Individualism and the Mental". *Midwest Studies in Philosophy, Volume IV: Studies in Metaphysics*, eds. Peter A. French, Theodore E. Uehling Jr., and Howard K. Wettstein: 73–121.

Burton-Roberts, Noel, Philip Carr, and Gerard Docherty. 2000. "Introduction". In *Phonological Knowledge: Conceptual and Empirical Issues*, eds. Noel Burton-Roberts, Philip Carr, and Gerard Docherty. Oxford: Oxford University Press: 1–18.

Caramazza, Alfonso. 1997. "How Many Levels of Processing are there in Lexical Access?" *Cognitive Neuropsychology* 14: 177–208.

—— 1999. "Lexicon, Neural Basis of". In Wilson and Keil 1999: 469–71.

Carey, Susan. 1985. *Conceptual Change in Childhood*. Cambridge, MA: MIT Press.

Carlson, Richard A. 2003. "Skill Learning". In Nadel 2003, vol. 4: 36–42.

Carroll, Lewis. 1895. "What the Tortoise Said to Achilles". *Mind* 4: 278–80.

Carruthers, Peter. 1996. *Language, Thought and Consciousness: An Essay in Philosophical Psychology*. Cambridge: Cambridge University Press.

—— 1998. "Thinking in Language? Evolution and a Modularist Possibility". In Carruthers and Boucher 1998: 94–119.

—— 2002. "The Cognitive Functions of Language". *Behavioral and Brain Sciences* 25: 657–74.

—— and Jill Boucher, eds. 1998a. *Language and Thought: Interdisciplinary Themes*. Cambridge: Cambridge University Press.

—— and Jill Boucher. 1998b. "Introduction: Opening Up Options". In Carruthers and Boucher 1998a: 1–18.

Chierchia, Gennaro. 1999. "Linguistics and Language". In Wilson and Keil 1999: xci–cix.

Chomsky, Noam. 1957. *Syntactic Structures*. The Hague: Mouton and Co.

—— 1959. Review of Skinner 1957. *Language* 35: 26–58.

—— 1965. *Aspects of the Theory of Syntax*. Cambridge, MA.: MIT Press.

—— 1966. *Cartesian Linguistics: A Chapter in the History of Rationalist Thought*. New York: Harper & Rowe.

—— 1969a. "Linguistics and Philosophy". In Hook 1969: 51–94.

—— 1969b. "Comments on Harman's Reply". In Hook 1969: 152–9.

—— 1972. *Language and Mind*. Enlarged edn. New York: Harcourt Brace Jovanovich.

—— 1975a. "Knowledge of Language". In Gunderson 1975: 299–320.

—— 1975b. *Reflections on Language*. New York: Pantheon Books.

—— 1975c. *The Logical Structure of Linguistic Theory*. New York: Plenum Press.

—— 1980a. *Rules and Representations*. New York: Columbia University Press.

—— 1980b. "Rules and Representations". *Behavioral and Brain Sciences* 3: 1–14.

—— 1980c. "Author's Response" to peer commentary on 1980b. *Behavioral and Brain Sciences* 3: 42–58.

—— 1982. *Some Concepts and Consequences of the Theory of Government and Binding*. Cambridge, MA.: MIT Press.

Chomsky, Noam. 1986. *Knowledge of Language: Its Nature, Origin, and Use*. New York: Praeger Publishers.

—— 1988. *Language and Problems of Knowledge: The Managua Lectures*. Cambridge, MA: MIT Press.

—— 1991a. "Linguistics and Adjacent Fields: A Personal View". In Kasher 1991a: 3–25.

—— 1991b. "Linguistics and Cognitive Science: Problems and Mysteries". In Kasher 1991a: 26–53.

—— 1993a. "Mental Constructions and Social Reality". In *Knowledge and Language Volume I: From Orwell's Problem to Plato's Problem*, eds. Eric Reuland and Werner Abraham. Dordrecht: Kluwer Academic Publishers: 29–58.

—— 1993b. "A Minimalist Program for Linguistic Theory". In *The View from Building 20: Essays in Honor of Sylvain Bromberger*, eds. Kenneth Hale and Samuel Jay Keyser. Cambridge, MA: MIT Press.

—— 1994a. *Language and Thought*. London: Moyer Bell.

—— 1995a. *The Minimalist Program*. Cambridge, MA: MIT Press.

—— 1995b. "Language and Nature". *Mind* 104: 1–61.

—— 1995c. "Base Phrase Structure". In Webelhuth 1995a: 383–439.

—— 1996. *Powers and Prospects: Reflections on Human Nature and the Social Order*. Boston: South End Press.

—— 2000a. *New Horizons in the Study of Language and Mind*. Cambridge: Cambridge University Press.

—— 2000b. *The Architecture of Language*. New Delhi: Oxford University Press.

—— 2003. "Reply to Rey". In Antony and Hornstein 2003: 274–87.

Churchland, Patricia S. 1986. *Neurophilosophy: Toward a Unified Science of the Mind–Brain*. Cambridge, MA: MIT Press.

Churchland, Paul M. 1981. "Eliminative Materialism and the Propositional Attitudes". *Journal of Philosophy* 78: 67–90. Reprinted in Churchland 1989: 1–22.

—— 1989. *A Neurocomputational Perspective: The Nature of Mind and the Structure of Science*. Cambridge, MA: MIT Press.

Clark, Andy. 1998. "Magic Words: How Language Augments Human Computation". In Carruthers and Boucher 1998a: 162–83.

Clark, R. 1994. "Finitude, Boundedness, and Complexity". In *Syntactic Theory and First Language Acquisition: Cross-Linguistic Perspectives. Vol. 2: Binding, Dependencies, and Learnability*, eds B. Lust, G. Hermon, and J. Kornfilt. Hillsdale, NJ: Lawrence Erlbaum: 473–89.

Cleeremans, Axel. 2003. "Implicit Learning Models". In Nadel 2003, vol. 2: 491–9.

Collins, John. 2003. "Cowie on the Poverty of the Stimulus". *Synthese* 136: 159–90.

—— 2004. "Faculty Disputes". *Mind and Language* 19: 503–33.

Corina, David P. "Sign Language and the Brain". In Wilson and Keil 1999: 756–8.

Cowie, Fiona. 1998. *What's Within: Nativism Reconsidered*. New York: Oxford University Press.

Crain, Stephen, Andrea Gualmini, and Paul Pietroski. 2005. "Brass Tacks in Linguistic Theory: Innate Grammatical Principles". To appear in a volume produced by the Sheffield Innateness Project.

—— and Paul Pietroski. 2001. "Nature, Nurture and Universal Grammar". *Linguistics and Philosophy* 24: 139–86.

—— and Paul Pietroski. 2002. "Why Language Acquisition is a Snap". *The Linguistic Review* 19: 163–83.

—— and Mark Steedman. 1985. "On Not Being Led up the Garden Path: The Use of Context by the Psychological Syntax Processor". In *Natural Language Parsing: Psychological, Computational, and Theoretical Perspectives*, eds. David R. Dowty, Lauri Karttunen, and Arnold M. Zwicky. Cambridge: Cambridge University Press.

—— and Rosalind Thornton. 1998. *Investigations in Universal Grammar: A Guide to Experiments on the Acquisition of Syntax and Semantics*. Cambridge, MA: MIT Press.

Croft, William, and D. Alan Cruse. 2004. *Cognitive Linguistics*. Cambridge: Cambridge University Press.

Culicover, Peter W. 1999. *Syntactic Nuts: Hard Cases, Syntactic Theory, and Language Acquisition*. Oxford: Oxford University Press.

Cummins, Robert. 1996. *Representations, Targets, and Attitudes*. Cambridge, MA: MIT Press.

—— and Robert M. Harnish. 1980. "The Language Faculty and the Interpretation of Linguistics". *Behavioral and Brain Sciences* 3: 18–19.

Curtis, Susan. 1981. "Dissociations Between Language and Cognition: Cases and Implications". *Journal of Autism and Developmental Disorders*, 11: 15–30.

Cutler, Anne. 1995. "Spoken Word Recognition and Production". In Miller and Eimas 1995: 97–136.

—— 1999. "Spoken-Word Recognition". In Wilson and Keil 1999: 796–8.

—— and Dennis Norris. 1999. "Sharpening Ockham's Razor". *Behavioral and Brain Sciences* 22: 40–1.

Davidson, Donald. 1980. *Essays on Actions and Events*. Oxford: Clarendon Press.

—— 1984. *Inquiries into Truth and Interpretation*: Oxford: Clarendon Press.

—— 1986. "A Nice Derangement of Epitaphs". In Lepore 1986: 433–46.

Davies, Martin. 1987. "Tacit Knowledge and Semantic Theory: Can a Five per cent Difference Matter?" *Mind* 96: 441–62.

—— 1989. "Tacit Knowledge and Subdoxastic States". In George 1989a: 131–52.

—— 1995. "Two Notions of Implicit Rules". In *Philosophical Perspectives, 9, AI, Connectionism, and Philosophical Psychology, 1995*, ed. James E. Tomberlin. Cambridge MA: Blackwell Publishers:

—— 1998. "Language, Thought, and the Language of Thought (Aunty's Own Argument Revisited)". In Carruthers and Boucher 1998: 226–47.

—— and Tony Stone. 1995. *Folk Psychology: The Theory of Mind Debate*. Oxford: Blackwell Publishers.

Davis, Martin. 1983. "Church's Thesis and Representation of Grammars". *Behavioral and Brain Sciences* 3: 404.

Dehaene, S. 1997. *The Number Sense: How the Mind Creates Mathematics*. New York: Oxford Universtiy Press.

Dell, Gary S. 1995. "Speaking and Misspeaking". In Gleitman and Liberman 1995: 83–208.

—— M. F. Schwartz, N. Martin, E. M. Saffran, and D. A. Gagnon. 1997. "Lexical Access in Aphasic and Nonaphasic Speakers". *Psychological Review* 104: 801–38.

——, Franklin Chang, and Zenzi M. Griffin. 1999. "Connectionist Models of Language Production: Lexical Access and Grammatical Encoding". *Cognitive Science* 23: 517–42.

Demopoulos, William, and Robert J. Matthews. 1983. "On the Hypothesis that Grammars Are Mentally Represented". *Behavioral and Brain Sciences* 3: 405–6.

Dennett, Daniel. 1978. *Brainstorms*. Cambridge, MA: Bradford Books.

—— 1980. "Passing the Buck to Biology". *Behavioral and Brain Sciences* 3: 19–20.

DePaul, Michael R., and William Ramsey, ed. 1998. *Rethinking Intuition*. Lanham: Rowman & Littlefield Publishers, Inc.

Devitt, Michael. 1981. *Designation*. New York: Columbia University Press.

—— 1990. "Transcendentalism about Content". *Pacific Philosophical Quarterly* 71: 247–63.

—— 1994. "The Methodology of Naturalistic Semantics". *Journal of Philosophy*, 91 (1994): 545–72.

—— 1996. *Coming to Our Senses*. Cambridge: Cambridge University Press.

—— 1997a. *Realism and Truth*. 2nd edn with new afterword. Princeton: Princeton University Press.

—— 1997b. "Responses to the Maribor Papers". In Jutronic 1998: 353–411.

—— 1998a. "Putting Metaphysics First: A Response to James Tomberlin". In *Philosophical Perspectives, 12, Language, Mind, and Ontology, 1998*. James E. Tomberlin, ed. Cambridge MA: Blackwell Publishers (1998), pp. 499–502.

—— 1998b. "Naturalism and the *A Priori*". *Philosophical Studies*, 92, 45–65.

—— 2001. "Sustaining Actualism". In *Philosophical Perspectives, 15, Metaphysics, 2001*, ed. James E. Tomberlin. Cambridge MA: Blackwell Publishers: 415–19.

—— 2002. "Deference: A Truth in Linguistic Relativity". Paper delivered at the annual conference of the Society for Philosophy and Psychology, Edmonton, June 2002.

—— 2003. "Linguistics is not Psychology". In Barber 2003a: 107–39.

—— 2005a. "There is no A Priori". In Steup and Sosa 2005: 105–15.

—— 2005b. "Reply to BonJour". In Steup and Sosa 2005: 118–20.

—— 2005c. "Scientific Realism". In *The Oxford Handbook of Contemporary Philosophy*, eds Frank Jackson and Michael Smith. Oxford: Oxford University Press: 767–91.

—— 2006. "Intuitions in Linguistics". *British Journal for the Philosophy of Science* (forthcoming).

—— and Georges Rey. 1991. "Transcending Transcendentalism: A Response to Boghossian". *Pacific Philosophical Quarterly* 72: 87–100.

—— and Kim Sterelny. 1987. *Language and Reality: An Introduction to the Philosophy of Language*. Cambridge, MA: MIT Press.

—— and Kim Sterelny. 1989. "What's Wrong with 'the Right View' ". In *Philosophical Perspectives, 3: Philosophy of Mind and Action Theory, 1989*, ed. James E. Tomberlin. Atascadero: Ridgeview Publishing Company, 497–531.

—— and Kim Sterelny. 1999. *Language and Reality: An Introduction to the Philosophy of Language*. 2nd edn. Cambridge, MA: MIT Press.

Donnellan, Keith S. 1972. "Proper Names and Identifying Descriptions". In *Semantics of Natural Language*, eds. Donald Davidson and Gilbert Harman. Dordrecht: Reidel: 356–79.

Dosher, Barbara A. 2003. "Working Memory". In Nadel 2003, vol. 4: 569–77.

Dretske, Fred. 1974. "Explanation in Linguistics". In *Explaining Linguistic Phenomena*, ed. D. Cohen. Washing DC: Hemisphere: 21–41.

Dronkers, Nina F. 1999. "Language, Neural Basis of". In Wilson and Keil 1999: 448–51.

Dummett, Michael. 1975. "What is a Theory of Meaning?" In Guttenplan 1975: 97–138.

—— 1993. *The Seas of Language*. Oxford: Oxford University Press.

Dwyer, Susan, and Paul Pietroski. 1996. "Believing in Language". *Philosophy of Science* 63: 338–73.

Ferreira, Victor S. 2003. "Production–Comprehension Interface". In Nadel 2003, vol. 3: 747–53.

Field, Hartry. 1978. "Mental Representation". *Erkenntnis* 13: 9–61. Reprinted with Postscript in Block 1981: 78–114. [Citations are to Block]

Fiengo, Robert. 2003. "Linguistic Intuitions". *Philosophical Forum*, 34: 253–65.

Fodor, Janet Dean. 1985. "Deterministic Parsing and Subjacency". *Language and Cognitive Processes* 1: 3–42.

—— 1989. "Empty Categories in Sentence Processing". *Language and Cognitive Processes* 4: 155–209.

—— 1992. "Learnability of Phrase Structure Grammars". In *Formal Grammar: Theory and Implementation*, Robert Levine, ed. New York: Oxford University Press: 3–68.

—— 1998. "Parsing to Learn". *Journal of Psycholinguistic Research*, 27: 339–74.

—— 2001. "Parameters and the Periphery: Reflections on *Syntactic Nuts*". *Journal of Linguistics* 37: 367–92.

—— Jerry A. Fodor, and Merrill F. Garrett. 1975. "The Psychological Unreality of Semantic Representations". *Linguistic Inquiry* 6: 515–31. Reprinted in Block 1981: 238–52. [Citations are to Block]

Fodor, Jerry A. 1975. *The Language of Thought*. New York: Thomas Y. Crowell.

—— 1981a. *Representations: Philosophical Essays on the Foundations of Cognitive Science*. Cambridge MA.: Bradford Books/MIT Press.

—— 1981b. "Introduction: Some Notes on What Linguistics is Talking About". In Block 1981: 197–207. Reprinted in Katz 1985.

—— 1983. *The Modularity of Mind: An Essay on Faculty Psychology*. Cambridge, MA.: MIT Press.

—— 1987. *Psychosemantics: The Problem of Meaning in the Philosophy of Mind*. Cambridge, MA: MIT Press.

—— 1990. *A Theory of Content and other Essays*. Cambridge, MA: MIT Press

—— 1998a. *Concepts: Where Cognitive Science Went Wrong*. Oxford: Clarendon Press.

—— 1998b. *In Critical Condition: Polemical Essays on Cognitive Science and the Philosophy of Mind*. Cambridge, MA: MIT Press.

—— 2001. "Doing Without What's Within: Fiona Cowie's Critique of Nativism". *Mind* 110: 99–148.

—— and T. G. Bever. 1965. "The Psychological Reality of Linguistic Segments". *Journal of Verbal Learning and Verbal Behavior* 4: 414–20.

—— T. G. Bever and M. F. Garrett. 1974. *The Psychology of Language: An Introduction to Psycholinguistics and Generative Grammar*. New York: McGraw-Hill Book Company.

—— and Ernest Lepore. 1992. *Holism: A Shopper's Guide*. Oxford: Basil Blackwell.

—— and Zenon W. Pylyshyn. 1988. "Connectionism and Cognitive Architecture: A Critical Analysis". *Cognition* 28: 3–71. Reprinted in McDonald and McDonald 1995: 90–163. [Citations are to McDonald and McDonald]

Fowler, C. A., and M. T. Turvey. 1978. "Skill Acquisition: An Event Approach with Special Reference to Searching for the Optimum of a Function of Several Variables". In *Information Processing and Motor Control*, G. E. Stelmach, ed. New York: Academic Press.

Frank, Adam. 1997. "Quantum Honey Bees". *Discover*: 80–7.

Frazier, Lyn. 1995. "Issues of Representation in Psycholinguistics". In Miller and Eimas 1995: 1–27.

—— and Janet Dean Fodor. 1978. "The Sausage Machine: A New Two-Stage Parsing Model". *Cognition* 6: 291–325.

—— and K. Rayner. 1982. "Making and Correcting Errors during Sentence Comprehension: Eye Movements in the Analysis of Structurally Ambiguous Sentences". *Cognitive Psychology* 14: 178–210.

Gallistel, C. R. 1990. *The Organization of Learning*. Cambridge, MA: MIT Press.

Garfield, Jay L. ed. 1987. *Modularity in Knowledge Representation and Natural-Language Understanding*. Cambridge, MA: MIT Press.

Garson, James. 2003. "Dynamical Systems, Philosophical Issues about". In Nadel 2003, vol. 1: 1033–9.

Gasper, Philip. 1986. Review of 1st edn of Devitt 1997. *Philosophical Review*. 95: 446–51.

Gazdar, Gerald, Ewan Klein, Geoffrey Pullum, and Ivan Sag. 1985. *Generalized Phrase Structure Grammar*. Oxford: Basil Blackwell.

Geach, Peter. 1967. "Intentional Identity". *Journal of Philosophy* 64: 627–32.

Gendler, Tamar Szabo. 2003. "Thought Experiments". In Nadel 2003, vol. 4: 388–94.

Gentner, Dedre, and Laura L. Namy. 2004. "The Role of Comparison in Children's Early Word Learning". In *Weaving a Lexicon*, D. G. Hall and S. R. Waxman, eds. Cambridge, MA: MIT Press: 533–68.

George, Alexander, ed. 1989a. *Reflections on Chomsky*. Oxford: Basil Blackwell.

—— 1989b. "How Not to Become Confused About Linguistics". In George 1989a: 90–110.

Gernsbacher, Morton Ann, and Michael P Kaschak. 2003. "Language Comprehension". In Nadel 2003, vol. 2: 723–5.

Gibson, Edward. 2003. "Sentence Comprehension, Linguistic Complexity in". In Nadel 2003, vol. 3: 1137–41.

Gladwell, Malcolm. 2005. *Blink: The Power of Thinking Without Thinking*. New York: Little, Brown.

Gleitman, Lila R., and Paul Bloom. 1999. "Language Acquisition". In Wilson and Keil 1999: 434–8.

—— and Mark Liberman. 1995. *Language: An Invitation to Cognitive Science, Second Edition, Volume 1*. Cambridge, MA: MIT Press.

Goldberg, Elkhonon. 2005. *The Wisdom Paradox: How Your Mind Can Grow Stronger as Your Brain Grows Older*. New York: Gotham Books.

Goldin-Meadow, Susan, and Ming-Yu Zheng. 1998. "Thought Before Language: the Expression of Motion Events Prior to the Impact of a Conventional Language Model". In Carruthers and Boucher 1998a: 26–54.

Gopnik, Alison, and Eric Schwitzgebel. 1998. "Whose Concepts Are They, Anyway? The Role of Philosophical Intuitions in Empirical Psychology". In DePaul and Ramsey 1998: 75–91.

Gordon, P. C., and R. Hendrick. "Intuitive Knowledge of Linguistic Co-reference". *Cognition* 62: 325–70.

Gorrell, Paul. 1999. "Sentence Processing". In Wilson and Keil 1999: 748–51.

Graves, Christina, J. J. Katz, Y. Nishiyama, Scott Soames, R. Stecker, and P. Tovey. 1973. "Tacit Knowledge". *Journal of Philosophy* 70: 318–30.

Grice, H.P. 1957. "Meaning". *Philosophical Review* 66: 377–88. Reprinted in Grice 1989.

—— 1989. *Studies in the Way of Words*. Cambridge MA.: Harvard University Press.

Grodzinsky, Yosef. 2003. "Language Disorders". In Nadel 2003, vol. 2: 740–6.

Gross, Maurice. 1983. "A Few Analogies with Computing". *Behavioral and Brain Sciences* 3: 407–8.

Gumperz, John J., and Stephen C. Levinson, eds. 1996. "Introduction to Part I". In *Rethinking Linguistic Relativity*, eds. Gumperz and Levinson. Cambridge: Cambridge University Press: 21–36.

Gunderson, Keith, ed. 1975. *Minnesota Studies in the Philosophy of Science, Volume VII: Language, Mind, and Knowledge*. Minneapolis: University of Minnesota Press.

Guttenplan, Samuel, ed. 1975. *Mind and Language*. Oxford: Clarendon Press.

—— ed. 1994. *A Companion to the Philosophy of Mind*. Cambridge, MA: Blackwell Publishers.

Hadley, Robert F. 1999. "Connectionism and Novel Combinations of Skills: Implications for Cognitive Architecture". *Minds and Machines* 9: 197–221.

Haegeman, Liliane. 1994. *Introduction to Government and Binding Theory*, 2nd edn. Oxford: Blackwell Publishers. 1st edn 1991.

Halle, Morris, Joan Bresnan, and George A. Miller, eds. 1978. *Linguistic Theory and Psychological Reality*. Cambridge, MA.: MIT Press.

Hannan, Barbara. 1993. "Don't Stop Believing: The Case Against Eliminative Materialism". *Mind and Language* 8: 165–79.

Harman, Gilbert. 1967. "Psychological Aspects of the Theory of Syntax". *Journal of Philosophy* 64: 75–87.

—— 1973. *Thought*. Princeton: Princeton University Press.

—— ed. 1974. *On Noam Chomsky: Critical Essays*. Garden City, N.Y.: Anchor Press/ Doubleday.

—— 1983. "Internally Represented Grammars". *Behavioral and Brain Sciences* 3: 408.

Harris, Catherine L. 2003. "Language and Cognition". Nadel 2003, vol. 2: 717–22.

Harris, Randy Allen. 1993. *The Linguistics Wars*. New York: Oxford University Press.

Hauser, Marc D., Noam Chomsky, and W. Tecumseh Fitch. 2002. "The Faculty of Language: What Is It, Who Has It, and How Did It Evolve?" *Science* 298: 1569–79.

Higginbotham, James. 1987. "The Autonomy of Syntax and Semantics". In Garfield 1987: 119–31.

—— 1989. "Knowledge of Reference". In George 1989a: 153–74.

Hillis, Argye E., and Alfonso Caramazza. 2003. "Aphasia". In Nadel 2003, vol. 1: 175–84.

Holding, Dennis H. 1992. "Theories of Chess Skill". *Psychological Research* 54: 10–16.

Hook, Sidney, ed. 1969. *Language and Philosophy: A Symposium*. New York: New York University Press.

Horgan, Terence, and John Tienson. 1999. "Rules and Representations". In Wilson and Keil 1999: 724–26.

Hornstein, Norbert. 1989. "Meaning and the Mental: The Problem of Semantics after Chomsky". In George 1989a: 23–40.

—— and David Lightfoot, eds. 1981a. *Explanation in Linguistics: The Logical Problem of Language Acquisition*. London: Longman.

—— 1981b. "Preface". To Hornstein and Lightfoot 1981a: 7–8.

Howe, Christine J. 1986. Review of Berwick and Weinberg 1984. *Mind and Language* 1: 83–8.

Hurford, James R., Michael Studdert-Kennedy, and Chris Knight, eds. 1998. *Approaches to the Evolution of Language: Social and Cognitive Basis*. Cambridge: Cambridge University Press.

Jackendoff, Ray. 1997. *The Architecture of the Language Faculty*. Cambridge, MA: MIT Press.

Johnson, Kent. 2004. "Systematicity". *Journal of Philosophy* 101: 111–39.

Johnson, Todd R., Hongbin Wang, and Jiajie Zhang. 2003. "Skill Acquisition: Models". In Nadel 2003, vol. 4: 30–6.

Jones, Gary. 2003. "Production Systems and Rule-Based Inference". In Nadel 2003, vol. 3: 741–7.

Jutronic, Dunja ed. 1997. *The Maribor Papers in Naturalized Semantics*, Maribor: Pedagoska fakulteta Maribor.

Kasher, Asa, ed. 1991a. *The Chomskyan Turn*. Oxford: Basil Blackwell.

—— 1991b. "Pragmatics and Chomsky". In Kasher 1991a: 122–49.

Katz, Jerrold J. 1981. *Language and Other Abstract Objects*. Totowa, N. J.: Rowman & Littlefield.

—— 1984. "An Outline of a Platonist Grammar". In Bever *et al.* 1984: 17–48. Reprinted in Katz 1985.

—— ed. 1985. *The Philosophy of Linguistics*. Oxford: Oxford University Press.

—— 1996. "The Unfinished Chomskyan Revolution". *Mind and Language* 11: 270–94.

Kelso, J. A. Scott. 1995. *Dynamic Patterns: The Self-Organization of Brain and Behavior*. Cambridge MA: MIT Press.

Kintsch, Walter. 1984. "Approaches to the Study of the Psychology of Language". In Bever *et al.* 1984: 111–45.

Kornblith, Hilary. 1998. "The Role of Intuition in Philosophical Inquiry: An Account with no Unnatural Ingredients". In DePaul and Ramsey 1998: 129–41.

Kripke, Saul A. 1980. *Naming and Necessity*. Cambridge, MA: Harvard University Press.

Kugler, P. N., and M. T. Turvey. 1987. *Information, Natural Laws, and the Self-Assembly of rhythmic Movement*. Hillsdale, NJ: Laurence Erlbaum.

Laird, J. E., A. Newell, and P. S. Rosenbloom. 1987. "Soar: An Architect for General Intelligence". *Artificial Intelligence* 33: 1–64.

Larson, Richard, and Gabriel Segal. 1995. *Knowledge of Meaning: An Introduction to Semantic Theory*. Cambridge, MA: MIT Press.

Lasnik, Howard, and Juan Uriagereka. 2002. "On the Poverty of the Challenge". *Linguistic Review* 19:147–50.

Laurence, Stephen. 1996. "A Chomskian Alternative to Convention-Based Semantics". *Mind* 105: 269–301.

—— 1998. "Convention-Based Semantics and the Development of Language". In Carruthers and Boucher 1998: 201–17.

—— 2003. "Is Linguistics a Branch of Psychology?" In Barber 2003a: 69–106.

—— and Eric Margolis. 2001. "The Poverty of Stimulus Argument". *British Journal for the Philosophy of Science* 52: 217–76.

Lees, Robert B. 1957. "Review of *Syntactic Structures*". *Language* 33: 375–407. Reprinted in *On Noam Chomsky: Critical Essays* ed. Gilbert Harman. Garden City, N. Y.: Anchor Press/Doubleday: 34–79. [Citation is to Harman]

Lepore, Ernest, ed. 1986. *Truth and Interpretation: Perspectives on the Philosophy of Donald Davidson*. Oxford: Basil Blackwell.

—— and Kirk Ludwig. 2000. "The Semantics and Pragmatics of Complex Demonstratives". *Mind*, 109: 199–240.

Levelt, William J. M., Ardi Roelofs, and Antje S. Meyer. 1999. "A Theory of Lexical Access in Speech Production". *Behavioral and Brain Sciences* 22: 1–38.

Lewandowsky, Stephan, and Simon Farrell. 2003. "Working Memory, Computational Models of". In Nadel 2003, vol. 4: 578–83.

Lewis, David K. 1969. *Convention: A Philosophical Study*. Cambridge, MA.: Harvard University Press.

—— 1994. "Reduction of Mind". In Guttenplan 1994: 412–31.

Lewis, John D., and Jeffrey L. Ellman. 2001. "Learnability and the Statistical Structure of Language: Poverty of Stimulus Arguments Revisited". *Proceeding of the 26th Annual Boston University Conference on Language Development*. Somerville, MA: Cascadilla Press: 359–70.

Lipton, Michael R. 1983. "Levels of Grammatic Representation: A Tempest in a Teapot". *Behavioral and Brain Sciences* 3: 409–10.

Logan, Gordon D. 1988. "Toward an Instance Theory of Automatization". *Psychological Review* 95: 492–527.

McClelland, James L. 1999. "Cognitive Modeling, Connectionist". In Wilson and Keil 1999: 137–41.

McDonald, Cynthia, and Graham McDonald, eds. 1995. *Connectionism: Debates on Psychological Explanation, Volume Two*. Cambridge, MA: Blackwell Publishers.

McGilvray, James. 1999. *Chomsky: Language, Mind, and Politics*. Cambridge: Polity Press.

Macintosh, Nicholas J. 1999. "Conditioning". In Wilson and Keil 1999: 182–4.

McLeod, Peter, and Zoltan Dienes. 1996. "Do Fielders Know Where to Go to Catch the Ball or Only How to Get There?" *Journal of Experimental Psychology: Human Perception and Performance* 22: 531–43.

Malcolm, Norman. 1968. "The Conceivability of Mechanism". *Philosophyical Review* 77: 45–72.

Malson, L. 1972. *Wolf Children and the Problem of Human Nature*. London: Monthly Review Press.

Maratsos, Michael P. 1989. "Innateness and Plasticity in Language Acquisition". In *The Teachability of Language*, M. L. Rice and R. L. Schiefelbusch, eds. Baltimore: Paul H. Brookes: 105–25.

—— 2003. "Language Acquisition". In Nadel 2003, vol. 2: 691–6.

Marr, David. 1982. *Vision: A Computational Investigation into the Human Representation and Processing of Visual Information*. San Francisco: W. H. Freeman and Company.

Masson, Michael E. J. 1990. "Cognitive Theories of Skill Acquisition". *Human Movement Science* 9: 221–39.

Mathews, R. C., R. R. Buss, W. B. Stanley, and R. Chinn. 1988. "Analysis of Individual Learning Curves in a Concept Discovery Task: Relations among Task Performance, Verbalizable Knowledge, and Hypothesis Revision Strategies". *The Quarterly Journal of Experimental Psychology* 40A: 135–65.

—— R. R. Buss, W. B. Stanley, F. Blanchard-Fields, J. R. Cho, and B. Druhan. 1989. "Role of Implicit and Explicit Processes in Learning From Examples: A Synergistic Effect". *Journal of Experimental Psychology: Learning, Memory, and Cognition* 15: 1083–100.

Matthews, Robert J. 1980. "Language Learning versus Grammar Growth". *Behavioral and Brain Sciences* 3: 25–26.

—— 1991. "The Psychological Reality of Grammars". In Kasher 1991a: 182–99.

—— 2003. "Does Linguistic Competence Require Knowledge of Language?" In Barber 2003a: 187–213.

Miller, G. A., and N. Chomsky. 1963. "Finitary Models of Language Users". In *Handbook of Mathematical Psychology*, Vol. II, eds. R. D. Luce, R. R. Bush, and E. Galanter, eds. New York: Wiley.

Miller, Joanne L. 1999. "Speech Perception". In Wilson and Keil 1999: 787–90.

—— and Peter D. Eimas, eds. 1995. *Speech, Language, and Communication*. San Diego: Academic Press.

Mills, Eugene. "Devitt on the Nature of Belief". In Jutronic 1997: 310–17.

Mon-Williams, Mark, James R. Tresilian, and John P. Wann. 2003. "Motor Control and Learning". In Nadel 2003: 121–6.

Moro, A., M. Tettamanti, D. Perani, C. Donati, S. F. Cappa, and F. Fazio. 2001. "Syntax and the Brain: Disentangling Grammar by Selective Anomalies". *NeuroImage* 13: 110–18.

Mulligan, Neil W. 2003. "Memory: Implicit versus Explicit". In Nadel 2003, vol. 2: 1114–20.

Nadel, Lynn, ed. 2003. *Encyclopedia of Cognitive Science*. London: Nature Publishing Group.

Neale, Stephen. 1989. "Paul Grice and the Philosophy of Language". *Linguistics and Philosophy* 15: 509–59.

—— 2004. "This, That, and the Other". In *Descriptions and Beyond*, Marga Reimer and Anne Bezuidenhout, eds. Oxford: Clarendon Press: 68–182.

Newell, A., and H. Simon. 1972. *Human Problem Solving*. Englewood Cliffs, NJ: Prentice-Hall.

Newell, Karl M. 1996. "Motor Skills". In *Encyclopedia of Leaning and Memory*, ed. Larry R. Squire. Macmillan Library Reference: 441–3.

Newport, Elissa L., and Ted Supalla. 1999. "Sign Languages". In Wilson and Keil 1999: 758–60.

Ni, Weijia, Stephen Crain, and Donald Shankweiler. 1996. "Sidestepping Garden Paths: Assessing the Contributions of Syntax, Semantics and Plausibility in Resolving Ambiguities". *Language and Cognitive Processes* 11: 283–334.

Niiniluoto, Ilkka. 1981. "Language, Norms, and Truth". In *Essays in Philosophical Analysis Dedicated to Erik Stenius on the Occasion of his 70th Birthday*, Ingmar Porn, ed. Helsinki: The Philosophical Society of Finland: 168–89.

Nygaard, Lynne C., and David B. Pisoni. 1995. "Speech Perception: New Directions in Research and Theory". In Miller and Eimas 1995: 63–96.

Palmeri, Thomas J. 2003. "Automaticity". In Nadel 2003, vol. 1: 290–301.

Pateman, Trevor. 1987. *Language in Mind and Language in Society: Studies in Linguistic Reproduction*. Oxford: Clarendon Press.

Peacocke, Christopher. 1986. "Explanation in Computational Psychology: Language, Perception and Level 1.5". *Mind and Language* 1: 101–23.

—— 1989. "When is a Grammar Psychologically Real?" In George 1989a: 111–30.

Pickering, Martin J. 2003. "Parsing". In Nadel 2003, vol. 3: 462–5.

Pietroski, Paul M. 2003. "The Character of Natural Language Semantics". In Barber 2003a: 217–56.

Pinker, Stephen. 1979. "Formal Models of Language Learning". *Cognition* 7: 217–82.

—— 1989. *Learnability and Cognition*. Cambridge MA: MIT Press.

—— 1994. *The Language Instinct: How the Mind Creates Language*. New York: William Morrow and Co.

—— 1995a. "Why the Child Holded the Baby Rabbits: A Case Study in Language Acquisition". In Gleitman and Liberman 1995: 107–33

—— 1995b. "Language Acquisition". In Gleitman and Liberman 1995: 135–82.

—— 1997. *How the Mind Works*. New York: W. W. Norton and Company.

—— and Paul Bloom. 1990. "Natural Language and Natural Selection". *Behavioral and Brain Sciences* 13: 707–27.

Poeppel, David, and Gregory Hickok. 2004. "Introduction: Towards a New Functional Anatomy of Language". *Cognition* 92: 1–12.

Port, Robert F. 2003. "Dynamical Systems Hypothesis in Cognitive Science". In Nadel 2003, vol. 1: 1027–32.

Posner, M. I. 1973. *Cognition: An Introduction*. Glenville IL: Scott, Foresman.

—— G. J. DiGirolamo, and D. Fernandez-Duque. 1997. "Brain Mechanisms of Cognitive Skills". *Consciousness and Cognition* 6: 267–90.

Poucet, Bruno. 2003. "Animal Navigation and Cognitive Maps". In Nadel 2003, vol. 1: 150–6.

Pritchett, Bradley L. 1988. "Garden Path Phenomena and the Grammatical Basis of Language Processing". *Language* 64: 539–76.

Pullum, Geoffrey. 1991. *The Great Eskimo Vocabulary Hoax and Other Irreverent Essays on the Study of Language*. Chicago: University of Chicago Press.

—— and Barbara Scholz. 2002. "Empirical Assessment of Stimulus Poverty Arguments". *Linguistic Review* 19: 9–50.

Putnam, Hilary. 1967. "The 'Innateness Hypothesis' and Explanatory Models in Linguistics". *Synthese* 17: 12–22. Reprinted in Block 1981: 292–9. [Citations are to Block]

—— 1975. *Mind, Language and Reality: Philosophical Papers Vol. 2*. Cambridge: Cambridge University Press.

Pylyshyn, Zenon W. 1980a. "Computation and Cognition: Issues in the Foundations of Cognitive Science". *Behavioral and Brain Sciences* 3: 111–32.

—— 1980b. "Author's Response" to peer commentary on 1980a. *Behavioral and Brain Sciences* 3: 154–68.

—— 1984. *Computation and Cognition: Toward a Foundation for Cognitive Science*. Cambridge, MA: MIT Press.

—— 1991. "Rules and Representations: Chomsky and Representational Realism". In Kasher 1991a: 231–51.

Quine, W. V. 1960. *Word and Object*. Cambridge MA: MIT Press

—— 1966. *The Ways of Paradox and Other Essays*. New York: Random House.

—— 1970. "Methodological Reflections on Current Linguistics". *Synthese* 21: 386–98.

Radford, Andrew. 1988. *Transformational Grammar: A First Course*. Cambridge: Cambridge University Press.

Ramsey, William. 1997. "Do Connectionist Representations Earn Their Explanatory Keep?" *Mind and Language* 12: 34–66.

Reber, A. S. 1967. "Implicit Learning of Artificial Grammars". *Journal of Verbal Learning and Verbal Behavior* 6: 855–63.

—— 1989. "Implicit Learning and Tacit Knowledge". *Journal of Experimental Psychology: General* 118: 219–35.

—— 2003. "Implicit Learning". In Nadel 2003, vol. 2: 486–91.

Reisberg, Daniel. 1999. "Learning". In Wilson and Keil 1999: 460–1.

Rey, Georges. 1997. *Contemporary Philosophy of Mind: A Contentiously Classical Approach*. Cambridge, MA: Blackwell Publishers.

—— 2003a. "Chomsky, Intentionality and a CRTT". In Antony and Hornstein 2003: 105–39.

—— 2003b. "Intentional Content and Chomskyan Linguistics". In Barber 2003a: 140–86.

—— 2006. "The Intentional Inexistence of Language—But Not Cars". In *Contemporary Debates in Cognitive Science*, ed. R. Stainton. Oxford: Blackwell Publishers: 237–55

Richard, Mark. 1990. *Propositional Attitudes: An Essay on Thoughts and How We Ascribe Them*. Cambridge: Cambridge University Press.

Richardson-Klavehn, Alan, and Robert A. Bjork. 2003. "Memory, Long-Term". In Nadel 2003, vol. 2: 1096–1105.

Riley, J. R., U. Greggers, A. D. Smith, D. R. Reynolds, and R. Menzel. 2005. "The Flight of Honey Bees Recruited by the Waggle Dance". *Nature* 435: 205–7.

Rosenbaum, David A., Richard A. Carlson, and Rick O. Gilmore. 2001. "Acquisition of Intellectual and Perceptual-Motor Skills". *Annual Review of Psychology* 52: 453–70.

Rumelhart, D. E., and J. L. McClelland. 1986. *Parallel Distributed Processing: Explorations in the Microstructure of Cognition, vol. 1, Foundations*. Cambridge, MA: MIT Press.

Rumfitt, Ian. 2003. "Savoir Faire". *Journal of Philosophy* 100: 158–66.

Sampson, Geoffrey. 1976. "The Simplicity of Linguistic Theories". *Linguistics* 167: 51–66

Samuelson, L. K., and L. B. Smith. 1998. "Memory and Attention Make Smart Word Learning: An Alternative Account of Akhtar, Carpenter, and Tomasello". *Child Development* 69: 94–104.

—— 2000. "Grounding Development in Cognitive Processes". *Child Development* 71: 98–106.

Sapir, Edward. 1931. "Conceptual Categories in Primitive Languages". *Science* 74: 578.

—— 1949. *Selected Writings in Language, Culture and Personality*, ed. David G. Mandelbaum. Berkeley: University of California Press.

Saussure, Ferdinand de. 1916. *Course in General Linguistics*, eds. Charles Bally and Albert Sechehaye, trans., Wade Baskin, New York: McGraw-Hill Book Co, 1966. 1st French edn., 1916.

Schacter, Daniel L. 1999. "Implicit vs Explicit Memory". In Wilson and Keil 1999: 394–5.

Schank, Roger. 1980. "An Artificial Intelligence Perspective on Chomsky's View of Language". *Behavioral and Brain Sciences* 3: 35–7.

—— and Lawrence Birnbaum. 1984. "Memory, Meaning, and Syntax". In Bever *et al.* 1984: 209–51.

Schiffer, Stephen. 1972. *Meaning*. Oxford: Clarendon Press.

—— 1987. *Remnants of Meaning*. Cambridge, MA: MIT Press.

—— 2002. "Amazing Knowledge". *Journal of Philosophy* 99: 200–02.

Scholz, Barbara, and Geoffrey Pullum. 2002. "Searching for Arguments to Support Linguistic Nativism". *Linguistic Review* 19: 185–223.

—— 2006. "Irrational Nativist Exuberance". In *Contemporary Debates in Cognitive Science*, ed. R. Stainton. Oxford: Blackwell Publishers.

Schutze, Carson T. 2003. "Linguistic Evidence, Status of". In Nadel 2003, vol. 2: 910–17.

Searle, John. 1972. "Chomsky's Revolution in Linguistics". *The New York Review of Books*. Reprinted in Harman 1974: 2–33. [Citation is to Harman]

Seidenberg, Mark S. 1995. "Visual Word Recognition: An Overview". In Millar and Eimas 1995: 137–79.

Singley, Mark K., and John R. Anderson. 1989. *The Transfer of Cognitive Skill*. Cambridge MA: Harvard University Press.

Smith, Barry C. 2001. "Idiolects and Understanding: Comments on Barber". *Mind and Language* 16: 284–9.

Smith, Brian Cantwell. 1999. "Computation". In Wilson and Keil 1999: 153–5.

Smith, N. and I-M Tsimpli. 1995. *The Mind of a Savant: Language-Learning and Modularity*. Oxford: Blackwell Publishers.

Smolensky, Paul. 1991. "Connectionism, Constituency and the Language of Thought". In *Meaning in Mind: Jerry Fodor and His Critics*, Barry Loewer and Georges Rey, eds. Oxford: Basil Blackwell: 201–27. Reprinted in Macdonald and Macdonald 1995: 164–98. [Citation is to Macdonald and Macdonald]

Soames, Scott. 1984. "Linguistics and Psychology". *Linguistics and Philosophy* 7: 155–79.

Sober, Elliott. 1980. "Representation and Psychological Reality". *Behavioral and Brain Sciences* 3: 38–9.

Sokolov, A. 1972. *Inner Speech and Thought*. New York: Plenum Press.

Sosa, Ernest, 1998. "Minimal Intuition". In DePaul and Ramsey 1998: 257–69.

—— and Mattias Steup, eds. 2005. *Contemporary Debates in Epistemology*. Cambridge, MA: Blackwell Publishers.

Spencer, N. J. 1973. "Differences Between Linguists and Nonlinguists in Intuitions of Grammaticality–Acceptability". *Journal of Psycholinguistic Research* 2: 83–98.

Sperber, Dan. 1996. *Explaining Culture: A Naturalistic Approach*. Oxford: Blackwell Publishers.

—— and Deirdre Wilson. 1995. *Relevance, Communication and Cognition*. 1st edn. 1986. Oxford: Blackwell Publishers.

—— 1998. "The Mapping Between the Mental and the Public Lexicon". In Carruthers and Boucher 1998a: 184–200.

Stabler, Edward P., Jr. 1983. "How are Grammars Represented?" *Behavioral and Brain Sciences* 6: 391–402.

Stanley, Jason, and Zoltan G. Szabo. 2000. "On Quantifier Domain Restriction". *Mind and Language* 15: 219–61.

—— and Timothy Williamson. 2001. "Knowing How". *Journal of Philosophy* 98: 411–44.

Stanley, William B., Robert C. Mathews, Ray R. Buss, and Susan Kotler-Cope. 1989. "Insight Without Awareness: On the Interaction of Verbalization, Instruction and Practice in a Simulated Process Control Task". *The Quarterly Journal of Experimental Psychology* 41A: 553–77.

Steedman, Mark. 2003. "Language, Connectionist and Symbolic Representations of". In Nadel 2003, vol. 2: 765–71.

Stemberger, Joseph P. 2003. "Speech Error Models of Language Production". In Nadel 2003, vol. 4: 156–62.

Sterelny, Kim. 2003. *Thought in a Hostile World.: The Evolution of Human Cognition*, Oxford: Blackwell Publishing.

Steup, Mattias, and Ernest Sosa, eds. 2005. *Contemporary Debates in Epistemology.* Cambridge, MA: Blackwell Publishers.

Stich, Stephen P. 1971. "What Every Speaker Knows". *Philosophical Review* 80: 476–96.

—— 1978a. "Empiricism, Innateness, and Linguistic Universals". *Philosophical Studies* 33: 273–86.

—— 1978b. "Beliefs and Subdoxastic States". *Philosophy of Science* 45: 499–518.

—— 1980. "What Every Speaker Cognizes". *Behavioral and Brain Sciences* 3: 39–40.

—— 1983. *From Folk Psychology to Cognitive Science: The Case Against Belief.* Cambridge, MA.: MIT Press.

Sun, Ron. 2003. "Connectionist Implementationalism and Hybrid Systems". In Nadel 2003, vol. 1: 697–703.

—— Edward Merrill, and Todd Peterson. 2001. "From Implicit Skills to Explicit Knowledge: A Bottom-Up Model of Skill Learning". *Cognitive Science* 25: 203–44.

Swinney, David A. 1999. "Aphasia". In Wilson and Keil 1999: 31.

Taatgen, Niels A. 2003. "Learning Rules and Productions". In Nadel 2003, vol. 2: 822–30.

Tanenhaus, Michael K. 2003. "Sentence Processing". In Nadel 2003, vol. 3: 1142–8.

—— and John C. Trueswell. 1995. "Sentence Comprehension". In Miller and Eimas 1995: 217–62.

Taylor, Kenneth A. 1994. "How Not to Refute Eliminative Materialism". *Philosophical Psychology* 7: 101–25.

Thompson, Henry. 1983. "Computation Misrepresented: The Procedural/Declarative Controversy Exhumed". *Behavioral and Brain Sciences* 3: 415.

Thornton, Rosalind. 1995. "Referentiality and *Wh*-Movement in Child English: Juvenile D-Link*uency*". *Language Acquisition* 4: 139–75.

Tomberlin, James E. 1998. "Naturalism, Actualism, and Ontology". In *Philosophical Perspectives, 12, Language, Mind, and Ontology, 1998*, ed. James E. Tomberlin. Cambridge MA: Blackwell Publishers: 489–98.

—— 2001. "How Not to be an Actualist". In *Philosophical Perspectives, 15, Metaphysics, 2001*, ed. James E. Tomberlin. Cambridge MA: Blackwell Publishers: 421–5.

Van Gelder, Tim. 1999. "Dynamic Approaches to Cognition". In Wilson and Keil 1999: 244–6.

Vigliocco, Gabriella, and Daniel P. Vinson. 2003. "Speech Production". In Nadel 2003, vol. 4: 182–9.

Wade, Nicholas. 2005. "A New Sign Language Arises, and Scientists Watch it Evolve". *New York Times*, February 1: F3.

Wanner, Eric. 1977. Review of Fodor, Bever, and Garrentt 1974. *Psycholinguistic Research* 6: 261–70.

Webelhuth, Gert (ed.). 1995a. *Government and Binding Theory and the Minimalist Program*. Oxford: Blackwell Publishers.

—— 1995b. "X-bar Theory and Case Theory". In Webelhuth 1995a: 15–95.

Wheeldon, Linda R., Antje S. Meyer, and Mark Smith. 2003. "Language Production, Incremental". In Nadel 2003, vol 3: 760–4.

Whorf, Benjamin Lee. 1956. *Language, Thought, and Reality*, ed. and intro. John B. Carroll. Cambridge, MA. MIT Press.

Wilson, Robert A. 1999. "Philosophy". In Wilson and Keil 1999: xiii–xxxvii.

—— and Frank C. Keil, eds. 1999. *The MIT Encyclopedia of the Cognitive Sciences*. Cambridge, MA: MIT Press.

Wisniewski, Edward J. 1998. "The Psychology of Intuitions". In DePaul and Ramsey 1998: 45–58.

Wolpert, Daniel M., and Zoubin Ghahramani. 2003. "Motor Learning Models". In Nadel 2003, vol. 3: 138–42.

Yamada, Jeni E. 1990. *Laura: A Case Study for the Modularity of the Mind*. Cambridge MA: MIT Press.

Yamadori, Atsushi, Takashi Yoshida, Etsuro Mori, and Hikari Yamashita. 1996. "Neurological Basis of Skill Learning". *Cognitive Brain Research* 5: 39–54.

Index

Abduction: criteria for 199, 253; from
    evidential role of intuitions 96–8,
    100, 112–19; "only-theory-in-town"
    12, 13–14, 198–201, 204, 219, 229,
    241, 252–6, 266, 271
adaptive control of thought (ACT), *see*
    production systems
Allen, C. 131
Anderson, John R. 5 n. 4, 12, 47, 210,
    214–16, 219, 240, 257 n. 14
Andrews, Avery 196 n. 3
Antony, Louise 8, 33
Armstrong, D. M. 133 n. 19, 146 n. 10
artificial grammar (AG) 114 n. 32, 217
associationism 55–6, 226–7
Aston, B. 116
Atkinson, Antony P. 94 n. 6
Au, T. K. 136
Avramides, A. 133 n. 19

Bach, Kent 128 n. 5
Baker, C. L. 70, 96, 100 n., 101 n. 6,
    119 n. 40, 183 n.
Baker, Lynne Rudder 126 n. 2
Barber, Alex viii, 6 n. 8, 129–30 n. 8,
    178 n. 19
Barkow, J. 94 n. 6
Baron-Cohen, S. 94 n. 6
Bealer, George 105 n. 14
bees and their dances 20–1, 22, 23, 26,
    29, 35, 36, 37, 38, 39, 49, 60, 67–8,
    134, 207, 216
behaviorism 6–7, 10, 55–6, 87–8, 120,
    125–6, 132 n. 17, 191, 252, 272
Bekoff, M. 131
Bennett, J. 133 n. 19, 186
Berkeley, George 199 n.
Bernal, Sara viii
Berwick, Robert 10, 32 n. 25, 36, 58 n.
    16, 65, 79–81, 83–4, 195–6, 200 n.,
    222

Bever, Tom 10, 28 n. 14, 65, 72–7, 80–3,
    100 n., 127, 195–6, 200, 209, 221
Bickerton, Derek 130 n. 11, 131
Birnbaum, Lawrence 197
Bjork, Robert A. 212
Bjorklund, David F. 211
blacksmiths and horseshoes 17–18, 21 n.
    6, 22, 23, 26, 39, 106
Blanchard-Fields, F. 116 n., 217
Blasi, Carlos Hernandez 211
Bloom, A. H. 136
Bloom, Paul 130 n. 12, 250–1, 263
Bloomfieldian linguistics 8 n. 11, 26, 27–8
Blumstein, Sheila E. 222 n. 24
Bock, Kathryn 68 n. 8, 169, 177, 196 n.
    2, 230–3
Boden, M. A. 68 n. 8
Boghossian, Paul A. 126 n. 2
BonJour, Laurence 105 n. 14
Boroditsky, Lera 136 n. 25
Botha, Rudolf P. 130 n. 11
Boucher, Jill 125, 160, 174 n. 8, 175 n. 10
Braddon-Mitchell, David 146, 147 nn.
    12–13
brain impairment: cognitive 11, 131, 137,
    163–5, 189–90, 263; linguistic 11,
    92–3, 131, 137, 163–71, 173,
    189–90, 208, 257, 259, 261, 263, 269
Bresnan, Joan 10, 36, 76–80, 83–4,
    195–6, 222
Broadbent, Donald E. 116
Broadbent, Margaret H. P. 116
Bromberger, Sylvain v
Brown, Liana E. 212
"brute–causal" processing vs "rational–
    causal" processing 12, 53–6, 59–60,
    61, 73, 88, 197, 198, 201, 206,
    208–9, 220–34, 239–41, 242–3,
    250, 267–8, 274, 275, 276; *see also*
    psychological reality, some possible
    positions on, versions (a) and (b)

Bub, Jeffrey viii
Burge, Tyler 139–40
Burton-Roberts, Noel 31, 90 n., 222 n. 25
Buss, R. R. 116 n., 217

Cappa, S. F. 168
Caramazza, Alfonso 167–70
Carey, Susan 131
Carlson, Richard A. 106 n., 211, 213, 215, 216 n. 20, 267 n. 26
Carr, Philip 31, 90 n., 222 n. 25
Carroll, Lewis 46, 50, 107–8
Carruthers, Peter 125, 130 n. 11, 152 n., 160, 174 n. 8, 175 n. 10
Cartesian access 96–8, 100–3, 106, 109, 112–19, 204 n.
central processor, *see* linguistic competence, relation to conceptual competence and the central processor
Champollian, Jean Francois 29 n. 18
Chang, Franklin 232
chess players and chess moves 18–19, 21, 22, 23, 24, 26, 29, 35, 36, 53, 58, 59, 106
Chierchia, Gennaro 154
Chinn, R. 116 n., 217
Cho, J. R. 116 n., 217
Chomskian Nativism 247–8, 253–7, 266, 270, 272, 275
Chomsky, Noam v, vii, 14–16, 39, 45 n. 1, 74, 108 n. 18, 131, 154, 166 n.; on conventions and idiolects, 11–12, 178–84, 190; on E-languages 26, 30; on Gricean semantics 174; on intuitions 3–5, 10, 95–6, 101 n. 7, 119; on knowledge of language 3–5, 10, 89–94; on the language faculty 13, 173–4, 262 n., 263–5; on LET 174; on LOTH 174–5; on language use 10, 62–71, 76–7, 79, 195, 200, 207, 223; on linguistics: what it is about 3–9, 26–36; on nativism 13–14, 130, 173–4, 177 n. 14, 244–7, 249–50, 251 n. 8, 252–6, 259, 268 n., 27; on realism 8, 28, 35; on RT 3–7, 10, 34, 46, 62–4, 71,
81, 87–96, 247, 253 n. 9; on RTM 6; on thoughts 11, 125, 163, 174–8, 190
Chomsky's tasks:
(i) 3, 4, 24, 26, 28–9, 30, 32–4, 134
(ii) 3, 4–5, 244
(iii) 3, 5, 66, 75, 176–7
Churchland, Patricia S. 125
Churchland, Paul M. 125
Clark, Andy 137, 150, 161
Clark, R. 255
Cleeremans, Axel 211 n., 212 n. 14, 217, 219, 221 n., 227
cognitive linguistics 174 n. 7
"cognizing" 4, 69, 96
Collins, John viii, 8 n. 11, 63, 254 n., 255, 268 n.
"communicative" vs. "cognitive" conceptions of language 125, 160–1
competence distinguished from outputs and inputs 8–9, 17–21, 23–41, 71, 273; *see also* major conclusions, first
competence hypothesis 76–7; strong 77–8
computer analogies 5, 46–7, 50–2, 54, 56 n. 15, 58, 62–9, 144 n. 6, 204, 207, 209, 215–16
conceptual analysis 105–6, 132 n. 16
conceptual competence: nature of, *see* thoughts, nature of; relation to linguistic competence, *see* linguistic competence, relation to conceptual competence and the central processor
conditioning 211, 216–17, 226 n. 29
connectionism 51, 55–6, 125, 147, 214, 217, 218, 221, 227, 228 n., 232–3, 238–40, 242
continuity hypothesis 251, 271
conventional meaning and syntax 12, 128, 132–41, 155–8, 178–90, 225–6; *see also* literal meaning and syntax; speaker meaning and syntax
Corina, David P. 167
Cosmides, L. 94 n.6
Cowie, Fiona viii, 8 n. 13, 39 n, 35, 87, 164 n., 165 n. 2, 249–50, 253–6, 259 n. 18, 266, 271

Crain, Stephen viii, 99 n., 110 n. 24, 237, 246 n., 249 n., 251, 255
creolization 251
Croft, William 174 n. 7
Cruse, D. Alan 174 n. 7
Culicover, Peter W. 251 n. 8
Cummins, Robert 8 n. 12, 146 n. 10
Curtis, Susan 137, 263
Cutler, Anne 169, 233 n., 238

Davidson, Donald 125 n., 132 n. 17, 178 n. 18, 179
Davies, Martin 52 n. 10, 92 n., 130 n. 9, 132 n. 16, 204 n.
Davis, Martin 58 n. 16
Dehaene, S 150
Dell, Gary S. 209, 232–3
Demopoulos, William 81
Dennett, Daniel 47 n. 6, 55, 64
Descartes' problem 176–7
Devitt, Michael v–vi, viii, 5 nn. 4 and 6, 7 n. 10, 8, 24 n. 10, 29–30, 32 n. 24, 36 n. 30, 37 n. 31, 39 n. 35, 46–7, 69 n., 89 nn. 1–2, 103–8, 113 n. 30, 119, 125–7, 132 n. 16, 133, 134–6, 138 n., 142–4, 152 n., 154 n. 17, 156 nn. 22–4, 157 n. 27, 165 n. 3, 174 n. 7, 182, 184 n., 185 n., 186 n. 27, 189, n., 199, 202, 203, 219 n.
Dienes, Zoltan 50
DiGirolamo, G. J. 218
Docherty, Gerard 31, 90 n., 222 n. 25
Donati, C. 168
Donnellan, Keith S. 138
Dosher, Barbara 240
Dow, James viii
Dretske, Fred 8 n. 12
Dronkers, Nina F. 168
Druhan, B. 116 n., 217
Duhem–Quine thesis 33, 114, 120
Dummett, Michael 34 n., 132 n. 17
Dwyer, Susan 6 n. 8, 48 n., 91 n., 96, 101 n. 6, 119 n. 40; on linguistics: what it is about 8, 26 n., 39–40
dynamical systems 213–14, 218, 221

E-languages 26, 30
Ellman, Jeffrey L. 249 n.
evidence: for grammars 4, 8–9, 10, 17, 31–4, 35, 37, 73–4, 95–7, 98–103, 108–15, 120, 191; for nativism 13, 246, 248–52, 254, 256, 262–3, 266, 269, 271–2; *see also* intuitions (intuitive judgments); Respect Constraint

Farrell, Simon 240
Fazio, F. 168
Fernandez-Duque, D. 218
Ferreira, Victor S. 233
Field, Hartry 47 n. 6, 144 n. 6
Fiengo, Robert 95 n.
Fitch, W. Tecumseh 130 n. 12, 131, 177 n. 14
Fitzgerald, Peter 116
Fodor, Janet Dean 32 n. 25, 35, 36, 78 n. 11, 97 n., 154, 237, 239–40, 241 n. 37, 251 n. 8, 255–6
Fodor, Jerry 28 n. 14, 29–30 n. 20, 33, 35, 35, 46 n. 5, 51, 52, 54 n. 12, 92 n. 5, 126 n. 2, 127, 144 n. 6, 156, 175 n. 10, 178 n. 17, 202, 216 n. 19, 228; vs. associationism 226–7; on intuitions 96, 97 n., 100 n., 112, 113 n. 31, 114; on LOTH viii, 145–6, 159–60, 174 n. 8, 205; on language use 65, 72–7, 80–3, 195–6, 198 n. 6, 200, 209, 210, 221; on linguistics: what it is about v, viii, 6, 8 n. 11, 39 n. on nativism 13–14, 247, 252–5, 268, 271; on RT viii, 3 n. 2, 6, 8 n. 11, 10, 72–6, 83, 195–6, 198 n. 6
formal vs syntactic properties 154–5
Fowler, C. A. 214
Frank, Adam 20, 29 n. 18
Frazier, Lyn 196 n. 1, 198 n. 5, 237, 239

Gagnon, D. A. 233
Gallistel, C. R. 21 n. 5, 54 n. 13, 218 n., 221 n., 226 n. 29

Garrett, Merrill 10, 28 n. 14, 35, 65, 72–7, 80–3, 97 n., 100 n., 127, 195–6, 200, 209, 221
Garson, James 213
Gasper, Philip 126 n. 2
Gazdar, Gerald 8 n. 11, 38 n. 33
Geach, Peter 188
Gendler, Tamar Szabo 105 n. 13
generation: actual vs. merely metaphorical 68–71, 274; by the I-language vs. by the grammar 71, 274
Gentner, Dedre 262
George, Alexander 8 n. 12
Gernsbacher, Morton Ann 234, 236, 240
Ghahramani, Zoubin 213
Gibson, Edward 237 n., 238
Gilbert, Margaret 8 n. 12
Gilmore, Rick O. 211
Gladwell, Malcolm 104 n.
Gleitman, Lila 250–1, 263
Goldberg, Elkhonon 103 n. 11
Goldin-Meadow, Susan 131
Gopnik, Alison 104
Gopnik, Myrna 164
Gordon, P. C. 98, 111 n. 25, 115 n. 36
Gorrell, Paul 234
Graves, Christina 92 n., 96, p7 n., 118 n., 247
Greggers, U. 20 n. 3
Grice, Paul 10, 128, 132–3, 172; *see also* Gricean semantics
Gricean semantics viii, 10–11, 40 n., 112 n. 29, 132–3, 141, 161, 178–9, 192, 220, 234–5; and linguistic relativity 135–7; and reference borrowing 138–41; wedded to LOTH 155–6, 162, 172–3, 261, 262; *see also* conventional meaning; literal meaning; speaker meaning
Griffin, Zenzi M. 232
Grodzinsky, Yosef 6 n. 8
Gross, Maurice 58 n. 16
Gualmini, Andrea 99 n.
Gumperz, John J. 135 n. 23

Hadley, Robert F. 227
Haegeman, Liliane 28 n. 14, 95, 101 n. 6, 183 n.
Haggard, Cynthia viii
Hannan, Barbara 126 n. 2
Harman, Gilbert 68 n. 8, 92, 149, 205–7, 268
Harnish, Robert M. 8 n. 12
Harris, Catherine l. 35
Harris, Randy Allen 8 n. 11, 29 n. 19
Hauser, Marc D. 130 n. 12, 131, 177 n. 14
Hendrick, R. 98, 111 n. 25, 115 n. 36
Hickok, Gregory 168
Higginbotham, James 101 n. 6, 178 n. 19
Hillis, Argye E. 167–70
Holding, Dennis H. 215 n.
Horgan, Terence 51
Hornstein, Norbert 38 n. 33, 101 n. 6
Horwich, Paul viii
Howe, Christine J. 79 n.
Hurford, James R. 130 n. 13

idiolects 12, 132, 178–84, 189 n., 190, 205; *see also* major conclusions, sixth
ignorance of language 5, 16, 89 n. 2, 109, 139, 252, 269, 271; *see also* major conclusions, second, third and seventh
inference to the best explanation, *see* abduction
innate ideas 14, 245–7, 269
instance theory 214, 218, 221
intentional realism 10, 108, 125–7, 141, 148, 158, 161
intuitions (intuitive judgments) 3–7, 10, 26 n., 32, 95–121, 181, 191, 204 n., 208, 217, 219, 223, 272; *see also* major conclusions, third
I-Representational Thesis 13–14, 247, 252–7, 266–72, 273, 275, 276; *see also* major conclusions, seventh

Jackendoff, Ray 173, 264
Jackson, Frank 146, 147 nn. 12–13
Johnson, Kent 146 n. 9
Johnson, Todd R. 215, 218, 227, 266 n.
Jones, Gary 214 n. 17
Jutronic, Dunja viii

Kant, Immanuel 69 n., 135
Kaplan, Ronald 10, 36, 76–80, 83–4, 195–6, 222
Kaschak, Michael P. 234, 236, 240
Kasher, Asa 176 n. 13
Katz, Jerrold 8, 26–7, 31 n. 22, 92 n., 96, 97 n., 118 n., 247
Kelso, J. A. Scott 213, 214 n. 16
Kintsch, Walter 226 n. 28
Klein, Ewan, 8 n. 11, 38 n. 33
Knight, Chris 130 n. 13
Knowledge: declarative (explicit) vs. procedural (implicit) 47, 211, 214–19, 227–8, 264, 266–7, 270; -how vs. -that (propositional) 10, 46–7, 50, 89–94, 106, 246–7; of language 3–8, 10, 34, 47, 89–94, 109, 246–7, 264; tacit 4–5, 49, 52 n. 11, 64, 91–2, 96, 97 n., 205–6, 247; *see also* learning, explicit vs. implicit; memory, explicit (declarative) vs. implicit (procedural)
Kornblith, Hilary 103 n. 9
Kotler-Cope, Susan 116 n., 217
Kripke, Saul A. 138
Kugler, P. N. 214

Laird, J. E. 214 n. 17
Lakoff, George v
language acquisition 3, 4–5, 10, 12–14, 15, 32–3, 40–1, 77, 84, 87, 99–100, 115–16, 120–1, 130, 133, 171, 173–4, 181, 189, 191–2, 197, 219, 221, 238, 242, 243, 244–72; *see also* major conclusions, seventh; tentative proposals, sixth and seventh
language expresses thought (LET) 10, 127–32, 141, 148, 151, 161, 163, 165–6, 172–4, 177, 189–92, 201–3, 257, 260–1, 273, 275
language faculty 4–14, 31 n. 23, 40, 69, 93–4, 96, 102, 112–14, 120, 125, 163–92, 203, 208–9, 228–9, 245–8, 251, 260–6, 271–2; *see also* linguistic competence; major conclusions, second and seventh; tentative proposals, second

language-of-thought hypothesis (LOTH) viii, 11, 13–14, 60, 92, 125, 142, 145–60, 161–2, 172–3, 174–5, 190–2, 201–3, 205–6, 208, 223, 225–7, 228, 243, 247, 257–60, 261, 264–6, 268–9, 271, 273, 275, 276 ; Public- 149–52, 158, 161–2, 258, 273; *see also* psychological reality, some possible positions on, (T); tentative proposals; thoughts, nature of
language use (processing), as brute–causal, *see* tentative proposals, fourth; not governed by the structure rules of language, *see* tentative proposals, third; *see also* linguistic competence
Larson, Richard 96, 176 n. 12
Lasnik, Howard 255 n.
Laurence, Stephen 97 n.; on conventions 133 n. 18, 180, 182 n., 189n.; on linguistics: what it is about 8, 28 n. 16, 30 n. 21, 32 n. 24, 33, 36 n. 30, 37 n. 31, 39–40; on nativism 248 n., 249 n., 253 n.10, 255
learning, explicit vs implicit 12, 107 n., 115–16, 211–12, 216–19, 221, 242, 245, 250, 264, 266–7; *see also* knowledge, declarative (explicit) vs. procedural (implicit); memory, explicit (declarative) vs. implicit (procedural)
Lebiere, Christian 214–15
Lees, Robert B. 119 n. 40
Lepore, Ernest 126 n. 2, 144 n. 5
Levelt, William J. M. 231–3
Levinson, Stephen C. 135 n. 23
Lewandowsky, Stephan 240
Lewis, David 21 n. 6, 133 n. 18, 146 n. 10, 180,
Lewis, John D. 249 n.
lexical function grammar (LFG) 10, 77–80, 196 n. 3, 208, 222
Lightfoot, David 38 n. 33
linguistic competence: acquired by implicit learning 12, 115–16, 219, 221, 242, 245, 250, 264, 266–7;

linguistic competence: (*cont.*):
 minimal view of 4, 128, 147–8, 201;
 relation to conceptual competence
 and the central processor 10–11, 13,
 94, 96, 106, 109–14, 117–18,
 129–32, 135–41, 144–5, 148, 153,
 163–7, 173–8, 189–91, 201–3,
 208–9, 220, 223, 227–8, 233–4,
 245, 248, 257, 260–6, 271–2, 275;
 as a skill or ability 12, 14, 89–94,
 106, 108–11, 218–20, 221–30, 232–
 43, 245, 248, 250, 256, 262–4, 266–
 70, 272; view (a) of, assuming
 LET 128–9, 148, 163–6, 189–90,
 201–3, 275; view (b) of, assuming
 RTM 144–5, 148, 172, 201–3, 275;
 view (c) of, assuming LOTH 11,
 148, 161, 172, 201–3, 275; *see also*
 language faculty; major conclusions,
 second and seventh; psychological
 reality, some possible positions on;
 tentative proposals
linguistic relativity 135–7, 141, 158–9, 263
linguistics, not part psychology, *see* major
 conclusions, first; methodological points
Lipton, Michael R. 58 n. 16
literal meaning and syntax 128, 132–4,
 156, 179–81, 186, 189 n., 234,
 235 n. 33; *see also* conventional
 meaning and syntax; speaker
 meaning and syntax
Locke, John 199 n.
Logan, Gordon D. 210, 214
logic machines and *wff*s 19–21, 22, 23,
 24–5, 29, 35, 37, 58, 59, 60, 68, 93,
 147 n. 13, 148–9, 152, 207
Longworth, Guy viii
Ludwig, Kurt 144 n. 5

McClelland, James L. 51, 214, 238
McDonald, Fritz viii
McGilvray, James 28 n. 15, 69 n.
Macintosh, Nicholas J. 56
McLeod, Peter 50
major conclusions:
 first 8–9, 40, 84, 120, 191, 275;
  argument for 17–41

second 9, 12, 14, 84, 97, 120–1, 191,
 197, 241 n., 242, 272, 275;
 argument for 87–121, 195–272
third 10, 120, 191, 208, 276; argument
 for 95–121
fourth 10, 14, 129, 141, 142, 148, 161,
 178, 191, 198, 243, 257, 260,
 265–6, 276; argument for 125–9
fifth 10–11, 141, 161, 174, 191, 276;
 argument for 37–8, 125–41
sixth 12, 183, 190, 276; argument
 for 178–92
seventh 14, 269, 271, 276; argument
 for 244–72
Malcolm, Norman 126 n. 2
Malson, L. 137, 263
map-like representations 11, 54 n. 13,
 146–7, 149, 158, 172, 202–3, 206–7,
 218 n., 221 n., 223, 259–61,
 268
Maratsos, Michael P. 257 n. 15, 259
Marcus parser 79–82
Margolis, Eric viii, 165, 248 n., 249 n.,
 253 n. 10, 255
Marr, David 49, 66–7, 69,
 114
Martin, N. 233
Masson, Michael E. J. 211, 214, 215
Mathews, R. H. 116 n., 217
Matthews, Robert viii, 8, 10, 63, 81–4,
 109 n. 20, 115 n. 36, 195–6, 197,
 200 n., 210, 221, 267
Maumus, Michael 19 n., 29 n. 18
Meeks, Roblin 28 n. 17
memory, explicit (declarative) vs implicit
 (procedural) 211–12, 217–18, 231;
 see also knowledge, declarative
 (explicit) vs procedural (implicit);
 learning, explicit vs. implicit
Mentalese, *see* language-of-thought
 hypothesis (LOTH)
Menzel, R. 20 n. 3
Merrill, Edward 47, 107 n.16, 211 n.,
 214–15, 217, 221 n. 23
methodological points:
 first 35, 57, 61, 76, 80, 81, 83, 195–6,
  274

second 35–6, 57, 61, 71, 76, 79, 83, 120, 142, 196, 274
third 36–7, 38, 57, 61, 63, 67, 72, 74, 76, 78, 79, 80–1, 83, 196, 274
fourth 37–8, 274
Meyer, Antje S. 226 n. 27, 231–3
Miller, G. A. 63, 79
Miller, Joanne 222 n. 26
Mills, Eugene 144 n. 6
Mon-Williams, Mark 212 n. 15, 213
Mori, Etsuro 217–18
Moro, A. 168
Mulligan, Neil W. 211 n.

Namy, Laura L. 262
Neale, Stephen 119 n. 40, 133 n. 19, 154
Newell, A. 214 n. 17, 215 n., 257 n. 14
Newell, Karl M. 211, 214
Newport, Elissa L. 15, 250
Ni, Weijia 237
Niiniluoto, Ilkka 109 n. 21
Nishiyama, Y. 92 n., 96, 97 n., 118 n., 247
nominalism 26–7, 30, 31, 33–4; *see also* Platonism; realism about language
Norris, Dennis 233 n.
Nygaard Lynn C. 186 n. 26

Palmiri, Thomas J. 210 n. 12
Paradox of Language Acquisition, 173, 264
Pateman, Trevor 96
Peacocke, Christopher 67 n.
Perani, D. 168
Pereplyotchik, David 19 n., 114 n. 33
Peterson, Todd 47, 107 n. 16, 211 n., 214–15, 217, 221 n. 23
phonology 15, 31, 90 n., 109 n. 20, 154, 170, 172 n., 184–7, 222–3, 224, 230–3, 265 n.
Pickering, Martin J. 236, 238
Pietroski, Paul viii, 6 n. 8, 15 n., 48 n., 91 n., 96, 99 n., 101 n. 6, 119 n. 40, 235 n. 32; on linguistics: what it is about, 8, 26 n., 39–40; on nativism 246 n., 249 n., 251, 255
Pinker, Stephen 33 n. 26, 78 n., 130 nn. 10 and 12, 134 n. 21, 153, 164, 167–8, 215, 251, 254, 258 n.

Pisoni, David B. 186 n. 26
Platonism 26, 31 n. 22; *see also* nominalism; realism about language
Poeppel, David 168
Port, Robert F. 213, 214 n. 16
Posner, M. I. 107, 218
Poucet, Bruno 218 n.
poverty of stimulus 249–51, 254, 271
pragmatic factors in language use 101–2, 110, 112, 129, 148, 163, 182, 187, 201, 220, 226, 230, 233–5, 237, 240, 253 n. 9
priority of conceptual competence over linguistic competence, ontological 10–11, 128–32, 137, 141, 148, 161, 163–5, 172–3, 202; Chomsky's views on 174–7; *see also* major conclusions, fourth and fifth
priority of theoretical interest in thought over language 11, 30, 38, 134–5, 141; Chomsky's views on 174–7; *see also* major conclusions, fifth
priority of theory of language over theory of competence 23, 29, 37–8, 40, 134–5; *see also* methodological points, fourth
priority of thought over language, explanatory 10–11, 132–3, 135–41, 155–8, 161, 172–3, 192, 261; Chomsky's views on 174–7; *see also* major conclusions, fifth
Pritchett, Bradley L. 84, 200 n., 240 n.
production systems 214–18, 240, 266, 267 n. 25
psychological reality, some possible positions on
 (M) 9, 57, 59, 61, 73–4, 80, 82–3, 117, 120, 128, 195, 198, 205, 243 n., 274
 (I) 57–61, 62–84, 90, 94, 96–7, 117, 120, 153, 190–1, 195–243, 244–5, 270–1, 274
 (II) 57–61, 62, 68–72, 75–6, 83–4, 90, 94, 96–7, 117, 120, 190–1, 195–243, 244–5, 270–1, 274

psychological reality (*cont.*):
(III) 58–61, 62–8, 71, 79, 81–3, 90,
97–8, 117–18, 153, 190–1,
195–8, 207–8, 220–42, 260, 274
(IV) 59, 61, 75–6, 195–243, 274
(V) 60, 76, 195–243, 275
versions (a) 59–61, 73, 191, 197–8,
206, 220–1, 229, 233, 242, 275
versions (b) 59–61, 73, 88, 191,
197–8, 201, 220–43, 275
(T) 60, 84, 90, 120, 125, 141, 142–62,
163, 177, 190–2, 198, 202, 208,
257–60, 264–6, 269, 271, 275
see also linguistic competence
Pullum, Geoffrey viii, 8 n. 11, 38 n. 33,
136 n. 24, 249 n., 251 n. 8, 255 n.
Pupa, Francesco 111 n. 26, 209–10 n.,
251 n. 8
Putnam, Hilary 138, 182, 248–50
Pylyshyn, Zenon 5 n. 5, 45 n. 1, 46 n. 3,
49, 50, 51–2, 54, 63 n. 3, 69, 76, 84,
96, 196, 228–9; on RT 197, 208,
209, 228
Pylyshyn's Razor 12–13, 14, 51–2, 56, 60,
71, 75, 79, 107, 117, 142, 191, 198,
204, 206, 211, 216, 221, 224, 239,
243, 269

Quine, W. V. 26, 37 n. 31, 87, 125 n.,
143, 187

Radford, Andrew 82 n., 95 n., 101
Ramsey, William viii, 56 n. 14, 147 n. 11
"rational–causal" processing, *see*
"brute–causal" processing vs
"rational–causal" processing
Rattan, Gurpreet viii
Rayner, K. 237
realism: about language 8, 12, 26–8, 35,
81, 109 n. 19, 184–9; about
thoughts, *see* intentional realism; *see
also* nominalism
Reber, A. S. 114 n. 32, 115, 211 n.,
216–17, 219, 221 n., 256
reference: borrowing 138–141, 182; doubts
about 15, 24 n. 10; fixing 138;
theories of 5, 138–9, 155–6

Reisberg, Daniel 210
'represent', senses of, 5–7, 97, 221
Representational Theory of Mind
(RTM) 6, 11, 46–7, 90, 92, 142–5,
148, 158, 161, 172, 176, 191, 201,
203, 206–7, 223, 229, 240, 242,
268, 273, 275; *see also* thoughts,
nature of.
Representational Thesis (RT) vii, 4–7,
9–10, 12–14, 33, 34, 40–1, 46, 52,
53, 57–8, 61, 62–4, 71–84, 87–121,
166, 190, 191, 196, 197–220, 228,
229–43, 244–5, 247, 252, 253 n. 9,
264–5, 266–7, 269, 270–2, 273,
293, 275; *see also* major conclusions,
second; psychological reality, some
possible positions on, (I) and (II)
Respect Constraint 23, 25, 32, 36–7, 40,
57, 61, 63, 67, 73–83, 196, 230, 273,
274; *see also* psychological reality,
some possible positions on, (M); rules
(or principles), "respected" by
competence (final state)
Rey, Georges viii, 7 n. 9, 12, 63 n. 2,
112 n. 27, 126 n. 2, 135, 144 nn.
5–6, 151 n., 163, 184–90, 225
Reynolds, D. R. 20 n. 3
Richard, Mark 145 n. 7
Richardson-Klavehn, Alan 212
Riley, J. R. 20 n. 3
Robbins, Philip viii
Roelofs, Ardi 231–3
Rosenbaum, David A. 211, 212
Rosenbloom, P. S. 214 n. 17
rules (or principles): represented vs.
"simply embodied" 7, 9, 45–52,
58–61, 63–4, 196–7, 273;
represented and used as data 53,
57–8, 60–1, 273; *see also*
psychological reality, some possible
positions on, (II); "respected" by
competence (final state) 9, 21–3, 25,
32–3, 35–9, 45 n. 2, 57, 61, 63, 67,
73–83, 99, 117, 166, 195–6, 205,
239, 240, 243 n., 246, 273, 274; *see
also* psychological reality, some
possible positions on, (M);

"respected" by initial state 246–52, 256–61, 265, 269, 271 275; structure vs processing 18–21, 24–5, 273; *see also* psychological reality, some possible positions on, (III)

Rumelhart, D. E. 214

Rumfitt, Ian 89 n. 2

Saffran, E. M. 233

Sag, Ivan 8 n. 11, 38 n. 33

Sampson, Geoffrey, 8 n. 12

Samuelson, L. K. 250 n.

Sapir, Edward 135

Saussure, Ferdinand de 24 nn. 9–10, 184 n.

Schacter, Daniel L. 211 n., 212

Schank, Roger 49, 65 n., 177 n. 16, 197

Schiffer, Stephen 89 n. 2, 133 nn. 18–19, 180

Scholz, Barbara viii, 249 n., 251 n. 8, 255 n.

Schutze, Carson T. 100

Schwartz, M. F., 233

Schwitzgebel, Eric 104

Searle, John 161 n.

Segal, Gabriel 96, 176 n. 12

Seidenberg, Mark S. 172 n.

sentence machine 25, 64–5, 68

sequential (or serial) reaction time (SRT) 217

Shankweiler, Donald 237

sign languages 131, 149–50, 167, 250–1

Simon, H. 215 n., 257 n. 14

Singley, Mark K. 215, 257 n. 14

skills and abilities, cognitive and motor 6–7, 12, 14, 21 n. 5, 45–52, 89–94, 106–11, 204, 210–20, 221–30, 232–43, 245, 248, 250, 256, 262–4, 266–70, 272

Smith, A. D. 20 n. 3

Smith, Barry C. 39, 178 n. 19

Smith, Brian Cantwell 56 n. 15

Smith, L. B. 250 n.

Smith, Mark 226 n. 27

Smith N. 94 n. 6, 164

Smolensky, Paul 56

Sneider, Wolfgang 211

Soames, Scott 8, 28, 33, 92 n., 96, 97 n., 118 n., 247

Sober, Elliott 45 n. 1, 64

Sokolov, A. 150

Sosa, Ernest 105 n. 14

speaker meaning 128, 132–4, 140, 155–8, 179–90, 225–6 *see also* conventional meaning and syntax; literal meaning and syntax

Spencer, N. J. 111 n. 25, 115 n. 36

Sperber, Dan 94 n. 6, 128 n. 4

Stabler, Edward P. 8 n. 12, 50–1, 53, 58, 81, 197, 204, 209, 268 n.

Stainton, Robert viii

Stanley, Jason 89 n. 2, 119 n. 40

Stanley, W. B. 116 n., 217

Stecker, R. 92 n., 96, 97 n., 118 n., 247

Steedman, Mark 237, 238, 261–2

Stemberger, Joseph P. 232

Sterelny, Kim v, viii, 5 n. 6, 8, 24 n. 10, 30 n. 21. 32 n. 24, 36 n. 30, 37 n. 31, 39 n. 35, 89 n. 1, 94 n. 6, 104 n., 113 n. 30, 119, 125 n., 132 n. 16, 133, 135–6, 138 n., 156 nn. 22 and 24, 157 n. 27, 184 n., 186 n. 27, 189 n.

Stich, Stephen viii, 91, 94 n. 7, 113 n. 30, 248

Stone, Tony 204 n.

structuralism 18, 26–7, 186 n. 27; post-186 n. 27

Studdert-Kennedy, Michael 130 n. 13

sui generis, language as 248, 251, 258, 261, 262, 271

Sun, Ron 47, 107 n. 16, 211–12, 214–15, 217, 221 n. 23, 227

Supalla, Ted 15, 250

Swinney, David A. 167

Szabo, Zoltan G. 119 n. 40

Taatgen, Niels A. 221 n.

Tanenhaus, Michael K. 129 n. 7, 235–8, 241

Taylor, Kenneth A. 126 n. 2

temporal consequences of priority claims about thought 10–11, 141, 161,

temporal consequences (*cont.*):
174, 191; for acquiring competence
in a language 130, 133, 137; for
conventional meanings and
syntax 133, 137, 160; for innate
linguistic capacities 130–1; *see also*
major conclusions, fifth
tentative proposals:
first 11, 13, 14, 152, 157, 162, 172,
190, 191, 208 n., 243, 265, 276;
argument for 142–62
second 11, 14, 173, 190, 223, 261,
265, 266, 272, 276; argument
for 163–74, 256–66
third 12, 207, 226, 229, 233, 240, 260,
276; argument for 18–21, 24–5,
37, 53, 59, 62–8, 76–7, 190–1,
207–8, 220–43
fourth 12, 220–1, 223, 229, 230, 233,
239, 240, 241 n., 243, 276;
argument for 220–43
fifth 13, 14, 243, 260, 265, 276;
argument for 195–243
sixth 13, 14, 257, 259, 260, 266, 269,
271, 276; argument for 256–60
seventh 13, 14, 260, 266, 269, 271,
276; argument for 256–60
Tettamanti, M. 168
thinking 50, 106–8, 111–12, 116, 118,
145–7, 150, 153, 161, 165, 211,
216, 226–7, 258, 263, 268–9, 272;
see also thoughts
Thompson, Henry 58 n. 16
Thornton, Rosalind 99, 110 n. 24
thoughts: realism about, *see* intentional
realism; nature of, viii, 6, 11,
13–14, 46–7, 60, 125, 127, 142–62,
174–8, 190–2, 201–3, 205–6, 226–7,
228, 247, 257–60, 268–9, 271, 273,
276; *see also* language expresses
thought (LET); priority of theoretical
interest in thought over language;
priority of thought over language,
explanatory; temporal consequences
of priority claims about thought;
tentative proposals, first and sixth
Tienson, John 51

Tomberlin, James E. 143 n. 4
Tooby, J. 94 n. 6
Tovey, P. 92 n., 96, 97 n., 118 n., 247
transcendental arguments 125–6
Tresilian, James R. 212 n. 15, 213
Trueswell, John C. 129 n. 7, 236–8, 241
Tsimpli, I-M. 94 n. 6, 164
Turvey, M. T. 214

Universal Grammar (UG) 171, 184,
244–8, 252–6, 260 n.; rules (or
principles) specified by, (UG-
rules) 13–14, 159, 244–52, 256–61,
265–72, 273, 275, 276
Uriagereka, Juan viii, 255 n.,
Use/mention sloppiness, 69–71, 74

Van Gelder, Tim 213, 214 n. 16
Vigliocco, Gabriella 151, 231–3
Vinson, Daniel P. 151, 231–3
Von Frisch, Karl 20, 29 n. 18

Wade, Nicholas 250–1
Wang, Hongbin 215, 218, 227, 266 n.
Wann, John P. 212 n. 15, 213
Wanner, Eric 151
Webelhuth, Gert 70, 183 n. 23
Weinberg, Amy 10, 32 n. 25, 36, 65,
79–81, 83–4, 195–6, 200 n., 222
wff machines and *wff*s 19–20, 24–5,
64–5, 68
Wheeldon, Linda R., 226 n. 27
Wheeler, Michael 94 n. 6
Whorf, Benjamin Lee 135–7, 158
Williamson, Timothy 89 n. 2
Wilson, Deidre 128 nn. 4–5
Wilson, Robert A. 56 n. 15
Wisniewski, Edward J. 104–5, 235 n. 33
Wolpert, Daniel M. 213

Yamada, Jeni E. 164
Yamadori, Atsushi 217–18
Yamashita, Hikari 217–18
Yoshida, Takashi 217–18

Zhang, Jiajie 215, 218, 227, 266 n.
Zheng, Ming-Yu 131